African Governance Report II
2009

Economic Commission for Africa

OXFORD
UNIVERSITY PRESS

Oxford University Press
Great Clarendon Street, Oxford OX2 6DP

Oxford University Press is a department of the University of Oxford. It furthers the University's
objective of excellence in research, scholarship, and education by publishing worldwide in

Oxford New York Auckland Cape Town Dar es Salaam Hong Kong Karachi Kuala Lumpur
Madrid Melbourne Mexico City Nairobi New Delhi Shanghai Taipei Toronto

With offices in
Argentina Austria Brazil Chile Czech Republic France Greece Guatemala Hungary Italy Japan
Poland Portugal Singapore South Korea Switzerland Thailand Turkey Ukraine Vietnam

Oxford is a registered trade mark of Oxford University Press in the UK and in certain other countries

Published in the United States by Oxford University Press Inc., New York

Cover photos (from left to right): UN Photo/Fred Noy, Nicole Brizard, Tim McKulka and Evan Schneider

British Library Cataloguing in Publication Data
Data available

Library of Congress Cataloging in Publication Data
Data available

Typeset by Communications Development Incorporated, Washington, D.C.
Printed in Great Britian
on acid-free paper by
Ashford Colour Press, Gosport, Hampshire

ISBN UNECA: 978-9-21-125110-4
ISBN Oxford University Press: 978-0-19-957429-2

1 3 5 7 9 10 8 6 4 2

Conclusion   263

Annex
ECA Project on Good Governance: Groundwork, Methodology and Indices   267

Boxes

Figures

Tables

There is a growing consensus in Africa that better governance is a key element in promoting growth and development and enabling African countries to achieve the Millennium Development Goals. The Economic Commission for Africa (ECA) is strongly committed to supporting the vision of improved governance by tracking the progress being made in this critical area through the publication of the *African Governance Report*.

The main message of this second edition of the *African Governance Report* (AGR II) is that Africa has made modest progress in improving governance using the benchmarks of the first edition of the report (AGR I). Though marginal, this progress has had positive spin-offs for the continent: declining levels of violent conflicts and civil wars, consolidation of peace and security, economic growth averaging 5% in recent years, modest improvement in the living standards of the African people and fewer deaths from the HIV/AIDS pandemic. Africa also continues to post remarkable progress in economic governance and public financial management. African economies are better managed, with improvements in the tax system and revenue mobilization, improved budgetary management and a more conducive environment for private investment and private-sector growth.

These gains in governance across the political, social and economic spheres must be consolidated and built upon. Several challenges still need to be addressed, including strengthening the confidence of the people in the electoral process and improving the capacity of electoral commissions to conduct free, fair and transparent elections. Similarly, issues such as unequal access to electoral resources and electoral malpractices must be addressed. While respect for human rights and the rule of law is on the ascendance, there are incidences of rights violations that must be overcome. In addition, the free flow of information is needed in the public sphere to further increase transparency and accountability.

The current global economic and financial crisis will undoubtedly have an impact on African economies, for aid and investment flows may be significantly altered and commodity prices adversely affected by reduced demand. But this situation also presents opportunities and challenges for Africa to diversify its economies, gradually create an industrial base, better mobilize investment resources nationally and regionally, and rely less on external sources of finance for development. Moreover, since the extent and scale of the global economic and financial crisis is yet to fully unfold, innovative governance mechanisms will be needed at national, regional and international levels to help African countries cope with the situation.

Governance remains a very sensitive issue, and a report of this nature and scope may be interpreted in some quarters as a scorecard on the governance situation in the countries covered. That, however, is not the intention of this report, which is aimed mainly at enabling governments and citizens alike to assess progress that has been made in governance and assist in identifying areas requiring further action. On its part, ECA has endeavored to maintain technical rigour throughout the study and is committed to ensuring a high-quality, objective, credible and transparent research process in which the views of all stakeholders are presented. Accordingly, the country reports are products of broad consultation with different stakeholders, and over time AGR's contribution to Africa's development process will no doubt be better appreciated and understood.

AGR II covers 35 African countries and is a significant improvement on the first report, which covered 27 countries. Our ultimate goal is to cover the entire continent when conditions permit and necessary resources are available. Meanwhile, I take this opportunity to thank our partners and the various stakeholders who participated for their valuable contributions to the production of AGR II.

I commend this report to all those interested in the progress of governance in Africa and its transformation into a more peaceful, stable, prosperous and better governed continent.

Abdoulie Janneh
Executive Secretary
Economic Commission for Africa

Acknowledgements

This report was prepared under the leadership of Mr. Abdoulie Janneh, Under-Secretary General and Executive Secretary of the Economic Commission for Africa (ECA). Keen to ensure the success and institutionalization of the report, Mr. Janneh supported all of the major proposals of ECA's Governance and Public Administration Division (GPAD), including its publication by Oxford University Press in order to ensure its wider circulation. GPAD is deeply grateful to Mr. Janneh. Deputy Executive Secretary Madame Lalla Ben Barka also actively supported the preparation of AGR II. As the chairperson of the Knowledge Management and Publications Committee of ECA, she kept the report regularly in the forefront of committee deliberations and was always willing to lend a helping hand whenever needed.

The AGR is a synthesis of the country reports, and ECA commends the 35 national research institutions that produced the reports for AGR II. The ECA staff were always at the heels of those institutions to ensure that they followed guidelines, met deadlines and observed quality control measures. ECA is quite pleased that apart from the excellent partnership it has fostered with those institutions, it has also contributed to building the capacity of those institutions for governance research and analysis.

AGR II was conducted under the directorship of Okey Onyejekwe, who provided guidance and an unswerving commitment to the entire project. Said Adejumobi coordinated and provided the technical and intellectual leadership in the production of the report, working tirelessly to bring the report to fruition. Emebet Mesfin diligently handled the administrative and logistical processes of the report, with Monique Nardi Roquette in charge of the country reports. The report also benefited from the intellectual inputs and administrative support of colleagues in GPAD: Kojo Busia, Sam Cho, Jalal Abdel Latif, Kaleb Demeksa, Guillermo Mangue, David Kamara, Guy Ranaivomanana, Hodane Youssouf, Gonazque Rosalie, Juliana Gonsalves, Almaz Mitikou, Taye Said, Yeshimebet Araya, Bethlehem Teshager, Rebecca Benyam, Tsigereda Assayehegn, Loule Balcha, Meaza Molla, Yetinayet Mengistu, Abijah Yeshaneh and Genet Beyene.

Other ECA staff members who provided invaluable administrative and technical assistance include Doreen Bongoy-Mawalla, Emmanuel Nnadozie, Patrick Osakwe, Kavazeua Katjomuise, Charles Ndungu and Max Jarrett.

The ECA owes a great debt of gratitude to those who prepared the chapters of the report. These include some staff of ECA and the Office of the High Commissioner for Human Rights in Geneva and Addis Ababa, and the consultants. They are, namely, Said Adejumobi, Ahmed Mohiddin, Abdul Aziz Jalloh, Asmelash Beyene, Dawit Makonnen, Ibrahim Wani, Patrice Vahard, Gonzaque Rosalie, Ebere Onwudiwe and Tegegne Gebre Egziabher.

Mehret Ayele and Kassahun Berhanu prepared useful background papers for some chapters in the report. Ayenew Ejigou and Legesse Ayane provided excellent statistical support for the entire project. The research assistance of several people is most appreciated: Boris Ephrem Tchoumavi, Gedion Gamora, Kidist Mulugeta, Saba Teklehaminot, Solomon Gashaw, Chimalan Ngu, Grace Gabala and Daniela Casula.

ECA is also grateful to the reviewers of the AGR chapters, some of who attended the AGR II Expert Peer Review Workshop in February 2008 in Addis Ababa, Ethiopia. They are Abdalla Bujra, Adigun Agbaje, Eghosa Osaghae, Melvin Ayogu, Patrick Molutsi, Janvier Nkurunziza, Abebe Shimeles, Zen Tadesse, Cyril Obi, Adebayo Olukoshi, Chantal Uwimana, Muna Ndulo and Chaloka Beyani.

The editors of the report—Communications Development Incorporated, especially Bruce Ross-Larson and Peter Whitten—and Oxford University Press provided invaluable support in finalizing and publishing the report. ECA wishes to thank them for their positive roles.

ECA is grateful to its partners who actively supported this report, including the German government through Deutsche Gesellschaft für Technische Zusammenarbeit, the United Kingdom through the Department for International Development, and the government of Netherlands. ECA hopes that the value of this report in facilitating good governance on the continent will encourage its partners to upscale their support for the project and other partners to come on board in supporting it.

As reflected above, this report is a highly collaborative work. ECA sincerely thanks all those who were involved in its production, including those whose names may not have been mentioned in this acknowledgement.

ecutive
mmary

e
orecard:
arginal
ogress on
vernance in
rica

The *African Governance Report* (AGR) assesses and monitors the progress on governance in Africa, identifies capacity gaps in governance institutions and proposes policy interventions to promote good governance. The report adopts a unique methodology, combining three research instruments—a national expert opinion panel, a scientific sample household survey and desk research. The first edition of the report, published in 2005, covered 27 African countries; this report covers 35 countries.

The main finding of this second edition of the *African Governance Report* (AGR II) is that there has been marginal progress on governance in Africa since the 2005 baseline study (AGR I). The aggregate index for all the indicators of the AGR II expert survey indicated a marginal increase of 2 percentage points from the 2005 study (from 51% to 53%). The core indicators of political representation and independence of civil society organisations and the media had a mixed result, with the former stagnating at 65% and the latter recording a marginal increase of 2 percentage points, from 53% to 55% (figure 1).

There is a slightly better observance of human rights and the rule of law in Africa. In these two areas there has been marginal progress—from 48% in 2005 to 50% in 2007 for human rights, and 49% to 52% for rule of law. Other areas of improvement include the effectiveness of the legislature, executive and judiciary, which all improved by 1 percentage point over the 2005 survey.

On the economy generally, Africa made some notable progress. Economic management (up 3 percentage points), pro-investment policies (6 percentage points) and efficiency of the tax system (3 percentage points) all drew positive evaluation from the expert panel survey. This positive perception of the economy is validated by Africa's average annual growth rate of about 5% over the last decade.

Corruption remains a major challenge in Africa. The corruption control index declined 3 percentage points (from 48% in 2005 to 45% in 2007). African countries need to improve their efforts to fight corruption.

The overall governance picture for Africa is therefore one of limited progress. There is a need to scale up efforts to improve governance in Africa because good governance is central to economic development and to realizing the Millennium Development Goals (MDGs).

Political governance (chapter 1)

Progress on political governance in Africa is mixed. A major finding of AGR II is the continuing liberalization of African polities, which presages a steady (albeit bumpy) development of multiparty politics in the continent. African countries continue to make progress on political inclusion, and voter turnout rates and political participation have increased across the continent. But the picture is not all rosy. Democratic culture has yet to be institutionalized, as vestiges of authoritarianism threaten the

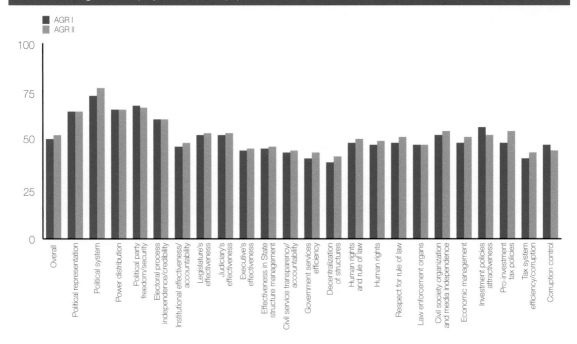

Figure 1 Comparison of survey results in AGR I and AGR II on key governance indicators

Scores, average across project countries (%)

Source: ECA surveys of experts, AGR I and AGR II.

democratic process and the politics of consociationalism and political accommodation are not yet rooted in the polity. Thus political tension, conflict and crises are emerging patterns of electoral politics in Africa.

Multiparty system flourishes, but with poor institutionalization
Since AGR I more African countries have opened up their political systems to competing political parties. Post-conflict countries like Liberia, Sierra Leone and the Democratic Republic of the Congo have joined the rank of democracies in Africa with multiparty systems. Across the continent democratic space

continues to expand, and more political parties compete for power.

But many ruling parties in Africa continue to suppress opposition parties with different degrees of severity. And access to the media, state funds and logistical facilities are skewed in favour of the ruling parties in most countries.

Organisational structures of African political parties remain largely undemocratic. The internal processes of many parties, especially in conducting party primaries, are rarely democratic. Wealthy individuals continue to have disproportionate influence in party affairs and selection of candidates. And parties are not sharply distinguishable by their programmes and policies, suggesting a dearth of ideas, perspectives and visions in the party system in Africa. This general trend of ineffective political parties is exacerbated by the hostility of incumbent parties to the frequently splintered opposition parties and the inability of the latter to form viable, competitive blocs. This situation has not changed since AGR I.

Multiparty democracy stands a greater chance in Africa if contending political parties are given equal opportunities and the parties become institutionalized. While there is a proliferation of parties in the continent, many are too weak to provide effective opposition alone.

Elections are more regular, but flawed in some countries

Elections have become the measure of democracy in Africa. In the decade 1996–2006, 44 elections were conducted in Sub-Saharan Africa; from 2005 to 2007, 26 presidential and 28 parliamentary elections were held on the continent. But the quality of elections remains suspect in many countries. Often they are less a peaceful means of transferring power than a trigger of conflict. Violence often follows elections in Africa, as evidenced by the recent experiences of Kenya and Zimbabwe—not a positive sign of the growth and consolidation of democracy.

In some countries the electoral authorities do not have the autonomy, funding and institutional capacity to conduct free, fair and transparent elections, calling into question the credibility and legitimacy of elections. Incumbent regimes often put unnecessary political pressure on the electoral authorities, undermining their integrity as independent referees in the electoral process. The result is that the choices of the people are subverted. On the other hand, there are other countries where the electoral process and the electoral authorities remain credible and trusted by the people.

Adherence to constitutionalism and the rule of law remains a major challenge

Respect for the rule of law and constitutionalism, though on the increase, is still limited in Africa. In some countries the executive has attempted to change the constitution to stay in power. Between 1990 and 2008 the constitution was amended in eight African countries to elongate the term of office of the president, mostly against popular opinion.

The media in Africa do not operate in a fully free environment—even in South Africa, Nigeria and Kenya, which are noted for the vibrancy and tenacity of their media. And even as civil society organisations continue to grow across Africa, there is some decline in their effectiveness in protecting and promoting human rights.

National governments in Africa are generally unwilling to allow the decentralization of power prescribed by their constitutions. The concentration of resources at the center impinges on the capacity of local governments to operate for the benefit of the local communities.

Social inclusiveness is on the increase

Virtually all the national constitutions of Africa prohibit discrimination on the basis of ethnic, religious, racial or geographical diversity. Some countries make a deliberate effort to ensure ethnic and racial balance in political representation. Overall, Africa is making remarkable progress in women's involvement and representation in public affairs. African countries place high in the global ranking of women's representation in national parliaments: Rwanda tops the list, ahead of older democracies such as the United Kingdom (ranked 53rd) and France (58th). Mozambique also ranked in the top 10, and 9 other African countries (South Africa, Tanzania, Uganda, Namibia, Lesotho, Seychelles, Tunisia, Senegal and Ethiopia) placed in the first 45 of a total of 189 countries from all regions of the world. This is major progress on social inclusiveness in governance in Africa.

Democracy is a work in progress in Africa

The will to make multi-party democracy work in Africa remains strong. At the continental and regional levels, several institutions—most notably the African Union, the Economic Community of West African States and the Southern African Development Community—have taken leadership in promoting democracy and good governance. In 2007 the African Union enacted the African Charter on Democracy, Elections and Governance. The growing demand for pluralism may carry the day for the entrenchment of democracy and good governance in Africa in the years ahead.

Economic governance and public financial management (chapter 2)

Several African countries have made substantial progress toward good economic governance and public financial management in the last few years. But a great deal remains to be done.

There have been marked improvements in recent economic performance in Africa

Africa has experienced solid improvement in economic performance. The continent as a whole grew at an average rate of 5.7% in 2006 and 5.8% in 2007 in real terms, up from an average of 3.4% in 1998–2002. The marked improvement was widespread across countries, with fewer countries recording negative growth than in the last decade, and an increasing number growing above 5%. In 2007 the growth of real GDP per capita exceeded 3% for the third consecutive year, reaching 3.2%, compared with about 1.5% in 2000.

African countries also made progress in creating a macroeconomic environment conducive to private-sector development and investment promotion. For the continent as a whole consumer price inflation is in single digits, government budget balances and current account performance have improved and external debt levels have declined. The debt burden has been eased by relief for low-income countries under the World Bank's Heavily Indebted Poor Countries initiative and the Multilateral Debt Relief Initiative of the International Monetary Fund.

. . . but macroeconomic challenges remain

Improvements in the balances of national budgets and current accounts over recent years were due to the strong performances of net oil-exporting countries on the back of high international oil prices. But rising food and fluctuating oil prices are beginning to pose a threat to price stability and put pressure on budget and current account balances, especially in net oil importers and low-income countries. Another major challenge facing African countries is management of exchange rates to support the competitiveness of the domestic economy while also ensuring that inflationary pressures are kept under control.

Public policy has a crucial role to play in making economic growth broad-based and inclusive

Economic growth in Africa has not been broad-based and inclusive, with a concomitant reduction in poverty levels, creation of jobs or improvements in social development, especially in Sub-Saharan Africa. In Sub-Saharan Africa unemployment rates remain high, the number of people living in extreme poverty is on the increase and progress in reducing under-five infant mortality rates has been slow. Northern Africa is performing well on social development indicators, though female unemployment rates remain high relative to those of males. Youth unemployment is still a major problem in Africa. Public policy has a crucial role to play in improving the quality of economic growth by facilitating private-sector development, improving basic public services and emphasizing social development.

There have been notable improvements in public financial management

Judging from recent trends in government revenue as a percent of GDP, African countries have, for the most part, dramatically increased their revenue mobilization since 2002. A growing number of countries are adopting a medium-term expenditure framework (MTEF) for their budgetary process. More countries are recording smaller budget deficits, meeting their revenue mobilization targets, demonstrating more transparency in monetary policies and improving the auditing of public funds. Despite these positive changes, several countries still score quite low on the control of corruption, the integrity of their tax systems, transparency and accountability.

Transparency and accountability in public finances are still problematic

Introducing transparency in government procurement remains a major challenge. The performance of African countries in budgetary oversight is somewhat negative, due largely to a lack of resources and procedures in the auditor general's office, deficiencies in the powers and exercise of oversight functions by parliament and lack of cooperation by the executive branch of the government. There is an urgent need for accelerated reform and capacity building in public management (public expenditure and financial management), especially to promote transparency and accountability and to control corruption.

Private sector development and corporate governance (chapter 3)

Since AGR I there has been little progress in creating an effective environment for developing the private sector and promoting good corporate governance. In some instances the fault lies in inappropriate policies. More significant is the lack of capacity to implement the strategies and policies adopted.

Progress has been slow in creating an enabling environment for private-sector development
There has been only meagre progress in growing the private sector. Privatization of state enterprises has slowed, perhaps due to the fact that most of the profitable enterprises have already been privatized. Few countries have full-fledged anti-monopoly regimes in place, though more are in the process of adopting such policies and legislation. There has also been limited progress in creating free-market economies, and African countries continue to rank low in the Index of Economic Freedom.

There has been significant progress in reducing administrative burdens on businesses, but the cost of doing business is still high
One area of significant progress is reducing the cost and burdens of doing business in Africa. From January 2005 to June 2007, 29 of the 32 countries surveyed in this report introduced 99 positive reforms: setting up one-stop institutions for investors, streamlining licensing procedures, reducing the cost, duration and procedures for creating or expanding an existing business and reducing the tax burden on businesses. Despite these reforms, African countries lag behind those in other regions on the ease of doing business. In Africa, especially Sub-Saharan Africa, it takes longer and is costlier to start a business and to obtain licenses, the labour market tends to be more rigid, taxes on businesses tend to be higher as a proportion of profits and it is relatively costly to export and import goods. This state of affairs is a cause for concern because there is compelling evidence that heavy regulations governing business and labour and higher corporate taxes are associated with lower levels of investment, employment, productivity and output in the registered sector. Those conditions also encourage a larger informal sector.

Lack of access to finance, land and quality infrastructure services remains a major obstacle to private-sector development
The private sector in Africa lacks access to finance due to the relatively low private savings rate, unsuitable assets for collateral, weaknesses in collateral and bankruptcy laws and

their enforcement, scarcity of credit information to enable lenders to assess potential borrowers and weak financial markets. Access to land is a significant feature of the business environment in Africa because agriculture is the livelihood for a majority of poor people. To facilitate access to land, governments must adopt and enforce policies on land tenure, redistribution, compensation and infrastructure that allow for land registration and transferability as well as enforcement of property rights by the legal and judicial systems. Africa also lags behind other developing regions in the quality, cost and predictability of infrastructure services.

Incentives to attract foreign direct investment remain important
With only a few exceptions, taxes and other incentives continue to be directed largely at attracting foreign direct investment (FDI) instead of boosting domestic investment. Some countries have established economic export processing zones where preferential economic policies—tax incentives, fewer restrictions on hiring expatriate labour, generous foreign exchange retention rates, access to land, developed infrastructure and streamlined procedures—are pursued to attract FDI. Still, the flow of FDI to Africa continues to be far less than the flows to other developing regions, and domestic investment is also low due to low income and savings. Further, the flow of FDI to Africa continues to be concentrated in a few countries rich in oil and other natural resources, with limited impact on domestic employment. The wisdom

of continuing with the strategy of attracting FDI is therefore questionable. Instead, countries should concentrate on improving their overall economic environment.

More countries are adopting regulations and institutions to enforce contracts and protect property rights
Constitutional provisions and legislation have been adopted to enforce business contracts and protect individual property rights, including intellectual property rights and shareholders' rights. The most popular reforms have been specialized commercial courts and simplified court procedures to increase the efficiency and reduce the cost of enforcing business contracts. Reforms aimed at making it easier and cheaper to register and transfer property titles have also been instituted. A number of countries have either adopted national codes on corporate governance or promulgated regulations on the operation of corporate entities, while others have enacted measures to ensure international credibility in accounting and audit practices.

Weaknesses in contract enforcement, protection of property rights and corporate governance persist
Enforcement of business contracts in most African countries is often tedious, time consuming and expensive, giving little incentive to businesses, especially small ones, to use the courts to settle business disputes. Registration of property and applications for intellectual property rights are complex and costly administrative procedures. In the majority

of project countries, less than half of the experts surveyed regarded government as effective in protecting property rights and enforcing business contracts.

Corporate governance has not advanced much in Africa, except for countries in Southern Africa. The data suggest that laws to protect shareholders, especially small shareholders, are not effective, and Africa ranks as the region with the lowest protection of shareholders. But the surveyed experts did rate African governments favourably in this area.

. . . due mainly to institutional capacity deficits, inappropriate legal and regulatory frameworks and poor governance in general
Even when a regulatory and institutional framework exists, implementation is compromised by the lack of effective enforcement mechanisms due to deficiencies in capacity. Institutions for protecting property rights, enforcing business contracts, setting standards for accounting and auditing procedures and requiring compliance with codes and standards of corporate governance remain weak. And they lack the skills and independence to achieve their objectives. The inappropriateness of global standards for local market conditions and economic structures, and the poor political and economic governance in general, including corruption and weak rule of law, also reduce the effectiveness of enforcement.

Checks and balances (chapter 4)
The distribution of political power among the three branches of

government is articulated in the doctrine of separation of powers and stipulated in a constitution. Separation of powers ensures that no branch of government is able to dominate the other branches and agencies of government. In a democracy the executive is periodically elected in open, competitive and fair elections. And in the performance of their functions the appointed civil servants support the executive. To sustain and promote good governance it is imperative to monitor and check the performance of the executive.

Executive dominance persists
Executive dominance is one of the disconcerting features of modern African governance systems, and checking executive power is a major factor in good governance. AGR I concluded that although the phenomenon of the "Big Man" in African governance systems is waning, the tendency of the executive to dominate continues to be a feature of many African states.

Not much has been done since the publication of AGR I to invigorate checks and balances, strengthen separation of powers or constrain the executive. The core structures of the separation of powers are in place in most African countries. There are established legislatures and judiciaries, but there is a lack of capacity, commitment to democracy and respect for the rule of law.

The way forward is to ensure that the modest gains in constraining the executive do not wither away. Measures should be taken to further strengthen them, and new ways should be explored to promote democracy and good governance in Africa.

Non-state actors check executive powers and other agencies of government

Non-state actors (civil society organisations, professional groups and the private sector) can play important roles in checking and balancing the executive and other agencies of government. Across the continent vibrant civil society organisations have emerged, and continue to do so. They have exposed abuses of power and demanded accountability and transparency. Between elections, civil society organisations keep the government on its toes, reminding ministers of their promises, insisting on accountability and transparency and generally keeping alive the democratic process. The majority of consulted experts in all of the reviewed countries shared the view that civil society organisations in most countries enjoy a considerable degree of operational independence and are not constrained by the state or harassed by incumbent political parties.

People's empowerment and vigilance constitute the most effective check on state power

In the last analysis, governance is about people and how they organize themselves to achieve their common objectives. In a democracy people are the ultimate source of constitutional and political legitimacy. They are the beneficiaries of good governance and victims of bad governance. To promote good governance and prevent bad governance, they must be empowered with knowledge about the role and responsibilities of government, their citizenship rights and obligations and the consequences if their rights are infringed upon or their obligations not exercised. Empowered people are likely to call to account those in authority and ensure that the institutions, principles and processes that support checks and balances are strengthened.

Effectiveness and accountability of the executive (chapter 5)

The executive plays a major role in the governance system of African countries. It ensures peace, security and stability, creates the enabling environment and regulatory framework for productive and creative activities and provides essential public services for the citizens. The effectiveness and accountability of the executive are therefore central to state performance. Effectiveness means the executive has the appropriate capacity and legitimacy for performing the expected functions. Accountability entails inclusiveness, popularity, transparency and responsiveness to the public.

Marginal improvement seen in the quality of the executive

While the quality of the executive has improved in some African countries, more needs to be done to improve the qualifications of the leadership on both the political and bureaucratic sides of the executive branch. The lack of intraparty democratic electoral processes in many African countries limits the emergence of leaders with competence and political will.

Institutional capacity of the public bureaucracy remains weak

A competitive, merit-based recruitment system ensures that the best people will be attracted to the public service. Although the principles of competitiveness and meritocracy in the recruitment of civil servants are generally recognized and acknowledged, their implementation has been slow in most countries, often neglected for political and ethnic reasons.

Low pay, poor working conditions and lack of training persist in the public sector of many African countries. Only a few countries have raised salaries to match the cost of living; in many others the salaries do not provide a decent livelihood, especially for the lower ranks of the service. Working conditions also need to be addressed, including adoption of modern information technology. While training facilities are available in almost all project countries, the nature and quality of the training leave much to be desired. With the exception of a few countries, public service reforms have not achieved the intended objectives.

Decentralization brings few gains in service delivery at the local level

African countries have embarked on decentralization programmes to raise the quality of services and bring them closer to the people. But inadequate capacity, poor management and low funding have been the bane of decentralization schemes. Many local authorities cannot provide clean and safe drinking water, maintain adequate standards of sanitation, light the streets, collect garbage, enforce planning laws, repair or build new roads, run markets in an efficient manner, provide amusement parks and regulate businesses in accordance with trading and business laws. Only in four project countries—Tunisia, Seychelles, Gambia and Botswana—did 40% or more of the experts indicate that local governments have the capacity to manage their responsibilities.

Many African governments recognize the positive role of traditional authorities in promoting good governance and facilitating efficient service delivery. But much needs to be done to overcome structural and organisational constraints affecting their efficacy as viable community institutions that can assist in promoting efficient service delivery at the local level.

The delivery of services in many African countries is far from satisfactory. In the health sector the quality of services remains poor. There are critical shortages of trained and qualified health personnel, particularly in rural communities. Hospitals and clinics are overcrowded and operate at less than capacity due to shortages of trained professionals and inadequate equipment.

More resources are needed for the delivery of social services, especially health, education, roads and electricity.

Transparency and accountability of the executive needs to be improved

Many African countries are establishing structures and institutional mechanisms to promote transparency and accountability in the public sector. Those efforts have achieved modest results. There are mixed results on the accountability of the executive in 2007, and the index on civil service transparency and accountability across all project countries increased only marginally from 44% in AGR I to 45% in AGR II.

Scaled-up efforts needed in the fight against HIV/AIDS

The HIV/AIDS pandemic has been contained in some countries and reduced in a few others. But it is still a devastating threat to the economies, societies and governance systems in Africa. A concerted approach in all areas of governance is needed to combat it. The medical and technological components to combat the phenomenon must be in place and updated as medical and technical knowledge improves. In the last analysis, however, the most critical factor is the people and what they can do to contain, moderate and eventually eliminate HIV/AIDS. They must be empowered to understand the pandemic and its impact on their lives and livelihood, lifestyles, cultures and traditions. This can only be achieved through sustained public information, better service delivery and improved livelihoods in the most affected countries.

Human rights and the rule of law (chapter 6)

Human rights and the rule of law are key indicators of good governance. In this regard, Africa has a mixed record: while the formal commitments taken at both the global and regional levels demonstrate a willingness to advance the cause of human rights and the rule of law across the continent, the reality on the ground is unsatisfactory. More efforts are needed, especially to enforce the rights provided for under the various international, regional and national instruments. Moreover, it is important to deepen a culture of human rights in Africa among political leaders, policymakers, bureaucrats and ordinary citizens.

Greater institutionalization of human rights machineries needed

Several African countries are parties to international and regional human rights treaties. In addition to the international commitments they have taken within the United Nations and the African Union, many countries have also established national human rights institutions. These institutions' functions and powers vary from country to country, and in some instances they need to be strengthened to comply with international standards.

In 2008 the African Union merged the Court of Justice of the African Union and the African Court on Human and Peoples' Rights into a single judicial body, the African Court of Justice on Human Rights. If the Court is granted autonomy and the necessary resources, coupled with the appointment of judges with impeccable credentials and integrity, it can be a major regional organ to redress human rights violations, abuses and impunity in Africa.

. . . to face significant enforcement challenges

Despite the improvement in human rights and the rule of law at the continental and regional levels, the domestication and enforcement of provisions at the national level is generally unsatisfactory. Often, formal commitments are negated by the failure of many states to give effect to the relevant treaties as legally binding instruments in national law. African law and practice are below international standards in several areas: gender equality, freedom of expression, religion, peaceful assembly and participation in public affairs. This gap between formal treaty commitments and reality is due to the weakness of state institutions, lack of political will and cultural and traditional prejudices. And public order is often used to justify unreasonable limitations on human rights and public liberties.

Need to deepen the human rights culture

Human rights and the rule of law are the subject of numerous bilateral and multilateral agreements. But internalizing the values contained in the agreements by the various stakeholders is far from a reality. Some states have used public security as a pretext to pass anti-terrorism laws that deny rights holders of their entitlements. The general public has quite a negative perception of law enforcement officials, including the police and the judiciary.

... to increase people's confidence in their institutions

Respect for human rights helps to reinforce the rule of law and increase the confidence of the citizenry in public institutions. But most African countries perform dismally on responding promptly on human rights violations. Impunity and lack of respect for due process of law by state institutions are considered common in many African countries. Only a few countries offer a different picture.

Generally, respect for human rights has improved modestly since AGR I. The overall index on human rights from the ECA survey results indicates a 2 percentage point increase since AGR I, from 48% to 50%. Respect for the rule of law also increased, from 49% to 52%.

Corruption in Africa (chapter 7)

Corruption remains the single most important challenge to the eradication of poverty, the creation of predictable and favourable investment environment and general socioeconomic development in Africa. The general perception of the expert panel is that the major institutions of government—executive, legislature and the judiciary—are corrupt in varying degrees. It is also understood that non-state institutions of civil society and the private sector are not immune to corruption. Corruption continues to deepen poverty and stall the realization of the Millennium Development Goals in Africa.

Concerted efforts made to tackle the problem, but challenges abound

International, regional and subregional instruments on corruption provide the benchmarks and parameters by which African countries can tackle the problem. Many countries have enacted progressive anti-corruption laws, although those laws may not be up to the standards of the international and regional instruments. Multiple anti-corruption institutions have been established in many countries, including those charged with money laundering, a permanent dedicated anti-corruption body, code of conduct bureau, an ombudsman and oversight agencies like the auditor general. There are parliamentary committees, and ad hoc bodies are regularly established to investigate specific cases of corruption or misadministration.

There have been major breakthroughs in anti-corruption investigation and convictions in several countries. In Nigeria the Economic and Financial Crimes Commission recovered about US$5 billion. But many national anti-corruption agencies are relatively weak, with inadequate legal provisions supporting them and a lack of autonomy, and they are subject to undue political interference.

African governments must give greater attention to anti-corruption agencies in four critical areas: the law establishing the agencies, which must conform with the minimum standards set by the United Nations and African Union conventions on corruption; the institutional and administrative autonomy they exercise; their funding; and the process for appointing and removing their members. In turn,

an anti-corruption body has to be accountable to the democratic institutions in its country, especially the parliament but also the people, through activities that are transparent.

Global initiatives reinforce Africa's fight against corruption
To complement the efforts of African countries, there are special initiatives at the international level to fight corruption, including the Extractive Industries Transparency Initiative (EITI), the Publish What You Pay Campaign, and the Kimberley Process. These initiatives have improved management and transparency and accountability in the extractive sector. But corruption in the extractive industry persists, and it has a direct impact on deepening poverty in many resource-rich countries in Africa.

Little progress made in asset repatriation from Western countries
Recovering and repatriating stolen African assets and resources from Western countries remains a dark spot in the global anti-corruption campaign. Western countries do not demonstrate enough commitment to tackle the problem. The legal regime in asset repatriation is complicated and cumbersome, and the costs of asset recovery make it an arduous, if not almost impossible, challenge for African countries.

The provisions of the United Nations Convention against Corruption on asset recovery must be enforced, while the United Nations Security Council should consider classifying the harbouring of stolen assets from poor countries as a global security risk, because it threatens the peace, progress and development of those countries.

Anti-corruption agenda needs to be scaled up

In the final analysis, the fight against corruption will involve considerable efforts by African countries in three areas:

1. *Institutions.* There must be conscious efforts to build key oversight institutions in Africa, namely the parliament, judiciary, the office of the auditor general, the ombudsman, the public procurement system and the various anti-corruption bodies. They need institutional autonomy, operational capacity, resources and a free and democratic environment in which to function.

2. *Anti-corruption constituency.* Civil society and the media, complemented by the key public anti-corruption institutions, can provide a powerful constituency in the fight against corruption in Africa. All the actors and institutions involved in the national anti-corruption campaign need to collaborate and regularly exchange ideas and information.

3. *Remuneration for public servants.* Public-sector workers need living wages to improve their morale and dedication to work and to prevent moonlighting and corrupt practices. Poor salaries encourage both petty

corruption and collaboration in grand corruption.

Institutional capacity building in governance (chapter 8)

Upon achieving independence, many African countries inherited weak and inefficient institutions that had been designed to serve colonial interests. The newly independent countries embarked on building schools, health facilities and universities. Then a shift in the policies of multilateral donors pressured governments to invest less in higher education. As universities declined, many educated Africans left for opportunities abroad. The capacity of universities was further undermined by the brain drain caused by oppressive military and authoritarian regimes.

Other developments heightened the need for capacity building in Africa: the structural adjustment programs of the 1980s, the shift to market economies, demands for transparency and accountability and the advent of information technology. The last few decades have witnessed efforts by national governments and their development partners to address the capacity challenge. The results achieved, however, have not equaled the resources allocated.

Capacity building is more than a technical exercise

Capacity building is about people. They have to be trained, adequately equipped and sufficiently remunerated. Capacity building is also about appropriate policies and infrastructure. But it should be recognized that it is more than a mere technical exercise. It is rooted in the political economy of a country, and any durable capacity-building programme has to design its intervention strategy with that in mind. The major capacity challenge for Africa is to promote the kind of culture of good governance necessary for sound economic management, efficient service delivery and empowerment of the people. Governance capacity is needed to create a capable democratic state, a virile civil society and a thriving private sector with a positive culture of corporate management.

The capacity challenges can be met
As it stands, many governance institutions in Africa—the legislature, executive, judiciary, civil service, political parties, civil society and the private sector—have a serious dearth of capacity. Sustaining and institutionalizing the modest gains in Africa will require a substantial scaling up of capacity development efforts by those institutions. Four interventions will help to address the capacity constraints in governance institutions:

Enhance the capacity of the legislature. The skills of standing committee members need to be strengthened, as well as the technical and professional support for the parliament. Members need resources to strengthen their relationships with constituencies. And training is needed to familiarize newly elected members with the workings of parliament.

Enhance the capacity of the executive. The executive needs to be strengthened by improving skills in policy analysis; formulating, managing and developing programs and monitoring them; strengthening the statistical office to enable it to generate reliable data for decision making and developing think tanks to broaden the sources of vital and credible information for policy discourse. Information technology should be harnessed to improve efficiency of service delivery, and executive capacity should be built to manage the changing role of the public sector in the context of globalization, the market economy, multiparty democracy and the information revolution.

Local governments need an enabling policy environment and adequate financial resources to improve their service delivery to the public. Their capacity for financial planning and management, policy and program design, implementation, monitoring and evaluation and improved accountability should be strengthened. Equally, local governments' capacity to respond to the needs of the community should be strengthened, especially by assisting them to develop a participatory planning and budgetary process that involves communities and other stakeholders in setting priorities and providing oversight.

Enhance the capacity of the judiciary. The judiciary needs adequate resources to improve its remuneration system so it can attract and retain qualified people. An efficient case management system should be built, and information technology harnessed. Continuous training should be provided at all levels to enhance the skills of the judicial staff. Resources should be made available for offices, courthouses and equipment that will improve the efficiency of the courts. Above all, a determined effort is needed to protect the independence of the judiciary in those countries.

Enhance the capacity of non-state actors. Non-state actors have to be able to participate in policy formulation and implementation, advocacy, negotiation and lobbying. Civil society organisations need strong skills to monitor public service delivery.

Funding policies of political parties should be reviewed to ensure that there is relatively equitable support for both large and small parties.

Governments should double their efforts to remove the policy, regulatory and infrastructure constraints that burden the private sector. The private sector should engage in a dialogue with other stakeholders in development, especially the public sector and civil society, to influence the policy agenda

The media in many countries need assistance to improve their skills through appropriate training.

In conclusion

Africa's ability to achieve sustained structural transformation in the decades ahead will depend on the political commitment to support capacity building and to effect the reforms that will enable effective use of that newly built capacity.

The linkages between good governance, democracy and development are recognized by Africa's major national and regional institutions. Across the continent there is a consensus that good governance advances political representation, civil liberties and constitutionalism and increases transparency and accountability. These elements of democracy boost the legitimacy of the state, which in turn promotes the peace and stability crucial for economic investment. In a continent noted for poverty, good governance is therefore a precondition for poverty reduction.

This chapter describes the progress on political governance in Africa, especially since the publication in 2005 of the first *African Governance Report* (AGR I) (UNECA 2005). It analyzes adherence to constitutionalism, evolution towards multiparty democracy, social inclusiveness in political representation, impact of public voices and the integrity and legitimacy of the electoral process. The central message is that progress has been mixed.

Since the foundational elections of the 1980s there have been numerous elections in Africa. But many countries have not had quality elections. Overall there has been notable progress on political governance in some countries, while improvements have been blunted or reversed in others. On balance the progress on political governance has been marginal.

Comparing AGR I and this report, AGR II, the aggregate data for indicators on political governance reveal that the overall index on political representation, independence of the electoral process and power distribution remained the same—65%, 61% and 66%, respectively—suggesting that in the aggregate there was little or no progress. On political party freedom and security, the overall index reveals a backslide of 1 percentage point from AGR I, but there was an increase of 3 percentage points on the rule of law and a similar improvement on independence for civil society organisations and the media. To sum up, there was marginal progress on political governance in Africa from the findings of AGR I to AGR II.

Democratic regime and structure of political representation

A positive shift in attitude toward democratic change of governments is now abroad in Africa. While the quality of elections may be suspect in some countries, there seems to be a general consensus in the population that elections are the best means for alternating political power and changing political regimes.

In the decade from 1996 to 2006, 44 elections were conducted in Sub-Saharan Africa; between 2005 and 2007, 26 presidential and 28 parliamentary elections were held on the continent.[1] In addition Liberia, Central African Republic and the Democratic Republic of Congo have joined the ranks of new African democracies since 2005. Of the 19 African countries with at least 2 successive elections, 12 of them show marked increases in voter registration, indicating greater participation, an element of democracy and good governance (IDEA, 2008; IPU 2008).

This report adds eight countries (Cape Verde, Republic of Congo, Djibouti, Madagascar, Rwanda, Seychelles, Sierra Leone and Togo) that were not part of AGR I.[2] When asked if they thought the political systems in their respective countries were competitive, an impressive number of households surveyed in the eight new countries agreed that politics in their country is pluralistic. Indeed, the survey shows a remarkable consensus in some countries, ranging from about 55% in Seychelles to over 87% in Rwanda.

While the general population in the eight countries may have a rosy perception of the competitiveness of the political system, the experts surveyed expressed skepticism about the general acceptance of the democratic framework. In only 3 of the 32 project countries did more than 50% of the experts agree that the democratic framework in their respective countries is accepted by all social and political groups (figure 1.1). Five countries scored between 39% and 45%, meaning that in over three-quarters of the project countries only 38% or less of the experts agreed that the democratic framework in their countries is accepted by, and entrenched in, all social and political groups. This is not altogether surprising, because it suggests that the

Figure 1.1 Expert opinion on acceptance of democratic framework

Democratic framework accepted by and entrenched in all social and political groups (share of experts surveyed, by country, %)

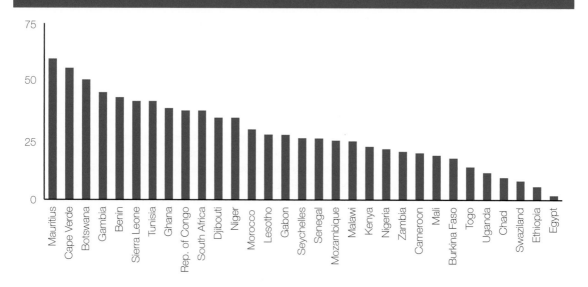

Source: ECA survey of experts 2007.

consolidation of democracy is still in its infancy in a majority of African countries. In Chad, Swaziland, Ethiopia and Egypt the presence of democracy may be so negligible in the opinion of the experts as to warrant little hope for its consolidation. In all, judging from the opinion of each country's experts, the democratic picture in Africa does not appear rosy in three-quarters of the countries in the survey.

Multiparty systems flourish, but with poor institutionalization
Many African countries have evolved from the one-party states of the post-independence period to multiparty systems. This is a welcome development because in Africa the competitiveness and stability of the party system have been found to be positively associated with democracy.[3] Since the "third-wave" of democratization began in the late 1980s, more African countries have opened their political systems to competing political parties. With the political conception of governance focusing on democratic rules and procedures, including political participation and representation, the liberalization of African polities foretells greater development of political parties on the continent.

Since 2001 Africa has held an impressive number of multiparty presidential and parliamentary elections. In the opinion of country experts the trend is toward democracies with more than two independent political parties but a dominant ruling party, followed closely by another set of countries with more than two strong political

---

Box 1.1 Democratic progress in Africa

In South Africa, Benin, Ghana, Cape Verde, Mauritius and Botswana, where successive elections have been adjudged free, fair and transparent, the trend is towards democratic consolidation. Nigeria, Ethiopia, Senegal, Egypt, Uganda, Kenya and Zimbabwe however, have had highly controversial elections. Of particular note are the elections generally acclaimed to be free, fair, transparent and credible in two post-conflict countries—Liberia (2005) and Sierra Leone (2007). Those positive elections constitute major democratic progress for Africa.

---

parties with independent political programmes.

Even Uganda, which had a no-party regime that was in practice a one-party system in all but name, has adopted a multiparty system. Domestic, regional and international pressures facilitated this change. Internal pressures for political reforms were high. The example of multiparty democracy in neighbouring countries—especially in Kenya and Tanzania, which share cultural, political and economic ties with Uganda—had a contagious effect. And external pressures from donor countries in the West further contributed to the change of mind in favour of reform (Kannyo 2004). Alluding to the external influence, President Yoweri Museveni observed, "The people who have opened their markets to us are the ones who want us to open political space to multiparty politics. . . .We should not take decisions that will scare away investors" (Kannyo 2004, 137).

In many countries there are micro-parties, which have few followers and are not worth more than the name they bear—a condition that makes it easy for incumbent political parties to maintain power. The 2007 elections in Seychelles, where all the opposition parties united to contest the elections under the banner of the Seychelles National Party, provides a good example of overcoming the weakness of having several micro-parties, even though the united opposition still lost the election to the incumbent Seychelles People's Progressive Front. International monitors judged the election to be free and fair, and the majority of the national households surveyed supported that verdict. In the ECA expert panel survey 55% of respondents believed that the political system is competitive, and close to 57% considered Seychelles to be a multiparty democracy with a dominant ruling party.

If the 2007 election in Seychelles is a good example of multiparty competition, Nigeria and Kenya's general elections in the same year and that of Zimbabwe in 2008 provided a clear example of derailed party competitiveness. The international and domestic observers of those elections judged them to be highly flawed.

In Benin, Cape Verde, Ghana, Malawi, Morocco and Sierra Leone a majority of the expert panel respondents were of the view that there is a stable multiparty democracy with two strong political parties with independent programmes. In Botswana, Ethiopia, Gabon, Burkina Faso, Niger, Nigeria, Lesotho, Senegal, Swaziland and Zambia a majority of the respondents felt that there was multiparty democracy with two independent political parties but with the ruling party being dominant.

Adherence to constitutionalism still weak

Democratic governance is based on the rule of law, while authoritarianism is based on the arbitrariness of state actions. A political system based on the rule of law institutes a set of rules shaping relations among citizens and between them and the state. Constitutionalism exists in a polity when rules codified in law establish the rights and obligations of both citizens and the state. In such a system no one, including a government official, is above the law. There is no rule of law when powerful government officials disobey democratically crafted laws and regulations.

Limited respect for the rule of law and constitutionalism in many African countries does not augur well for democratic consolidation. In some countries the ruling party has attempted to change the constitution to stay in office (table 1.1). Between 1990 and 2008, eight African countries amended their constitutions to extend the president's term of office. Most of these actions were contrary to popular opinion. In 1997–2000 the constitution of Burkina Faso was amended twice on the issue of presidential tenure. Originally, the constitution limited presidential tenure to a once-renewable period of one term. In 1997 the constitution was amended to make the president eligible for office indefinitely. Three years later the clause limiting the president to two five-year terms

> ‘ **Since 2001 Africa has held an impressive number of multiparty presidential and parliamentary elections**

Table 1.1 Third-term amendments in Sub-Saharan Africa since 1990

Countries in which constitution contains a two-term limit on the presidency in which constitutional amendment has been attempted or not attempted		
Two-term limit reached (21 countries)		
Constitution amendment not attempted	Constitution amendment attempted	
	Without success (3 countries)	With success (8 countries)
Benin (Kerekou)	Malawi (Muluzi)	Burkina Faso (Campaore)
Cape Verde (Monterio)	Nigeria (Obasanjo)	Cameroon (Biya)
Ghana (Rawlings)	Zambia (Chiluba)	Chad (Deby)
Kenya (Moi)		Gabon (Bongo)
Mali (Konare)		Guinea (Conte)
Mozambique (Chissano)		Namibia (Nujoma)
São Tomé and Príncipe (Trovoada)		Togo (Eyadema)
Sierra Leone (Kabbah)		Uganda (Museveni)
Tanzania (Mkapa)		

Source: Extracted, but data updated, from Vencovsky 2007, 17.

was restored. The controversy arose again in 2005. Although President Blais Compaore had served two terms of seven years each, the Constitutional Council declared that he was eligible for re-election, much to the displeasure of the opposition parties and the critical segment of civil society (ECA 2007a). A similar attempt to extend the term of the presidency was made in Cameroon, generating serious conflict.

According to the experts surveyed, respect for the rule of law or constitutionalism is low in most African countries (figure 1.2). In close to 70% of the project countries, fewer than half the experts said that their governments respect due process and the rule of law. This suggests that there is still an authoritarian hangover among the ruling democrats in Africa's emerging democracies. There are, however, hopeful signs from Ghana, Mauritius, Benin, Cape Verde and Botswana, where a strong majority of the experts were of the opinion that there is respect for the rule of law and the constitutional order. Interestingly, the same countries also registered impressive scores for democratic acceptance, suggesting gradual institutionalisation and grounding of democracy in these democratic pace-setting nations.

Leadership systems: presidential, parliamentary or hybrid

The term *leadership system* refers to the institutional arrangements between legislative and executive authorities in African countries. The

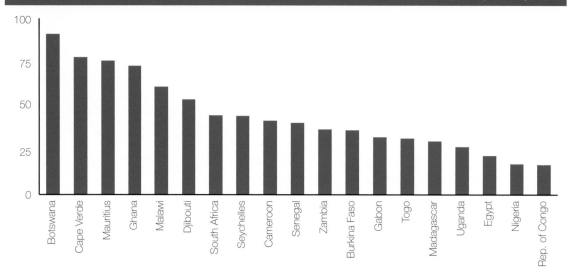

Figure 1.2 Expert opinion on government's respect for the rule of law

Country fully or mostly respects due process and the rule of law (share of experts surveyed, by country, %)

Source: ECA survey of experts 2007.

common prototypes of that relationship are parliamentary and presidential systems. The parliamentary system merges legislative and executive power because the government is drawn from the legislature, meaning that members of the government are also members of parliament. In this system the government has to maintain the confidence of the legislature to stay in power, encouraging accountability on the part of the government. A parliamentary system also encourages effective government. As long as the government has the support of the legislature, it will usually get its legislative programmes approved, making it more effective than governments under a presidential system.

A presidential system of government is defined by the separation

of powers and checks and balances. The members of the legislature and the heads of the executive branch are separately elected into independent law-making and law-implementing institutions, prohibiting the kind of membership overlap that marks the parliamentary system. The main advantage of the presidential system is the web of checks and balances that is supposed to prevent abuse of power by government. The checks and balances allow the different branches to have a say in the powers given to each other by the constitution. The division of power in a presidential system helps to protect civil liberties and human rights of citizens from the abuse of government.

The most common forms of government in Africa are the hybrid and presidential systems (figure 1.3).

Most African countries that inherited the parliamentary system from Great Britain have since dropped it for either the presidential or the hybrid system, primarily because it is difficult to operate a parliamentary system in a country with ethnic heterogeneity. When ethnic politics or outright rigging of elections enable strong political parties to control the legislature through a unified and dependable majority, the government can become dictatorial. The resultant rancour and instability are magnified by opposition politics, a primary feature of the parliamentary system. Nigeria, Uganda, Zimbabwe and Gambia now have presidential systems while the other Anglophone countries—Kenya, Ghana, Zambia, Botswana and South Africa—have opted for the hybrid system.

Constitutional framework: federalism and unitary systems
The most popular forms of a constitution are the federal and unitary

systems of government. In a federal system there are two or more layers of political authorities, which are constitutionally recognized, with clear lines of responsibilities and sharing of political power. Although the layers of authority are to be coordinate and independent, in reality the central authority often exercises more powers than the subnational units. In a unitary system political power is concentrated in the central government, with subnational units

Figure 1.3 Structure of government in AGR II project countries

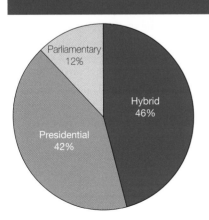

Hybrid
Botswana, Chad, Egypt, Ghana, Kenya, Mali, Namibia, Niger, Senegal, South Africa, Tanzania, Zambia, Djibouti, Madagascar, Sierra Leone

Presidential
Benin, Burkina Faso, Cameroon, Gabon, Gambia, Malawi, Mozambique, Nigeria, Uganda, Zimbabwe, Seychelles, Togo, Tunisia, Rep. of Congo

Parliamentary
Ethiopia, Lesotho, Mauritius, Cape Verde

Source: Compiled from ECA's country reports 2007.

either created by it or enjoying delegated powers from it.

Historical, cultural and even physical characteristics determine whether a country opts for a federal or unitary system. In some states in Africa colonialism was a historical determinant in the adoption of unitary government, as in Kenya and Ghana. In Nigeria and Ethiopia the federal system was conceived as a political instrument to tackle the problem of social pluralism and ethnic heterogeneity. Historical realities and developmental experiences largely inform the constitutional framework a country adopts.

The major question for both unitary and federal systems is how to decentralize power and ensure that government is closer to the people, represents their interests and delivers services efficiently and effectively. While a federal system appears more amenable to political decentralization, the precepts in Africa are often at variance with the practice. Some federal systems have unitary tendencies, while some unitary systems have been able to facilitate genuine decentralization.

Whether a federal or unitary system is being practiced, local authorities must have adequate resources and the capacity to deliver services efficiently to the people. Unfortunately, most local authorities lack the wherewithal to discharge their responsibilities. In some countries local governments serve as institutions of political gratification, used by the ruling party to compensate political allies and potentates. In

> **The high rate of voter turnout, which cuts across gender, ethnic and racial divides, suggests greater political inclusion and participation in the electoral process in many African countries**

others local governments are viewed as substandard or inferior layers of government, which affects the ability of the local authorities to attract the needed manpower and human resources (figure 1.4).

In Zambia the national government deliberately included local authorities in the preparations of the second national strategic plan to fight HIV/AIDS. By including the local authorities in the preparations of the strategy and by anchoring the plan on the local (district) governments, the national government provided a model of how to empower communities to formulate and implement policies (Chuma 2005). It encourages local capacity, especially when supported by the provision of adequate resources to the district government.

Social inclusiveness and political representation

During the long years that authoritarianism held sway in Africa, political exclusion was the organizing principle of political life, as a narrow, elite-dominated politics and controlled state institutions. In those years a great majority of Africans—particularly women, the young, the poor and ethnic minorities—were excluded from political participation.

Today Africa continues to make progress in some areas of social inclusion. The high rate of voter turnout, which cuts across gender, ethnic and racial divides, suggests greater political inclusion and participation in the electoral process in many African countries. In Uganda and Rwanda affirmative action

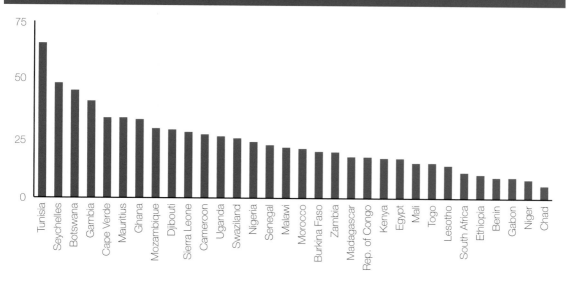

Figure 1.4 Expert opinion on local government capacity

Adequate or some capacity to manage decentralised responsibilities effectively (share of experts surveyed, by country, %)

Source: ECA survey of experts 2007.

policies ensure that women and the physically challenged are represented in parliament and the cabinet.

As in AGR I, many of the households surveyed preferred voting as a form of political participation. Many of the household respondents in the eight countries added in AGR II indicated that they participate in voting as a form of political participation. Togo, Sierra Leone, Seychelles, Rwanda and Madagascar have the highest household ratings for participation.

Regional, ethnic, religious and racial representation

Virtually all national constitutions in Africa prohibit discrimination on the basis of ethnic, religious, racial or geographical diversity. Ghana's constitution not only prohibits such discrimination but also requires the state to promote the integration of all Ghanaians irrespective of differences. According to ECA's Ghana country report, the composition of the executive and the legislature of the country largely reflect the social composition of the country as stipulated by the law (article 35(5) of the 1992 Constitution).[4] But in almost all African countries low literacy and the rural-urban dichotomy appear to thwart political inclusion. The information required for effective participation does not get to the illiterate and the rural dwellers as easily as it gets to the educated and urban citizens. Extreme poverty also diminishes the ability of many Africans to get political information.

Many African countries make deliberate efforts to ensure ethnic and racial balance in political representation. In Nigeria and Ethiopia promoting political inclusiveness informed the adoption of federalism. In South Africa decades of racial discrimination under apartheid led to affirmative action policies that today favour historically disadvantaged groups, especially the blacks. Many African countries have unwritten codes that both the president and the vice-president must be from different parts of the country and sometimes from different religious creeds. It is through this process of conscious but delicate political balancing that many African countries seek to negotiate social cohesion and political stability.

But in Nigeria, Liberia, Sierra Leone, Côte d'Ivoire, South Africa, Rwanda, Uganda and other countries, years of predatory ethnic and racial rule have weakened the bonds between citizens and government. The resultant polarization led to communal violence and even civil wars in those countries, and the arrival of democracy has yet to completely dispel the distrust created by a history of discriminatory politics.

In a culturally heterogeneous continent ethno-regional discrimination lies in part at the heart of political disunity. But many African countries now appear to realize that conflicts caused by exclusion are inimical to good governance because one obviously needs a nation first, before good governance.

Access to land, equitable distribution of resources and the sharing of political power in heterogeneous societies continue to generate communal and ethnic tensions and conflicts. Some of those conflicts are of low intensity, as in the Niger Delta region in Nigeria, and some have been more explosive, as in Sudan, Rwanda, Burundi and Somalia. The challenge is to include all ethnic, racial and gender categories in the political process. While majority rule may be the hallmark of liberal democracy, the protection of minority rights constitutes the major strength and resilience of any democratic system.

Gender representation

In many African countries more women are participating in government and the political process, due partly to conscious policy design by regional institutions like the African Union, subregional organisations like the Southern African Development Community (SADC) and national governments. The African Union has a policy of 50% gender parity in its activities and institutions and encourages its member states to follow suit. The SADC has set a 30% baseline for women's participation in state institutions. Many member states of SADC are struggling to meet the minimum standard.

Box 1.3 Ghana: a conducive environment for freedom of expression

In Ghana the Kuffor administration kept its electoral promise and repealed the criminal libel law. Internet access is unhindered, and the right to peaceful assembly and association fully guaranteed. Except for large demonstrations that may require police presence, permits are not required for meetings and other small-scale demonstrations. It is no wonder that Ghana's democracy is gradually consolidating.

Some African countries have put in place affirmative action policies to accelerate the inclusion of women in the administrative machinery of the state and the political process. In Djibouti the National Strategy for the Integration of Women in Development was established in 1998 to facilitate women's participation in the public life of the country. The Department of Women's Empowerment and Family Affairs was created and situated in the presidency. Currently, women constitute 20% of the civil service but only 9% of government employees belonging to the A category, the highest administrative level. In the judiciary the first female president of the Supreme Court, two magistrate court presidents, and two women members of the Constitutional Council have been appointed. In addition, the first woman head of department in the Ministry of Justice has been appointed. At the political level there is a mandatory quota of 10% for women in the nomination list of political parties.

Togo presents a picture of under-representation of women in state institutions. Only 5 of 35 cabinet members are women (14%). In the National Assembly only 6 out of 81 deputies are women (14%). And only 0.2% of the members of parliamentary committees and executive committees of the main political parties are women (ECA 2007i). As a result, the expert panel opinion in Togo indicates that 46.5% of the respondents are of the view that government services do not address the needs of women.

While African countries need to do more to increase the participation

Box 1.4 Civil society organisations launch campaign for freedom of information law in Africa

In September 2007 in Lagos, Nigeria, 30 NGOs from 16 African countries launched the Africa Freedom of Information Center to support campaigns throughout Africa for FoI adoption and implementation. This exemplary transborder cooperation in advocacy is led by a steering committee of six organisations: Human Rights Network, Uganda; Commonwealth Human Rights Initiative, Ghana; International Commission of Jurists, Kenya; International Federation of Journalists, Senegal; Citizen's Governance Initiatives, Cameroon and Media Rights Agenda, Nigeria. The founding of the Center may lead to the building of informational infrastructures and exchange of ideas, experiences and good practices between the CSOs that work on good governance and democracy in different African countries.

of women in government, they are heading in the right direction. Rwanda is ranked first in the world on women's representation in a national parliament. And Rwanda and Mozambique made the top 10. Further, 11 African countries (Rwanda, Mozambique, South Africa, Tanzania, Uganda, Namibia, Lesotho, Seychelles, Tunisia, Senegal and Ethiopia) were ranked in the top 45 of 189 countries from all regions.

Public voices and the legitimacy of the political framework

To what extent do African governments enjoy popular acceptance and legitimacy? Part of the answer lies in the freedom and independence enjoyed by the media and civil society. In a democracy citizens are the essential actors and have the right and even the obligation to participate in the institutions and processes of their political systems. The media and civil society are two principal channels for citizens to express critical and supportive opinions on public affairs. The freedom and independence of the media and civil society, a measure of the liberalization of the public space, are essential indicators of the vigour of public voice in a given polity.

The term *public voice* refers to the combination of civic engagement, civic monitoring and media independence, as well as citizens' freedom of expression. Public voice as a trait of popular sovereignty is the main source of a government's legitimacy. Public voice or opinion is the definitive measure of emerging African democracies: where it exists in earnest, it reflects citizen valuation of government programmes and the virtue of public officials. The scale of public officials' popularity is a measure of their legitimacy in the eyes of citizens.

Objective impediments to the effectiveness of public voice in Africa

It is common to blame African governments for the limited expression of the public voice in their countries. But governments rarely constitute the only obstacle to effective public opinion. Many African countries contain heterogeneous nationalities that pose formidable language, literacy and geographical barriers to developing an effective public voice.

Multiple languages, poverty and illiteracy

The majority of African countries were unable to enforce a common national language for all their citizens at independence. In its place the ruling elites substituted the

languages of the departing colonial powers in countries that had very low levels of literacy. In many countries the whole population is yet to be conversant with that lingua franca, particularly the poor and illiterate masses living in urban squalor and the countryside. To the extent that the great majority of uneducated Africans cannot communicate in the government languages of English, French or Portuguese, or afford to buy or read newspapers, they are effectively excluded from expressing their opinions or having an effectual voice on public affairs.

Underdeveloped communication infrastructure

In culturally heterogeneous Africa there is limited communication infrastructure—the roads, railways, airports and telecommunication that can link geographically dispersed ethnic groups. There are, therefore, few lines of communication between the different ethno-regional groups, a condition that prevents the exchange of ideas and information. This is still true for most of the democratizing African countries of today. The result is that most African countries do not have a common set of political beliefs— a situation that continues to hamper the development of an effective public voice in the continent.

The media: deepening democracy through information flow

The new mass media in Africa are facilitating a national market place of ideas, where opinions on public affairs compete for acceptance. More individuals in Africa now receive information about their

> ❛ **Public voice or opinion is the definitive measure of emerging African democracies**

governments, both local and national, and views on public affairs that originate outside their localities and ethno-regional communities.

In the past, when government dominated the media, news coverage focused mostly on positive presentation of government activities. This unbalanced and biased news amounted to propaganda, leaving the general citizenry uninformed and unable to participate effectively in public affairs. The AGR I survey showed that while there had been a liberalization of the media space, there was still a heavy reliance on the government-owned media. A great majority of the African households surveyed in AGR I preferred government radio and television to the private alternative. (This was not true, however, of the print media.) Since then the private media have come of age, and many of them serve as reliable sources of information, education and entertainment.

The phenomenal growth of the media in Africa can be seen in Cape Verde and Madagascar. Generally, the government respects the freedom of expression and of the press in Cape Verde (ECA 2007b). The country's media sector has grown from a single radio and television station in the 1990s to seven radio stations today, and in 2006 the state authorized the establishment of four private television stations. Table 1.2 shows a similar trend for the electronic media in Madagascar.

The media are generally considered free and effective in Madagascar, where 33% of the consulted experts expressed the view that the media works in a relatively free environment. In Togo the media sector has expanded from one public television station to four, to numerous private radio stations, and to five weekly magazines and about forty registered but irregular print titles (ECA 2007i).

It is not only the media that are making a difference in governance in Africa. The revolution in information technology—e-mails, mobile phones and text messages—has made communication and campaigning by political parties much easier. Election results are tracked from different constituencies and polling stations by different stakeholders and communicated informally through text messages, reducing election rigging in Africa.

The media: constraints and challenges

Despite the liberalization of the media space, the flourishing of private media organisations and the better access to information by citizens, the media continue to confront major constraints and challenges in Africa. In a 2006 special report the Committee to Protect Journalists listed three African countries—Equatorial Guinea, Libya and Eritrea—among the ten most-censored countries worldwide.[5] Journalists and media workers continue to suffer arrests, disappearances, unlawful detention and imprisonment and laws that limit their capacity to report objectively and act independently. In Sierra Leone media workers are subject to conviction and imprisonment under

> *Since AGR I the private media have come of age in Africa, and many of them serve as reliable sources of information, education and entertainment*

the criminal libel and false news law if they report stories that may cause disaffection against the government or injure the reputation of the government and its officials. The Sierra Leone Association of Journalists has challenged those laws in court.[6]

In Nigeria, in the heat of the third-term campaign by the erstwhile Obasanjo administration, African Independent Television, a media house that covered the deliberations of the Nigerian Senate on the issue, had its Abuja office shut down and marked for demolition by the Federal Capital Development Authority, which alleged that the building was sited in an inappropriate location. In Gabon the National Communications Council suspended *Edzombolo*, a private bimonthly magazine, for three months, and its director was accused of publishing "defamatory and insulting news about prominent state personalities".

Apart from state violations, there are other threats to effective media performance in many African countries. Most journalists receive poor remuneration and have a low standard of living, which makes them vulnerable to compromising the integrity of news coverage by allowing government's influence or private financial inducement to determine what they report. In many African countries the journalists do not have adequate training or the modern tools of the profession.

But some countries do provide a favourable environment for media practice. Ghana's constitution guarantees the freedom and independence of the media but also goes further and explicitly prohibits censorship. One exemplary provision, Article 162(3), requires that there be "no impediments to the establishment of private press or media; and in particular, there shall be no law requiring any person to obtain a license as a prerequisite to the establishment or operation of a newspaper, journal or other media for mass communication or information".[7]

Responses from the panel of experts were varied on the freedom enjoyed by the mass media in African countries. Only Ghana was identified by the majority of the experts as a country where the media operate under a completely free environment. Most of the remaining countries were depicted as places where media freedom is either complete or violated only infrequently by the government or the ruling party. The majority of the consulted experts in Benin, Botswana, Cape Verde, Malawi and Mauritius, among others, support this view. The fact that a significant number of countries were reported as allowing media freedom at varying levels is an encouraging sign, indicating that the media could be one of the pillars of national integrity and contribute to the entrenchment of a system of accountability, transparency and checks and balances.

Freedom of information bill

In general, the media in Africa seem determined to create a conducive environment for holding governments accountable, as evidenced by the push for the enactment of a

> *The fact that a significant number of countries were reported as allowing media freedom at varying levels is an encouraging sign*

freedom of information bill (FoI) in some African countries. The bill extends the right of the public to have access to information that is held by public authorities. Not surprisingly, many governments are opposed to such a bill. In Africa an FoI bill has yet to become a public issue in many countries.

In Nigeria, where promoters of the FoI bill have made some progress, the president vetoed the bill after the National Assembly passed it in 2007. But the bill appears to have a new lease on life under the new administration of President Musa Yar'dua, who has made the rule of law and due process the watchwords of his administration. A signature petition launched in September 2007 by the Nigerian FoI Coalition garnered over a million signatures in just one week. Such bills are also being seriously considered in Kenya, Ghana and Tanzania.

Civil society

Civil society organisations (CSOs) have grown rapidly since the transition to democracy in many African countries. The last five years have witnessed increased effectiveness by CSOs. But the performance and efficacy of CSOs are not uniform across project countries. In some countries there has been a decline in CSO activities, especially in human rights.

Among the works by CSOs in promoting good governance is monitoring the abuses and rights violations by law enforcement agencies. In Ghana 40% of the experts surveyed in AGR I agreed that civil society

organisations regularly monitored human rights violations. In this study only 36% of the same experts still held that view.

An exemplary confederation of NGOs in Senegal stands as a promoter of good governance. The government allows reasonable independence for its CSOs. In 2002, 73.3% of experts surveyed thought the civil society in Senegal was independent of the government, and the present study shows an increase of 1.9 percentage points in this indicator. In Nigeria, where civil society is vibrant, only 15.2% of the expert panel agreed that civil society effectively contributes to the promotion of accountability and transparency in government, while 25% claimed that CSOs do not make any contributions at all to these two major areas. The question of the relevance of CSOs is germane to the emerging democracies of Africa since there is still evidence of government animosity toward civil society inquisitiveness.

The ability of CSOs to influence government programmes and activities fluctuated across countries from the period of AGR I to AGR II. In Benin, Burkina Faso, Malawi, Mozambique and Uganda a majority of the consulted experts perceived CSOs to have a better and stronger influence on government programmes and activities, while the opposite is true in Chad, Ethiopia, Gambia, South Africa and Uganda (figure 1.5).

CSOs in Africa must adapt to the challenge of the new democratic

'The last five years have witnessed an increased effectiveness of CSOs. But the performance and efficacy of CSOs are not uniform across project countries

Strong or fairly strong influence on government policy and programmes (share of experts surveyed, by country, %)

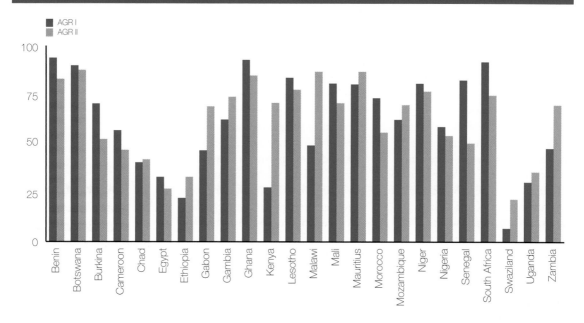

Source: ECA survey of experts 2007.

environment by, for example, learning the public relations, lobbying and information-gathering techniques required for advocacy and compromise in a democratic regime. Some CSOs have adapted reasonably well by focusing on budget monitoring and tracking, lobbying for legislative reforms, seeking electoral and judicial reforms and serving as watchdogs on the transparency and accountability of state institutions.

Most CSOs in Africa have no independent funding sources other than donor support, so their activities are channeled toward donor priorities. They can rarely set their own

agendas or dictate the pace of their programmes. They become caught up in the funding and reporting cycle of their international development partners, which leaves little space for autonomy of action and agenda setting. African governments should consider supporting African CSOs, especially those that have a reasonable track record and a culture of transparency and accountability in their internal management.

Making choices through voting
The increase in the rate of voter turnout in many African countries has not been matched by the quality of the electoral process and electoral

outcomes. Electoral irregularities, rigging and fraud have led some to question the extent to which voting and elections reflect the choices of the people.

Still, voting is a major means of political participation in Africa and a gauge of confidence in the democratic process. The demand for participation in the political process is evidenced by the very high voter participation rate in the eight new AGR project countries, ranging from a 79.4% voter turnout in Togo to 97.7% in Seychelles—a clear indication of progress since AGR I. When the share of households surveyed across project countries was averaged for AGR II, the average turnout rate showed an increase of 4.2 percentage points.

Integrity and legitimacy of the electoral process

Elections have yet to be free and fair in most African countries, even though the intensity of voter fraud is not uniform among the emerging democracies.

All electoral processes and structures—the electoral law, demarcation of constituencies, electoral system, registration of political parties, voter registration exercise, electioneering, processes of voting, counting of votes, declaration of election results and the adjudication of electoral disputes—must be perceived as credible, transparent and legitimate if a democratic system is to be stable (Adejumobi 2000). But there are often disputations and disagreements about the inclusiveness and fairness of those processes

in countries where the ruling party is accused of manipulating the electoral process. In Nigeria, for example, voter registration has been an enduring problem.

The expert respondents were asked whether the electoral law, independent electoral commission and electoral district demarcation were accepted by all the political parties (figure 1.6). In several countries—Benin, Botswana, Cape Verde, Ghana, Mauritius, Niger, Mali, Sierra Leone, South Africa, Morocco, Mozambique, Nigeria and Malawi—a majority of the panel members were of the view that the electoral system was generally acceptable to all political parties, while in Ethiopia, Uganda, Burkina Faso and Madagascar the political parties regard the electoral system marginally acceptable. In Egypt, Chad and Swaziland the perception is that the electoral system is largely or totally unacceptable to all political parties.

Electoral systems in Africa
Broadly speaking, there are two major types of electoral systems: the plurality/majority system and the proportional representative system. Variants of both and mixed types are found in Africa (box 1.5).

Many African countries use the plurality or majority electoral system—the first-past-the-post, winner-take-all system in which the winning candidate gains more votes than any other candidate. The main purpose of this system is to represent the plurality or majority of voters in a constituency. With the exception of its at-large voting variant, it guarantees

> **Elections have yet to be free and fair in most African countries**

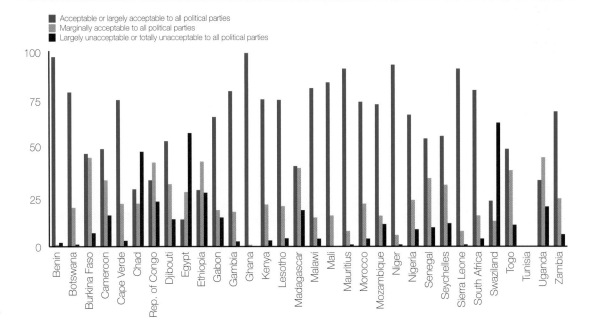

Figure 1.6 Expert opinion on the credibility of the electoral system

Share of experts surveyed, by country (%)

■ Acceptable or largely acceptable to all political parties
▨ Marginally acceptable to all political parties
■ Largely unacceptable or totally unacceptable to all political parties

Source: ECA survey of experts 2007.

representation for all parts of the country. There are different configurations of the plurality/majority electoral system, including single-member district plurality voting, instant run-off voting, two-round run-off voting and at-large voting.

Under proportional representation, the number of seats a party wins in an election is proportional to its support among voters. If a parliamentary district has 100 voters, for example, a political party that wins 60 votes wins 60% of the seats in that district.

The extent to which a parliament is representative depends on whether

the electoral system is capable of reflecting the diversity of interests, ideologies, concerns and common interests of the political forces of a country (IDEA 2007). Generally, proportional representation provides fairer representation for weaker political parties and less privileged national groups such as women and minority ethnic groups, and it provides more opportunity for inclusive governance. The plurality or majority system provides better-focused constituency representation and stronger political accountability by the electorate. In deeply divided societies, however, the electoral system should provide a platform for social inclusiveness and political legitimacy, and serve as an instrument of conflict management and resolution. This is the major challenge for reformers of the electoral system in most African countries.

Political parties

Political parties are non-state institutions with the primary function of nominating and electing candidates for office. In fulfilling these functions, political parties help to facilitate political participation, political education and recruitment. It is in this sense that political parties are important institutions of good governance. But the existence and growth of political parties is directly related to the requirements for their formation and registration, their internal governance, the level of freedom allowed to opposition parties, and the rules governing party financing and the media.

Registration of political parties

AGR I noted that requirements for party registration had been significantly liberalized in many African countries. That trend has continued. In Madagascar 180 political parties exist, although only 9 have a major presence. During the May 2007 elections in Burkina Faso, 126 political parties were recognized, although only 47 stood for electoral competition.

The right to create and join political parties is often defined by the country's constitution or its electoral law, which specify the requirements and processes for the registration of parties. Local sociopolitical conditions determine the ease or stridency of the qualifications and party registration

---

Box 1.5 Electoral system typology of project countries

Plurality or majority electoral system

First-past-the-post electoral system

The candidate who gains more votes than any other candidate is elected, regardless of whether he or she won by absolute majority or not. The voters vote for candidates rather than political parties.

Botswana, Côte d'Ivoire, Ethiopia, Gambia, Ghana, Kenya, Madagascar, Malawi, Nigeria, Sudan, Swaziland, Tanzania, Uganda, Zambia, Zimbabwe

Two-round system

Under the two-round system a second election is held if no candidate or party achieves a given level of votes, frequently a 50%-plus-one absolute majority in the first round of election. In the case where more than two candidates contest the second round, the candidate who wins the highest number of votes in the second round is elected.

Central African Republic, Egypt, Gabon, Mali, Mauritania, Republic of Congo, Togo

Block vote system

Voters have as many votes as there are competing candidates, and candidates with the highest vote totals win. Voters usually vote for candidates rather than political parties.

Mauritius

Party block vote

Voters do not choose between candidates; they vote for political parties. The party that wins the most votes gets every seat in the electoral district.

Cameroon, Chad, Djibouti

Proportional representation

The number of seats that a party wins in an election is proportional to the number of its support among voters.

Algeria, Benin, Angola, Burkina Faso, Burundi, Cape Verde, Equatorial Guinea, Guinea-Bissau, Morocco, Mozambique, Namibia, Nicaragua, Niger, Rwanda, São Tomé and Príncipe, Sierra Leone, South Africa.

Single nontransferable vote system

Voters cast a single vote in a multimember district. The candidates with the highest vote totals win. Votes are for candidates rather than political parties.

Democratic Republic of Congo, Eritrea, Liberia, Libya, Somalia

Source: IDEA 2006.

processes in each country. In some countries political parties are compelled to draw support throughout the country to ensure national unity and social cohesion, especially in plural and socially segmented societies.

In Southern Africa generally, the processes of registering political parties are relatively unencumbered. In Botswana, where multiparty democracy has a long, stable history and acceptance among contending groups (the country has been a constitutional democracy since political independence in 1966), an organisation seeking to be a political party need only register with the Registrar of Societies on prescribed application forms. The only other requirements are that the organisation aspiring to be a political party must have at least ten members, a set of objectives and a constitution that comply with the national constitution and regulations, rules and by-laws that govern its operations. In South Africa the process for registering political parties is similarly uncomplicated. The Bill of Rights there establishes a number of rights for all individuals, including the right to form a political party and to campaign for a political party or for a cause. The country's constitution simply requires registration with the Independent Electoral Commission, submission of party lists to the chief executive officer of the Commission by a specified date and payment of a deposit to the Commission as specified by the Regulations for the Registration of Political Parties.

In Francophone West Africa political parties are mostly registered as

associations, and registration is usually done by a ministry—the Ministry of the Interior in Togo and the Ministry of Territorial Administration and Decentralization in Guinea. In Anglophone West Africa political parties are registered by the electoral commissions (Nigeria, Liberia and Ghana). But in Sierra Leone a separate institution, the Political Parties Registration Commission, handles the registration of political parties. While differing somewhat, the processes of registering political parties in all these countries are fairly relaxed (Adejumobi 2007).

Egypt's Law on Political Parties, which transformed the country from a one-party to a multiparty system, contains some stipulations for forming and continuing political parties. A party's goals, principles and objectives must conform to the principles of Islamic Shari'a, and the party must agree to maintain national unity, social peace, the democratic socialist system and the socialist gains of the Egyptian people. In addition, its platform must be shown to be different from those of existing political parties, and the aspiring party must not be based on class, ethnicity or discrimination against any religion or gender. One of the main obstacles to party pluralism in Egypt was the Political Parties Affairs Committee, the body charged with approving the establishment of new political parties. Until 2005 its membership included a number of government officials, and it did not approve the establishment of any new party to join the four parties established during the

> ‘ *Requirements for party registration have been significantly liberalized in many African countries*

transition to the multiparty system in 1977. It took the intervention of the Supreme Administrative Court to resolve the issue.

In Tanzania and Uganda party registration is not cumbersome, but there are some provisions that make it rigorous to form new parties. Registration of parties in Tanzania is a two-stage process. Under the Political Parties Act of 1992 every political party is to be first provisionally registered and issued a certificate of provisional registration. Within 180 days those parties must apply to the registrar for full registration. The party must have no fewer than two hundred members who are qualified to be registered as voters for the purposes of parliamentary elections from each of at least ten regions of the country; submit the names of the national leadership of the party, which must be drawn from Tanzania Zanzibar and Tanzania Mainland and submit to the registrar the location of its head office in the country. This cumbersome procedure has limited the number of registered parties to 18.

If a party wants to register in Uganda, it must submit a "list of full names and addresses of at least 50 members of the political party or organisation from each of at least two-thirds of all the districts of each of the traditional geographical regions of Uganda listed in the Second Schedule, being members ordinarily resident or registered as voters in the district" (ECA 2007j, 12). This provision makes an otherwise simple registration regime somewhat rigid in Uganda.

The political party space remains largely liberalized in Africa. Political parties are flourishing in many African countries, but their quality, standard and value remain suspect. As democratic culture deepens and the democratization process is entrenched, it is possible that those parties will be streamlined and consolidated, and only few of those existing now will survive.

Democratic deficit in most political parties

The internal governance and functioning of political parties are crucial to their effective performance and institutionalization. Parties that are democratic in their internal governance are more likely to inculcate democratic values in their members, advancing the spread of democratic political culture. They are more likely to be accountable than their authoritarian counterparts and therefore could be more attractive to more people.

But there is a considerable democratic deficit in most political parties in Africa. In Nigeria virtually all the political parties have a serious crisis of internal governance. In the ruling People's Democratic Party (PDP), which describes itself as the largest political party in Sub-Saharan Africa, a recent committee report clearly indicated that the party is largely undemocratic.[8] The report noted that the party had been run in a nondemocratic and noninclusive way for about eight years since its establishment and recommended that the party "commit itself to internal democracy and due process, to ensure transparency and integrity

> *The political party space remains largely liberalized in Africa. Political parties are flourishing in many African countries, but their quality, standard and value remain suspect*

of all party decisions and elections". The PDP is a manifestation of the general failure of the party system in Africa.

There is usually a divergence between the precepts and actual internal governance of political parties. As noted in AGR I, some countries directly encourage internal democracy of political parties through electoral laws and even constitutional provisions. In Ghana the 1992 Constitution explicitly requires that "the internal organisation of all political parties shall conform to democratic principles, and no organisation shall operate as a political party unless it is registered as such". But in Ghana the expert opinion noted that political party rules and regulations and governance within parties are generally weak and discriminatory. Indeed, in Ghana, Kenya and Malawi there is a serious lack of internal party democracy in candidate selection, leadership contests, regular membership conventions, internal rules and accountability of the party leadership (Salih 2006). The ECA Malawi country report noted that candidates are simply handpicked, and in some instances people impose themselves as leaders on the parties without any democratic processes (ECA 2007f).

In Tanzania "many political parties have not formalised internal democracy including membership consultations in critical decisions such as who should be nominated to compete with other candidates. . . . [A]ll of them display a strong propensity towards centralised system when it comes to nomination of candidates

for parliamentary elections" (ECA 2007h, 10). In Egypt political parties are required to have a platform that sets out a democratic process for forming the organisational tiers of the party and electing its leaders and members of steering bodies. But parties in the country rarely follow these rules.

In other countries the issue of internal party governance is the prerogative of the parties without any external regulatory framework. In Botswana each party is guided by its constitutional and organisational arrangements, though all of them require party candidates for parliamentary or local elections to be subjected to primary elections and approval by a central committee. In Zambia the management of political parties is determined by mutually agreed intraparty electoral rules and regulations, which are not always followed in practice. According to ECA's Zambia country report, the Patriotic Front has never had an election for the position of party president. Instead, the founding leader has led the party since its formation, and calls for subjecting him to elections have been rejected on the grounds that the party does not have the resources to conduct a national party conference. The Movement for Multiparty Democracy, another major Zambian political party, has a different provision to frustrate internal party democracy—a clause in its constitution that allows a serving party president to nominate his successor.

Parties founded and sustained by wealthy individuals are invariably

> *Some countries directly encourage internal democracy of political parties through electoral laws and even constitutional provisions*

more authoritarian in governance because members rarely challenge the leader openly. Such political parties are rarely sustainable; with the death or diminished resources of the leader, the party almost immediately begins to falter and eventually collapses.

Limited space for opposition political parties

Frequently, ruling parties in Africa try to suppress opposing parties. Since AGR I the record of African states remains mixed on this measure of political rights in multiparty democracies. In many countries the ruling parties continue to deny opposition parties adequate police protection, disrupt their meetings and rallies, harass their leadership and deny them access to state resources and the public media.

Many countries have legal provisions that seek to promote a level playing field among political parties. But these laws are rarely respected or fully implemented. The ruling party often gains undue advantages by deploying its power of incumbency to corrupt the electoral process. It denies campaign permits to opposition parties and candidates. It inequitably distributes state grants to parties. It prosecutes, harasses, intimidates and sometimes imprisons opposition party leaders. And it uses state resources to further the ruling party's political agenda.

In the more stable democracies of Africa—Botswana, Mauritius, South Africa and Ghana—opposition political parties seem to have more space for action and are better protected; yet the power of incumbency is still dominant. In Ghana the ruling party regularly deploys the power of incumbency during elections. Public officials use official vehicles and drivers and their own time to campaign for the ruling party, even though prohibited by the Political Parties Act. Still, freedom of movement is guaranteed in Ghana for all political party candidates during election campaigns. Despite the incumbency advantages, a majority of the experts surveyed (54%, up from 49% in AGR I) believed that the government provided reasonably good security to all legally registered opposition parties, enabling them to travel around the country. About a quarter of the respondents (23%) felt government provides full security to all legally registered opposition parties.

In many budding democracies in Africa the opposition parties face a hostile political environment. The Uganda country report observed that the ruling party usually misuses the Police Act. The police often stop or disperse the meetings and rallies of opposition political parties while allowing the meetings and rallies of the National Resistance Movement, the ruling party, and its supporters. Before the 2006 presidential election there was an attempt to deny the main opposition party's presidential candidate, Dr. Kiiza Besigye, the opportunity to register or campaign. A few weeks after his return to the country from a four-year exile in South Africa he was arrested and charged with rape and treason. He had to campaign while on bail, his campaign was severely

Frequently, ruling parties in Africa try to suppress opposing parties

curtailed (ECA 2007j) and he lost the election. In Ethiopia a 2005 report by Freedom House noted that "campaigning opportunities have not been equal for various contestants in past elections. Access to print and broadcast media have been widely uneven; permits for campaign events have been issued prejudicially; and access to public facilities has been skewed in favour of Ethiopian Peoples Revolutionary Democratic Front (EPRDF) and its allies" (Clark 2005, 3).

Unequal access of parties to public media

Where the state media are significant during elections, it is important that all political parties have equal access. But access by political parties in Africa to television, radio and newspapers varies from country to country, even though there has been a remarkable media explosion with the current democratization. Political parties usually do not have equal access to public media, which can be skewed in favour of the ruling party in contravention of the electoral law regulating media access during elections.

To ensure equal access to public media by all political parties, some countries establish national media regulatory agencies to enforce equitable media access. This is the practice in many Francophone African countries. In Senegal the National Council for the Regulation of Radio and Television regulates all audiovisual media access by political parties. Similar agencies exist in Guinea, Burkina Faso, Mali, Togo and Côte d'Ivoire (Adejumobi 2007). Despite

these regulatory frameworks, public media access still often tilts in favour of the ruling parties. The ECA country report for Burkina Faso observed that while the High Council for Communication encourages fairness in access to public media, opposition parties complain that in the pre-election period the activities of the opposition parties are rarely covered by the public media but there is full coverage of the ruling party, which helps to sustain public focus on the incumbent and reinforce its dominance (ECA 2007a).

For general elections in Senegal there is no equality of access to public media according to the law. Airtime is distributed among political parties at two levels. On the first level, access is distributed equally among competing parties; on the second it is on the basis of parties' representation in parliament (ECA 2007g). The latter criterion often gives undue advantage to the ruling party, which usually controls the parliament. In Togo, because of the unequal access of parties to the public media, leaders of the opposition parties usually express themselves more through private mass media.

In Malawi the state broadcasting corporation is considered to be biased in favour of the ruling party, giving it overwhelming coverage (about 98%) and preventing the private media from covering the opposition parties. The Malawi Communications Regulatory Authority threatened to close down a private radio station for refusing its order to stop broadcasting political news that was essentially covering the opposition parties

> **Access by political parties in Africa to television, radio and newspapers varies from country to country, even though there has been a remarkable media explosion with the current democratization**

(ECA 2007f). Given this context, most of the expert respondents (82%) were of the opinion that the media did not operate in a free environment and were influenced largely by the government.

In Botswana no laws govern the parties' access to publicly owned media. It is generally left to the national public broadcasters, Radio Botswana and Botswana TV, to cover political party activities in accordance with their editorial policies and programme requirements. Given the unequal capacity of the political parties, media access is often skewed. Thus only a small percentage (17%) of the expert respondents felt that access to public media and other resources was equal for all political competitors in the country.

Ghana's constitution requires that all presidential candidates and political parties be given the same amount of time and space on the state-owned media to present their programmes to the people. But the provisions are not often complied with during election campaigns. A report by the Accra-based Centre for Development and Democracy revealed that the ruling party enjoyed overwhelming advantage in public media coverage, reflecting the expert panel's view that the public mass media was relatively inaccessible to opposition political parties. Only 24% of the expert panel, down from 41% in AGR I, said the public mass media were equally accessible to all registered political parties.

Political parties have greater access to the media in South Africa than

in most African countries. The Independent Communication Authority of South Africa regulates media access. Its broadcasting regulations are legally binding under the Independent Broadcasting Authority Act. During the prescribed election period political parties are allowed free broadcast time according to a formula that considers the need for all parties to be heard, the number of seats held by each party in the respective legislatures and the number of seats or legislatures being contested by a party. The system appears sensitive to the needs of new parties because the formula allows for parties with no representation to achieve one-fourth of the maximum points available to any party. The Independent Communication Authority determines the sequence of party broadcasts by drawing lots. Broadcasters are required to allow the discussion of conflicting views and to treat all contesting parties equitably. Throughout the designated election period it is required that parties be given the opportunity to respond when criticized in a broadcast. Even with these legal provisions, there are incidences of disproportionate coverage of the ruling party by the public broadcasting stations in the country's recent elections (Lodge and Scheidegger 2006).

In Cape Verde, Mozambique, Benin and Morocco a majority of the expert panel respondents were of the view that the public media is equally or largely accessible to all registered political parties, while the reverse is the case in Ethiopia, Lesotho, Democratic Republic of the

> ' *Political parties have greater access to the media in South Africa than in most African countries*

Congo, Swaziland, Egypt, Uganda, Madagascar, Zambia, Malawi and Tunisia.

Party funding

Liberal democracy is an expensive project. Multiparty competitive elections cost money. Political parties have to pay for election campaigns, party administration, print and electronic advertising and other expenses. They also have to buy or rent offices, pay their staff, conduct policy research, participate in voter registration exercises and perform other party functions that are expensive. The quest for funds by political parties can induce corruption, which is why many governments, including many developed democracies, regulate party funding and provide some quantum of support for political parties, especially in election periods.

There are three types of state support for political parties. Some countries provide financial support based on fixed criteria, usually according to a party's performance in elections or its representation in parliament (Nigeria, Democratic Republic of the Congo, Malawi, Lesotho, Egypt, Togo, Cape Verde, Cameroon and Namibia). Others do not provide financial support to parties but instead make available other forms of electoral resources, such as vehicles, buildings and printed campaign materials (Ghana). Still, others provide no support to parties (Botswana, Tanzania, Kenya). In the third approach political parties are considered to be private entities to be privately funded and run like any other non-state entity.

Increasingly, governments are seeking to regulate the funding of political parties, even if they do not provide state financial support. Regulation promotes a culture of public accountability by the parties, because political parties are institutions with deep public interest. It also ensures that political parties are not controlled by vested interests, especially the rich. And regulation prevents parties from becoming conduits of foreign support and foreign agendas. In fact, many African countries outlaw foreign financial grants to political parties except contributions from the national diaspora, which have to be channeled through or reported to the state.

Nigeria obliges all political parties to submit to the Independent National Electoral Commission all of their sources of finance and to publish a statement of party assets and liabilities. Parties are required to disclose their election accounts to ensure that no party possesses funds or other assets outside the country. In addition, assets or funds remitted to political parties from abroad are to be transferred to the commission within 21 days of receipt, with such information as may be required. The commission is also empowered to give directions to political parties regarding the records of financial transactions. But these rules are rarely obeyed in Nigeria, and the commission has never sanctioned political parties for not complying with required financial regulations or auditing their accounts regularly.

In Togo political parties derive their funding from membership

> *Increasingly, governments are seeking to regulate the funding of political parties. Regulation promotes a culture of public accountability by the parties*

contributions, donations and their activities, as well as some government financial grants. The law requires that to qualify for state funding political parties have to receive no fewer than 5% of the votes at the national parliamentary elections. But the grant to a party must not exceed 25% of the sum of the party's resources.

In Egypt the Law on Political Parties stipulates that the state shall provide to each registered party an annual financial stipend. The amount is 100,000 L.E. annually for each party for the first ten years following its founding. Beyond this period a political party shall be eligible for such amount if it wins at least one seat in the People's Assembly or the Shura Council. A party will also receive 5,000 L.E. for every seat it wins in the latest elections of the People's Assembly or the Shura Council, up to a maximum of 500,000 L.E. for each party. A party's income is restricted to the annual subscription fees of its members, the money it receives as state funding determined according to each party's electoral power, the donations it receives from citizens of Egypt and the returns on the investment of its assets in non-trading operations (for example, the profits from sales of the party newspaper). The law requires each registered party to report its annual balance sheet to the auditor-general, the body responsible for performing auditing operations on the sources of income of each functioning party. Again, the laws are rarely implemented. Egypt's auditor-general has yet to find a case of financial malpractice by any of the established parties. This does not mean that such incidents have never happened (ECA 2007c).

South Africa is more generous than most countries in state funding of political parties, though it discriminates against newly formed parties. The South African constitution requires that the government provide funding for political parties participating in national and provincial legislatures on an "equitable and proportional basis". The implication of the word "participating" is that the funding provision is restricted to parties already in parliament, meaning that new parties are not entitled to public funding.

State funding in South Africa appears to be used as an instrument to encourage the national breadth of political parties. Ninety percent of public funds granted to parties are allocated in proportion to the strength of representation of the party in the national and provincial legislatures. The remaining 10% is shared by the nine provincial legislatures on the basis of the number of seats each has as a portion of total provincial legislative seats. The provincial legislature then distributes the money equally among the represented parties. As a result, political parties with seats in more provinces receive a larger share of the equitable part of the fund than parties that do not, even if they hold fewer provincial seats in total. For example, in 2006 the African Christian Democratic Party, which had eight members of parliament in six legislatures, received a larger equity

> *Many African countries outlaw foreign financial grants to political parties except contributions from the national diaspora*

transfer than the Inkatha Freedom Party, which had 32 members concentrated in two legislatures. Parties with representation in the National Assembly, but without any representation in the provinces (such as Azapo), receive no money through the equity formula.

The following African countries provide public funding for political parties:

- Angola, which also prohibits funding of political parties by foreigners and foreign governments.

- Malawi, where political parties that receive more than 10% of the vote qualify for public funding.

- Lesotho, where half of the funds provided by the Independent Electoral Commission are shared equally by registered political parties and the remaining half shared according the number of candidates fielded for election.

- Namibia, where public funds are distributed to the political parties in parliament in proportion to the votes received in the previous election.

- Seychelles, where the registrar of political parties allocates public funds in proportion to the number of votes obtained by parties in the previous election, although parties that did not participate also receive some funding.

There is an urgent need to review and reform the party financing regime and the regulatory framework in many African countries

There is an urgent need to review and reform the party financing regime and the regulatory framework in many African countries. An argument can be made for scaling up state financing in many countries, and some creative rethinking is needed on the criteria for determining state financial allocation to parties, to give preference to the weaker and vulnerable parties—as opposed to the current systems, in which stronger parties have an advantage.

Electoral commissions
Electoral commissions, which go by different names in different countries, are charged with the responsibility of managing elections. Their ability to do so depends on their independence. Typically, the commissions are established by law or by national constitutions. Their performance in conducting free and fair elections determines the legitimacy they enjoy among citizens.

The composition, structure, functioning, autonomy and effectiveness of electoral commissions differ from country to country. In many African countries electoral commissions lack adequate autonomy and capacity, which undermines their legitimacy and performance. Incumbent regimes often seek to manipulate the electoral commissions in order to influence the outcome of elections. In Nigeria, Kenya, Egypt, Ethiopia, Gambia, Burkina Faso, Senegal, Zimbabwe, Uganda and Cameroon opposition political parties and civil society have questioned the autonomy and credibility of the electoral commission. In South Africa, Sierra Leone, Liberia, Ghana, Cape Verde and Namibia the electoral commissions have maintained relative autonomy and credibility, earned by their efficient and impartial management of the electoral process.

Namibia has a unique procedure for the composition of its electoral commission, which enjoys a high level of credibility and integrity. Under the Electoral Amendment Act of 1998, a selection committee screens prospective candidates. Based on performance in open interviews, the committee recommends eight candidates to the president, who appoints five of the eight. The duration of office for the commissioners should not exceed five years, though they are eligible for reappointment. The commission is under obligation to submit annual reports to the president and speaker of the National Assembly, describing the discharge of its administrative functions and matters relating to the electoral process.

Cape Verde is another success story. The National Commission of Elections is an independent, permanent organ that works closely with the National Assembly. The commission comprises five members chosen by the National Assembly by a two-thirds majority vote. The commission chooses its president and vice-president from its own members. The term of office is six years, renewable once. The commission is independent, and its members cannot be removed without proven cases of gross misconduct. Cape Verdeans are highly satisfied with its integrity and performance. Two-thirds of the expert respondents are of the

opinion that political parties and candidates accept the legitimacy of the electoral authority, and 86% considered the electoral law to guarantee the autonomy and independence of the electoral system (ECA 2007b).

Tanzania presents an interesting balance between the search for autonomy and the popular perception of the electoral authority's performance. Its constitution states that "for the better carrying out of its functions, the electoral commission shall be an autonomous department". To strengthen the commission's autonomy, article 74(11) of the constitution reads, "[T]he electoral commission shall not be obliged to comply with orders or directions of any person or any government department or the views of any political party". Furthermore, to insulate it from undue litigation, article 74(12) states that no court shall have power to inquire into anything done by the electoral commission in the discharge of its functions, and when a candidate has been declared by the commission to have been duly elected president, no court of law shall have any power to inquire into the election of that candidate (Article 41(7)). But these constitutional provisions do not seem enough to insulate the commission from political pressures. Or from critics, who point to the fact that the president appoints members of the electoral commission and that the commission relies on the goodwill of the executive for its funding. When asked about views on the impartiality of the electoral commission, a slight majority of the experts (51.6%) indicated that

> ‘ *In many African countries electoral commissions lack adequate autonomy and capacity, and incumbent regimes often seek to manipulate the electoral commissions*

the incumbent government controls the electoral commission; only 21% held the view that the commission is always or largely impartial.

Several countries—Uganda, Kenya, Nigeria, Senegal, Zimbabwe, Gambia, Cameroon and Ethiopia—provide examples of a growing crisis in electoral management and the dwindling credibility of the electoral authority. In Senegal the Independent National Electoral Commission is a legally independent institution, imbued with relative financial autonomy. Yet serious issues arose over the management of the February 2007 elections. Opposition parties and civil society groups questioned the partiality of the electoral commission, alleging that it acted in favour of the ruling party. The expert panel opinion from the Senegal country report corroborates that view (ECA 2007g). In 2002 about 68% of the experts believed that the electoral commission was impartial, but by 2007 the score had dropped to 24%. Only 45% held the view in 2007 that the political community recognizes the legitimacy of the electoral authority, down from 60% in the 2002 survey.

The Electoral Commission of Kenya has 22 commissioners, including a chairman and vice-chairman, who take decisions by a simple majority (European Union Election Observer Mission 2008). The commission commenced work with the 1992 general elections. During the Inter-Party Group negotiations (the period of Kenya's democratic transition), the political parties agreed to share responsibility

for the nomination of commissioners with final approval of the president. Shortly before the 2007 elections, however, the president decided to unilaterally replace nine of the commissioners without consulting the other political parties. This action attracted sharp criticism from opposition political parties and eroded public confidence in the electoral authority. The new commissioners were perceived as biased in favour of the ruling party, and most of them lacked experience in electoral administration (European Union Election Observer Mission 2008), which may have affected the conduct of the December 2007 general elections in the country.

The Kenya country report noted that "the institution lacks capacity to manage elections" (ECA 2007d, 5). This fact was confirmed by none other than the chairman of the commission, Samuel Kivuitu, when he noted that the electoral process was far from free and fair, and that reforms are needed to improve the situation. The chairman pointed to the powerlessness of the Electoral Commission to curb electoral violence, saying that "the electoral offences Act is a dead law because the office of the Attorney General does not seem to know it exists" (ECA 2007d, 14–15). He further noted that "terms of service are not spelt out anywhere, and security of tenure for commissioners was illusory as the vital decisions are in the hands of the president who is a player in the electoral game" (ECA 2007d, 15). In this context the stage appeared set for the electoral mishap in December 2007. In its report on

> *In several countries there is a growing crisis in electoral management and a dwindling credibility of the electoral authority*

the 2007 elections the EU Election Observer Mission stated:

> [T]he ECK [Electoral Commission of Kenya] failed to meet international standards of transparency in key areas of its mandate. Crucial safeguards against malpractices such as those designed to ensure full confidence in the results were lacking. . . . ECK made no provision for results to be pasted at the constituency tallying centers. Furthermore since results are not published down to the level of polling stations, they cannot be systematically corroborated by party agents and observers. . . . ECK chairman, Kivuitu admitted publicly on 2nd January 2008 that he acted under pressure when announcing the results. The declaration of presidential winner in the absence of all original result certificates and the external pressure on the ECK to prematurely announce the presidential results are indications of a breach of the Constitution and the electoral law (constitution, Article 41, 9; ECK Regulations, Section 41, 2a) (European Union Election Observer Mission 2008, 16).

The elections, to say the least, were not credible or transparent, free or fair.

In Uganda the electoral commission is established by the constitution and intended to be independent. But as the Uganda country report noted, "[B]ecause of the appointment mode of the electoral commission is composed of only members and/or supporters of the NRM and President Museveni, it is a clearly partisan commission" (ECA 2007j, 14). In the expert opinion survey a majority of respondents did not regard the commission as legitimate or impartial in managing the electoral process. The view that the government or ruling party controlled the electoral commission was held by 41%; only 21% regarded the electoral commission to be largely or fairly impartial (figure 1.7).

Securing the autonomy (both political and financial) necessary for the electoral commissions to discharge their responsibilities creditably is a challenge. Both respect for the spirit of the law and restraint on the part of ruling parties in unduly seeking to influence the electoral commissions are required. In addition, there is a need to address the problems of personnel, logistics and limited infrastructure for electoral management.

Continental and regional strides in political governance

The struggle for good governance in Africa has not been limited to states. Several multilateral institutions— the African Union and regional economic communities such as the Economic Community for West Africa and the Southern African Development Community—have taken up the mantle of leadership in the promotion of democracy and good governance in African countries. The Constitutive Act of the African Union emphasizes

' Securing the autonomy necessary for the electoral commissions to discharge their responsibilities creditably is a challenge

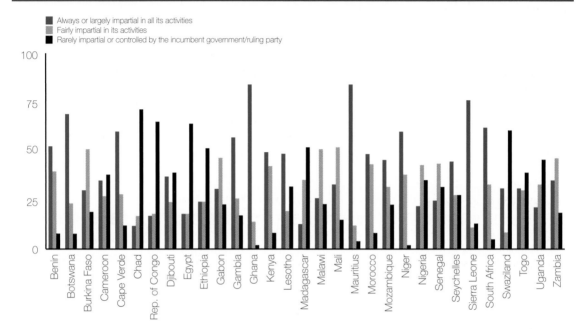

■ Always or largely impartial in all its activities
■ Fairly impartial in its activities
■ Rarely impartial or controlled by the incumbent government/ruling party

Source: ECA survey of experts 2007.

democracy, good governance, rule of law and human rights. The New Partnership for Africa's Development, the economic programme of the African Union, adopts an integrated approach to development that emphasizes the connections between democracy, good governance, peace, security and development in Africa. The New Partnership for Africa's Development therefore includes provisions on political and economic governance and the African Peer Review Mechanism, a voluntary, nonadversarial, self-assessment peer-review process by African countries. This voluntary system assists participating countries in developing and promoting laws, policies and

practices to enhance political stability, economic growth and sustainable development.

On 30 January 2007 in Addis Ababa, Ethiopia, the 8th Ordinary Session of the African Union Assembly adopted the African Charter on Democracy, Elections and Governance. The document, developed as part of the African Union's determination to promote democracy and good governance in member states, is aimed at solidifying the political reforms that have been achieved in the continent. Several provisions underscore the African Union's resolve to promote good governance in member states: a statement accentuating the importance of pre-election observation missions; a call for state parties to invite the AU Commission to monitor elections; a stipulation of the need for independent and unbiased national election bodies; a requirement that state parties provide an environment that will enable independent and impartial domestic NGOs to monitor elections and many other provisions to facilitate free and fair elections.

In its charter the African Union underlines its rejection of illegal assumption of political power in member states. Article 23 stipulates that "illegal means of accessing or maintaining power constitute an unconstitutional change of government". It goes further to define "illegal means" to include an inventory of most of the ills that have bedeviled those trying to consolidate democracy and political stability in much of the continent, including the use of military coups, mercenaries, armed rebels and dissidents to overthrow democratically elected governments and incumbents' undemocratic attempts to amend the constitution to prolong their tenures.

Africa's regional economic communities have also been active in promoting democracy and good governance, with the Economic Community of West African States (ECOWAS) at the forefront.[9] In addition to its acclaimed peace operations in Liberia from 1990 to 1997, in Sierra Leone (1997–2000), in Guinea-Bissau (1999) and in Côte d'Ivoire (from 2003), which led to recent democratic elections in

Box 1.6 Sierra Leone's National Electoral Commission enjoys high credibility and legitimacy

The Sierra Leone National Electoral Commission conducts all public elections in the country. Although its commissioners, including its chairperson, are appointed by the president in consultation with the opposition parties in parliament, all political parties and other stakeholders generally regard it to be independent. Approaching the 2007 elections, the commission demarcated the constituencies, accepted by all the political parties to be fair, and registered 2.6 million voters, of whom 75.8% turned out to vote in the parliamentary and presidential elections in August 2007, the most successful multiparty election in Sierra Leone's political history.

Liberia (Adejumobi 2006) and Sierra Leone, the ECOWAS member states in 2001 adopted the Protocol on Democracy and Good Governance to aid its work on conflict resolution, peacekeeping and security in the region. The protocol emphasized that the organisation will no longer tolerate the seizure of political power and continuation in office by unconstitutional means in member states, and called on all members to guarantee the rule of law, freedom of association and assembly, press freedom, human rights, transparent elections and the implementation of other elements of democracy.

Like ECOWAS, the Southern African Development Community[10] (SADC), formed in 1992, has also enjoined its member states to develop democratic institutions and practices and to observe universal human rights as contained in the Charter and Conventions of the Organization of African Unity (now the AU) and the United Nations. SADC's Principles and Guidelines Governing Democratic Elections is informed in part by the AU's

Guidelines for African Union Electoral Observation and Monitoring Missions and the AU's Declaration on the Principles Governing Democratic Elections in Africa.

Concluding remarks

Progress has been mixed in Africa's quest for democracy. Some countries have advanced remarkably, while others have stagnated and a few have had apparent reversals. Ghana, Benin, Cape Verde, Botswana, Mauritius and Tanzania have passed the two-elections test— that is, conducting two successive democratic elections and ensuring orderly regime change. Impressively, the post-conflict countries Liberia and Sierra Leone also recently conducted general elections regarded by domestic and international observers as free, fair, transparent and credible. But Nigeria, Kenya, Senegal, Zimbabwe, Uganda and Ethiopia conducted controversial and questionable elections, signaling democratic decline in those countries.

Adherence to constitutionalism and respect for the rule of law are still low. Space for opposition political parties to operate is shrinking, and access to public resources by parties is uneven, with the ruling party mostly at an advantage. The media have blossomed, but violation of the media's rights is still rampant. The electoral process does not have the required public confidence to keep the democratic project on a speedy momentum in many countries. Put differently, the demand of the African people for democracy is very high, as evidenced by high voter turnouts and general political participation. But the supply from the leadership is low. There is a need to create a convergence between the aspirations of the people and the quality of leadership and political governance.

Notes

1. Presidential elections were held in Sierra Leone, Mali, Nigeria, Mauritania, Senegal, Madagascar, Zambia, Gambia, Democratic Republic of the Congo, São Tomé and Príncipe, Seychelles, Chad, Comoros, Benin, Uganda, Cape Verde, Tanzania, Gabon, Burkina Faso, Liberia, Guinea-Bissau, Togo, Djibouti, Central African Republic and Egypt. Parliamentary elections held in Madagascar, Sierra Leone, Cameroon, Mali, Republic of Congo, Senegal, Seychelles Nigeria, Burkina Faso, Benin, Lesotho, Gambia, Gabon, Mauritania, Zambia, Democratic Republic of Congo, São Tomé and Príncipe, Uganda, Cape Verde, Tanzania, Gabon, Zimbabwe, Liberia, Burundi, Mauritius, Ethiopia, Zimbabwe and Central African Republic.

2. The study in the eight new countries was conducted using all three research instruments (C1, C2 and C3). The update of the 27 countries from AGR I was conducted using only the expert panel and instrument (C1) and desk study (C3). Figure 1.1 uses the C2 instrument (household opinions), the reason only the new countries are in figure 1.1.

3. Party system competitiveness is defined as the effective number of parties; party system stability is the

> *Progress has been mixed in Africa's quest for democracy. Some countries have advanced remarkably, while others have stagnated and a few have had apparent reversals*

average age of parties. See Kuenzi and Lambright 2005.

4. Article 35(5) of the Constitution of Ghana, 1992, states that "the state shall actively promote the integration of the peoples of Ghana and prohibit discrimination and prejudice on the grounds of place of origin, circumstances of birth, ethnic origin, gender, or religion, creed or other beliefs".

5. The non-African countries on the list are Burma, North Korea, Belarus, Syria, Turkmenistan, Uzbekistan and Cuba. See www.cpj.org/censored/censored_06.html.

6. For more information, see www.justiceinitiative.org/db/resources2?res_id=104048.

7. Appropriately, however, for protecting the reputations, rights and freedoms of others persons, provisions of Articles 162 and 163 of the Constitution are subject to implementing laws.

8. The Committee is known as the National Reconciliation Committee, led by a former vice-president, Dr. Alex Ekwueme. *Guardian* (Lagos), 17 March 2008.

9. Members of ECOWAS are Benin, Burkina Faso, Cape Verde, Côte d'Ivoire, Gambia, Ghana, Guinea, Guinea Bissau, Liberia, Mali, Niger, Nigeria, Sierra Leone, Senegal and Togo.

10. Members of SADC are Angola, Botswana, Democratic Republic of Congo, Lesotho, Malawi, Mauritius, Mozambique, Namibia, South Africa, Swaziland, Tanzania, Zambia and Zimbabwe.

References

Adejumobi, Said. 2000. "Elections in Africa: A Fading Shadow of Democracy?" *International Political Science Review* 21(1): 59–73.

———. 2006. "Reviving a Failed State: The 2005 General Elections in Liberia." *Journal of African Elections* 5(1): 126–152.

———. 2007. *Political Parties in West Africa: The Challenges of Democratization in Fragile States.* Stockholm: IDEA.

Chiroro, B. 2006. "The Dilemma of Opposition Political Parties in Southern Africa." *Journal of African Elections* 5(1).

Chuma, A. 2005. Remarks to the Local Government Association of Zambia Annual General Meeting and AMICAALL General Assembly, Livingston.

Clark, J. 2005. "Countries at the Crossroads 2005—Ethiopia." *Freedom House Report.* www.unhcr.org/cgi-bin/texis/vtx/refworld/rwmain?page=printdoc&docid=473869

CPJ (Committee to Protect Journalists). 2006. "North Korea Tops CPJ List of '10 Most Censored Countries.'" www.cpj.org/censored/censored_06.html.

Diamond, L., and M. Plattner, eds. 2006. *Electoral Systems and Democracy.* Baltimore: Johns Hopkins University Press.

ECA (Economic Commission for Africa). 2005. *African Governance Report.* Addis Ababa.

———. 2007a. Burkina Faso country report. Addis Ababa.

———. 2007b. Cape Verde country report. Addis Ababa.

———. 2007c. Egypt country report. Addis Ababa.

———. 2007d. Kenya country report. Addis Ababa.

———. 2007e. Madagascar country report. Addis Ababa.

———. 2007f. Malawi country report. Addis Ababa.

———. 2007g. Senegal country report. Addis Ababa.

———. 2007h. Tanzania country report. Addis Ababa.

———. 2007i. Togo country report. Addis Ababa.

———. 2007j. Uganda country report. Addis Ababa.

European Union Election Observer Mission. 2008. *Kenyan Final Report on General Elections of 27 December 2007.*

Freedom House. 2005. Freedom of the Press—Morocco. www.freedomhouse.org/inc/content/pubs/pfs/inc_country_detail.cfm?country=6795&pf.

IDEA (International Institute for Democracy and Electoral Assistance). 2006. *Electoral Systems Design: The New International IDEA Handbook.* Stockholm.

———. 2007. *Political Parties in Africa: Challenges for Sustained Multiparty Democracy.* Stockholm.

———. 2008. *Voter Turnout.* www.idea.int/vt/survey/index.cfm.

IPU (Inter-Parliamentary Union). 2008. *Women in National Parliaments.* www.ipu.org/wmn-e/classif.htm

Kannyo, E. 2004. "A New Opening in Uganda." *Journal of Democracy* 15: 126–139.

Kuenzi, M. and G. Lambright. 2005. "Party Systems and Democratic Consolidation in Africa's Electoral Regimes." *Journal of Party Politics* 11(4): 423–446.

Lijphart, A. 1994. *Electoral Systems and Party Systems: A Study of Twenty-Seven Democracies, 1945-1990.* New York and London: Oxford University Press.

Lodge, T. and U. Scheidegger. 2006. "Political Parties and Democratic Governance in South Africa." Electoral Institute for South Africa (EISA) Research Report 25.

Obiorah, N., ed. 2004. *Political Finance and Democracy in Nigeria: Prospects and Strategies for Reform.* Lagos: CLASA.

Ogbodo, J. 2008. "Alex Ekwueme Report: Great Expectations as Peoples Democratic Party Begins Work." *Guardian Newspaper* (Lagos), 17 March.

Salih, M. 2006. "Globalization and Party Politics in Africa: The Influence of Party Based Democracy Networks." in Peter Burnell, ed., *Globalizing Democracy: Party Politics and Political Parties.* London: Routledge.

Vencovsky, D. 2007. "Presidential Term Limits in Africa." *Conflict Trends* No. 2.

African leaders recognize that good economic governance is an integral part of sustainable development and a key to poverty reduction. One objective of the African Union's New Partnership for Africa's Development (NEPAD) is for Africa to promote democracy, good governance and peace in close partnership with development partners. Developed countries on their part have also committed to supporting good economic governance in Africa, as demonstrated by the declarations at the various summits of the Group of 8 major industrialized countries (G-8), in the 2007 G-8 Action Plan for Good Financial Governance in Africa and the 2005 Paris Declaration on Aid Effectiveness.

In general, economic governance is concerned with creating a macroeconomic environment and an institutional and legal framework conducive to private-sector investment, employment creation, economic growth and efficient, effective management of public funds and resources. Good economic governance exists in those economies where the institutions of government:

- Manage funds and resources efficiently and effectively.

- Formulate, implement and enforce sound policies, rules and regulations.

- Can be monitored and held accountable.

- Respect the rules and norms of economic activity.

- Promote economic activity unimpeded by corruption and other activities inconsistent with the public trust.

The key elements contributing to an environment of good economic governance are transparency, accountability and an enabling environment for growth (ECA 2002).

Efficient economic governance enhances the capacity of the state to deliver on its mandate to improve the standard of living of its citizens. Besides the material benefits— improved health, literacy and public services—broad-based economic growth reduces poverty and increases employment. Economic growth provides the funds to finance investments in primary and secondary education, health, water, sanitation and other infrastructure services, all of which contribute to the quality of life and sustained economic growth. And growth makes investment in market-supporting institutions, such as the rule of law, property rights and a competent bureaucracy, viable.

But positive outcomes of economic growth are not automatic. They depend on a host of factors, the most important being public policy. Government policy that develops the private sector will ensure that economic growth is broadly based.

Macroeconomic performance

The causes of sustainable economic growth are economic institutions, geographical factors and government policies (Acemoglu, Johnson and Robinson 2005; Easterly and Levine

2003). Economic institutions that protect property rights, enforce contracts and reduce the cost of doing business provide incentives for the accumulation of capital, innovation and adoption of technology to foster growth. Countries endowed with natural resources in high demand will tend to have high rates of economic growth, while countries without easy access to international trade and those with adverse soils, ecological conditions and high disease burdens will tend to have lower productivity and slower economic growth rates. A macroeconomic environment that encourages private enterprise to flourish—low and stable inflation rates, a competitive exchange rate, sound public financial management, openness to international trade and low-cost infrastructure services—will foster economic growth.

Economic growth
Compared with the early 1990s, when economic growth averaged an anemic 1% per year, Africa has experienced a marked improvement in growth in the last decade. The continent as a whole grew in real terms at an average rate of 5.7% in 2006 and 5.8% in 2007, up from an average of 3.4% for the period from 1998 to 2002 (table 2.1). The average growth rate in Africa was 4.3% for the ten years up to 2007, which still lags behind East Asia and South Asia but is better than Latin America and the Caribbean region.

The marked improvement was widespread, with few countries recording negative growth and an increasing number growing above 5%. Sub-Saharan Africa, North Africa and Nigeria grew at virtually the same rate of 4.5–4.6% over the decade from 1998, while South Africa posted average real GDP growth of 3.5% in the same period. Net fuel exporters grew at an average of 4.7% in 1998–2007, while net oil importers registered an average growth rate of 4.4% over the same period. In 2006

Table 2.1 Africa: real GDP growth rates, 1998–2007 (annual percentage change)

Economy	Average 1998–2002	2003	2004	2005	2006	2007[a]	Average 1998–2007
Total Africa	3.4	4.6	4.8	5.2	5.7	5.8	4.3
Sub-Saharan Africa (excluding Nigeria and South Africa)	3.5	3.3	5.8	5.9	6.1	7.0	4.6
North Africa	3.8	5.2	4.8	4.5	5.8	5.6	4.5
Nigeria	2.7	10.7	4.0	7.1	5.2	5.5	4.6
South Africa	2.7	2.8	3.7	5.1	5.0	4.8	3.5
Net fuel exporters	3.5	5.8	4.7	5.9	5.9	6.6	4.7
Net fuel importers	3.3	3.5	4.9	4.7	5.5	5.1	4.0

Note: Weighted average of individual country growth rates of GDP based on GDP in 2000 prices and exchange rates.

a. Estimated.

Source: UNDESA 2008.

only one African country had negative growth, compared with 16 in 1990. And 23 countries registered growth of above 5% in 2006, compared with 14 in 1990 (table 2.2).

The improvement in African living standards is evident even after allowing for population growth. Growth of real GDP per capita in 2007 exceeded 3% for the third consecutive year, reaching 3.2%, compared with about 1.5% in 2000. Only 8 countries had a negative real per capita growth rate in 2006 compared with 20 in 2000, and 6 countries recorded growth above 5% (table 2.3).

The healthy economic growth in African countries was due to a confluence of factors: higher international prices for commodities, debt relief, political stability and improved macroeconomic management. Countries rich in natural resources benefited from the higher prices of commodities in world markets and increased foreign direct investment flows to the extractive sector. Increased government spending also supported economic growth in resource-rich countries and in low-income countries that qualified for debt relief under the Heavily Indebted Poor Countries (HIPC) initiative of the World Bank and the Multilateral Debt Relief Debt Initiative (MDRI) of the International Monetary Fund. The end of violent conflicts and subsequent relative political stability in Angola, Republic of Congo, Côte d'Ivoire, Liberia, Mozambique and Sierra Leone have helped to reverse their economic fortunes during the past decade.

Table 2.2 Africa: real GDP growth rates (number of countries)

Country growth rates	1990	2000	2005	2006
Negative	16	9	1	1
0–3%	9	16	12	2
3–5%	13	12	13	15
Above 5%	14	14	25	23
Not available	1	2	2	2
Total	53	53	53	53

Source: AfDB 2007b.

Table 2.3 Africa: Real per capita growth rates (number of countries)

	1990	2000	2005	2006
Negative	25	20	4	8
0–1.5%	10	10	13	5
1.5–5%	12	17	29	32
Above 5%	5	4	5	6
Not available	1	2	2	2
Total	53	53	53	53

Source: AfDB 2007b.

Macroeconomic environment
Macroeconomic stability and a predictable policy environment are indispensable for effective private-sector development, investment promotion and sustained economic growth, as well as for effective delivery of public services. An unstable macroeconomic environment creates uncertainties about relative prices, undermining long-term planning and deterring investment. High-inflation environments complicate government planning and make the delivery of public services more problematic. Governments running large budget deficits may have to

compete with the private sector to borrow funds, pushing up the cost of borrowing and crowding out private-sector investment. Servicing of large external debt diverts resources away from public investment in education, health, infrastructure and economic institutions that in turn support private-sector development. Over the last decade African countries have made good progress in creating a macroeconomic environment conducive to private-sector development and investment promotion.

Inflation

Consumer price inflation for Africa as a whole fell from an average of 7.6% annually in 1998–2002 to 5.8% in 2005, before rising to an estimated 6.2% in 2007 as a result of increases in the international price for food and oil. The improved performance was even more impressive for Sub-Saharan Africa (excluding Nigeria and South Africa), where inflation has been reduced by more than half. Even in Nigeria inflation fell significantly from 2005 to 2007. The inflation rate in net fuel importing countries also fell by 3.9 percentage points in 2007 compared with 1998–2002.

Public finance

Budget performance. In the past, macroeconomic instability in African countries was largely fuelled by persistent government deficits financed by printing money. Government deficits are caused by weak revenue mobilization, profligate government spending and anticipatory spending, including anticipation of donor inflows. Poor budgetary discipline will raise demand-pull inflation,

crowding out the private sector from the financial market because of high interest rates and unsustainable debt profiles, all of which slow private-sector growth and reduce business confidence in the economy.

Of the 35 countries under survey, 20 improved their budget balances in 2007 compared with their 1997–2002 average, including all net oil exporters and all middle-income net oil importers except Egypt. Ten countries registered a budget surplus in 2007, including all five net oil exporters, three resource-rich countries—Botswana, Namibia and South Africa—and two resource-scarce countries— Lesotho and Morocco. The budget improvements resulted from the increase in government revenue due to the rise in international demand for commodities, reductions in central government spending relative to GDP, enhanced revenue mobilization and debt relief. In Nigeria, although government revenue fell from 20.9% of GDP in 1997–2002 to 16.2% in 2007, government spending also fell from 23.2% of GDP to 15.3%, translating into an improvement in budget outcome from a deficit of 2.3% of GDP to a surplus of 0.9%.

Government revenue. Revenue mobilization is a vital part of public financial management and governance, which relies heavily on an efficient tax system. Since 2002 African countries have dramatically increased their revenue mobilization to finance their economic development agenda.

Among the 35 survey countries, 28 registered much higher government

> *Since 2002 African countries have dramatically increased their revenue mobilization to finance their economic development agenda*

revenue as a percentage of GDP in 2007 than their 1997–2002 average. Among the net oil exporters, government revenue fell as a percentage of GDP in Gabon and Nigeria despite the rise in international oil prices. In contrast, government revenue in Chad rose substantially from 2005 to 2007 due to both higher oil production and higher oil prices.

As expected, government revenue as a share of GDP tends to be higher in middle-income countries than in low-income countries because better management of tax systems tends to increase with income. Seven low-income countries—Burkina Faso, Ethiopia, Madagascar, Rwanda, Sierra Leone, Tanzania and Uganda—had government revenue of less than 15% of GDP, the minimum level considered desirable for low-income countries. Low-income countries need to improve domestic revenue mobilization to finance development spending without hurting investment and private-sector development. As tax rates on profits in African countries tend to be higher than elsewhere, raising rates is not an option in most countries. The introduction of indirect taxes would be at odds with a government's pro-poor policies because for the poor they represent a higher proportion of their income. Instead, countries should broaden their tax bases by strengthening their tax management systems to reduce tax evasion and by limiting exemptions, which will reduce the complexity of the tax system and raise revenue to invest in education, health, infrastructure and market-supporting

institutions—thus improving the business environment.

External debt. External debt levels have also declined across the continent. The stock of outstanding external debt declined as a percentage of GDP from an average of 62.4% for 1998–2001 to 47.9% for 2000–2005, and to 23.1% in 2007 (ECA 2008), mainly due to the improvement in the economic performance of African countries and debt relief under the HIPC initiative and the MDRI for low-income countries.

External sector

The current accounts for African countries have improved, moving from a surplus of 0.7% of GDP in 1999–2005 to a surplus of 5.3% in 2006, before falling to an estimated surplus of 2.9% of GDP in 2007 (table 2.4). Again, the improvement of the current account balances in recent years was due to the strong performances of net oil-exporting countries. The current account surplus increased from 3.7% of GDP in 1999–2005 to 10.0% in 2007 for net oil exporters, while the deficit for net oil importers widened to 4.3% of GDP in 2007 from 2.0% in 1999–2005. The deterioration in the balance on the current

The current accounts for African countries have improved due to the strong performances of net oil-exporting countries

Table 2.4 Africa: current account balance (% of GDP)

Economy	1999–2005	2006	2007[a]
Africa	0.7	5.3	2.9
Net oil exporters	3.7	14.0	10.0
Net oil importers	−2.0	−3.6	−4.3

a. Estimated.
Source: AfDB and OECD 2008.

account for net oil importers was the result of high oil prices.

A major challenge facing African countries is the management of exchange rates to ensure the competitiveness of their domestic economies while also controlling inflationary pressures. Most of the countries that experienced significant real appreciation in exchange rates benefited from higher prices for commodities in the international markets. The countries from the CFA franc zone—Benin, Burkina Faso, Niger, Senegal and Togo—experienced real appreciation because the CFA franc is tied to the strong euro. The economies of these countries will tend to lose competitiveness. The eight countries experiencing real depreciation in their currencies are in danger of developing inflationary pressures unless appropriate measures are taken.

Structural transformation

Structural transformation is the process by which nonagricultural sectors increase their shares of employment and output. It therefore involves a net resource transfer from agriculture to other sectors over the long term.

Structural transformation has four major indicators: a declining share of agriculture in economic output and employment, a rising share of urban economic activity in industry and modern service, migration of rural workers to urban settings, and demographic transition to lower rates in births and deaths. All these features are critical to reducing agriculture's share in the total labour force and promoting economic growth.

In Sub-Saharan Africa the share of the labour force in agriculture was reduced by 8.5 percentage points from 1996 to 2006, while in North Africa it was reduced by 1.1 percentage points (table 2.5).

Countries more advanced in their demographic transition (with low fertility rates) are doing well in transforming their economies (ECA 2005). They have lower shares of their total work force in agriculture, higher agricultural labour productivity and higher infrastructure development. Table 2.6 shows structural transformation for selected survey countries (where data is available), using trends in share of the labour force in 1990 and 2000.

Of the survey countries, Namibia, Cameroon, Nigeria and Togo reduced the share of their labour force by more than five percentage points between 1990 and 2000. At the other extreme Burkina Faso achieved no structural transformation over the same period.

While some structural transformation took place between 1990 and 2000, it was not to a sufficient degree, and African economies are still dominated by low productivity in the agricultural sector. The decline in the share of agriculture is accompanied in most cases by an increase in the share of employment in the services sector and the informal sector, which is an extension of the agrarian economy.

With 70% of poor Africans living in rural areas, poverty in the continent is largely a rural phenomenon.

In Sub-Saharan Africa the share of the labour force in agriculture was reduced by 8.5 percentage points from 1996 to 2006, while in North Africa it was reduced by 1.1 percentage points

Table 2.5 Employment in Africa across economic sectors in 1996 and 2006 (% of total)

Region	Agriculture		Industry		Services	
	1996	2006	1996	2006	1996	2006
North Africa	35.5	34.4	19.8	20.0	43.7	45.6
Sub-Saharan Africa	74.4	65.9	7.5	10.0	18.1	24.1

Source: ILO 2007.

Increasing rural employment and income is therefore crucial to reducing poverty. An increase in nonagricultural rural incomes will likely improve the living standard of the rural poor, but it could also drive a structural transformation of the whole economy.

Social development

Recent economic growth in Africa has been solid, with real GDP growth of 4.3% over the past decade. Economic growth alone, however, is not enough to improve living standards. To foster economic development, economic growth must be broadly based, lifting the standard of living of the majority of the population. Analysis of performance relative to the Millennium Development Goals (MDGs) can reveal the extent to which economic growth in African countries has made inroads in fostering growth in employment, reducing income poverty, improving education and health, promoting gender equality, empowering women and increasing access to water and sanitation.

Employment

With a higher unemployment rate than other regions, African countries must include employment creation in their development

Table 2.6 Share of African labour force in agriculture (%)

Selected survey countries	1990	2000
All countries	73	68
Botswana	46	45
Ghana	59	57
Kenya	80	75
Namibia	49	41
Cameroon	70	59
Nigeria	43	33
Senegal	77	74
Tanzania	84	80
Togo	66	60
Zambia	74	69
Burkina Faso	92	92
Malawi	87	83
Mali	86	81
Niger	90	88
Uganda	85	80

Source: ECA 2005.

programmes. The unemployment rate in Africa fell only marginally from 8.5% in 1997 to 8.2% in 2007; corresponding figures for North Africa were 11.7% and 10.9% (table 2.7). Those figures are considerably higher than in South Asia or the rest of the world.

High youth unemployment is a particular problem in Africa, where the

Table 2.7 Labor market indicators in Africa, 1997–2007

Economies	Unemployment rate (% of labor force)				Annual labor force growth (%) 1997–2007[a]	Annual GDP growth (%) 1997–2007[a]
	1997	2002	2005	2007[a]		
Sub-Saharan Africa	8.5	10.2	9.7	8.2	3.0	4.1
North Africa	11.7	13.7	11.6	10.9	3.3	4.9
South Asia	4.7	5.1	5.3	5.1	2.4	6.4
World	6.1	6.6	6.4	6.0	1.7	4.2

a. Estimated.

Source: ILO 2007 and ILO 2008.

unemployment rate for the 15-to-24-year-old age group is about twice that of the overall labour force (table 2.8). The youth unemployment rate in Sub-Saharan Africa fell only slightly from 2002 to 2006, and only at a slightly better pace in North Africa over the same period. Whereas the female unemployment rate in Sub-Saharan Africa is similar to that of males, the female unemployment rate in North Africa was 17.1% in 2006 compared with 9.6% for males.

Job creation is an even more pressing challenge in Africa, given the relatively high growth of the labor force. The labor force in Africa grew just over 3.0% per year on average from 1997 to 2007, compared with 2.4% in South Asia and 1.7% globally (table 2.7). Given these statistics, it would seem that the recent improvement in economic growth has so far not resulted in a significant growth in employment. One reason is that economic growth was driven in the main by extractive industries, which have little direct or indirect impact on employment. And the growth rates were not high enough to generate employment for those already in the labor force as well as for new entrants in the job market.

Income poverty and inequality

In general, poverty reduction has been limited in Africa since the 1990s. Although the percentage of those in the labor force actively looking for work without success is 8.2% in Sub-Saharan Africa and 10.9% in North Africa, the percentage of employees who are poor is much higher.

The number of African workers living on less than a dollar a day

Table 2.8 Women and youth unemployment rates, Africa, 1996–2006 (% of labor force)

Group	1996	2002	2005	2006[a]
Women				
Sub-Saharan Africa	9.2	10.2	9.7	9.7
North Africa	19.3	19.7	17.2	17.1
Youth				
Sub-Saharan Africa	17.6	18.7	17.8	17.8
North Africa	28.6	29.0	25.6	25.7

a. Estimated.

Source: ILO 2007.

increased from 132 million in 1997 to an estimated 158 million in 2007 (table 2.9). In 2007 an estimated 53.0% of workers lived in extreme poverty in Sub-Saharan Africa. This figure rises to 85.4% if US$2 a day is considered as the poverty line. In North Africa, by contrast, 1.6% of those employed lived on less than a dollar a day in 2007, and 42.0% lived on less than two dollars a day in 2007, compared with 50.1% in 1997.

Using an improved dataset, the World Bank revised poverty estimates in 2008 as part of its 2005 International Comparison Program. The Bank proposed a new international poverty line of US$1.25 a day at purchasing power parity (PPP) for 2005 (Chen and Ravallion 2008). Based on the new poverty line, the global poverty count for 2005 was estimated, and past estimates were revised as far back as 1981. The new dataset shows that the incidence of global poverty is higher than previously estimated. But the incidence of poverty has been declining since the 1980s, as previously predicted.

The number of people in the world living on less than US$1.25 at PPP fell from 1.9 billion in 1981 to 1.4 million in 2005 (table 2.10).

Table 2.9 Working poor indicators in Africa, 1997–2007

	Number (million)			Share of total employment (%)		
	1997	2002	2007[a]	1997	2002	2007[e]
US$1 a day						
Sub-Saharan Africa	130.7	143.6	157.3	57.4	55.6	53.0
North Africa	1.2	1.0	0.9	2.6	2.0	1.6
Africa	131.9	144.6	158.2			
US$2 a day						
Sub-Saharan Africa	197.8	224.0	253.3	86.8	86.7	85.4
North Africa	22.5	24.4	25.2	50.1	48.7	42.0
Africa	220.3	248.4	278.5			

a. Estimated.

Source: ILO 2008.

Table 2.10 Population living below US$1.25 a day, 1981–2005 (millions)

	1981	1990	1996	2002	2005
East Asia and Pacific	1,087.6	893.4	642.2	543.9	336.9
Sub-Saharan Africa	202.0	283.7	347.8	373.2	384.2
World	1,904.2	1,815.5	1,673.8	1,627.0	1,399.6

Source: Chen and Ravallion 2008.

Table 2.11 Population living below US$1.25 a day, 1981–2005 (% of population)

Economy	1981	1990	1996	2002	2005
East Asia and Pacific	78.8	56.0	37.1	29.6	17.9
Sub-Saharan Africa	50.8	54.9	57.5	52.7	50.4

Source: Chen and Ravallion 2008.

Table 2.12 Distribution of Gini coefficients for selected African countries

Range	Countries
30–39	Benin, Egypt, Ethiopia, Malawi, Mauritius, Tanzania, Tunisia
40–44	Burkina Faso, Cameroon, Republic of Congo, Gabon, Ghana, Kenya, Mali, Mozambique, Niger, Senegal, Uganda
45–49	Gambia, Madagascar
50–55	Lesotho, Nigeria, Rwanda, Swaziland, Zambia
56–60	Botswana, Cape Verde, Namibia, South Africa
Above 60	Sierra Leone

Source: AfDB and OECD 2008.

This reduction in global poverty was mainly due to the massive fall in the number of people in East Asia and the Pacific region living in extreme poverty from just over a billion in 1981 to 337 million in 2005.

The number of people living in extreme poverty in Sub-Saharan Africa rose by 182 million to 384 million between 1981 and 2005. As a percentage of the population, those living in poverty increased from 50.8% in 1981 to 57.5% in 1996, before trending downward to reach 50.4% in 2005 (table 2.11). It would seem that the economic growth starting in the latter part of the 1990s is starting to tackle the persistent challenge of extreme poverty in Sub-Saharan Africa.

Although economic growth has resulted in a fall in the share of people living in poverty in Africa, it has not translated into an improvement in the distribution of income. Figure 2.1 shows that the share of national consumption going to the poorest quintile of the population in 2004 was unchanged from its 1990 level of 3.4%, while in North Africa it increased slightly from 6.2% to 6.3% over the same period.

Table 2.12 shows the degree of inequality as measured by the Gini coefficient for survey countries with available data for 2000 onwards.[1] For the 30 countries in the table, the Gini index for income inequality ranges from a low of 30 in Ethiopia to a high of 62.9 in Sierra Leone (on a scale of 0 to 100).

The Southern Africa region has the least egalitarian income distribution in Africa. Six countries from the region—Botswana, Lesotho, Namibia, South Africa, Swaziland and Zambia—rank in the top ten of the most unequal countries in the sample.

Apart from African countries, 14 countries in the Latin America and Caribbean region and Papua New Guinea have a Gini coefficient above 50 (UNDP 2008).[2]

Education

Only 13 of the 53 African countries are likely to achieve the target of universal primary education by 2015, as set in the MDGs. Millions of children are not attending school, especially in rural areas, more than half of them girls. All North African countries are on track to reach the target with an average primary enrolment ratio of 95% in 2005 after allowing for drop-outs. The average primary enrolment ratio for Sub-Saharan Africa was 70% in 2005, up from 57% in 1999.

Only Algeria, Cape Verde, Egypt, Mauritius, Seychelles, Tanzania and Tunisia are likely to ensure that by 2015 all children will be completing primary school. But Ethiopia has made considerable progress on the education goal in the last 15 years.

Health

Life expectancy at birth is 50 years for all of Africa and 46 years for Sub-Saharan Africa. The life expectancy in North Africa is 71 years (World Bank 2006). In Sub-Saharan Africa, Mauritius and Cape Verde have the highest life expectancy, averaging 73 years and 70 years, respectively. Due to the HIV/AIDS pandemic, the spread of malaria and tuberculosis and regional conflicts, life expectancy at birth in the rest of the region remains the lowest in the world. Zimbabwe, Lesotho and Botswana all have life expectancy at birth below 40 years.

Reducing mortality rates for children under five years of age in Africa has been slow, especially in Sub-Saharan Africa, where 166 infants

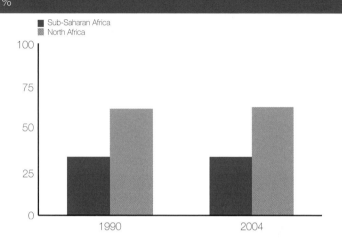

Figure 2.1 Share of poorest quintile in national consumption, 1990 and 2004

%

■ Sub-Saharan Africa
■ North Africa

Source: UNDESA 2007.

out of every thousand live births died in 2005, compared with 185 in 1990. In 2005 in North Africa 35 infants died for every thousand live births, compared with 88 in 1990.

Only three countries in Sub-Saharan Africa—Cape Verde, Comoros and Eritrea—have managed to reduce the under-five mortality rate by at least 37% between 1990 and 2004. Several other countries in the region—Botswana, Central African Republic, Côte d'Ivoire, Equatorial Guinea, Kenya, Rwanda, South Africa, Swaziland and Zimbabwe—have even slipped back, due largely to the HIV/AIDS pandemic, conflicts and the fact that the percentage of children receiving vaccination is estimated to be only 65%.

Only 11 African countries are on track to reduce the maternal mortality ratio by three-quarters, as set in the Millennium Development Goals. The provision of skilled care at childbirth is one of the key elements necessary to reduce maternal mortality. But in Sub-Saharan Africa the proportion of deliveries attended by skilled health care personnel increased by only 3 percentage points between 1990 and 2004. On the other hand, for the same period, the proportion increased from 40% to 75% in Northern Africa.

Access to improved source of drinking water

Worldwide in 1990, 1.2 billion people lacked access to an improved source of drinking water, and 2.7 billion worldwide lacked access to improved sanitation. In Africa 277 million lacked access to clean water, and 393 million had no access to sanitation. Target 10 of Millennium

Development Goal 7 calls for "[h]alving by 2015 the proportion of people without sustainable access to safe drinking water and basic sanitation".

Progress toward target 10 will bring many benefits, including salutary effects on the achievement of other goals, especially those related to poverty, health, education and gender equity. Sustainable access to clean water and sanitation will reduce the incidence of water-related diseases such as diarrhea, dysentery and typhoid and, as a consequence, health-related costs and child mortality. It will reduce income poverty and free girls and women for productive and educational activities because they will have closer access to water facilities. It will improve girls' education through separate sanitation facilities. And it will promote economic equity and ensure a sense of human dignity (UNDP 2006).

By the end of 2004, 191 million more Africans had access to an improved drinking water source than in 1990. At the current rate of increase in coverage of 13.6 million people per year, an additional 150 million people will have access to safe drinking water by the end of 2015. But to attain the MDG target of halving the proportion of people without sustainable access to safe drinking water, an average of 28.9 million people per year must be added to bring the total population covered to 78% of the total population in 2015 (figure 2.2). The 550 million people in Africa with access to safe drinking water in 2004

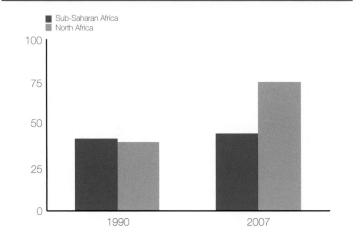

Figure 2.2 Population with access to improved drinking water source in 1990 and 2007

% of total

Source: UNICEF and WHO 2006.

represented 62% of the population; 337 million people still had no access.

This analysis hides huge disparities in access to safe drinking water between regions and between urban and rural areas. Whereas North Africa (NA) is on track to meet the target with coverage of 91% in 2004, coverage in Sub-Saharan Africa (SSA) was only 56%. The proportion of the population to have access to a safe drinking source is expected to increase only marginally to 57% by 2015, well below the target.

In 2004 only 42% of the rural population in SSA had access to an improved source of drinking water, compared with 80% in urban areas. But 42% was an improvement over the 36% in 1990. In contrast, the coverage in urban areas fell from 82% in 1990, as a result of rapid population growth.

The urban-rural gap is even more startling when one looks at country data (table 2.13). Fourteen countries have an urban-rural gap in coverage of 40% and above.

Access to improved sanitation
From 1990 to 2004 an additional 146 million people in Africa enjoyed access to improved sanitation, increasing the coverage from 38% to 44% (figure 2.3). But at the end of 2004, 498 million people in Africa still did not have that access. Furthermore, the progress is still too slow for the continent to reach the MDG target by 2015. At the current rate of progress only 45% of Africans will have access to

Table 2.13 Urban-rural gap in drinking water coverage in selected African countries (% of population)

Country	Drinking water coverage (%)			Urban-rural gap (%)
	Average	Urban	Rural	
Burkina Faso	61	94	54	40
Cameroon	66	86	44	42
Madagascar	46	77	35	42
Mali	50	78	36	42
Guinea	50	78	35	43
Morocco	81	99	56	43
Niger	46	80	36	44
Togo	52	80	36	44
Mozambique	43	72	26	46
Gabon	88	95	47	48
Zambia	58	90	40	50
Congo, Rep.	46	82	29	53
Congo, Dem. Rep.	58	84	27	57
Ethiopia	22	81	11	70

Source: UNICEF and WHO 2006.

Figure 2.3 Population with access to improved sanitation in 1990, 2004 and 2015

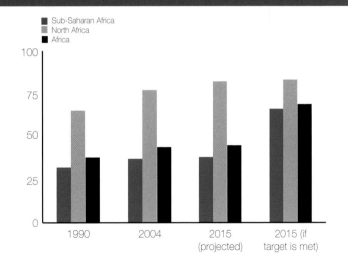

Source: UNICEF-WHO 2006.

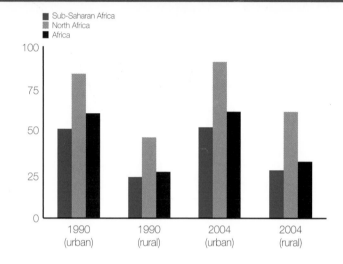

Figure 2.4 Urban and rural population with access to improved sanitation in 1990 and 2004

%

- Sub-Saharan Africa
- North Africa
- Africa

100

75

50

25

0

| 1990 (urban) | 1990 (rural) | 2004 (urban) | 2004 (rural) |

Source: UNICEF-WHO 2006.

improved sanitation by 2015—well below the target of 69%.

North Africa is on track to meet the sanitation target, while SSA is not. The growth in coverage of 7.6 million per year for SSA over 1991–2004 is well below the 31.3 million per year required to meet the goal by 2015.

At the end of 2004, 53% of the urban population in SSA had access to improved sanitation, a small increase from 52% in 1990. In contrast, the equivalent figures for NA were 84% and 91% in 1990 and 2004, respectively. The rural population with access to improved sanitation in 2004 was lower than that for the urban population for both SSA and NA in both magnitude and as a proportion of the population

(figure 2.4). The rural population without access to improved sanitation in SSA in 2004 was 339 million (72%) compared with 124 million (47%) of the urban population. Although the effort to improve access to sanitation in SSA was concentrated in urban areas, with an average yearly increase of 4.6 million people served (compared with 3.0 million in rural areas), rapid population growth caused coverage in urban areas to increase by only 1.0% in 2004.

Gender equality and empowerment of women

Ensuring access to education for girls is a major challenge for many African countries. The ratio of girls to boys in gross primary education increased during 1991–2005 from 0.84 to 0.89 in Sub-Saharan Africa and from 0.82 to 0.93 in North Africa. However, the same ratio dropped from 0.82 to 0.80 for secondary enrollment and from 0.69 to 0.63 for tertiary education in Sub-Saharan Africa from 1991 to 2005 (UNDESA 2007).

Some countries, such as Burkina Faso and Mali, have made significant progress towards gender parity through school feeding programmes. Rwanda also made significant progress in gender parity as a result of its post-conflict reconstruction programme, which benefited from generous donor support. Close monitoring of the gender gap and a better targeting of policy interventions are needed to accelerate progress towards gender equity. To fill this gap, ECA has developed the African gender and development index

(AGDI), which measures integration of women in all aspects of a country's economic and political life (ECA 2004).

Women have consistently increased their numbers in parliaments over the years, but they are still underrepresented in politics and at the highest level of economic institutions and sectors. Over the period 1990–2007, the share of women in parliaments increased from 7% to 17% in Sub-Saharan Africa and from 3% to 8% in Northern Africa (figure 2.5). Rwanda is the only African country that has come close to parity.

Economic growth and development

Better macroeconomic management, increased government spending and growing demand for commodities have contributed to improved economic growth in African countries over the last decade. But it is not apparent that this growth has been broadly based and inclusive—in other words, the economic growth has not translated into poverty reduction and employment creation.

If growth is to reduce poverty, it needs to be pro-poor. The basic features of pro-poor growth are:

- Utilizing more effectively the labour and other resources of the poor (labour absorbing).

- Emphasizing social needs (women, minority, health, education and participation).

- Orienting policies to pro-poor goals (public spending for

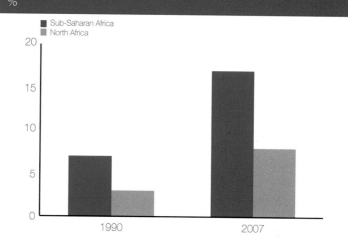

Figure 2.5 Share of women in African parliaments, 1990 and 2007

Source: UNDESA 2007.

education, health and family-planning services).

- Improving access to credit and promoting small and medium-size enterprises that will generate employment.

Agricultural productivity is the backbone of a pro-poor growth policy. But emphasis on agriculture and the rural sector should not gainsay the role of manufacturing, in particular labour-intensive industries, in creating employment opportunities for the uneducated poor, sometimes even more dramatically than agriculture. In fact, small and medium-size enterprises account for approximately 60% of the workforce in urban areas and 25% of industrial output. Because they provide employment for workers with limited formal training and use local inputs generally produced by the poor, their further development is essential for employment creation and poverty reduction.

Public policy has a crucial role to play in job creation in several respects. It can:

- Facilitate private-sector development by promoting competition in the economy.

- Ensure that entrepreneurs are free to operate throughout the economy.

- Reduce the burdens of doing business.

- Grant tax and other incentives to private investors.

- Adopt measures to develop small and medium-size enterprises.

- Protect property rights.

- Enforce business contracts.

- Encourage good corporate governance.

If African governments take steps along these lines to improve their policies and increased financial assistance becomes available, significant progress toward the MDGs is possible. In the past decade countries that have implemented sound pro-poor economic policies and improved their systems of governance have seen accelerated growth and a reduction in poverty.

African countries need to take three necessary steps:

- Deepen macroeconomic reforms and enhance domestic competitiveness and efficiency as foundations for a favourable investment climate and pro-poor growth.

- Strengthen democratic institutions and systems for public budgeting and financial management to ensure that governments are accountable to their people, especially for effective delivery of public resources.

- Invest adequate resources in human development.

In 11 of the 27 countries where data are available, more than 50% of the experts surveyed felt that policies

---

Box 2.1 Status of women in Sub-Saharan Africa

Women provide approximately 70% of the agricultural labour and produce about 90% of all food in Sub-Saharan Africa. The women's economic activity rate, a measure of the percentage of people furnishing the supply of labour for the production of economic goods, ranks highest when compared with other regions of the world, including the OECD countries, with a value of 61.9%. But women are predominately employed in the informal sector or they occupy low-skill jobs. This can be illustrated by considering the percentage of women in wage employment in the nonagricultural sector: Sub-Saharan Africa scores lowest among all regions of the world with 8.5%.

The weak status of women in the formal economy of Sub-Saharan Africa has many explanations. Lack of access to the key resources of education and health care are two important factors. The Gender, Institutions and Development Database (GID-DB) of the OECD Development Centre reveals that primary education of females is still at a strikingly low rate of 67% despite endeavours such as the second Millennium Development Goal to achieve universal primary education by the year 2015. Not surprisingly, illiteracy remains a major challenge. Among women above the age of 15, only 51.0% are able to read and write, compared with 67.1% of men.

Source: AfDB and OECD 2007.

for sustainable economic development are actively or largely actively pursued by the government. The top four countries in this regard were Tunisia, Malawi, Botswana and South Africa (figure 2.6).

In 15 of the 27 countries less than 40% of the experts responded that policies for sustainable economic development are actively or largely actively pursued by the respective government. The fact that in several countries less than half of the experts believe that policies for sustainable economic development are pursued by their government suggests a lack of strong commitment to sustainable economic development.

A correlation between GDP growth and experts' opinions in 2005 on the pursuit of sustainable development shows mixed results. In Botswana, Cape Verde, Kenya and South Africa, where over 50% of the experts responded that the government actively or largely pursues policies for sustainable economic development, growth was over 5%.

On the other hand, in Burkina Faso, Republic of Congo and Sierra Leone, where the GDP growth in 2005 was 7.1%, 7.1% and 7.2% respectively, less than 40% of the experts responded that the government actively or largely pursues policies for sustainable economic development. This is a clear indication that sustainable economic performance is determined by several factors, such as basic infrastructure, technical capacity and resource availability. Good policies play only a limited role.

Box 2.2 Best-practice countries in growth and poverty reduction: Ghana, Uganda and Mozambique

Ghana. With the support of its development partners, sustained efforts by the government to reduce poverty and improve the standard of living of Ghanaians have shown good results. Economic growth averaged 4.5% from 1983 through 2000 but accelerated to 5.8% in 2004 and 6.1% in 2006. Poverty levels dropped from 52% in 1992 to 28.5% in 2005.

Uganda. The country's firm commitment to poverty reduction, as spelled out in the Poverty Eradication Action Plan and supported by development partners' contributions, has brought the country closer to reaching the Millennium Development Goals. Economic growth averaged 5.4% from 2000 through 2004. Poverty declined rapidly from 1992 to 2006 as a result of broad-based economic growth. The poverty headcount dropped from 56% in 1992 to 31% in 2006. Still, poverty remains high in rural areas and in northern and eastern Uganda.

Mozambique. Since the devastating civil war ended in 1992, Mozambique has enjoyed a remarkable recovery. It achieved an average annual economic growth rate of 7.7% from 2000 through 2004 and registered 7.9% in 2006. As a result of high growth and pro-poor policies, the poverty headcount index fell by 15 percentage points between 1997 and 2003, raising almost 3 million people out of extreme poverty.

Source: World Bank country briefs 2007.

Public financial management

Effective public financial management requires a disciplined budgetary process, programming that is outcome-based and accurate diagnosis of the causes of poverty. Implementation of public spending should be monitored to ensure that it actually achieves the intended outcomes, and oversight should ensure that public services actually reach the intended beneficiaries. The key issues in financial management are the degree of discipline, efficiency in revenue mobilization and extent of transparency, accountability and control.

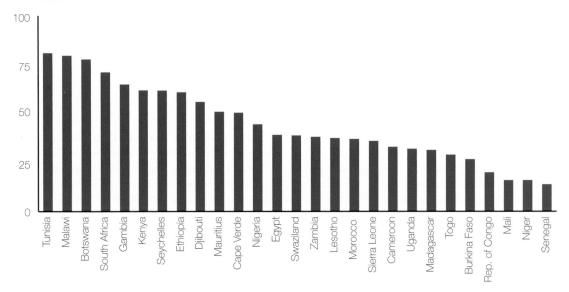

Figure 2.6 Expert opinion on government's pursuit of sustainable economic development

Actively or largely actively pursued by the government (share of experts surveyed, by country, %)

Source: ECA survey of experts 2007.

Conceptually, good public financial management deals with three issues:

- The capacity of a government to provide resources for a desired outcome, subject to the constraint that the fiscal position is sustainable, both in the medium and long term.

- The gap between the current level of expenditure and the maximum level of expenditures a government can undertake without impairing its solvency.

- The funds available to government as a result of enhanced resource mobilization, and the reforms to secure the policies that will direct the funds to a specified set of development objectives.

Budgetary control systems
Effective budgetary control systems apply a medium-term expenditure framework, procurement rules and procedures and internal auditing and internal control systems.

Medium-term expenditure framework and similar schemes
A medium-term expenditure framework (MTEF) links policymaking, planning and budgeting, enabling expenditures to be driven by policy priorities and disciplined by budget realities, injecting a medium-term perspective and allowing for policies that enhance long-term development. A three-year MTEF is a

rolling budget that covers the current fiscal year and the next two years. It contains a macroeconomic framework with a forecast of revenues and expenditures in the medium term, a multiyear sectoral programme with cost estimates, a strategic expenditure framework, a plan for allocating resources among sectors and detailed sectoral budgets. (Note that an MTEF can be more than three years. Mozambique's, for example, is four years.)

The MTEF budget process in Ghana is a three-year, performance-oriented process. The framework and the budget and public expenditure management systems were introduced as part of the government's Public Financial Management Reform Programme to address the weaknesses within the planning and budgetary system. With the MTEF Ghana has improved its macroeconomic planning and forecasting, economic analysis of expenditure allocations, strategic planning and management and performance-based budgeting.

South Africa's MTEF requires all public entities to prepare budgets over a three-year planning period, and the entire government budget is presented in its entirety in that form. The government releases a medium-term budget policy statement (MTBPS) in October of each year (roughly halfway through the fiscal year), setting out the broad parameters of its economic outlook, revenue expectations and budget priorities for the next three years. One of the benefits of the MTBPS and the MTEF has been greater

predictability in fiscal policy. This predictability has enabled longer-term planning, not only by the government but also by the private sector, and it has reduced the potentially destabilizing financial speculation that thrives on uncertainty and rumours.

In Kenya the budgetary process is coordinated by the MTEF/PRSP secretariat, located in the Ministry of Planning and National Development. The process was established in all ministries in 1998 to ensure that policies, planning and budgetary processes are linked so resources are focused on priority areas. The ministry provides the fiscal framework, including reliable forecasts of revenue and expenditure ceilings, and all ministries have been applying the MTEF to their planning and budgeting since 2001. Entrenchment of the MTEF in budget preparation has not been fully embraced, as reflected by large variances between budget out-turns and the approved budget.

Government procurement rules and procedures

A procurement system based on transparency, competition, fairness and accountability is critical for building the confidence of the public and the international community. Yet in several African countries the procurement system is troubled by a gap between intentions and practice, weakness in structure, poor management and corruption.

In many African countries the legislation and regulations that establish rules and procedures for government

> **In many African countries government procurement rules demonstrate an adherence to transparency, but in practice there is much less transparency**

procurement demonstrate an adherence to transparency and avoidance of corruption. But in practice there is much less transparency, and corruption is higher than would be expected from the constitutive documents. Transparency International rates Kenya as one of the most corrupt countries in the world, with a corruption perception index (CPI) score of 2.1. (A CPI score ranges from ten—an indication that a country is corruption-free—to zero, which indicates that most transactions in the country are contaminated by corruption.)

The surveyed experts were asked their perception of transparency in government procurement. They were given three categories from which to choose: fully transparent or usually transparent, sometimes transparent, and rarely or never transparent. Figure 2.7 shows the percentage of experts who responded that government procurement is fully or usually transparent in their respective countries. According to the survey results, among the 28 countries where data was available, in only four countries (Tunisia, Cape Verde, Mozambique and Botswana) did more than half of the experts feel that government procurement is fully transparent or usually transparent. In general, the fact that in 24 out of the 28 countries less than half the experts responded that government procurement is fully transparent or usually transparent clearly implies that the procurement system in many African countries lacks transparency and has a high degree of corruption and rent seeking.

Figure 2.7 Expert opinion on transparency in government procurement

Fully or usually transparent (share of experts surveyed, by country, %)

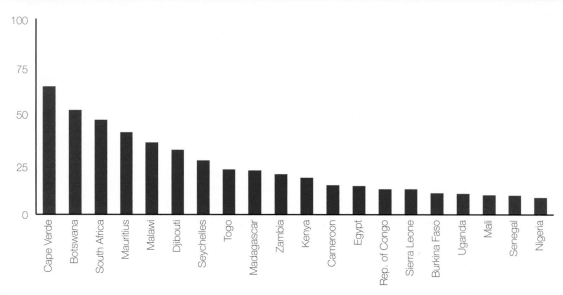

Source: ECA survey of experts 2007.

Nonetheless, several African countries have made progress toward greater transparency in their fiscal systems. Botswana has instituted an open procedure for consulting stakeholders to ensure that all relevant interests and views are considered in formulating policy and legislation. Namibia has a fairly transparent fiscal system due to elaborate budget procedures to ensure that the public is fully informed about the process and content of the budget. Since the new cabinet took office in Egypt in October 1999 considerable progress has been made toward greater transparency. The Ministry of Finance publishes data on economic performance and the domestic and external debt of the country.

Internal auditing and internal control systems

In South Africa the Public Finance Management Act (1999) details the responsibilities of the political and administrative heads of departments. It ensures that all government institutions and public entities have accounting officers who are responsible for budgetary control and subject to stringent reporting requirements, such as preparation of financial statements that have to be audited and submitted within seven months after the end of a fiscal year. The executive authorities are required to observe budgetary limits, take into account monthly financial reports and issue directives with financial implications.

In Botswana individual government units make regular reports to the auditor general, who is mandated by the constitution to submit regular reports to the executive

and parliament on public accounts to ensure that laws, regulations and directives are followed.

Budgetary oversight

In most African countries the auditor general's report is sent to parliament for discussion and action, sometimes under specific provisions and deadlines. In most cases a special parliamentary committee, usually the public accounts committee, examines the report in detail. Several African countries have taken steps to ensure that the parliamentary committees examine the auditor general's report in an objective and nonpartisan manner. On the whole, however, the performance of African countries in this area is somewhat lacking, mostly due to limited resources in the auditor general's office, deficiencies in the powers and exercise of oversight functions by parliament and a lack of cooperation by the executive branch.

The auditor general and controller general

In most countries the controller and auditor general (AG) are appointed by the executive, sometimes in consultation with or on the nomination of the prime minister. The constitutions and laws in most African countries provide for the auditor general's independence and security of tenure. In addition, the texts empower AGs to enquire into all aspects of public accounts, including the authority to request all relevant documents, question all concerned officials and hold public hearings.

In Botswana the AG is a specified office, meaning that although the

> *On the whole, the performance of African countries in budget oversight is somewhat lacking*

person is appointed by the president, the incumbent's tenure is constitutionally protected, similar to that of a high court judge. The auditor general cannot be dismissed without due cause or process, but may choose to retire at one's own will.

In Malawi the president appoints the AG, who must then be confirmed by the National Assembly. The Public Appointments Committee of the National Assembly may inquire as to the competence of the person appointed. A presidential appointment based upon the approval of the National Assembly provides some safeguards in that the National Assembly may reject the presidential appointee if it feels that the person is not competent to hold the post. In March 2007 the National Assembly rejected a presidential appointee on the grounds that he had a poor track record, had no audit experience in the civil service and was chiefly an accountant and not an auditor.

Parliamentary oversight

Parliamentary involvement in the budgetary processes promotes good governance by encouraging participation, transparency, accountability and national ownership of the budget (ECA 2007). Parliamentary activism in budgeting will lead to fiscal discipline if the involvement is successful in strengthening accountability mechanisms and in reducing the vulnerability of the public finances to corruption.

In Botswana a major problem arises with follow-up action against errant public officers. Neither the AG nor the Public Accounts Committee has the power to sanction. The committee's reports may lead to referral of an accounting officer to face sanctions, such as a surcharge or dismissal. But beyond the reports it cannot enforce the recommendations to ensure that the public officer is actually disciplined or prosecuted.

The audit cycle in Malawi is modeled on the Westminster system. It starts with government departments and public bodies preparing their accounts for the previous year for the AG to audit. After auditing the accounts, the AG produces a report for parliament, which in turn refers it to the relevant parliamentary committees, most notably the Public Accounts Committee, which examines the report and conducts public hearings at which officials from ministries and government departments answer queries raised in the report. When this process is over, the committee lays the report and its recommendations before the plenary sessions of parliament for debate. Although the committee can summon departmental controllers to appear before it to answer queries, it lacks sufficient enforcement mechanisms, and its recommendations are sometimes ignored by those empowered to take action. Incentives for members of parliament to pressure and follow up on government action or inactions are also limited. Treasury memoranda are rarely received by the committee, and even when they are produced, members' inability to understand the reports and limited time to examine them renders them ineffective.

> **Parliamentary involvement in the budgetary processes promotes good governance by encouraging participation, transparency, accountability and national ownership of the budget**

Anti-corruption bodies

Although Botswana has functional systems of accounting, auditing and parliamentary oversight for public resources, there have been instances of corruption and other crimes. Botswana's legal framework to combat financial corruption is provided by the Corruption and Economic Crime Act, the Proceeds of Serious Crimes Act, the Banking Act of 1995 and the Banking (Anti-Money Laundering) Regulations of 2003. At the regional level, in 2001 Botswana ratified the Protocol against Corruption in the Southern African Development Community, and the country ratified the Rome Statute of the International Criminal Court in 2000.

The authorities in Togo have taken several steps to fight corruption, notably the creation in 2001 of the National Commission to Fight Corruption and Economic Sabotage. The commission is charged with compiling all necessary information on corruption and economic sabotage and undertaking appropriate legislative measures. It oversees and reports on corrupt activities of all persons involved in the administration of government services and local authorities and any other public services.

In Namibia the independent Anti-Corruption Commission was inaugurated in February 2006 and charged with receiving, initiating and investigating allegations of corruption, giving advice on preventing corruption, educating the public and examining the systems of organisations to ensure that corruption is prevented. In performing these tasks, the commission is obliged to cooperate with other authorities, including those of other countries.

Monitoring corruption

Between April 2004 and March 2006 Namibian newspapers published 1,364 articles on 184 cases of corrupt activities, a significant increase over the numbers reported in AGR I. In Botswana major investigations by the Directorate on Corruption and Economic Crime in 2005 involved fraud, money laundering and public procurement. Of the 1,951 cases reported that year, 642 qualified for investigation.

In Malawi the Anti-Corruption Bureau receives and investigates numerous complaints about corruption involving public officials. In 2006 the bureau completed investigations of 358 cases, of which 232 were closed for various reasons, such as lack of evidence of corruption or the complaints themselves not being genuine. The majority of the cases did not constitute corruption, an indication that most Malawians have not been properly educated on what corruption is. In the prosecution of corruption cases Malawi's legal system moves slowly: in 2006 the bureau prosecuted 245 cases, but only 26 were concluded.

The revenue management system

Most African countries face major difficulties with their tax policies and administration. On the one hand, there is an obvious need for more revenues to enable resource-poor states to provide even the basic public services. But those with

> *Most African countries still have to improve the management of their revenue collection system*

wealth are few and do not want to pay tax. Those without much economic power are many but have almost nothing to tax. On top of that harsh reality, most African countries still have to improve the management of their revenue collection system.

Sources of government revenue

External grants account for a substantial part of both the recurrent and capital budgets of several African countries, and in a few cases income from public enterprises is another important source of government revenue.

For most African countries, indirect taxes are the most important source of revenue. But indirect taxes are considered regressive because for the poor these taxes represent a higher proportion of their income.

Resource-rich countries receive rent from nonrenewable resources such as oil, diamonds and other minerals. Income from them tends to be highly volatile, resulting in highly volatile budgeting. In African countries where rent from these resources is high, evidence shows that broad-based development, good economic management and overall economic and political governance are often disregarded.

Efficiency of the tax system

Efficient management of the tax system enables the public sector to mobilize resources for economic development. It also engenders confidence and trust in public financial management, which is an important component of good governance.

African countries are trying to reduce budget deficits, meet resource mobilization targets and manage the tax system more efficiently. Despite efforts to broaden the tax base and reduce evasion, corruption and lack of transparency in the tax system, many countries need to take more steps to achieve satisfactory results.

Panel experts were asked how they perceived the efficiency in the tax collection system in 2002 (AGR I) and again in 2007 (AGR II). Figure 2.8 shows the change in the views of those who responded that the tax collection system is efficiently or largely well managed.

Of the 24 countries where comparable data are available, in 4 countries (Kenya, Gambia, Lesotho and Botswana) there was an increase of over 20 points between 2002 and 2007 in the percentage of experts who responded that the tax collection system is efficiently or largely well managed. In 4 other countries (South Africa, Cameroon, Benin and Ghana) there was a significant decrease of over 10 percentage points. Nigeria and Mali score the lowest for both survey years.

An important indicator of resource mobilization is the degree to which revenue collected meets the amount targeted. Revenue shortfall is a major reason for budget deficits and lack of budgetary discipline. African countries need to increase the efficiency of their resource mobilization to finance their ambitious economic development programmes and meet the Millennium Development Goals. Benin, Malawi, Nigeria and South

> **Despite efforts to broaden the tax base and reduce tax evasion, many African countries need to take more steps to achieve satisfactory results**

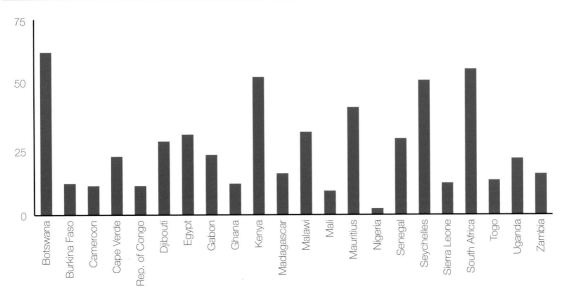

Figure 2.8 Experts who responded that the tax system was efficiently or largely well managed, 2002 and 2007

Share of experts surveyed, by country (%)

Source: ECA survey of experts 2002 and 2007.

Africa have recently succeeded in meeting or exceeding their targets.

Other African countries, including Burkina Faso, Ghana and Mauritius, are failing to meet their targets for resource mobilization. Deficiencies in the tax collection system—evasion, corruption, abuse and misapplication of provisions on tax exemption, political interference and the low capacity of tax collection agencies—are at the root of these failures.

Tax evasion, corruption and transparency

Tax evasion, corruption and lack of transparency in the tax system are major impediments to good public financial management. If left unchecked, they can quickly spread and destroy the moral fiber of society as well as economic and political structures. Vigorous action by African countries is required to combat these threats.

The experts on the panel were in asked in 2002 (AGR I) and again in 2005 (AGR II) how they perceived the tax collection system is affected by tax evasion: never or rarely affected by tax evasion, sometimes affected by tax evasion, mostly affected by tax evasion or always affected by tax evasion.

In none of the 24 survey countries where data were available did more

collection system is never or rarely affected by tax evasion.

Equity in the tax system

In tax analysis the equity of a tax system is usually divided into horizontal equity and vertical equity. Horizontal equity requires that people in similar circumstances be treated similarly. Vertical equity requires that people in different circumstances be treated differently. A good example of tax equity is Seychelles (box 2.3).

The experts on the panel were asked how they perceived the equitability of the tax system in 2002 (AGR I) and again in 2007 (AGR II): always or mostly equitable, sometimes equitable, rarely equitable or never equitable. In only one country (Botswana, 75%) did more than half of the experts feel the tax system is always or mostly equitable in both 2002 and 2007. In South Africa, Cameroon and Morocco there was a significant decrease between 2002 and 2007 in the percentage of experts who felt the tax system is always or mostly equitable. In 13 of the 24 countries fewer than 30% of the experts responded that the tax system is always or mostly equitable for both years. Judging from the survey results, the tax system in many African countries is to a great extent inequitable.

Management of public enterprises
The performance of public enterprises in several African countries has been disappointing since the 1970s. While they were created to alleviate the shortcomings of the private sector and spearhead economic development, many of them have

than 35% of the experts believe that the tax collection system is never or rarely affected by tax evasion in either 2002 or 2007—a clear indication of the rampant nature of tax evasion in African countries. Moreover, in eight countries there was a significant decrease in the percentage of experts who felt the tax stifled entrepreneurial development and fostered economic stagnation. State-owned enterprises have served as platforms for patronage and the promotion of political objectives and have suffered from corruption due to lack of transparency and accountability. In many African countries public enterprises were misused, then blamed for poor performance.

A public enterprise is an organisation established by government under public or private law as an autonomous or semi-autonomous legal entity that produces or provides goods and services on a full or partial self-financing basis and in which the government or other public body participates by having shares or representation in its decision-making structure.

The major considerations when discussing SOEs in Africa are:

- The size of the public-sector enterprises and the effectiveness of strategies and policies of divestiture.

- Independence of a public enterprise's management.

- Profitability, efficiency and effectiveness of public enterprises.

- Corruption, transparency and accountability of public enterprises.

Size of public enterprises and policies of divestiture

In Nigeria the public sector has not been significantly reduced despite the policy reforms of the 1980s. One of the primary goals of deregulation, liberalization and privatization programmes was to introduce competition in the private-sector economy and subsequently reinforce efficiency. But the 88 public enterprises privatized before 2000 remain the only ones to be privatized.

Delays in privatization make many people skeptical about the seriousness of a government's announced intentions to create a competitive environment. About 32% of the respondents in the experts' survey felt that government never takes effective measures to ensure competition or rarely takes effective measures. But 37% were of the view that government does take effective measures.

Since 1991 the Zambian government has been undertaking a spirited privatization and commercialization of public enterprises. At the beginning of 2001 the country had 280 public enterprises, from mining to trading, wholesale to fishing. The majority of them were thoroughly inefficient and only survived with state subsidies. Most of them have been privatized; by 2006 only 16 public enterprises remained.

Independence of public enterprises management

In Zambia the role of government in managing public enterprises has significantly diminished. But in the energy and telecommunications sectors it exercises great control over policymaking and appointment of senior officials. Allegiance to the president and the ruling party is

> *The performance of public enterprises in several African countries has been disappointing since the 1970s*

perceived to be a key qualification for appointment as head of any of these institutions.

The management of public enterprises in Botswana was perceived to be independent of the government or ruling party by only 43% of the expert panel respondents. Approximately 26% of the respondents thought it was either fully dependent or hardly independent. Only 13% stated it was fully independent. Most boards of public enterprises are dominated by government representatives who are mostly permanent secretaries, compromising the independence of the enterprises.

Profitability, efficiency and effectiveness

Several public enterprises in Africa are unprofitable. Air Malawi, the country's sole designated flag carrier, registered a net loss before tax of about K700 million in the 2005/06 fiscal year. The poor performance was largely attributed to managerial inefficiencies and weak governance as the airline embarked on an ambitious programme of fleet and route expansion without regard to its ability to pay for it.

In Zambia the government is concentrating on enhancing efficiency in the energy sector and telecommunications sectors through commercialization and privatization. The main objectives of the parastatal reform programme are to scale down the government's direct involvement in commercial activities by disposing of entities that could be better run by the private sector, reduce budgetary outlays to state-owned

' *In general, corruption in the management of public enterprises in Africa remains a serious problem*

enterprises, promote competition, improve the efficiency of state-owned enterprises, encourage wider share ownership and minimize the involvement of government bureaucracy in the operations of enterprises.

Corruption, transparency and accountability

The panel experts were asked how they perceived the management of public enterprises: free or largely free from corruption, fairly free from corruption, largely corrupt or completely corrupt (figure 2.9).

In Tunisia, Botswana and South Africa close to 50% and more of the experts surveyed felt the management of public enterprises is free or largely free from corruption. At the other extreme, less than 20% of the experts in 19 of the 30 countries surveyed felt the same. In general, the survey results indicate that corruption in the management of public enterprises in Africa remains a serious problem.

Management of monetary and financial systems

The integrity of monetary and financial systems is indispensable for sustainable economic growth and effective functioning of the market economy. Monetary authorities (central banks) have a wide range of responsibilities: overseeing monetary policy, implementing currency stability and ensuring low inflation and full employment. Central banks also issue currency, function as the bank of government, regulate the credit system, supervise financial institutions, manage exchange reserves and act as a lender as last resort.

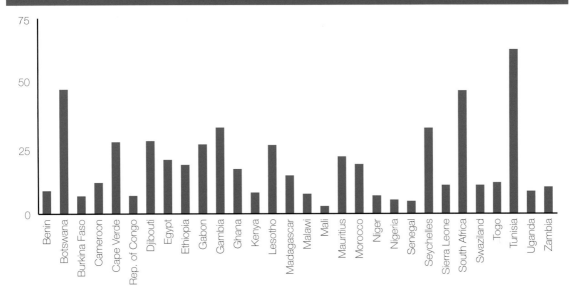

Figure 2.9 Expert opinion on corruption in public enterprises in Africa

Free or largely free of corruption (share of experts surveyed, by country, %)

Source: ECA survey of experts 2007.

Autonomy of monetary authorities
Central bank autonomy is important. But it does not mean that a central bank is not accountable. A central bank must be sensitive to the broad social, political and economic environment within which monetary policy is set, and it must make every effort to explain its policies to the government and to the general public. A central bank and the finance ministry should work together in confidence, but without decisions being imposed on the central bank.

In many countries a major threat to monetary stability is excessive borrowing by the government and intervention by the executive in the central bank's conduct of monetary and financial policies. To counter this threat, the central banks and other agencies that control monetary policies and regulate and supervise banks and other financial institutions must enjoy a high degree of independence and autonomy from the executive.

Most African countries have adopted constitutional or legislative provisions that grant autonomy and independence to the central bank. In reality, however, many central banks enjoy less autonomy and independence than is provided for in their constitutive documents. Some powers may be reserved for the government, central banks may have to consult the government on certain matters, the government may have financial leverage over the banks, real and effective limits on government borrowing may not exist and members of the board of central banks may be appointed by the government—all of which raise fundamental questions of institutional checks and balances, the role and accountability of the executive and respect for the rule of law.

Although the central bank of Malawi has the legal autonomy to manage its affairs and implement monetary policies, the government has the final say on some of the bank's policies. On some policy issues the bank drafts a policy and seeks approval from government before issuing the policy. The fact that the Reserve Bank Act does not place any limitations on the amount the government may borrow from the Reserve Bank enables the government to use political influence to borrow money. This loophole allowed the Muluzi administration to borrow substantially from the Reserve Bank in order to finance the short-term balance-of-payments deficit at a time when donors stopped supporting Malawi, leading to high inflation and crowding out of the private sector.

Effectiveness of monetary authorities

To be effective, monetary authorities must ensure transparency, a sound system for banking regulation and supervision and integrity in the monetary and financial systems.

Transparency

Several African countries have increased the transparency of their monetary and financial systems— at least on paper. In practice, however, their independence is sharply curtailed. And weak regulatory and supervisory institutions have limited their effectiveness.

The Bank of Botswana ensures transparency through the annual publication of a monetary policy statement outlining the objectives and targets of its monetary and anti-inflation policies. Adjustments to the Bank's rate are publicly announced, explained and justified. The exchange rate policy is fully explained, and information is made available on the basket of currencies (though the exact weight of the different currencies used to calculate the exchange rate is not specified). The Bank of Botswana requires commercial banks and credit institutions to provide it with details of all charges payable for the operation of accounts and other services rendered.

In the French-speaking countries of West and Central Africa, monetary policy is under the control of the Central Bank of West African States and the Bank of Central African States. These two central banks and monetary unions originated in the colonial period as part of the Franc zone. There was a fixed exchange rate between the French franc and the currencies in the two monetary unions, and France guaranteed their free convertibility. France essentially determined the monetary policies of these two monetary unions and central banks, an arrangement that gave them a high degree of integrity and stability. Since 1999 the currencies of these French-speaking countries have been pegged to the euro. But France still maintains a dominant role in monetary policy through its

> **Several African countries have increased the transparency of their monetary and financial systems. In practice, however, their independence is sharply curtailed**

membership in the governing body of the two central banks.

Banking regulation and supervision

Regulation and supervision are essential for a stable and healthy financial system. Supervision entails not only the enforcement of rules and regulations but also judgments concerning the soundness of a financial institution's assets, its capital adequacy and its management. Several African countries have improved their financial regulatory and supervisory bodies, but limited institutional capacity has been a major stumbling block to more progress.

In Kenya the Central Bank of Kenya, the Capital Markets Authority, the Commission of Insurance and the Retirement Benefits Authority, all of which report to the Treasury, are responsible for regulating and supervising the financial sector. On the whole, the Central Bank of Kenya has successfully regulated and controlled the banking system, but it faces problems in controlling non-performing loans in the commercial banks. The Capital Markets Authority has mobilized domestic and foreign capital for investment, reorganized the legal framework and become involved in the creation of an integrated East African capital market. Likewise, the Commission of Insurance has effectively supervised the insurance industry.

The regulation and supervision of South Africa's financial sector is considered quite good. The South African Reserve Bank seems to be shifting its concentration from day-to-day supervision of bank operations to oversight of the financial system as a whole. The Reserve Bank carries out its supervisory functions through off-site inspections. South African banks are generally well managed, with a sophisticated system for risk management and corporate governance. But there are weaknesses among small banks.

In French-speaking West and Central Africa, the regulation and supervision of banks has significantly improved since 1990. The Banking Commission was created for West Africa in 1990 and another for Central Africa in 1993, both of which have more regulatory and supervisory powers. These measures have greatly improved the quality of regulation and supervision in these regions.

Integrity in monetary and financial systems

The level of integrity in the monetary and financial systems can be measured using contract intensive money (CIM) as an indicator of the level of integrity for the 35 countries in the survey.[3] The closer the CIM value is to 1, the more money is held in the form of bank deposits rather than currency, which many believe is a key measurement of the integrity and reliability of the monetary and financial system. A low CIM value, on the other hand, suggests that individuals have little faith in the monetary and financial system and prefer to hold their assets in currency. Most middle-income countries have a CIM value above 0.9, while low-income countries tend to have CIM values ranging from .3 to 0.9 (table 2.14).

> *Several African countries have improved their financial regulatory and supervisory bodies, but limited institutional capacity has been a major stumbling block to more progress*

Table 2.14 Integrity and reliability of selected national monetary and financial systems in Africa, 2005 and 2006: contract intensive money (CIM) value and country ranking

AGR II survey countries	CIM raw data		AGR II survey countries	CIM raw data	
	2005	2006		2005	2006
Botswana	0.96	0.97	Tanzania	0.79	0.79
Namibia	0.96	0.97	Gabon	0.76	0.78
South Africa	0.95	0.96	Burkina Faso	0.72	0.77
Mauritius	0.94	0.94	Uganda	0.77	0.76
Swaziland	0.93	0.94	Gambia	0.77	0.75
Seychelles	0.93	0.92	Ghana	0.71	0.75
Cape Verde	0.89	0.91	Malawi	0.78	0.75
Lesotho	0.92	0.91	Senegal	0.76	0.74
Kenya	0.88	0.88	Togo	0.80	0.74
Zambia	0.86	0.87	Madagascar	0.71	0.72
Djibouti	0.86	0.86	Sierra Leone	0.68	0.69
Mozambique	0.86	0.86	Benin	0.70	0.65
Cameroon	0.82	0.84	Mali	0.59	0.61
Rwanda	0.82	0.82	Republic of Congo	0.55	0.59
Nigeria	0.79	0.81	Niger	0.56	0.53
Ethiopia	0.80	0.79	Chad	0.38	0.42

Source: Mo Ibrahim (2008).

Concluding remarks

Several African countries have made substantial progress in the last few years toward good economic governance and public financial management. Economic growth, public financial management and accountability have improved considerably in Africa. More countries are recording smaller budget deficits, meeting their revenue mobilization targets, demonstrating more transparency in monetary policies and improving the auditing of public funds. But a great deal remains to be done. Several countries still score quite low on control of corruption, integrity of the tax system, transparency and accountability.

Improved economic policies have made inflation, budget deficits, exchange rates and foreign debt repayments more manageable for several African countries. Their economies are more open to trade and private enterprise, governance is improving and there are more assaults on corruption. These improved economic fundamentals have helped to spur growth. The solid economic performance across Africa in 1995–2005 contrasts sharply with the economic collapse of 1975–85 and the stagnation experienced in 1985–95.

Since 2001 African countries have dramatically increased their revenue mobilization. More countries are adopting a medium-term expenditure framework in their budgetary processes. But introducing transparency in government procurement remains a major challenge. Other areas of concern are efficiency in managing the tax system and improving its equitability.

Further improvement in Africa appears to be most urgent in public-sector governance, where there is a need for accelerated reform and capacity building in public management and especially in transparency, accountability and control of corruption.

For public policy processes to be effective and reduce poverty, the following observations are fundamental:

• Participatory processes build effective pro-poor policies.

• Disciplined, outcome-oriented budgetary processes can assist a development orientation.

• Accurate diagnosis of the nature and causes of poverty can feed directly into the design of programmes.

• Implementation of public spending can be more effectively monitored to ensure that it actually achieves intended outputs, and there should be checks that public services actually reach the intended beneficiaries.

Given the critical importance of good governance for continuing economic and social progress,

African countries must forge effective participatory governance and empower their citizens through popular participation and decentralization. Many African countries lack the capacity to implement well-intentioned reforms and measures. Taking this shortcoming into account, African governments and the international community must focus not only on devising schemes and policies for economic management but also on ensuring that the capacity to implement these reforms is available.

Notes

1. The Gini coefficient index of 0 indicates complete equality while a value of 100 is maximum inequality.

2. According to UNDP (2008), the countries with a Gini coefficient above 50 are Argentina (51.3); Chile (54.9),Panama (56.1); Brazil (57.0); Colombia (58.6); Dominican Republic (51.6); Peru (52.0); Ecuador (53.6); Paraguay (58.4); El Salvador (52.4); Honduras (53.8); Bolivia (60.1); Guatemala (55.1); Lesotho (63.2); Swaziland (50.4); Papua New guinea (50.9); Haiti (59.2); Zimbabwe (50.1); Gambia (50.2); Zambia (50.8); Central African Republic (61.3); Niger (50.5); and Sierra Leone (62.9)

3. Contract intensive money (CIM) is the ratio of noncurrency money to total money supply, or $(M2-C)/M2$ where $M2$ is a broad definition of the money supply and C is currency held outside banks.

References

Acemoglu, Daron, Simon Johnson and James Robinson. 2005. "Institutions as the fundamental Cause of Long-run Growth." In Philippe Aghion and Steve Durlauf, eds., *Handbook of Economic Growth*. Amsterdam: Elsevier B.V.

AfDB (African Development Bank). 2007a. *African Development Report*. Tunis.

———. 2007b. *Selected Statistics on African Countries 2007*, Vol. XXVI.

AfDB (African Development Bank) and OECD (Organisation for Economic Co-operation and Development). 2007. *African Economic Outlook 2006/2007*. Paris.

———. 2008. *African Economic Outlook 2007/2008*. Paris.

Chen, Shaohua and Martin Ravallion. 2008. "The Developing World Is Poorer Than We Thought, But No Less Successful in the Fight against Poverty." World Bank Policy Research Working Paper 4703. Washington, DC: World Bank.

Easterly, William and Ross Levine. 2003. "Tropics, germs, and crops: how endowments influence economic development." *Journal of Monetary Economics* 50: 3–39.

ECA (Economic Commission for Africa). 2002. *Guidelines for Enhancing Good Economic Governance and Corporate Governance in Africa*. Addis Ababa.

———. 2004. *The African Gender and Development Index*. Addis Ababa.

———. 2005. *Economic Report on Africa*. Addis Ababa.

———. 2007. "The Role of African Parliaments in the Budgetary Processes Especially in the Medium Term Expenditure Framework." Addis Ababa, April 2007.

———. 2008. *Economic Report on Africa*. Addis Ababa.

ILO (International Labour Organisation). 2007. *Key Indicators of the Labor Market*, 5th edition. Geneva.

———. 2008. *Global Employment Trends 2008*. Geneva.

IMF (International Monetary Fund). 2007. *Regional Economic Outlook: Sub-Saharan Africa*. Washington, DC.

———. 2008a. *Regional Economic Outlook: Sub-Saharan Africa*. Washington, DC.

———. 2008b. *Regional Economic Outlook: Middle East and Central Asia*. Washington, DC.

The Ibrahim Index of African Governance. 2008. *Reliability of Financial Institutions (Contract Intensive Money)* The Mo Ibrahim Foundation. Can be accessed at: http://www.moibrahimfoundation.org/index-2008/bycategory/sustaionable-eco-opp.asp

UNDESA (United Nations Department of Economic and Social Affairs). 2007. *The Millennium Development Goals Report 2007*. New York.

———. 2008. *World Economic Situation and Prospects 2008*. New York.

UNDP (United Nations Development Programme). 2006. *Human Development Report 2006 Beyond scarcity: Power, poverty and the global water crisis*.

———. 2008. *Human Development Report 2007/2008 Fighting climate change: Human solidarity in a divided world*.

UNICEF (United Nations Children's Fund) and WHO (World Health Organisation). 2006. *Meeting The MDG Drinking Water and Sanitation Target: The Urban and Rural Challenge of the Decade*. Geneva.

World Bank. 2007. *Africa Development Indicators 2007*. Washington, DC.

———. 2006. *Africa Development Indicators 2006*. Washington, DC.

In the late 1980s African countries made a commitment to promote development of the private sector. There was a consensus among African countries and donors that the private sector was the most efficient engine for sustainable economic growth, structural transformation and poverty eradication.

In the founding document of the New Partnership for Africa's Development (NEPAD) in 2001, African leaders committed to ensuring a sound and conducive environment for private-sector activities, with particular emphasis on encouraging domestic entrepreneurs, promoting foreign direct investment and trade with special emphasis on exports and developing enterprises of all sizes. The NEPAD Declaration on Democracy, Political, Economic and Corporate Governance of 2002 promulgated eight codes and standards, including the goal "to promote market efficiency, to control wasteful spending, to consolidate democracy, and to encourage private financial flows—all of which are critical aspects of the quest to reduce poverty and enhance sustainable development" (NEPAD 2002, 6).

Private investment creates jobs, increases the capacity of the economy to produce goods and services, promotes diversification in production and exports and provides taxes to finance investment in education, health and infrastructure. And the private sector may, in partnership with the state, provide public services more efficiently.

Ideally, private-sector development will encourage the growth of companies of all sizes in all key sectors of the economy. Development of the private sector should be both vertical within sectors and horizontal across sectors. The strategic focus of African governments has been on increasing both domestic and foreign private investments in the economy—but with more emphasis on foreign direct investment (FDI) than on domestic investment. The emphasis on FDI is based on the notion that domestic income and savings are too low to generate significant capital for investment, which must therefore come from external sources.

The conventional wisdom has been that African governments need to provide direct assistance to develop the private sector—doing more than just creating an enabling environment. These additional measures include:

- Creating specific institutions to facilitate the development of the private sector.

- Simplifying the tax systems and providing tax and other incentives for investors.

- Improving access to finance and infrastructure.

- Reducing the burden and cost of doing business.

- Providing training and support for entrepreneurship.

- Protecting property rights and enforcing business contracts.

Box 3.1 The role of the Ministry for Private Sector Development in Ghana

Recognizing the importance of the private sector, Ghana created the Ministry for Private Sector Development and Presidential Special Initiatives in 2001. The Ministry developed the National Medium-Term Private Sector Development Strategy to:
Clarify the respective roles of the state and of the private sector in achieving a golden age of business;

Set out a prioritised, costed and sequenced action plan with clear targets and milestones, setting out the steps to be undertaken by government and private-sector stakeholders in order to continue to move towards the Government's objective of a positive business environment in Ghana; and

Present a coherent institutional framework for implementing the strategy, and ensure effective and efficient use of resources through effective monitoring and evaluation.

This prominence given to private-sector development and the associated policy changes has had major success. The 2007 and 2008 reports of The World Bank's Doing Business project ranked Ghana as a top-ten reformer after introducing three reforms in 2005/06 and five in 2006/07 (World Bank 2006d; 2007a). As a result of the reforms, which are summarised in the table below, Ghana jumped 22 places in the Ease of Doing Business ranking to 87th out of 178 countries.

Year	Reform	Outcome
2007	Computerization of business registry.	Reduced time to start a business from 81 days in 2005/06 to 42 days in 2006/07.
	Abolished requirement to register the deeds of sale at the land commission.	Cut the time to register property from 169 days in 2005/06 to 34 days in 2006/07.
	Allowed out-of-court enforcement of collateral for secured creditors.	The Strength of Legal Rights index increased from 4 in 2005/06 to 5 in 2006/07.
	At the Tema port: • Construction of new terminal. • Allow into the port area only trucks ready to load or unload.	• Time to export fell from 47 days in 2004/05 to 19 days in 2006/07. • Time to import fell from 55 days in 2004/05 to 29 days in 2006/07.
	Six commercial courts are now fully operational in Accra.	Time to enforce a business contract fell from 552 days in 2005/06 to 487 days in 2006/07.
2006	Reduced property registration tax.	Costs to register property fell from 2.1% of property value in 2004/05 to 1.3% in 2006/07.
	Reduced corporate income tax rate from 32.5% to 28%.	Total tax rate on businesses fell from 36.1% of profits in 2005/06 to 32.9% in 2006/07.

Source: Ghana country report 2007; World Bank 2006d, 2007a.

- Ensuring competition.

- Pursuing an anticorruption strategy.

- Treating the private sector as a legitimate and effective

partner in promoting sustainable growth, development and poverty eradication.

Since the late 1980s an increasing number of African countries have taken steps along these lines.

Another factor contributing to the development of the private sector is good corporate governance, especially accountability and transparency in the conduct of corporate affairs; the application of internationally accepted standards and practices of accounting and audit; and the protection of shareholders' rights. Good corporate governance promotes efficient, effective, profitable, competitive and sustainable enterprises that contribute to the welfare of the society by creating wealth and employment (AfDB 2007).

According to the first *African Governance Report* (AGR I), most African countries consider the private sector a partner in economic development and have provided a range of incentives, including tax reductions, physical infrastructure and other cost-reduction mechanisms to attract private investment (ECA 2005). Policies and regulations to protect rights to property and encourage public-private partnerships were introduced. But there were also numerous impediments to stronger development of the private sector: high administrative and financial barriers to investment; crime and insecurity; limited access to credit; inadequate and ineffective protection of property rights, including intellectual property rights such as patents, and shareholders' rights; and weak enforcement of business contracts.

A major conclusion of AGR I was that a significant gap exists between policy formulation and implementation. There is ample evidence that the incentives provided to the private sector have had at best only a limited impact on the flow of FDI, and even then only at the margin. Even when policies and strategies for the development of the private sector have been sound, their implementation has not been effective due largely to lack of capacity. The fundamental problem seems to be the absence of capable states, as all evidence suggests that a capable state is a prerequisite for the development of the private sector.

Private-sector development—creating an enabling environment

Starting in the 1980s with the call of the Bretton Woods institutions and donors for adoption of economic stabilization and structural adjustment programmes in Africa, more and more African countries have emphasized sound macroeconomic policies and public financial management. The elements of these programmes are low inflation, low budget deficits, realistic and stable exchange rates, a limited role for the government in the economy, reductions of restrictions on private businesses and more emphasis on export promotion. Low inflation, a stable exchange rate and low budget deficits are essential because they ensure stability and thus predictability in the economy, which in turn encourages domestic and foreign entrepreneurs to invest in the economy.

Since the late 1980s most African countries have identified the private sector as the main engine of economic growth and development and have adopted specific strategies and

> *Since the late 1980s most African countries have identified the private sector as the main engine of economic growth and development and have adopted specific strategies and policies to this effect*

policies to this effect. This strategy can be seen the Ministry of Private Sector Development in Ghana (see box 3.1).

Competition in the economy
A key aspect of the economic reforms embarked on by African countries since the late 1980s is reducing government's role in the economy by privatizing public enterprises. Progress toward privatization was made during the 1990s, but it was hindered by strong opposition, the fact that many state enterprises were not sufficiently profitable to attract private-sector interest and the limited capacity of African countries to carry out privatization programmes. The pace of privatization in Africa has therefore slowed considerably since 2000. But efforts to ensure competition in the economy have continued.

Government intervention is needed to promote competition by prohibiting anticompetitive activities, ensuring that businesses do not attain dominant positions in particular industries, and regulating industries with natural monopoly characteristics, such as utilities. But in most African countries policies and laws to prevent anti-competition practices are still in their preliminary stage.

AGR I identified Botswana, Egypt and Senegal as having a competition policy or in the process of instituting one. These countries have now been joined in AGR II by Namibia, Malawi, South Africa and Zambia, and to some extent Djibouti and Ethiopia.

But anticompetition practices are still prevalent in several countries.

> *A key aspect of the economic reforms embarked on by African countries since the late 1980s is reducing government's role in the economy by privatizing public enterprises*

A recent study on competition in East and Southern Africa showed instances of anti-competition practices in both the public and private sectors. In Botswana anticompetition practices such as price fixing, bid rigging and unfair trade practices were observed (Monnane 2006). Namibia has natural monopolies in telecommunications, utilities and rail transport (Shilimela 2006). In Cape Verde contractors complain about unfair competition practiced by informal operators on their doorsteps.

The experts consulted for this report were pessimistic about the effectiveness of measures taken by African governments to ensure a competitive economy. Only in South Africa did more than a majority state that the government takes or largely takes effective measures to ensure competition. In all other countries except Malawi and Botswana, less than 40% of the experts believed that the government takes effective or largely effective measures to ensure competition. In Madagascar and Republic of Congo only a few responded in the positive.

Freedom of entrepreneurs
Freedom of trade, occupation and profession is entrenched in the constitution of some African countries. The freedom of entrepreneurs to operate throughout the economy and of individuals to seek gainful employment and practice their professions is vital for creating integrated national economies and stimulating private-sector development. African countries are not doing well in this area.

According to the *Economic Freedom of the World Annual Report* for 2007 (Fraser Institute 2007), only 4 out of 39 African countries—Mauritius, Botswana, Lesotho and South Africa—were ranked 60th or better in the Economic Freedom of the World (EFW) rankings for 2005 (figure 3.1).[1] Twenty-eight of the 33 countries for which comparative data are available have improved their EFW index compared with 1990.[2] Uganda and Zambia experienced the biggest improvements, more than doubling their EFW indices for 1995–2005.

Over 65% of the experts in Cape Verde, South Africa, Botswana, Malawi and Mauritius indicated that the government always or often ensures that entrepreneurs are free to operate throughout the country. In Kenya, Sierra Leone, Seychelles and Uganda between 50% and 60% of the experts indicated the same. In the remaining countries less than half of the experts believed that the government ensures free operation of entrepreneurs.

Figure 3.2 compares responses to the same question in AGR I. Of the thirteen countries for which comparable information is available, the trend is positive in six and negative in seven. If anything, African countries have

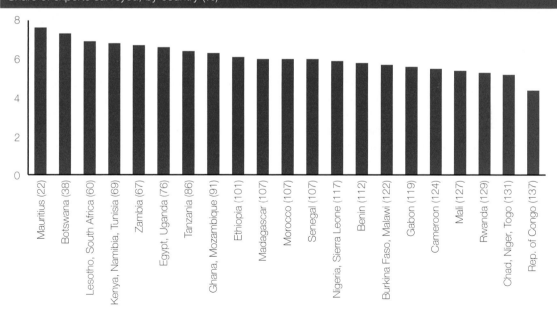

Figure 3.1 Economic freedom in Africa, 2005

Share of experts surveyed, by country (%)

Note: The EFW index ranges from 0–10. The higher the number, the greater degree of economic freedom. The numbers in parentheses are the economic freedom rankings out of 141 countries. The EFW indexes for Cape Verde, Djibouti, Gambia, Seychelles and Swaziland were not available.

Source: Fraser Institute 2007.

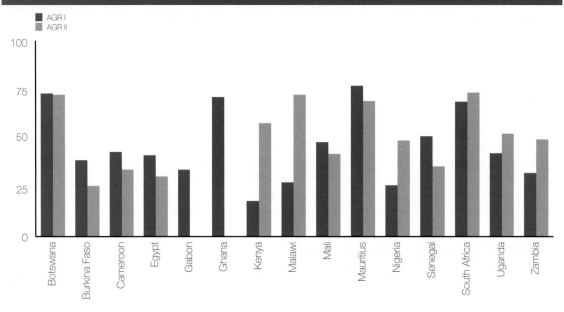

Figure 3.2 Expert opinion on whether government always or often makes sure that entrepreneurs are free to operate throughout the country, AGR I and AGR II

Share of experts surveyed, by country (%)

Source: ECA survey of experts 2007.

taken a backward step in ensuring the freedom of entrepreneurs.

Cost, duration and procedures for doing business

The need for licenses, permits and paperwork add to the cost of registering a business and divert managers' time away from running the business. These barriers to entry slow down the creation of new businesses. The available evidence suggests that a 10% decrease in the costs of starting a business raises the rate of creation of new registered firms by 1% (Klapper 2006; Klapper and Delgado 2007).

As the cost of complying with laws and regulations and tax rates on profits rises, compliance declines and businesses are encouraged to operate in the informal sector, while those in the formal sector are more likely to engage in tax evasion.

In the case of the labour market, employment regulations are required to protect workers from arbitrary, unfair or discriminatory actions by employers. But rigid regulations, while benefiting a select group of incumbent workers, shut out other potential employees from jobs in the formal sector altogether (World Bank 2006d). Governments need to maintain a balance between correcting market failures and creating an administrative, legal and regulatory environment that does not put unnecessary burdens on businesses.

Many African countries have taken initiatives to reduce the burden of doing business by setting up one-stop institutions for investors, streamlining licensing procedures, reducing the cost, duration and number of procedures for starting a new or expanding an existing business and reducing the tax burden on businesses. From January 2005 to June 2007, 29 of the countries surveyed in this report introduced 99 positive reforms in the areas covered by the World Bank's Doing Business project (table 3.1). Reforms to simplify the procedures and reduce the cost of starting a business were the most popular. The next most popular reform was reducing the number of procedures, time and cost to register property. The most reforms during the study period were undertaken by Ghana and Mauritius, each with eight, followed by Egypt with seven and Kenya with six.

Despite these reforms, African countries are lagging behind other regions in ease of doing business. In Sub-Saharan Africa it takes longer and is costlier to start a business and obtain licenses, the labour market tends to be more rigid than elsewhere, taxes on businesses tend to be higher as a proportion of profits and it is relatively costly to export and import goods. This state of affairs is a cause for concern, for there is compelling evidence that higher costs of starting a business, regulation of labour and higher corporate taxes correlate with lower levels of investment, employment, productivity and output in the registered sector,

Table 3.1 Number of pro-business reforms by African countries, 2005/06 and 2006/07

Number of reforms	Country
8	Ghana, Mauritius
7	Egypt
6	Kenya
5	Morocco, Nigeria, Rwanda, Tanzania
4	Burkina Faso, Mozambique, Lesotho, Mali, Niger, Tunisia
3	Madagascar, South Africa, Uganda
2	Benin, Djibouti, Gambia, Seychelles Sierra Leone
1	Botswana, Chad, Ethiopia, Malawi, Senegal, Swaziland, Togo

Source: World Bank 2006d; 2007a.

breeding a larger informal sector (Besley and Burgess 2004; Djankov et al. 2008; Djankov et al. 2002; Botero et al. 2004).

In overall ranking on the ease of doing business, only three African countries—Mauritius, South Africa and Namibia—are in the top 50 of 178 countries, while 14 of the countries covered by AGR II are in the bottom fifth (World Bank 2007a).[3]

Although the World Bank data suggest some progress in removing restrictions in doing business in Africa, this optimism is not shared by the experts in most of the countries covered in this report. In South Africa, Cape Verde, Mauritius, Botswana and Djibouti more than 50% of the experts believed that the government always or often takes effective measures to remove restrictions on businesses. Approximately 40–50% of the experts in Uganda,

Box 3.2 Reducing the cost of doing business in Egypt and Mauritius

According to the World Bank, Ghana, Mauritius and Egypt were the top reformers in Africa in easing the cost of doing business from January 2005 to June 2007. Ghana and Mauritius introduced eight reforms (see box 3.1 for the Ghanaian reforms), while Egypt introduced seven, five of them from April 2006 to June 2007, making the country the top reformer in the world for that period.

Egypt has succeeded in reducing the time needed to start a new company from 22 days in 2004/05 to 9 in 2006/07 and costs to start a business from 105% of the gross national income per capita in 2004/05 to 29% in 2006/07—a result of reducing the minimum amount of capital required to establish a company from LE 50,000 to only 1,000, and creating a one-stop shop for business registration. The property registration tax was cut from 3% of property value to a fixed tax of LE 2,000, translating into a 4.9% fall in registration costs and a 39% rise in revenue from property registration six months following the reform. One-stop shops at the ports reduced the number of days to export from 27 to 15 and cut the time to import from 29 days to 18.

Mauritius made it easier to start a business by launching a virtual one-stop shop that uses an electronic database to link the commercial registry and tax and local authorities. This reform reduced the number of days to start a business from 46 to 7 and propelled Mauritius to the top-ten list of countries where it was easiest to start a company in 2006/07. The country also consolidated its development and building permits, and it is now issued within two weeks, cutting the time to obtain the licenses, permits and utility connections and for dealing with the relevant inspectors and other requirements for building a warehouse by 55 days to 107 days. The property registration tax was halved to 5% of property value, and physical inspection of cargo was limited to 30% by introducing a computerized risk management system of customs clearance. These reforms helped to place Mauritius as the top African country for ease of doing business.

Source: World Bank 2006d, 2007a.

among the most important considerations for firms (World Bank 2005a). Taxes affect the incentive to invest by weakening the link between effort and reward and by increasing the cost of inputs used in the production process (World Bank 2005a). Simplifying the tax structure and ensuring that the tax burden compares favourably with that in other countries are important steps for attracting domestic and foreign investment.

African governments have been active for some time in providing tax incentives to encourage investment, especially FDI. The incentives include tax reductions and deductions for tax purposes, tax holidays, location incentives, avoidance of double taxation and improving tax services. In fact, virtually all African countries provide different forms of tax reductions and deductions. Ghana, Kenya, Namibia, Sierra Leone, South Africa and Malawi provide tax holidays and location incentives, and Ghana, Kenya, South Africa and Botswana have provisions to avoid double taxation.

Only in three countries (Botswana, Seychelles and Mauritius) did half or more of the experts believe that the tax system encourages local investment in all or most sectors. This response could be due to difficulties in tax administration and management and in some cases the bureaucratic procedures for granting these benefits. Another factor that explains the experts' views is that many of these incentives tend to be tilted in favour of foreign investments. And the weak relation

Senegal, Cameroon and Kenya gave this response, while in the remaining countries less than 40% of experts said the same thing.

Tax incentives

A recent survey on investment climate found that the tax rate is

between tax incentives and local investment points to the fact that tax incentives alone are not enough to stimulate local investment.

Since AGR I there has been an improvement in the response of the experts to this question in 13 of the 15 countries. In contrast, in many countries most experts agreed that tax incentives encourage foreign direct investment in all or most sectors.

In AGR I only in 3 (Namibia, Botswana and Gambia) of the 27 countries did 50% or more of the experts believe that the tax system encouraged local investment. In the present study 50% or more of the experts in 3 (Botswana, Seychelles

and Mauritius) of the 22 countries gave the same answer. Similarly, while AGR I found that 50% or more of the experts in 8 countries (Namibia, Botswana, Ghana, Lesotho, Burkina Faso, Uganda, Swaziland and Zambia) agreed that tax incentives encouraged FDI, the comparable figure in the current study is 10 (Botswana, Zambia, Uganda, Ghana, Mauritius, Cape Verde, Seychelles, Kenya, Djibouti and Senegal) of 22 countries (figure 3.3). Twelve countries registered an improvement in their scores since AGR I, two recorded lower scores, while the score for South Africa remained essentially the same.

Experts surveyed in both studies agree that tax incentives stimulate

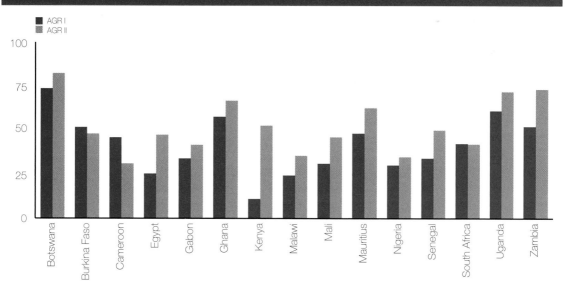

Figure 3.3 Comparison of expert opinion on the impact of tax incentives on foreign investments, AGR I and AGR II

Share of experts surveyed, by country (%)

Source: ECA survey of experts 2007.

FDI more than local investment, though the difference is not substantial. More important is whether tax incentives do encourage private investments, especially FDI. According to the United Nations Conference on Trade and Development, incentives have positive effects on the flow of FDI only at the margin (UNCTAD 1996). Other studies have concluded that incentives rarely make up for deficiencies in a country's economic environment in attracting FDI and that most private investments would have been made without these incentives. Most FDI flows to Africa, in fact, go to countries that are rich in mineral resources, notably oil. In light of these findings, African countries may wish to reconsider the merits of providing tax incentives to attract private investments.

Access to finance

A major obstacle facing the private sector in Africa is lack of access to finance. There is a relatively low private savings rate in Africa because of low income per capita, high young-age dependency ratios and high dependency on overseas development assistance (Elbadawi and Mwenga 2000). According to the United Nations Economic Commission for Africa, domestic savings as a percentage of GDP was 19.0% in 1998–2001 and 22.0% for 2002–2005, and is estimated at 26.0% in 2007 as a result of the strong price for commodities (ECA 2008). Excluding North Africa, the corresponding figures are 17.8%, 20.0% and 22.1%, respectively.

Africa has insufficient assets to act as collateral, weaknesses in collateral and bankruptcy laws and their enforcement and a lack of quality information to enable lenders to assess the creditworthiness of potential borrowers, all of which limit businesses' access to formal credit markets. There is statistically significant evidence that legal creditor rights and information-sharing institutions are important determinants of private credit development (Djankov, McLiesh and Shleifer 2007).

A functioning credit market requires that lenders have a fair idea of the creditworthiness of prospective borrowers. The availability of credit information, such as that provided in some countries by credit registries, facilitates lending activity. The low Depth of Credit Information Index (DCII) for Sub-Saharan Africa indicates that information necessary to ascertain the creditworthiness of potential borrowers, compared with other regions, is lacking.[4] South Africa provides the highest quality credit information among African countries with the maximum score of 6 on the DCII, followed by Namibia and Swaziland with 5, then Botswana, Egypt, Kenya and Tunisia with 4. The remaining countries surveyed in this report had scores below 3, with 12 having a score of 0. Botswana, Cape Verde, Mauritius, Namibia, South Africa and Swaziland are the only countries in the survey with credit registries covering more than 20% of adults (World Bank 2007a). This is a cause for concern because recent evidence has shown that credit registries, both private and public, are strongly associated with private credit in low-income countries (Djankov, McLiesh and Shleifer 2007).

Borrowers can also have access to credit by pledging suitable collateral for loans. Whether lenders accept a particular type of asset as collateral depends on the ease and expense of enforcing loan agreements and applicable collateral and bankruptcy laws. Sale of the collateral by the creditor is not permitted in some countries without involving the courts. Involving the courts provides some protection for debtors from wrongful seizure of their assets by creditors but adds to creditors' time and costs to enforce loan contracts, thereby discouraging lending. In some countries secured creditors are not given priority over collateral; in Malawi, for example, the Employment Act of 2000 ranks labour claims ahead of secured creditor claims (Djankov, McLiesh and Shleifer 2007).

Sub-Saharan Africa has a Strength of Legal Rights Index (SLRI) score comparable with South Asia, the Middle East and North Africa, and Latin America and the Caribbean.[5] According to the World Bank's Doing Business database, the collateral and bankruptcy laws of Kenya were the most supportive of lending activities in Africa in 2007, with an SLRI score of 8 (out of 10). Botswana, Malawi and Nigeria had a score of 7, while Zambia's was 6.

Financial markets in African countries tend to be weak and therefore unable to satisfy the large demand for financial services by the business sector (Atieno 2006). This is particularly true of the banking sector in many countries of Sub-Saharan Africa, where a few banks provide a small range of uncompetitive services. The total assets of banks exceed $10 billion only in Nigeria ($22 billion) and South Africa ($219 billion) and are less than $1 billion in 24 Sub-Saharan countries (World Bank 2006a). The banking sector also suffers from internal weaknesses and tends to be risk-averse and cautious in lending. When credit is provided, terms and conditions are often exorbitant and beyond the capacity of most potential borrowers.

Stock markets in Africa are few in number and have been largely inconsequential in facilitating economic growth and investment. Their development is constrained by small markets, lack of human capital, market fragmentation, shortage of equity capital, information inefficiency, inadequate regulatory regimes and lack of investor confidence (ECA 2008). As a result, there are few opportunities for sharing risks, trading shares and providing liquidity (World Bank 2006a). Outside of South Africa, the few stock markets that exist are small.

Some African countries have tried to promote access to credit for the private sector by making it easier for lenders to assess the creditworthiness of potential borrowers and by improving creditor rights. Egypt established its first private credit bureau in 2006/07, and Mauritius set up a public credit registry in 2005/06. In 2006/07 Kenya and Tunisia expanded the information available in credit registries. Kenya

> **Financial markets in African countries tend to be weak and therefore unable to satisfy the large demand for financial services by the business sector**

compelled banks to report defaults to private credit bureaus, and in South Africa lenders are legally required to check the debt levels of current and potential borrowers. In Ghana a new insolvency law allowed out-of-court enforcement of collateral for secured creditors (World Bank 2006d, 2007a).

African countries should expand the range of assets that can be used as collateral, establish collateral registries to register charges on assets, give secured creditors priority to collateral and facilitate the sharing of credit information with proper safeguards to protect the privacy of borrowers. Given the weaknesses in enforcing business contracts in African countries and the strong positive association of private credit to the introduction of credit registries, a focus on information-sharing institutions might bring a bigger economic payoff in the short term.

Other investment incentives and support for the private sector
African countries have been emphasizing the development of infrastructure through public investments as far back as the 1960s. Now efforts are being made to bring the private sector into the development of infrastructure and improve the management of public utilities to broaden cost-effective service and attract private investments, especially FDI, to the sector. The trend in Africa has been to privatize key infrastructure sectors such as energy and telecommunications.

Still, Africa is behind other developing regions in the availability and quality of infrastructure, lagging at least 20% behind the average for International Development Association (IDA) countries on almost all measures of infrastructure development. The quality of service is low, supplies are unreliable and disruptions are frequent and unpredictable—all of which increase production costs and discourage investors. The unmet infrastructure needs of Africa are estimated at $22 billion, plus an additional $17 billion for operations and maintenance (World Bank 2007b), meaning that most Africans have limited access to infrastructure. Only 30% of Africans have access to electricity, compared with 75% for other least-developed countries (LDCs), access to water and sanitation is about 65% compared with 89% for other LDCs, access to roads is 34% compared with 50%, and the penetration rate for telecommunication is less than 13%, compared with the world average of 40% (AfDB, 2006).

African countries have failed so far to attract much private investment in infrastructure. But this trend is changing. Private-sector provision and management of infrastructure increased from $4 billion in 2004 to $6 billion in 2006, though about 84% of this investment went to telecommunications and energy.

Directly or indirectly, agriculture is the source of livelihood for a majority of poor people, especially in rural areas. In Sub-Saharan African countries (excluding South Africa) agriculture accounts for an average of 34% of GDP and 64% of employment (World Bank 2007c).

> ❝ **African countries have failed so far to attract much private investment in infrastructure. But this trend is changing**

Consequently, access to agricultural land is important for alleviating poverty. But land ownership on the continent is legally insecure. Only 2–10% of the total land area is covered by the formal legal system (Dam 2006). The rest is communal land, operating under traditional institutions. Communal ownership implies the absence of individual property titles, which are important in providing incentives to invest in land and use the formal titles as security for access to credit.

To facilitate access to land, governments must adopt and enforce policies on land tenure, redistribution and compensation and create a legal infrastructure that allows for land registration and transferability as well as enforcement of property rights. South Africa is attempting to redress the unequal distribution of land through its land reform policy of 1994, including restitution, redistribution and land reform. Some achievements have been recorded, although targets set in the land reform policy, such as transfer of 30% of the land from minority to majority, are yet to be achieved. In Madagascar the government has improved the land system and procedures for acquiring title. In Malawi the government is in the process of drafting a land policy to address the problems associated with access to land.

Some countries have established economic export processing zones with preferential policies—tax incentives, fewer restrictions on hiring expatriate labour, generous foreign exchange retention rates, access to land, developed infrastructure and streamlined procedures—to attract FDI. Seychelles, Kenya, Namibia, Cape Verde, Malawi, Djibouti, Madagascar, Mauritius and Togo have established such zones. But there are serious doubts about whether such zones do in fact encourage foreign investments that would not have been made otherwise.

Support for the informal sector

The informal sector includes enterprises that are outside state regulations. They are not registered, and they pay no taxes on their profits. Most of them are micro, very small and small enterprises individually owned and operated with the help of a few workers, often relatives. The sector is large and growing in most African countries. As a percentage of gross national income it ranges from under 30% in South Africa to nearly 60% in Nigeria, Tanzania and Zimbabwe. The average for Sub-Saharan Africa is 42.3% (Verick 2006). The contribution of the informal economy to employment is also high, averaging 78% in Sub-Saharan Africa. The informal sector has also grown relative to the formal sector in its share of output and employment (Xaba, Horn and Motola 2002).

Enabling the informal sector to become part of the formal sector allows the government to improve the enforcement of regulations to protect consumers, employees and the environment, and it broadens the tax base of the government. Legal registration will improve access of enterprises to the formal

' The informal sector is large and growing in most African countries. As a percentage of gross national income it ranges from under 30% in South Africa to nearly 60% in Nigeria, Tanzania and Zimbabwe

credit system and to public services, which will facilitate their expansion, increase productivity and create employment.

The informal sector in Africa faces several obstacles in achieving these benefits. A major problem in this regard is lack of access to finance. This is especially true of micro and small enterprises, most of which are not legally registered, may even lack a fixed permanent address and cannot offer collateral for loans by banks and other financing institutions. The result is that business finance for most enterprises in the informal sector comes from individual savings or loans from unregulated financing sources, often at very onerous terms.

> *Development of small and medium-size enterprises is a focus for African governments, but the results have not been encouraging*

Almost all African countries allow the informal sector to operate more or less freely and adopt specific policies and programmes to develop the sector. Some governments try to facilitate access to credit (Djibouti and Ghana), training for workers (Ghana and Nigeria) and partnerships and linkages with established enterprises (Nigeria and South Africa). But according to the experts interviewed only in 5 of 22 countries did more than half of the experts reply that the government always or usually supports the informal sector and encourages its development.

There are several explanations for the decline in government support for the informal sector. While African countries are on record as being favourable to the development of domestic entrepreneurs, most of whom are in the informal sector, they give far more effort to

attracting FDI. Access to infrastructure and export and processing zones go more often to foreign investors than to the informal sector. While several African countries have created microcredit schemes to assist the informal sector, the funds available are miniscule when compared with the needs of the sector.

Development of small and medium enterprises

Small and medium-size enterprises (SMEs) are a focus for African governments. The measures taken by African governments to encourage the development of SMEs are similar to those applied in the informal sector, including credit, training and capacity building to support SMEs.

While several countries have adopted specific policies and programmes for SMEs, the results have not been encouraging. The South African government has tried to support entrepreneurial and business development through a number of programmes and institutions, but performance of the sector until 2005 was not proportionate to the efforts. Limited access to credit, raw materials and markets remain the main bottlenecks.

Flow of foreign and domestic private investment

The flow of FDI into Africa reached a record US$36 billion in 2006 (UNCTAD 2007). But table 3.2 shows that Africa's share of FDI flows is smaller than other regions, and the improvement in this area has been only slight.

FDI flows to Africa are highly concentrated (table 3.3). The top

Table 3.2 World FDI flows, 2000–06 (in % unless stated otherwise)

Region/economy	Average 2000–2003	2004	2005	2006
World total (billion US$)	861.0	742.1	945.8	1, 305.9
World	100.0	100.0	100.0	100.0
Developed economies	73.6	56.4	62.4	65.6
Developing economies	23.3	38.1	33.2	29.0
Africa	1.6	2.4	3.1	2.7
Latin America and the Caribbean	8.2	12.7	7.9	6.4
Asia and Oceania	13.3	23.0	22.1	19.8
South East Europe and Commonwealth of Independent States	3.1	5.4	4.3	5.3

Source: UNCTAD 2007.

ten recipients of FDI in Africa in 2004, 2005 and 2006 accounted for 68.5%, 69.9% and 91.0%, respectively, of the FDI flows to the continent. Eight of the top ten recipients of FDI in Africa are oil-exporting countries. Whereas FDI flows into North Africa increased by 72% to US$23.3 billion in 2006, those into Sub-Saharan Africa dropped by 24% from the previous year, largely because of outflows by transnational corporations in South Africa (UNCTAD 2007).

The concentration of FDI in oil-producing countries is an impediment to broad-based and sustained growth. Investments in extractive industries generate economic rents for as long as resources last and are in demand, with little direct or indirect impact on employment. Dependence on resource rents cause real appreciations of the exchange rate, stifling the development of other economic sectors by making other domestic products uncompetitive in export markets. Sustainability requires

Table 3.3 Concentration of FDI flows to Africa, 2004–2006 (US$ million)

Country	2004	2005	2006
Egypt	2,157	5,376	10,043
Nigeria	2,127	3,403	5,445
Sudan	1,511	2,305	3,541
Tunisia	639	782	3,312
Morocco	1,070	2,946	2,898
Algeria	882	1,081	1,795
Libya	357	1,038	1,734
Equatorial Guinea	1,651	1,873	1,656
Angola	1,449	1,303	1,140
Chad	495	613	700
Total top 10 African countries	12,338	20,720	32,264
Rest of Africa	5,680	8,928	3,280
Total	18,018	29,648	35,544

Source: UNCTAD 2007.

development of both upstream and downstream industries, requiring the development of local labour skills and technological capabilities. Furthermore, resource-dependent governments rely less on taxation of individuals and businesses, eroding accountability to taxpayers and fostering the politics of patronage (Collier 2007). The result is usually a low-growth environment characterized by under-investment and investments with low rates of return.

Domestic investment in Africa has been stagnant—an estimated 19.7% of GDP in 1998-2001, 20.1% of GDP in 2002-2005 and a projected 22.1% of GDP in 2007. Excluding North Africa, the corresponding figures are 18.4%, 19.0% and 19.8% of GDP, respectively. Domestic investment as a percentage of GDP is 31% in East Asia, by comparison. Such low domestic investment rates in Africa are clearly incompatible with accelerated and sustained growth led by the private sector.

The main reason for the low domestic investment in Africa is the low domestic savings rate. From 2000 to 2004 domestic savings as a percentage of GDP was 17% in Sub-Saharan Africa, compared to 21% for Latin America and the Caribbean, 26% for the Middle East and North Africa and 35% for East Asia and the Pacific. The figure for Sub-Saharan Africa also hides wide disparities among countries. Botswana, the Republic of Congo, Gabon and Nigeria, all of which export oil or diamonds, have domestic savings rates ranging from 32% in the case of Nigeria to 51% in the case of the Republic of Congo.

Public-private partnerships

Partnership between governments and the private sector must be understood against the backdrop of

suspicion, if not outright hostility, toward the private sector in many African countries from the 1960s to the 1980s. With the shift in the 1980s toward recognizing the private sector as vital in promoting sustainable growth and development, it was essential that governments reassure the private sector about its role and importance in the economy. Governments have tried to provide this assurance by making statements about the importance they attach to the private sector. And Ghana created the Ministry for Private Sector Development.

African governments realize that they alone do not have the resources to stimulate sustainable growth. Further, many public services and enterprises had been wasteful and ineffective due to mismanagement and corruption. The conclusion drawn in the 1980s was that not only commercial enterprises but also such social services as health and education should be placed in private hands as much as possible. The argument was also made that carrying out the traditional economic functions of government—creating an enabling environment and regulating the conduct of business— requires expertise and other inputs from the private sector. Public-private partnerships would ensure that the activities of the two sectors are mutually reinforcing rather than contradictory. In the light of these considerations, African governments have been endeavouring to associate the private sector in economic decision making and creating mechanisms to strengthen collaboration between the two parties.

> *Partnership between governments and the private sector must be understood against the backdrop of hostility toward the private sector in many African countries from the 1960s to the 1980s*

Engaging the private sector in economic decision making

There are various ways to draw the private sector into economic decision making—from ad hoc and informal consultations with individual entrepreneurs and organisations such as chambers of commerce to formal mechanisms that provide membership for the private sector in economic and social councils. Botswana, Senegal, Ghana, Tanzania and Malawi have consultative forums to strengthen public-private partnership. Often, governments resort to a variety of methods to engage the private sector. It should be stressed that participation by the private sector is purely advisory, with final decision-making power resting with the governments.

Only in five countries (Botswana, Mauritius, Malawi, Mali and Ghana) did more that half of the experts indicate that the government always or usually involves the private sector in any area of policymaking. In 13 of the remaining countries, 40% or less of the experts gave the same response. In two countries (Zambia and Congo) the percentage was less than 20%.

A comparison of the responses of the experts in AGR I and this study shows a positive trend in 9 of the 15 countries and a negative trend in the remaining 6 countries (figure 3.4). The increase in the case of Kenya is particularly remarkable and raises questions about its reliability. The findings of both AGR I and AGR II

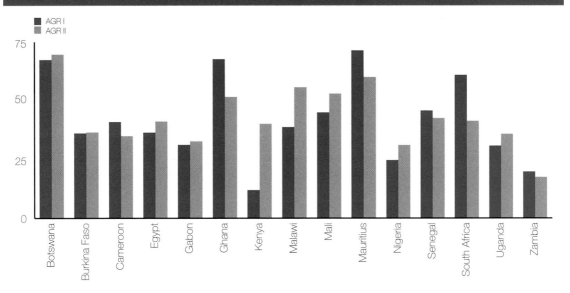

Figure 3.4 Expert opinion on whether government always or usually involves the private sector in policymaking that affects its development

Share of experts surveyed, by country (%)

Source: ECA survey of experts 2007.

suggest that the involvement of the private sector in policymaking is still more the exception than the rule.

Effectiveness of public-private collaboration

The experts were also generally of the view that the public and private sectors are not effective partners in development. In none of the 22 countries did 25% or more of the experts believe that the private and public sectors are partners in development with effective collaborative mechanisms; in some countries the proportion was as low as 5%.

Public-private partnership in Africa remains weak. The failure to engage the private sector in policymaking is a reflection of the continuing tendency of the governing class in many, if not most, African countries to seek to monopolize power to the exclusion of all other groups. There is also the legacy of mistrust of the private sector, despite official pronouncements to the contrary. Inherent weaknesses in the private sector, such as internal divisions and the tendency of entrepreneurs to focus on what is good for them—as individuals or members of a particular ethnic, regional, racial or religious group, rather than what is good for the private sector and the economy as a whole—is also a problem.

Finally, the limited capacity of the private sector to collect and analyze economic, social and political data and develop sound policy recommendations reduces its credibility in the eyes of government and detracts from its ability to act as a viable partner. Surmounting these

> ‘ **The failure to engage the private sector in policymaking is a reflection of the continuing tendency of the governing class in many African countries to monopolize power to the exclusion of all other groups**

obstacles will require sustained efforts to educate the private sector on its appropriate role in development and enhancing its capacity to organize, engage in sound analytical and policy analysis and play a more effective advocacy role.

Contract enforcement and property rights

Economic progress depends on institutions that enforce contract rights and codify and protect private, exclusive and transferable property rights. There is ample empirical evidence of the link between such institutions and economic performance (De Long and Shleifer 1993; Besley 1995; Acemoglu et al. 2001; Acemoglu and Johnson 2005).

Enforcement of contracts and protection of property rights require a strong, efficient and politically independent judiciary and law enforcement system and a competent bureaucracy to define, register and record titles to property and their transference. The independence of the judiciary takes on added significance when private parties have to enforce contracts involving the state or when they have to protect their property from expropriation by the state and its agents.

Enforcement of business contracts

Third-party enforcement of contracts is less important for disputes between parties from the same community and culture and where there are ongoing and repeated interactions between contracting parties. But in modern economies, where commercial transactions take place across geographical areas and

Box 3.3 Reforms in contract enforcement in Africa

In recent years many African countries have taken steps to improve the enforcement of business contracts. The most popular reforms have been specialized commercial chambers in general courts and separate commercial courts. The main benefit of specialized courts is having judges with expertise in handling commercial cases and their streamlined procedures. The table below summarises reforms undertaken to introduce specialized commercial courts.

Burkina Faso	Since October 2006 commercial chambers have been operating in the general courts in Ouagadougou and Bobo-Dioulasso.
Chad	The commercial court in N'Djamena started operating in October 2006.
Congo, Dem. Rep.	Specialized commercial courts started operating in Gombe in August 2006 and in Kinshasa in November 2006.
Gambia	Established a commercial division in the high court during 2005/06.
Ghana	Six commercial courts are now fully operational in Accra.
Malawi	The commercial division of the Blantyre High Court started hearing cases above 50,000 kwachas in May 2007.
Mauritania	During 2006/07 commercial courts replaced commercial chambers in the general courts.
Mozambique	Specialized commercial chambers have been operated in the general courts in Maputo since March 2007.
Nigeria	Lagos State introduced a specialized commercial division in the high court during 2005/06
Rwanda	In March 2006 commercial chambers started operating in the high courts; 3 separate commercial courts were established in May 2007

Following the introduction of specialized commercial courts, the time to enforce contracts fell from 552 to 487 days in Ghana, from 730 to 457 days in Nigeria and from 766 to 434 days in The Gambia.

One way to reduce delays is to simplify trial procedures. In 2004 Burundi introduced a simplified procedure for debt recovery, requiring the creditor only to present the judge with evidence of the transaction and nonpayment, leading to a reduction in debt recovery by nearly three months. Simplifying trial procedures for claims below a given threshold may also speed up enforcement. In some countries creditors are charged a fee to obtain an original copy of the judgment. In 2006/07 Burkina Faso reduced this registration tax from 4% to 2% of the judgment amount.

Source: World Bank 2005a, 2006d and 2007a.

contracts are long-term and complex, court enforcement of contracts becomes important. In African countries, as in other developing countries, such long-term and complex contracts are prevalent in the construction and infrastructure sectors, which are vital for economic development.

All African countries have provisions for the enforcement of business contracts as part of their general civil code or specific laws of contract or tort. The Economic and Monetary Union of West African States (UEMOA) has adopted the harmonized code of the Organization of Business Law in Africa (OHADA), which covers commercial and corporate law, recovery procedures, arbitration, and accounting law.

Some countries have established separate courts to deal with commercial cases. Burkina Faso, Ghana, Malawi, Gambia, Mozambique and Nigeria have either introduced specialized commercial chambers within general courts or set up separate commercial courts. In addition to the formal court system, alternative dispute resolution mechanisms are used. Ghana has an alternative dispute resolution mechanism to expedite legal actions, and in the Republic of Congo arbitration is one mechanism by which contracts are enforced.

Despite the adoption of these laws and the establishment of institutions for their enforcement, there is strong evidence suggesting that the enforcement of business contracts is often tedious, time-consuming and expensive. It took an average of 660 days to settle a business dispute in Africa in 2006/07, compared with 699 days for the Middle East and North Africa and 1,047 days for South Asia. Among the countries covered by the survey, only in Namibia (270 days) and Rwanda (310 days) did the settlement of a business dispute through the local courts occur within one year.

The surveyed experts confirmed that property rights and contracts are not effectively enforced. Only in seven countries were more than half of the experts positive about government effectiveness in enforcing contracts and protecting property rights.

> *The enforcement of business contracts is often tedious, time-consuming and expensive in Africa*

Protection of private property rights

Protection of individual property rights, especially in land, is as important as enforcing business contracts. There are three important ways that secure private property rights increase investment. First, a high risk of expropriation by private individuals or by the state dampens incentives to invest in the maintenance and improvement of property. Second, secure private property rights enable owners to use the property as collateral for loans, improving businesses' access to finance. Third, secure and transferable property rights will tend to increase investment if it encourages trade to those who value the property more than the current owner (Besley 1995).

All African countries have provisions in their constitutions or laws protecting individual properties. The constitutions of Botswana, Burkina Faso, Djibouti, South Africa and Zambia guarantee the security of property but subject to expropriation under certain circumstances. In Botswana, Ethiopia, Ghana, Mauritius, Sierra Leone and Zambia, separate laws have been enacted and institutions created to protect property rights, particularly as it relates to land and housing.

Despite the legal protection of property rights in many countries, major challenges remain in making it effective. In Ghana, for example, unclear demarcation and ownership of land results in conflict, making it difficult to secure land for productive ventures. There are instances of corruption in land allocation and titling that hamper the security of property rights in Zambia. While the constitution accords equal rights for all in Malawi, there is a great deal of discrimination in access to land based on social and economic status and gender. It is difficult to fight the government. Other obstacles are the long and costly procedures to defend an individual property right, restriction of land ownership to nationals, and ethnic and other cleavages that prevent ownership outside one's place of origin.

Registering property can be a complex and long procedure. In 2006/07 it took an average of 102 days to register property in Africa, at an average cost of 10.7% of the property value, significantly higher than any other region. It takes over a year to register property in Gambia and Rwanda, and businesses can expect to pay more than 20% of the value of property they are registering in the Republic of Congo, Nigeria, Mali and Chad.

While the burden of registering property and transferring property titles in Africa is still high, some reforms are making it easier and cheaper. Ghana cut the time from 169 to 34 days by abolishing the requirement to register the deeds of sale at the land commission. The time to register property in Kenya was reduced by nine days by opening the land valuation market to new suppliers. The efficiency gains from digitizing property records in Tunisia contributed to a fall in registration time from 57 to 49 days. Benin, Burkina Faso, Mauritius and Niger lowered registration costs by 4–5%

Box 3.4 Measures to ensure good corporate governance in South Africa

South Africa has implemented several innovative corporate governance reforms. The first King Report on Corporate Governance for South Africa (King I Report) was issued in 1994, and a second, more comprehensive King II Report was issued in 2002 by the Institute of Directors of South Africa. The King II report promotes the highest standards of corporate governance and identifies seven primary characteristics of good corporate governance: discipline, transparency, independence, accountability, responsibility, fairness and social responsibility. These principles were integrated into the Code of Corporate Practice and Conduct in South Africa, which applies to affected countries. The Code does not have the force of law.

Additional initiatives in South Africa were the Insider Trading Act of 1998 and the Revised Listing Requirements for companies listed on the Johannesburg Stock Exchange (JSE), which came into effect in 2003 (Vaughn and Ryan 2006). The Insider Trading Act prohibits insider dealing, provides for civil and criminal penalties for such dealing and allows the Financial Service Board to investigate matters relating to such dealing. The JSE Revised Listing Requirements requires listed companies to comply with the recommendations contained in King II. It requires listed companies to adopt the International Financial Reporting Standards (Vaughn and Ryan 2006).

---

by reducing the property registration tax. The property registration tax in Egypt was cut from 3% of property value to a fixed tax of 2,000 Egyptian pounds, translating into a 4.9% fall in registration costs and a 39.0% rise in revenue from the property registration tax.

Guarantees of intellectual property rights

The protection of intellectual property rights (IPRs) is part of African countries' efforts to encourage domestic innovation and technological adoption. In countries where IPRs are not protected, innovations and entrepreneurship are discouraged and do not serve as engines of development.

Since intellectual property is intangible and easily moved across international boundaries, international agreements provide stronger protection than national laws (World Bank 2005b). Several African countries have signed international and regional agreements relating to industrial and intellectual property. Others have national laws and regulations, and many have taken both steps. The major international and regional agreements for the protection of intellectual property rights to which African countries adhere are the World Intellectual Property Organization (WIPO), the World Trade Organization (WTO), the Universal Copyright Convention, the Paris and Berne Conventions for the Protection of Industrial Property, the African Regional Property Organization and the African Regional Industrial Property Organization.

Botswana, the Republic of Congo, Madagascar, Malawi, Mauritius and Namibia have signed international agreements or become members of international organisations for the protection of intellectual property, and the East African countries have modeled their intellectual property laws on international conventions and agreements. Kenya has a legal framework for industrial property (patents and trademarks), copyright laws, and plant breeders' rights, while Uganda and Tanzania have copyright and trademark laws but use the African Regional Industrial Property organisation for their industrial property laws.

AGR I noted that despite enacting legal provisions and signing regional and international agreements, many African countries do not effectively protect IPRs. And there is no indication that the protection of IPRs has improved in recent years.

Corporate governance

The *Cadbury Report* (1992) defined corporate governance broadly as "the system by which companies are directed and controlled".[6] That is, companies and the directors who oversee them operate within boundaries set by rules and regulations, by the providers of funds, by the shareholders at the general meeting, by the constitutions of companies themselves and by public opinion (Cadbury 2002).

Until recently most African countries paid little attention to issues of corporate governance, in the mistaken view that it has little impact on the economy and is the responsibility of the private sector. Governments had little expertise to address the problem and feared that an active regulatory role would frighten private investments, especially FDI. One exception was government intervention in some cases of labour disputes, price fixing and other anti-competition practices, blatant cases of corruption, and failure to pay taxes and other fees.

But attitudes are beginning to change in African countries, largely through external encouragement and advocacy, and to a more limited extent because of pressure from civil society organisations. These efforts are still largely limited to adopting codes on good corporate governance and measures to ensure international

> ❛ **Despite enacting legal provisions and signing regional and international agreements, many African countries do not effectively protect intellectual property rights**

credibility in accounting and audit practices. The focus is on engendering trust and credibility in how enterprises are managed in order to encourage private investments. Rarely do these efforts extend to corporate social responsibility and how to ensure that corporate governance makes an effective contribution to realizing broad political, social and economic goals.

Transparency and accountability in corporate governance

To ensure good corporate governance, all firms, including small enterprises, must be run in a transparent and accountable way. Transparency is the extent to which outside stakeholders have sufficient access to information about the financial affairs of companies to allow them to make informed judgments. Financial statements that provide reliable and clear information about a company and how the information was arrived at promotes transparency and engenders trust between providers of finance and the company.

The key mechanisms for accountability are rules on accounting and audit procedures and the disclosure of financial and other information on the state of the enterprise to shareholders, government officials and the public. The main measures taken by African countries to ensure sound accounting and audit standards and procedures are establishing organisations that set standards and regulate accounting and audit procedures, adopting national legislation to regulate accounting and audit activities, and facilitating adherence

to and membership in regional and international agreements and organisations that deal with accounting and audit.

The most significant measure to ensure confidence in accounting and audit practices and procedures is adherence to international standards. Accurate financial reporting contributes to private-sector growth by strengthening a country's financial system, reducing the risk of financial crisis, contributing to foreign direct and portfolio investment, and helping to mobilize domestic saving. It also facilitates access by small corporate borrowers to credit from the formal financial sector by allowing investors to evaluate corporate prospects (Hegarty, Gielen and Barros 2004).

Most African countries have adhered to one or more international and regional agreements on accounting and audit. The UEMOA countries have many arrangements in place, such as SYSCOA, the Permanent Council on the Accounting Profession, the National Order of Accounting Experts and Chartered Accountants, and the Official Management Centers. African countries also belong to the International Accounting Standards Board, the International Federation of Accountants and the International Organization of Supreme Audit Institutions.

Despite these efforts, progress in ensuring respect for internationally recognized accounting and audit standards and practices has been limited. A case in point is Ghana,

> *Until recently most African countries paid little attention to issues of corporate governance, but attitudes are beginning to change*

where accounting and auditing practices suffer from institutional weakness in regulation, compliance and enforcement. The laws and regulations governing financial reporting are weak, and national ethical requirements for auditors are not in line with international requirements or even in full compliance with Ghana's national accounting standards.

Figure 3.5 indicates that the experts surveyed are not impressed with the efforts of their governments to ensure transparency and accountability in corporate governance. Only in three countries (South Africa, Botswana and Cape Verde) did more than half of the experts believe that the government always

ensures transparency and accountability in corporate governance. In two other countries (Mauritius and Malawi), a little over 40% shared this view. In the rest of the countries only a minority expressed a positive opinion.

Codes on corporate governance

A number of African countries have adopted codes on corporate governance. The countries of UEMOA have adopted the West African Accounting System (SYSCOA) within the framework of OHADA. SYSCOA contains provisions to ensure the reliability of accounting and financial information, adapt corporate accounting models to international standards, promote modern management in corporations

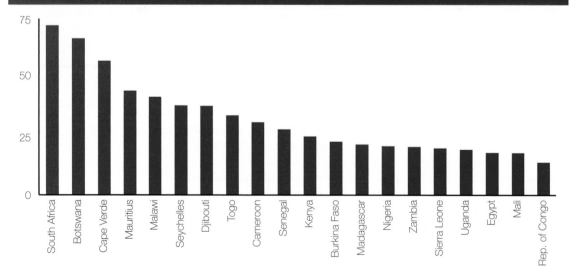

Figure 3.5 Expert opinion on government efforts to ensure transparency and accountability in corporate governance

Always or often ensures transparency and accountability in corporate governance (share of experts surveyed, by country, %)

Source: ECA survey of experts 2007.

and share information with various stakeholders. Egypt, Malawi, Mauritius, Mozambique, Nigeria, South Africa and Zambia have adopted national codes on corporate governance. Botswana, Ghana, Namibia, Seychelles and Madagascar make use of provisions in legislation regulating the operations of corporate entities.

The African Development Bank (AfDB) describes varying progress in corporate governance among the subregions in Africa (AfDB 2007):

- Nearly all the countries of Southern Africa have done a great deal to promote an understanding and implementation of good corporate governance, using the second King Report as a benchmark.

- In East Africa Kenya, Uganda and Tanzania have made steady progress in establishing self-regulatory institutions to promote good corporate governance.

- In Central Africa there is a uniform framework for the harmonisation of business laws, practices and procedures based on Francophone civil law. But strengthening institutions to promote good corporate governance and create an enabling environment for sound corporate practice has not progressed due to the military conflicts in the subregion.

- West Africa has witnessed a number of initiatives aimed at good corporate governance and

a number of collaborative efforts through various subregional agencies and common market institutions. There is a considerable degree of harmonization through the West Africa Business Association in the banking sector and OHADA for business laws and accounting standards.

- North Africa has made good progress in implementing harmonised standards of corporate governance through the Middle East and North Africa Corporate Governance Initiative.

African countries urgently need to upgrade corporate governance in several areas:

- Improve company law.

- Introduce standards of corporate governance.

- Develop regulatory bodies.

- Strengthen capital markets.

- Safeguard against corruption, bribery and mismanagement.

- Promote transparency in economic life.

- Develop the capacity of firms.

- Establish systems to ensure compliance with good principles of corporate governance.

Many of the structures to do so are already in place, but their effectiveness is limited by lack of capacity.

> *Many of the structures to upgrade corporate governance in Africa are already in place, but their effectiveness is limited by lack of capacity*

Protection of shareholders' rights

Corporate governance protects the interest of shareholders. The rights of shareholders and their equitable treatment are among the OECD principles of corporate governance (OECD 2004).[7] Protecting shareholders also helps businesses have access to equity finance. Investors are more likely to buy shares in the company if the directors disclose the affairs of the company, if the directors are liable for using the company's assets for their own private use, if it is easier for shareholders to sue directors for misconduct and if there is a high level of protection afforded to shareholders.

Several African countries have laws to protect shareholder's rights: Djibouti, Egypt, Gambia, Kenya, Malawi, Mauritius, Morocco, South Africa and the countries of UEMOA within the framework of OHADA. Still, shareholders face serious obstacles, especially small shareholders, in protecting their rights. Sometimes they have only limited information. The ownership structure of a family corporation might result in shareholders being dominated by a small group of family members. The shareholders have limited influence in appointing directors. As a group the shareholders are not organized. And seeking redress from the courts requires time and cost.

Consequently, in 2006/07 Africa was the region with the lowest protection of shareholders as measured by the World Bank's investor protection index.[8] Three African countries—South Africa, Mauritius and Mozambique—have an investor protection index equal to or higher than the average index for OECD countries, which is 6. South Africa has the strongest shareholder protection regulations in Africa with an index of 8 and ranks tenth in the world in this area. Mauritius, with a ranking of 7.7, has the eleventh strongest investor protection regulations in the world. At the other extreme, Swaziland has the weakest investor protection regulations in Africa, with an IP index of 2.

The World Bank studied the observance of OECD corporate governance in Africa and found varying levels of success in observing shareholders' rights (World Bank 2005b). The assessment concluded that in Ghana basic shareholders' rights are generally well protected and information is available to shareholders in a regular and timely manner. The problem, however, is with enforcement, especially the disclosure of material facts, monitoring for content and ownership disclosures. Private registries are not regulated, and it is impossible even for a sizeable shareholder to nominate a director against the will of the board and management. Controlling shareholders monopolize the annual general meetings through the board.

In South Africa every shareholder has a right to vote at general meetings and on the appointment and removal of directors and auditors, on amendments to articles and on authorization and issuance of share capital. However, shareholders are passive and do not exercise these rights (World Bank 2003). In a few

> *Several African countries have laws to protect shareholder's rights. Still, shareholders face serious obstacles, especially small shareholders, in protecting their rights*

countries small shareholders have taken steps to overcome their weakness by forming small shareholders associations. In Nigeria shareholders have established associations as a result of their dissatisfaction with the performance of directors and auditors. The most prominent of these bodies are the Nigerian Shareholders' Solidarity Association, the Association for the Advancement of Rights of Shareholders and the Independent Shareholders Association.

The experts are somewhat positive regarding the protection of the rights of shareholders in Africa. In 13 out of the 22 countries, 50–87% of the experts believed that the rights of shareholders are effectively protected. This seems to be at variance with the above analysis on the protection of small shareholders rights.

In general, corporate governance has not advanced much in Africa except for countries in the Southern African region. Corporate governance is still viewed solely in terms of its impact on stimulating private investments, to the comparative neglect of understanding how corporate governance encourages good citizenship by the private sector. Accounting and audit standards and practices fall short of what is internationally acceptable, and the protection of shareholders' rights, especially small shareholders, leaves much to be desired. To address these problems, the UN Economic Commission for Africa in 2002 recommended that African countries endeavour to respect seven international, regional

and domestic codes on economic and corporate governance (ECA 2002). Four of the codes relate to corporate governance in general: the International Accounting Standards of the International Accounting Standards Board, the International Standards on Auditing of the International Federation of Accountants, the Core Principles for Effective Banking Supervision of the Basel Committee on Banking Supervision and the OECD's Principles of Corporate Governance. Little progress has been made by African countries in implementing UNECA's recommendation.

Conclusion

African countries have taken a number of steps in the last decade to strengthen the private sector and make it the engine of accelerated growth, development and structural transformation. The principle measures employed have been creating an enabling environment for the development of the private sector by promoting competition in the economy, ensuring that operators are free to operate throughout the economy, reducing the burdens of doing business, granting tax and other incentives to private investors, adopting special measures for the development of the informal sector and SMEs, strengthening public-private partnerships, enforcing business contracts, protecting property rights and encouraging good corporate governance.

Compared with the situation that existed from the 1960s to the 1980s, African countries have recorded some progress in each of the above

> ' In general, corporate governance has not advanced much in Africa except for countries in the Southern Africa region

areas. But there was very limited improvement between AGR I and AGR II. More important, the impact of these measures on the flow of both domestic and foreign investments has been negligible.

There is a gap between well intentioned strategies, policies and institutions and effective and efficient implementation. The emphasis of African countries has been on the former, at the expense of implementation and enforcement. This has been an unfortunate mistake. The fundamental problem is not an error in judgment or emphasis but the lack of capacity for effective and efficient implementation and enforcement.

Capacity building is a complex, dynamic—and long—process. It entails continuous mobilization and effective utilization of a variety of resources and is central to all aspects of governance, including private-sector development and corporate governance. A strong and dynamic private sector requires a strong and capable state. The fundamental challenge facing African countries in promoting the development of the private sector is therefore how to enhance capacity and build the capable state.

> ' *The fundamental challenge facing African countries in promoting the development of the private sector is how to enhance capacity and build the capable state*

Notes

1. The 2007 report states that the key ingredients of economic freedom are personal choice, voluntary exchange coordinated by markets, freedom to enter and compete in markets and protection of persons and their property from aggression by others. The EFW index measures the degree of economic freedom in five major areas: size of government (expenditures, taxes and enterprises), legal structure and security of property rights, access to sound money, freedom to trade internationally and regulation of credit, labour and businesses. The EFW index ranges from 0 to 10, with a higher number representing more economic freedom.

2. Of the countries in figure 3.2 for which data is available on the EFW index for 2005, comparative data for 1990 was not available for Angola, Burkina Faso, Ethiopia, Lesotho, Mauritania and Mozambique.

3. Of the countries not surveyed in this report, sixteen of them were in the bottom fifth of the Ease of Doing Business ranking, including the bottom three—Guinea-Bissau, Central African Republic and Democratic Republic of Congo.

4. The Depth of Credit Information Index measures the rules affecting the scope, accessibility and quality of credit information available through either public or private registries. The index ranges from 0 to 6. Higher values indicate the availability of more credit information to facilitate lending decisions (World Bank 2006d).

5. The Strength of Legal Rights Index measures the degree to which collateral and bankruptcy laws protect the rights of borrowers and lenders. Scores range from 1–10. Higher scores indicate that collateral and bankruptcy laws facilitate lending by giving power to creditors in loan agreements (World Bank 2006d).

6. The *Cadbury Report* (1992) was prepared at the instigation of

the London Stock Exchange by the Committee on the Financial Aspects of Corporate Governance under the chairmanship of Sir Adrian Cadbury.

7. The principles are the rights of shareholders to (1) receive relevant information about the company in a timely manner, have the opportunity to participate in decisions concerning fundamental corporate changes, and share in the profits of the corporation among others; and (2) equitable treatment of shareholders, especially minority and foreign shareholders. Principle II, The Rights of Shareholders and Key Ownership Functions, states, "The corporate governance framework should protect and facilitate the exercise of shareholders' rights." Principle III, The Equitable Treatment of Shareholders, states that "[t]he corporate governance framework should ensure the equitable treatment of all shareholders, including minority and foreign shareholders. All shareholders should have the opportunity to obtain effective redress for violation of their rights."

8. The investor protection index is the average of three indices: the extent of disclosure index, the extent of directors' liability index and the ease of shareholder suit index. Higher values indicate higher shareholder protection (World Bank 2006d).

References

Acemoglu, Daron, Simon Johnson, and James Robinson. 2001. "The Colonial Origins of Comparative Development: An Empirical Investigation." *American Economic Review* 91: 1369–1401.

Acemoglu, Daron, and Simon Johnson. 2005. "Unbundling Institutions." *Journal of Political Economy* 113(51): 949–995.

AfDB (African Development Bank). 2006. "Infrastructure development and regional integration: getting the policy framework right." Concept paper for the 2006 annual meetings. Ouagadougou, Burkina Faso.

———. 2007. *Corporate Governance Strategy.* Tunis.

Atieno, Rosemary. 2001. "Formal and Informal Institutions' Lending Policies and Access to Credit by Small Scale Enterprises in Kenya." African Economic Research Consortium Research Paper Number 111.

Besley, Tim. 2005. "Property Rights and Investment Incentives: Theory and Evidence from Ghana." *Journal of Political Economy* 103(5): 903–937.

Besley, Tim, and Robin Burgess. 2004. "Can Labor Regulation Hinder Economic Performance? Evidence from India." *Quarterly Journal of Economics* 119(1).

Botero, Juan, Simeon Djankov, Rafael La Porta, Florencio Lopez-de-Silanes, and Andrei Shleifer. 2004. "The Regulation of Labor." *Quarterly Journal of Economics* 119(4): 1339–1382.

Cadbury, Adrian. 2002. *Corporate Governance and Chairmanship: A Personal View.* Oxford: Oxford University Press.

Collier, Paul. 2007. *The Bottom Billion: Why the Poorest Countries are Failing and What Can be Done About it.* Oxford: Oxford University Press.

Committee on the Financial Aspects of Corporate Governance. 1992. *Report of the Committee on the Financial Aspects of Corporate Governance 1992* (The Cadbury Report). ecgi.org/codes/documents/cadbury.pdf.

Dam, Kenneth W. 2006. *The Law-Growth Nexus: The Rule of Law and Economic Development.* Washington, D.C.: Brookings Institution Press.

De Long, Bradford, and Andrei Shleifer. 1993. "Princes and Merchants: European City Growth Before the Industrial Revolution." *Journal of Law and Economics* 36: 671–702.

Djankov, Simeon, Tim Ganser, Caralee McLiesh, Rita Ramalho, and Andrei Shleifer. 2008. "The Effect of Corporate Taxes on Investment and Entrepreneurship." National Bureau of Economic Research Working Paper 13756.

Djankov, Simeon, Rafael La Porta, Florencio Lopez-de-Silanes, and Andrei Shleifer (2002). "The Regulation of Entry." *Quarterly Journal of Economics* 117(1): 1–37.

Djankov, Simeon, Caralee McLeish, and Andrei Shleifer. 2007. "Private Credit in 129 Countries." *Journal of Financial Economics* 84: 299–329.

ECA (Economic Commission for Africa.) 2002. "Guidelines for Enhancing Good Economic and Corporate Governance in Africa." Addis Ababa.

———. 2005. *African Governance Report.* Addis Ababa.

———. 2008. *Economic Report on Africa: Africa and the Monterrey Consensus.* Addis Ababa.

Elbadawi, Ibrahim A., and Francis M. Mwega. 2000. "Can Africa's saving collapse be reversed?" *World Bank Economic Review* 14(3): 415–443.

Fraser Institute. 2007. *World Economic Freedom Annual Report 2007.* Vancouver, British Columbia: Fraser Institute.

Hegarty, John, Frederic Gielen, and Ana Cristina Hirata Barros. 2004. "Implementation of international accounting and auditing standards: lessons learned from the World Bank's Accounting and Auditing Report on the Observance of Standards and Codes (ROSC) programme." www.worldbank.org/ifa/lessonslearned_ROSC_AA.pdf.

King Committee on Corporate Governance. 1994. *King Report on Corporate Governance for South Africa 1994* (King I Report). Johannesburg: Institute of Directors.

———. 2002. *King Report on Corporate Governance for South Africa 2002* (King II Report). Johannesburg: Institute of Directors.

Klapper, Leora. 2006. "Entrepreneurship: How Much Does the Business Environment Matter?" Viewpoint series, Note 31. Washington, D.C.: World Bank Group.

Klapper, Leora, and Juan Manuel Quesada Delgado. 2007. "Entrepreneurship: New Data on Business Creation and How to Promote It." Viewpoint series, Note 316. Washington, D.C.: World Bank Group.

Monnane, M. Monnane. 2006. "Competition scenario in Botswana." Research paper prepared for Botswana Institute for Development Policy. Jaipur, India: Consumer Unity and Trust Society International.

NEPAD (New Partnership for Africa's Development). 2002. *Declaration on Democracy, Political, Economic, and Corporate Governance.*

OECD (Organisation for Economic Co-operation and Development). 2004. *OECD Principles on Corporate Governance.* Paris.

Rehabeam, Shilimela. 2006. "Competition Scenario in Namibia." Jaipur, India: Consumer Unity and Trust

Society International. www.cuts.org/7up3/Namibia_CRR.doc.

South Africa, Republic of. 1998. Insider Trading Act. Act No. 135. *Government Gazette*, vol. 402 no.19546.

UNCTAD. 2007 *Investment Report of the World*. Geneva.

Vaughn, Melinda, and Lori Verstegen Ryan. 2006. "Corporate Governance in South Africa: A bellwether for the continent?" *Corporate Governance* 14(5).

Verick, Sher. 2006. "The impact of globalization on the informal sector in Africa." www.iza.org/conference_files/worldb2006/verick_s872.pdf.

World Bank. 1994. *World Development Report 1994: Infrastructure for Development.* New York: Oxford University Press.

———. 2003. *Global Economic Prospects and the Developing Countries: Investing to Unlock Global Opportunities.* Washington, D.C.

———. 2005a. *African Development Indicators.* Washington, D.C.

———. 2005b. *World Development Report 2005: A Better Investment Climate for Everyone.* Washington, D.C.

———. 2006a. *African Development Indicators.* Washington, D.C.

———. 2006b. *World Development indicators.* Washington, D.C.

———. 2006c. *World Development Report: Equity and Development*

———. 2006d. *Doing Business 2007: How to Reform.* Washington, D.C. www.doingbusiness.org.

———. 2007a. *Doing Business 2008: Comparing Regulation in 178 Economies.* Washington, D.C. www.doingbusiness.org.

———. 2007b. *African Development Indicators.* Washington, D.C.

———. 2007c. *World Development Report 2008: Agriculture for Development.* Washington, D.C.

Xaba, Jantjie, Pat Horn, and Shirin Motola. 2002. "The informal sector in Sub-Saharan Africa: Working paper on the informal economy." Geneva: International Labor Organization.

What a government does and how it does it depends on the people who manage and control the three branches of government—executive, legislature and judiciary. How the three branches interact—and how people in civil society organisations and the media react to the policies and activities of the government—determines the effectiveness of a country's governance.

The tendency of the executive branch to monopolize power and abuse discretionary authority has been observed throughout the ages. A major challenge confronting advocates of good governance in Africa is to constrain the executive's power while not diluting its ability to fulfil its constitutional obligations and electoral mandate. Various constitutional and governance reforms have been undertaken to restrain the executive, yet the tendency for the executive to dominate the other institutions of government continues to be a major concern for those promoting good governance in Africa.

The executive is responsible for formulating and implementing national policies and designing and initiating legislation to support the policies. It enacts rules, procedures and the regulatory framework for public, commercial and entrepreneurial endeavours and enforces compliance with them. It is the main provider of public goods and services, ranging from health, education, commerce and transportation to security, defense and maintaining law and order. It controls major material and financial resources, mobilizing people and providing employment and income. It prepares the national budget and ensures its adoption by the legislature. And it appropriates and allocates national resources to government institutions and agencies.

The executive appoints ranking bureaucrats, directors of national institutes, heads of parastatal bodies and watchdog organisations such as the ombudsman, human rights commission and anti-corruption commission. It controls the bureaucracy, making decisions on promotions, transfers, deployment, remuneration and working conditions of the ranking civil servants. In a highly centralized governance system with a strong presidency, as in Kenya, the executive appoints all important administrative positions. It appoints the chief justice, judges and magistrates and controls the budget of the judiciary. It also has the constitutional power to dissolve the legislature at its own discretion, thus perpetually threatening the legislators and in the process undermining their independence and effectiveness. In such circumstances it is very difficult, and certainly politically problematic, for the legislature to try to check the powers or regulate the discretionary authority of the incumbent executive.

In Ghana and many other African countries the constitution empowers the president to appoint as many members of parliament as ministers or assistant ministers as deemed necessary, potentially diminishing the independence of the legislature and its effectiveness in checking the executive. And in Nigeria the executive is perceived as extraordinarily powerful, dominant across the entire governance system (box 4.1).

This chapter explores how the executive in Africa has been sufficiently or effectively checked and balanced by the other branches of government—the legislature and judiciary—as well as by civil society organisations and the media. The major finding of the chapter is that while constitutional reforms and institutional changes are ongoing in Africa, executive power still predominates, vitiating the principle of checks and balances.

Separation of powers facilitates and ensures checks and balances

The constitution determines the distribution of political power in a democracy. The purpose and effectiveness of political power are products of the dynamic interactions between the constitutional provisions, the political predispositions and capabilities of those managing the executive, legislative and judicial branches and the major actors in civil society.

The politicians in control of a democratic government are periodically elected. While in charge of the institutions of government they are expected to be accountable to the legislature. Legislators are expected to apply checks and balances to the policies, performance and activities of those in other key governance institutions to ensure that they conform to the provisions of the constitution and the rule of law and due process of law, and that they deliver their electoral mandates. Those who support the government in formulating and implementing policies—civil servants and law enforcement personnel—are required to be accountable and transparent in the performance of their duties. Between elections civil society organisations, the press and media monitor and report on the activities of the government to ensure that it delivers on its electoral promises, is responsive to the needs and wishes of the people, does not abuse its powers or discretionary authority, is accountable and transparent in its performance and, in general, conforms to constitutionalism and the political culture and traditions of the people.

The principal objective of the doctrine of separation of powers is to prevent one branch of government from gaining a dominant position in its relations with the other branches. Checks and balances are usually built into a constitution. The executive can also initiate checks and balances by, say, establishing independent watchdog institutions and agencies such as an ombudsman, a human rights commission and administrative tribunals

---

Box 4.1 Nigeria: executive dominance persists

The Nigerian president makes all important state appointments, including members of boards of parastatals and commissions. Although the theory of separation of powers operates in Nigeria, the executive heads—the president at the national level, the governors at the state level and the government chairmen at the local level—have power disproportionate to the other two arms of government. Unless most federal functions are decentralized by devolution to the state and local governments, the president in Nigeria will continue to have powers above and beyond the other organs of government.

Source: ECA 2007i, 114.

or creating internal mechanisms and codes of conduct to ensure conformity to the provisions of the constitution and to strengthen accountability and transparency. The auditor general has a constitutional mandate to monitor and certify public expenditures, ensuring financial accountability of the executive to the legislative branch.

The separation of powers is essentially a constitutional and legal provision. Whether the principle is observed ultimately depends on the political realities of a country—the level of democratization and good governance, the political culture, social conventions and the political will of the leadership across the governance system. Though all the core legal structures of the separation of powers might be in place, the checking and balancing of the executive could still be weak.

The need to contain executive dominance is widely recognized. The separation of powers is also acknowledged, but its operation continues to be weak. Although the phenomenon of the "Big Man" in African governance may be fading, as suggested in the first *African Governance Report* (AGR I), the tendency of the executive to dominate continues in many African countries (ECA 2005).

New institutions, such as an ombudsman and a human rights commission, have created a better environment for checks and balances and general oversight of the executive. The Kenya National Human Rights Commission has exposed extra-judicial executions by the Kenya Police in 2007. During the Kenyan general elections the same year, the commission exposed election irregularities allegedly carried out on behalf of the executive.

Despite constitutional reforms, the executive still dominates

Over the past two decades many African countries have reviewed and rewritten their constitutions. Implicit in the constitutional reinventions were reforms and restructurings of the executive, legislative and judicial branches of government and the administrative apparatus to enhance their capacities and make them more accountable and transparent. Decentralization measures and strengthening of local institutions and civil society organisations were put in place to enhance capacity and promote local government ownership, accountability and transparency— thus developing public trust in government and state legitimacy. Measures were put in place to strengthen the media, to ensure the widest possible dissemination of information and knowledge.

Civil society organisations and the mass media, vigilant in identifying abuses of power, have proved effective in promoting good governance. Many African governments have created new institutions and administrative tribunals to protect and promote basic human rights and freedoms, partly in response to the abuses of power revealed by civil society organisations and the media and partly in recognition of their own failures to contain excessive executive influence.

Although the phenomenon of the "Big Man" in African governance may be fading, the tendency of the executive to dominate continues in many African countries

The principle of separation of powers is now entrenched in the constitutions of almost all African countries. The reforms in recent decades have created a more propitious environment for democracy and good governance. The once-dominant civilian and military authoritarian regimes—as in Ghana, Liberia, Nigeria and Lesotho—were obliged to embrace a multiparty system. Single-party systems—such as those in Angola, Cameroon, Republic of Congo, Djibouti, Ethiopia, Côte d'Ivoire, Kenya, Malawi, Mozambique, Mali, Seychelles, Swaziland, Sierra Leone and Zambia—have also embarked on multiparty systems and decentralization.

Since the publication of AGR I there have not been any successful constitutional measures to reduce or moderate the dominance of the executive. An attempt was made in Kenya in late 2005 to introduce a people-negotiated new constitution, known as the Boma Constitution. (Boma was the venue where the representatives of Kenyans from all walks of life and different political parties met for more than two years to deliberate on a new constitution for their country.) The Boma Constitution, "the product of the most extensive constitutional consultations in Africa's history" (APRM 2006), was embedded with devolutionary principles and strong decentralization measures. But it was significantly altered by the incumbent government to retain executive dominance. When the altered constitution was submitted to a popular referendum, the people overwhelmingly rejected it—a clear verdict that the majority

of Kenyans were not happy with a constitution that vested too much power in the executive.

In Uganda President Yoweri Museveni amended the constitution to permit him to assume a third term. Because the new constitution removed any limits on executive tenure, it is possible that executive dominance in Uganda will be in perpetuity. President Obasanjo of Nigeria attempted a similar undertaking—changing the Nigerian constitution so he could contest a third term—but it was overwhelmingly rejected by the people.

Although the constitutions of South Africa and Egypt provide for the executive's accountability to the legislature, in practice it has been difficult for the legislatures to call to account their respective executives (ECA 2007l; ECA 2007d). Even so, an encouraging trend has emerged recently in Egypt following a constitutional amendment in 2005 that provided for the election of the president on the basis of universal suffrage for the first time. A further amendment in March 2007 provided for a more strict observance of the relevant laws and codes of conduct for the election of the president. Despite these changes the Egyptian executive still appears to dominate the other branches (ECA 2007d).

The overwhelming majority of experts affirmed that the principle of checks and balances was indeed enshrined in their constitutions, albeit in varying degrees of operational effectiveness. Botswana, Cape Verde, Ghana, Malawi, Mauritius,

> ' **The principle of separation of powers is now entrenched in the constitutions of almost all African countries**

Nigeria, Seychelles and Sierra Leone, among others, have a significant degree of constitutional checks and balances between the various branches of government. Egypt, the Republic of Congo, Kenya, Madagascar, Morocco, Zambia and Madagascar were identified as countries where the constitutions provided limited or very few possibilities for checks and balances.

Effectiveness of the executive

To perform its functions effectively, the executive must be vested with requisite powers and endowed with appropriate institutional capacity. If the executive is vested with overwhelming powers, the temptation to dominate the other branches of government will be greatly enhanced. But if the executive is endowed with limited constitutional powers or constrained by administrative procedures, it may lack the capacity to address the major issues confronting the country.

Studies for AGR II affirmed that elections have become the legitimate means of acquiring power and assuming office in African countries. According to the great majority of consulted experts, the executive is constituted through a fully competitive political process and multiparty elections. The implication is that the executive is imbued with legitimacy and constitutional powers to discharge its responsibilities to the country. The responses obtained from the majority of the consulted experts—falling within a minimum of 66.3% for Togo and a maximum of 100% for Cape Verde, Malawi

and Zambia—affirmed that the formation of the executive branch takes place through a fully competitive electoral process. A notable exception is Egypt, where only 16.2% of the consulted experts stated that the executive was formed on the basis of the competitive electoral processes. Clearly, competitive elections are now the accepted means for people to acquire political power and constitute the executive. This also signifies that competitive multiparty democratic politics is now well established, though the way it is practiced might vary from country to country.

Many African countries are decentralizing executive power and devolving some central government functions to local governments, primarily through administrative, not constitutional, means. They permit the administrative performance of specific functions at the local level but do not transfer the actual constitutional powers to initiate, implement and sustain the functions. Even so, such decentralizing strengthens local governance capacity, empowers people, enhances ownership and cultivates habits of accountability and responsiveness in governments. But the tendency of the executive to co-opt members of the legislature and strengthen the fusion between the two branches—at the expense of legislative oversight of the executive—is an enduring phenomenon in Africa. And it has created difficulties for the independent functioning of the legislature and judiciary.

The June 2005 interim report of the Constitution Review Commission

> *Many African countries are decentralizing executive power and devolving some central government functions to local governments, primarily through administrative, not constitutional, means*

of the government of Zambia noted that the constitution vested excessive powers in the president on the pretext of ensuring good governance and "promoting national unity" (ECA 2007o, 74). Executive dominance in other African countries poses a serious challenge to checks and balances between the branches of government. One observer argues that "nearly all presidential countries show a considerable degree of power concentration in the form of executive dominance" (Cranenburgh 2003 191–95).

For the executive to perform its functions adequately, it must not be subordinated to either internal or external political forces. In Nigeria the phenomenon of the "political godfather", where powerful political figures sponsor candidates for elective positions and control them when in power, has impaired the performance of the executive and sometimes the legislature. And the Nigerian experience is not an isolated case in Africa.

Some of the country reports (Cape Verde, Botswana, Mauritius, Djibouti, Gambia, Malawi, Seychelles and Tunisia) revealed that the executive branch is fairly free from subordination to external agencies in all or most major areas of policy. There are variations in the extent of executive subordination, ranging from those who are free in all or most major areas of policy to those free from subordination in a few or no major areas of policy. Most executives in the countries under review are reported to enjoy varying degrees of independence from

subordination to external agencies in all or most major areas of policy. An average of 28% of the consulted experts were of the view that executive independence is limited to either a few or none of the major policy areas.

Effectiveness of the legislature

The separation of powers entails the checking and balancing of the executive by the other branches of government. In a democracy an important function of the legislature is to ensure that the executive is monitored as it formulates and implements public policies. The majority of the consulted experts in Botswana, Cape Verde, Malawi, Mauritius and Tunisia perceived that the legislature is always or usually effective in controlling the executive and holding it accountable. Mali, and to some extent Kenya, are identified by the majority of the experts as the only countries where the legislature is only occasionally effective in controlling the executive. On the whole, the record of legislative effectiveness in controlling the executive in most of the countries under review is far from satisfactory (figure 4.1).

The capacity of the legislature to perform its functions efficiently and effectively is a major concern in many African countries. Many African legislatures lack the independence to perform their constitutional functions because they depend on the executive for their human and material resources and funding.

In the absence of legislative capacity, the struggle to attenuate executive

> *The capacity of the legislature to perform its functions efficiently and effectively is a major concern in many African countries*

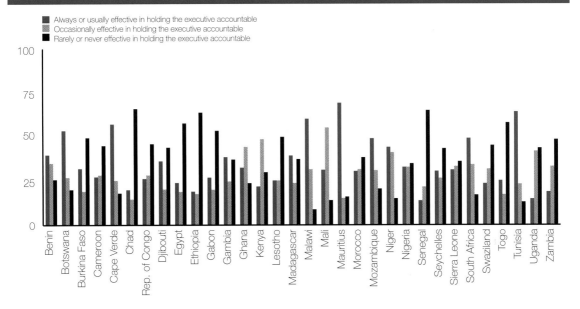

Figure 4.1 Expert opinion on the extent of legislative control of the executive

Share of experts surveyed, by country (%)

■ Always or usually effective in holding the executive accountable
▨ Occasionally effective in holding the executive accountable
■ Rarely or never effective in holding the executive accountable

Source: ECA survey of experts 2007.

dominance in African governance is likely to continue for a long time. Unless legislative effectiveness is promoted or the powers of the executive are constrained, the democratic system of governance is likely to be undermined. People might lose confidence in the legislature as the institution that articulates their interests, promotes and protects their rights and enacts policies for their welfare. Reform measures would also empower the non-state actors—CSOs, press and media—to be more vigilant in identifying abuses of power and in checking and balancing the executive and its agencies.

The effectiveness of a legislature is influenced, even today, by the type of political system that emerged in a country immediately after independence and the behaviour of the first generation of post-colonial political and military leaders. Ensuring accountability of the executive to the legislature is difficult under a

Box 4.2 Question time in the parliament

Question time is a key institution in the Westminster model of parliament adopted by many African countries. Members of parliament pose direct questions to government ministers. On special days the prime minister appears in parliament to listen and respond to the questions. In Madagascar the entire cabinet, including the prime minister, appears before the National Assembly on live radio and television to report on its annual activities and results. The report is followed by a tough questions-and-answers session on the individual presentations. This process makes a reality of the government's accountability and transparency to parliament and through it to the people.

one-party political system, the case in many African countries immediately after independence. Today those countries are at the stage of transition from authoritarian rule to multiparty democracy.

How anti-colonial struggles were organized and independence was achieved—through restrictive or inclusive mass mobilization and peaceful or violent struggles—as well as the post-colonial behaviour of the political leadership created the context for the new country's governance. Depending on the quality and commitment of the political leadership, the context could be manipulated by the "Big Man" to retain and strengthen the executive power. Cape Verde, Kenya, Mozambique and South Africa achieved independence through mobilization and violent struggle, yet due to the quality of their political leadership they have evolved into different political environments and attitudes towards executive authority. Benin, Mali, Malawi, Tanzania and Zambia managed to transform themselves from one-party rule to multiparty democracy in the 1990s. Nonetheless, consolidating democratic institutions by enhancing and strengthening accountability mechanisms is a continuous process (Doorenspleet 2005).

Notwithstanding the persistent shortcomings of African legislatures, there are some hopeful signs that the executive is likely to be confronted in the future by legislatures determined to assert their constitutional obligations and electorally mandated responsibilities. In an unprecedented step the Zambian legislature initiated a legal action against a former head of state, subjecting him to a motion of impeachment that resulted in the rise to power of the incumbent president (Munalula 2007). In Ghana the legislature is growing more assertive and incrementally effective in holding the executive accountable on several counts (ECA 2007e).

Reforms in many of the countries under review are enhancing the institutional capacity of legislatures and the capabilities of legislators. Zambia provides power to the parliament by creating constituency offices, enacting a code of conduct and addressing other institutional weaknesses (ECA 2007o). In Botswana standing and ad hoc committees of parliament monitor sectoral activities undertaken by the executive branch (ECA 2007b).

It could be argued that legislatures in some African countries are becoming more assertive in performing their functions and fulfilling their constitutional responsibilities. But executive dominance persists in some African countries despite the reforms, due partly to the ruling party's majoritarian influence and the weakness and fragmentation of opposition parties.

Periodic, open and fair elections are one of the major foundations of a democratic system of governance. A large majority of the consulted experts affirmed that national parliaments were constituted as a result of fully competitive elections. Exceptions were Cape Verde and

Madagascar, where 100% and 72% of the experts, respectively, noted that legislatures are constituted through a mixture of appointments of a small minority of legislators while the rest of the parliamentary seats are filled through competition in multiparty elections. Notwithstanding such a minor variation, constituting legislatures through fully competitive multiparty elections in most of Africa indicates that pluralism and multiparty politics are gaining ground.

The independence of the legislature is extremely important; otherwise it would not be able to perform its function of articulating and promoting the people's interests and checking and balancing the executive. Indeed, it is only when all the branches of government enjoy their respective institutional independence and are endowed with the appropriate capacities that democratic governance is likely to be sustained. A majority of the consulted experts in less than half the countries under review noted that their respective legislatures are free from subordination to external agencies in all or most areas of legislation. In Cape Verde, Mauritius, Ghana, Botswana and Tunisia the legislatures are free from subordination to external agencies in all or most of the major areas of legislation (figure 4.2). And there are instances where legislatures are rarely or never free

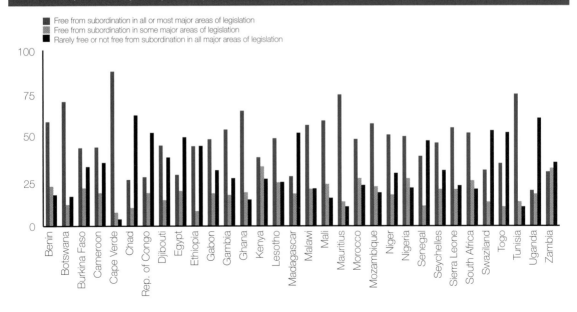

Figure 4.2 Expert opinion on the extent of legislative independence in major areas of legislation

Share of experts surveyed, by country (%)

■ Free from subordination in all or most major areas of legislation
■ Free from subordination in some major areas of legislation
■ Rarely free or not free from subordination in all major areas of legislation

Source: ECA survey of experts 2007.

from subordination to external agencies, as in Chad, Madagascar, Swaziland and Uganda.

Overall, the responses of the consulted experts on the effectiveness of the legislatures in their respective countries varied widely. The majority of experts from Benin, Cape Verde, Botswana, Ghana, Gabon, Nigeria, Sierra Leone, South Africa and Tunisia noted that the legislature is always or usually effective. Chad, Egypt, Madagascar, Malawi, Senegal and Uganda are identified by more than 60% of the experts as countries having legislatures that are sometimes, rarely or never effective. The majority of experts in the remaining countries under review

felt that legislatures are sometimes or rarely effective in discharging their responsibilities as provided for in their constitutions (figure 4.3).

Parliamentary committees play an important role in effective legislatures. Numerous standing and select committees deal with subjects that need the approval of parliament. They hold hearings at which the details of legislation supportive of executive policies or projects are explained, defended, critiqued, modified—and on rare occasions rejected. The committees invite people with special interests, and it is there that civil society organisations and those in the private sector articulate the interests of their

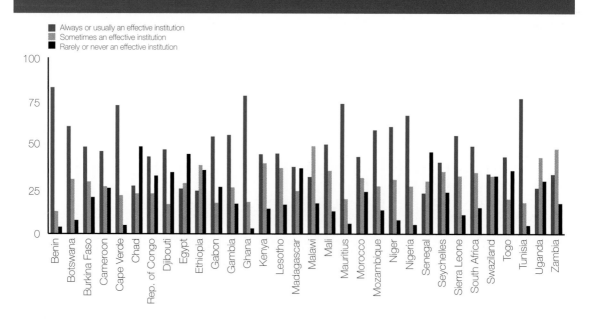

Figure 4.3 Expert opinion on the extent of legislative effectiveness

Share of experts surveyed, by country (%)

- Always or usually an effective institution
- Sometimes an effective institution
- Rarely or never an effective institution

Source: ECA survey of experts 2007.

stakeholders, defend their rights and call into question government's accountability and transparency. Many of these committee meetings are held in public with the media and press present.

Among the most powerful standing committees in parliamentary democracies is the public accounts committee, which oversees the expenditure of government revenues and receives reports from the auditor general. The country reports affirm the role of the committees in monitoring and scrutinizing government expenditure and in allocating the legislatively approved public resources. The public accounts committees in Nigeria, Botswana and South Africa are particularly noted for checking government expenditures. But the capacity of parliamentarians to be effective on financial and budgetary issues remains limited in many African countries.

Parliamentary committees also investigate the activities of the executive. In Ghana ministerial nominees require prior approval by the relevant parliamentary committee. In Zambia committees established by the legislature study, report, and make recommendations on the mandate, management and operations of the executive. They also scrutinize measures taken and recommend reviewing policies or existing legislation. It could be argued that sufficient constitutional and legal bases exist to empower parliamentary committees to embark on institutional checks and balances. But they are fairly ineffective in doing so.

Even so, parliamentary committees have had some notable achievements. For example, the Defense Committee of the South African parliament took up a case of a dubious arms deal that culminated in the exposure and prosecution of executive officers implicated in the transactions.

In a democratic system of governance the opposition plays an important role in ensuring that those in power—the ruling political party and the ranking civil servants—behave according to the constitution of the country, observe the rule of law and due process of law and respect the political culture and traditions of the country. In general, the opposition performs these functions by checking, challenging and questioning the performance of the executive and its supporters in the legislature. Through persuasive debates the opposition offers itself as a competent alternative to the ruling party. In a parliamentary system most of this debate takes place during the question time (box 4.2).

The strength of the opposition political party (or parties) in parliament is one factor that determines the degree and extent of checks and balances in a democratic pluralist system. Where parliamentary opposition groups are weak, the system of checks and balances is likely to be undermined or eroded owing to the immense leverage that ruling parties enjoy in dominating and influencing lawmaking.

In most countries under review the majority of the consulted experts

Where parliamentary opposition groups are weak, the system of checks and balances is likely to be undermined or eroded

were of the opinion that parliamentary opposition groups have weak or no significant influence on government policy, programmes or legislation. Notable exceptions are Malawi and Mozambique, where parliamentary opposition groups have a range of influence varying from considerable to moderate to fairly strong.

Effectiveness of the judiciary

An independent and effective judiciary determines the security of life and property, the legitimacy of government and an environment of peace and stability for people to feel free to engage in productive and creative activities. As an impartial arbiter between government and the citizens, the judiciary ensures government's accountability to the provisions of the constitution and its political legitimacy in case of disputed election results.

The judiciary is not immune to the influence of vested interests or dominance by the other organs of government. There has been considerable executive dominance over the judiciary in the appointment and promotion of judges, creating the phenomenon of the executive-minded judiciary—judges who anticipate the wishes of the incumbent governments or protect their leaders and supporters. The judiciary must not only be independent in fact; it must also be perceived as independent by the citizens. Following the disputed election results of December 2007, opposition groups in Kenya refused to refer their electoral grievances to the judiciary for arbitration, as demanded by the government,

because they felt the courts were not independent of the incumbent government.

Botswana is noted as a country where the judiciary is reasonably independent. In Nigeria the judiciary is considered exceptionally independent and fiercely nonpartisan in a governance system where the executive is perceived to be extremely powerful and dominant. This is not so in Kenya, however. A mission report by the International Commission of Jurists (ICJ) on the rule of law and the judicial system under the democratisation process in Kenya observed that there are several problems in the system that have to be improved upon for there to be a real rule of law in the country (ICJ 1997). Asked about the judiciary's independence, the majority of consulted experts in Botswana, Egypt, Malawi, Mauritius, Cape Verde, Ghana, Tunisia and South Africa reported that it is fully or largely independent of other branches of government in its operations. In most of the remaining countries the majority of the consulted experts reported that the judiciary is either somewhat independent, hardly or fully independent or largely independent (figure 4.4).

A merit-based system for recruiting and appointing judges can ensure that the judiciary achieves and maintains its independence, integrity and effectiveness. A majority of consulted experts in Botswana, Cape Verde, Ghana, Mauritius, Malawi, Sierra Leone, Nigeria, South Africa, Tunisia and Zambia perceived that judges are always

> *The judiciary must not only be independent in fact; it must also be perceived as independent by the citizens*

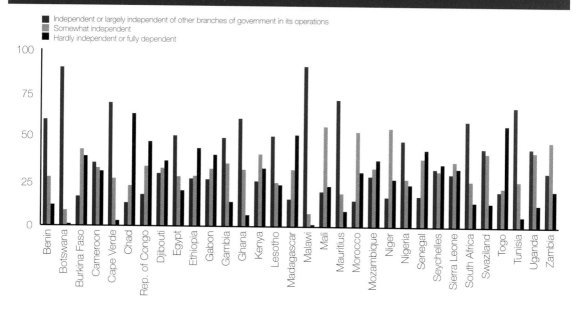

Figure 4.4 Expert opinion on the extent of judicial independence

Share of experts surveyed, by country (%)

Legend:
- ■ Independent or largely independent of other branches of government in its operations
- ■ Somewhat independent
- ■ Hardly independent or fully dependent

Source: ECA survey of experts 2007.

or usually appointed and promoted on the basis of merit and qualifications (figure 4.5). Chad, Congo and Togo are the notable exceptions. It could be tentatively concluded that in most African countries a merit system is used in various degrees in appointing and promoting judges. Consolidating this mode of judiciary recruitment and appointment is now necessary, and people must be continuously aware of the executive's temptations to encroach on the other institutions of governance.

Effectiveness of non-state actors

Non-state actors (civil society, professional groups and the private sector) can also check and balance the executive and other agencies of

government in a functioning democracy. Across Africa, vibrant civil society associations and organisations continue to emerge. Democracy is an ongoing process that requires continuous adaptation and adjustments to respond to peoples' needs. Between elections a civil society organisation (CSO) can keep the government on its toes by reminding ministers of their promises, insisting on accountability and transparency and generally keeping alive the democratic process.

The blossoming of CSOs in Africa might suggest that the pendulum in the relationship between the state and its citizens has finally swung away from state-centric big government to people-centred governance.

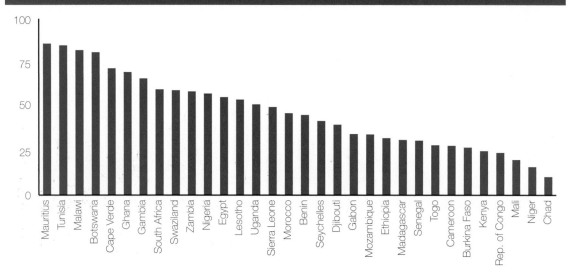

Figure 4.5 Expert opinion on the mode of appointing and promoting judges

Always or usually appointed and promoted on their own merits and qualifications (share of experts surveyed, by country, %)

Source: ECA survey of experts 2007.

But it is difficult to generalize because different countries have reacted with different strategies to the growing number of policy-oriented, advocacy, human rights and anti-corruption CSOs. Some countries have acknowledged CSOs and granted them considerable autonomy to pursue their goals within the confines of existing laws. In Zambia this trend is signified by the Non-Governmental Organizations Bill of 2007, which specifies the role of CSOs in national development and provides space for CSOs to operate. (ECA 2007n). Active non-state actors can also be found in South Africa, Ghana, Botswana and Benin, while in other countries, such as Egypt, they are constrained by stringent laws (ECA 2007d). In Senegal civil society is allowed by

law to operate freely (ECA 2007j). The Senegalese constitution guarantees both the empowerment of citizens and their access to information. Nigeria, South Africa, Ghana and Botswana, too, have provided an enabling constitutional environment conducive for CSOs to perform their various functions as vibrantly and effectively as possible under the law.

Inadequate funding, lack of qualified managers and weak organisational infrastructures continue to be the major operational challenges confronting CSOs, even in such resource-rich countries as Nigeria (ECA 2007i). Non-state actors in Africa have nonetheless achieved varying levels of success in their struggles to influence policy that improves the welfare of the people. Their participation in governance has considerably expanded the political space, facilitating the involvement of many people, informing and empowering them and thus strengthening their confidence to call to account those in authority. But the effectiveness of CSOs is subject to debate. It varies from country to country, largely determined by how they have been allowed to function independently, their ability to secure funds on their own, their relations with government and whether they are organisationally strong.

In Ghana and South Africa some CSOs are deeply engaged in governance and democracy issues and in protecting and promoting human rights, but they tend to represent only a very small proportion of the non-state actors and are often dependent on foreign donors for running and managing their activities. One study found that for various reasons in South Africa and Ghana (and some other countries not included in this report) CSOs have been constrained in generating their own funds and have not been effective enough (Robinson and Friedman 2005). Where CSOs engage in such fields as welfare and service deliveries, their freedom of operation tends to be much greater, as in Benin, Botswana, Ghana and South Africa.

A majority of the consulted experts in all the reviewed countries share the view that CSOs enjoy a considerable degree of operational independence and are not constrained by the state or harassed by the incumbent political parties. Botswana, Cape Verde, Ghana, Malawi and Benin are commended by more than 80% of the consulted experts for allowing CSOs to enjoy a wide latitude of freedom. The experts in several other countries noted moderate or strict control of CSOs by organs of the state or the ruling party. But it is encouraging that many African governments have allowed, or at least tolerated, the existence and operation of CSOs. Such a policy is critical for promoting and reinforcing checks and balances.

Effectiveness of civil society organisations in conflict management

The role of CSOs in conflict management is gradually expanding. State intervention has failed to address many conflicts, demanding the intervention of CSOs and traditional African governance institutions, especially where they are trusted. At times the state could be part of the problem, either in fact or in perception, or is unacceptable to the parties as an impartial arbitrator.

There is a need for recognized neutral actors, such as respected civil society groups, to take part in preventing and managing conflicts. But CSOs are not often consulted by governments on matters of conflict prevention or resolution. Mali and Tunisia are the notable exceptions, where more than half of the consulted experts stated that CSOs were always consulted on matters of conflict prevention and management.

It could be argued that one of the major reasons for a government's

> *The role of CSOs in conflict management is gradually expanding. There is a need for recognized neutral actors, such as respected civil society groups, to take part in preventing and managing conflicts*

reluctance to involve non-state actors in conflict prevention and resolution is its preference for its own administrative measures. But as active and concerned members of the evolving democratic societies in Africa, CSOs need to partner with government in conflict prevention and resolution. As they become part of the process, they can contribute their expertise, experience and commitment. In Africa CSOs have played important roles in conflict management, especially in conflict and post-conflict countries. During the wars in Sierra Leone and Liberia, CSOs were critical to the informal negotiations and pressures on the warring parties to come to a truce and concede to peace deals. Women's organisations were central to peace negotiations in Sierra Leone. In addition, CSOs were very useful in facilitating post-conflict reconciliation, healing and a culture of forgiveness. In Sierra Leone, for example, a CSO named The Movement to Unite People was involved in post-conflict reconciliation and rehabilitation of the child soldiers through public education, reintegration, support programmes and community dialogue with the local leaders (Adejumobi 2004).

Influence of civil society organisations in policy formulation and public accountability
Involving CSOs in policymaking and programme formulation and implementation is likely to have a positive impact. The participation of CSOs is deemed important for representing and protecting stakeholder rights and interests, promoting their welfare and forging a sense of ownership of policies and programmes.

> **During the wars in Sierra Leone and Liberia, CSOs were critical to the informal negotiations and pressures on the warring parties to come to a truce and concede to peace deals**

Although CSOs are recognized more, their impact on public policy is unclear. A majority of the consulted experts in most African countries under review regard the influence of CSOs on government policies and programmes as either limited or rare. No country covered by this study is described by a majority of its experts as a place where CSOs have either a strong or a fairly strong influence on government policies and programmes. More than 80% of the experts from Cameroon, Republic of Congo, Egypt, Gabon, Madagascar, Nigeria, Senegal and Togo held the view that CSOs have limited, rare or no influence on official policies and programmes. These responses can be partly explained by the fact that the opening up of the public space and the autonomy of the non-state actors is a recent phenomenon, a work in progress still fraught with unexpected impediments from the executive.

The country reports elicited the opinions of experts on CSOs' impact on promoting accountability and transparency in government. A majority of the experts in Malawi, Ghana, Zambia, Tunisia, Senegal, Benin, Sierra Leone, Niger and Botswana noted that CSOs have made effective or moderate contributions in promoting accountability and transparency in government, whereas in the other countries their influence is considered to be insignificant and therefore ineffective (figure 4.6).

Effectiveness of the media
Government accountability and transparency depend on the media's

Figure 4.6 Expert opinion on the role of civil society organisations in promoting accountability and transparency in government

Share of experts surveyed, by country (%)

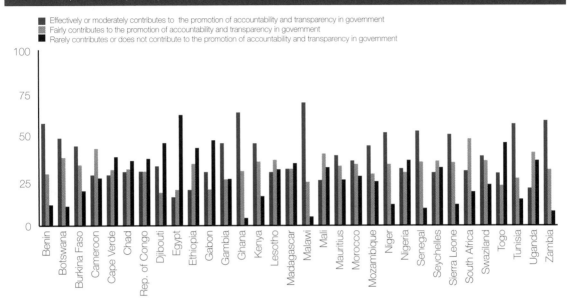

■ Effectively or moderately contributes to the promotion of accountability and transparency in government
■ Fairly contributes to the promotion of accountability and transparency in government
■ Rarely contributes or does not contribute to the promotion of accountability and transparency in government

Source: ECA survey of experts 2007.

circulation of information, ideas, opinions, experiences and views. By facilitating debates and discussions on political, economic and social issues, the media enable citizens to make intelligent decisions, as well as to call to account those in power. Privately owned media—newspapers, radio and television—have informed and educated people on domestic governance issues and parliamentary proceedings and provided them with alternative sources of information. Through investigative journalism the media provide alternative interpretations of public issues and events. They also provide information on governments—what they are expected to do, and how, when and why.

With the advent of multiparty politics, democratization and liberalism in general, privately owned radio and television stations and the Internet have been a watchdog on governments in Africa. Moreover, they have created alternative sources of information about the government, and the government spokesperson has lost the once-held monopoly on information and credibility. The popularity of the Internet and the investigative journalism of the media have uncovered and identified abuses of power and discretionary authority, and widely disseminated allegations of public corruption and other unethical activities by government officials.

But constraints on the media continue. Some of them affect the media's ability to build capacity; others shape the environment it operates in. Not all African governments view the media as a partner. Indeed, some African governments perceive the media as agents of foreign interests, while some media seem perpetually to criticize governments irrespective of what the governments are doing. In countries where private interests own and control the media, the owners tend to abdicate their traditional roles of disseminating objective information and providing reasoned editorial views. Instead, they become strong supporters of incumbent government officials, who in turn reciprocate with favours.

The effectiveness of the media also depends upon their trained manpower for investigative journalism and their ability to produce quality reporting. Even where there are drawbacks, however, many countries have made significant strides toward recognizing the media's role in promoting checks and balances in government. In many African countries constitutional provisions ensure the media's unhindered operation, including their right to criticize governments. In Benin, Mali and Namibia, for example, freedom of the press is guaranteed in the constitution. The same is true in Botswana, Ghana, Mauritius and South Africa, where the media operate independent of interference from the governments, signified by their bold and open criticisms of government policies (Doorenspleet 2003).

> **Some African governments perceive the media as agents of foreign interests, while some media seem perpetually to criticize governments**

Still, some ugly events have threatened the freedom of the press and risked the lives of those collecting and publishing news and information. In March 2006 the police in Kenya forcibly invaded the premises of the East African Standard newspapers, radio and television on the pretext that the company was about to print material prejudicial to the country's security. Armed and with their faces covered, the police destroyed equipment, took some computers and other electronic equipment, harassed, threatened and intimidated those on duty, and set fire to all the printed newspaper editions of the day. Responding to the public outrage and complaints by the media establishment in the country, the minister of security and internal affairs quipped that those who "rattle the snake" should expect "the consequences". This comment and government reactions were meant to instill fear in the media and restrain them from performing their duties objectively and professionally.

Concluding remarks

Governance is about holding and using power. How the institutions of government interact with one another, and with the people and organisations in civil society, determine the efficiency and effectiveness of the system of governance. Government is essentially a collection of people, elected or appointed. The executive is the most powerful branch of government in any system of governance, and there are understandable reasons for this to be so. But this power makes it necessary to impose checks and balances within the government—primarily on the executive but on the other branches as well. Unrestrained power promotes arbitrariness and bad governance. In Africa checks and balances are essential in the light of the history of bad governance and its consequences.

Many African countries have instituted checks and balances in their constitutions, and they have adopted various political and administrative reforms in support of good governance, accountability and transparency. The CSOs, the press and other media have been vigilant and active in exposing abuses of power and discretionary authority, demanding accountability and transparency from governments. Big government is incrementally, albeit gradually, being transformed into good government.

The core structures of the separation of powers are in place in almost all African countries. There are written constitutions, but constitutional practice is lacking, and there is very little respect for the rule of law and the due processes of law. The legislature and the judiciary—the other core structures of the separation of powers—are also in place. But for various reasons they are weak and not performing their functions, and in various degrees they are dominated by the executive. With few exceptions, the "Big Man"—the omnipotent, untouchable executive—has withered away. And the residual few are increasingly becoming an embarrassment to the rest of Africa. But the dominant executive continues in many African countries.

Since AGR I few attempts have been made to reinforce the principles of the separation of powers, enhance checks and balances or constrain the executive. On the contrary, some attempts were made to further entrench the incumbent executives or prolong the dominance of the executive branch of government in the governance system. Constitutionally entrenching the structures that ensure separation of powers is essential. But in the light of experience so far, it is not sufficient.

Strengthening the core structures of the separation of powers is crucial. But doing so depends on the commitment and political will of the managers of those institutions, especially the executive. As long as those in authority are convinced that they have the power to encroach on the other branches of government, they will continue to do so. In a democracy people are the ultimate source of constitutional and legal authority, good governance and political legitimacy. They are also the beneficiaries of good governance and victims of bad governance. What is needed is comprehensive and continuous empowerment of the people. Once appropriately empowered, sufficiently knowledgeable about their citizenship entitlements and rights and aware of their constitutional and civic obligations—and the consequences of infringing upon or not fully exercising those rights and obligations—people are likely to call to account those in authority and ensure that the institutions and processes of checks and balances are strengthened.

> **Constitutionally entrenching the structures that ensure separation of powers is essential. But in the light of experience so far, it is not sufficient**

References

Adejumobi, S. 2004. "Conflict and Peace Building in West Africa: The Role of Civil Society and the African Union." *Conflict, Security, and Development* 4(1): 59–77.

APRM (African Peer Review Mechanism). 2006. Kenya Country Review Report, no. 3, 25.

Carbone, M. Giovanni. 2003. "Political Parties and Party Systems in Africa: Themes and Research Perspectives." *World Political Science Review* 3(3).

Cranenburgh, Oda Van. 2003. "Power and Competition: The Institutional Context of African Multiparty Politics." In M. Salih, ed., *African Political Parties: Evolution, and Governance.* London: Pluto Press.

Diamond, L., Andreas Schedler, and Marc F. Plattner. 1999. "Introduction." In Andreas Schedler, Larry Diamond, and Marc F. Plattner, eds., *The-Self Restraining State: Power and Accountability in New Democracies.* London: Lynne Reinner Publishers.

Doorenspleet, Reneske. 2005. "Citizen's Support for Legislature and Democratic Consolidation: A Comparative Study with Special Focus on Mali." In M. Salih, ed., *African Parliaments: Between Governance and Government.* New York: Palgrave Macmillan.

ECA (Economic Commission for Africa). 2005. *African Governance Report.* Addis Ababa.

———. 2007a. Benin country report. Addis Ababa.

———. 2007b. Botswana country report. Addis Ababa.

———. 2007c. Cape Verde country report. Addis Ababa.

———. 2007d. Egypt country report. Addis Ababa.

———. 2007e. Ghana country report. Addis Ababa.

———. 2007f. Kenya country report. Addis Ababa.

———. 2007g. Mauritius country report. Addis Ababa.

———. 2007h. Namibia country report. Addis Ababa.

———. 2007i. Nigeria country report. Addis Ababa.

———. 2007j. Senegal country report. Addis Ababa.

———. 2007k. Seychelles country report. Addis Ababa.

———. 2007l. South Africa country report. Addis Ababa.

———. 2007m. Tunisia country report. Addis Ababa.

———. 2007n. Uganda country report. Addis Ababa.

———. 2007o. Zambia country report. Addis Ababa.

Freedom House. 2007. *Freedom in Sub-Saharan Africa 2007: A Survey of Political Rights and Civil Liberties.* www.freedomhouse.org/uploads/special_report/57.pdf.

Hearn, Julie. 1999. "Foreign Aid, Democratization and Civil Society in Africa: A Study of Uganda, Ghana and South Africa." IDS discussion paper 368. Sussex: Institute of Development Studies, University of Sussex. www.ids.ac.uk/ids/bookshop/dp/dp368.pdf.

Hout, Wil. 2005. "Parliaments, Politics and Governance: African Democracies in Comparative Perspective." In M. Salih, ed., *African Parliaments: Between Governance and Government.* New York: Palgrave Macmillan.

ICJ (International Commission of Jurists). 1997. *Democratisation and the Rule of Law in Kenya: ICJ Mission Report.* Geneva: International Commission of Jurists.

Ikome, Francis, Zondi Siphamandla, and Ajulu Che. 2006. "Enhancing Institutional Effectiveness in Sub-Saharan

Africa: Reflections on trends in Kenya, Ghana and Senegal." Institute for Global Dialogue Series no. 4. Midrand, South Africa.

Madison, James, Alexander Hamilton, and John Jay. 1788. *The Federalist Papers.* Reprinted and edited by Clinton Rossiter, 1961. New York: New American Library.

Munalula, Mulela M. 2007. "Legal Perspectives on the Search for Legitimacy in African Governance System." In J. Oloka Onyango and Nansozi K. Muwanga, eds., *Africa's Governance Models: Debating Form and Substance.* Kampala: Fountain Publishers.

Robinson, Mark and Steven Friedman. 2005. "Civil Society, Democratization and Foreign Aid in Africa." IDS Discussion Paper 383. Sussex: Institute of Development Studies, University of Sussex. www.ids.ac.uk/ids/bookshop/dp/dp383.pdf.

Salih, Mohammed A. 2003. "Conclusions." In M. Salih, ed., *African Political Parties: Evolution, Institutionalization and Governance.* London: Pluto Press.

Selolwane, D. Onalenna. 2007. "In Search of Legitimate Governance and Electoral Substance: From Theory to Practice." In J.O. Onyango and Nansozi K. Muwanga, eds, *Africa's Governance Models: Debating Form and Substance.* Kampala: Fountain Publishers.

Widner, Jennifer. 1999. "Building Judicial Independence in Common Law Africa." In Andreas Schedler, Larry Diamond, and Marc F. Plattner, eds., *The Self-Restraining State: Power and Accountability in New Democracies.* London: Lynne Reinner Publishers.

In a democracy the elected leaders and the appointed civil servants are accountable for their actions and are expected to be transparent in making and implementing their decisions. The elected leaders should be responsive to the needs and wishes of the voters. The appointed civil servants are expected to conform to the codes and conduct of public service. Both the elected leaders and appointed civil servants are expected to conform to the constitution, the rule of law and due process of law in the performance of their functions.

The legitimacy of the state is undermined if the executive fails to perform its functions. Similarly, the failure of the executive to deliver on its electoral promises is likely to undermine popular trust in government. The executive must therefore have the institutional capacity and political will to perform its functions efficiently and effectively. Failure to conform to the constitution, the rule of law and the traditions and political culture of the people is also likely to erode the legitimacy of the state and undermine the trust in government.

The effectiveness of an institution is the product of its capacity and how managers utilize that capacity. Institutional capacity entails the ability to identify problems, design and implement policies in response to the problems, and monitor and evaluate the impact of the policies. Institutional effectiveness is a major factor in consolidating or undermining the trust in government and the legitimacy of the state. Failure to deliver basic public goods and services is likely to weaken the confidence of the people in the governance system, thus undermining its legitimacy.

Quality of the executive and the public sector

The quality of the executive depends on the qualifications, skills, experience, integrity and political will of the two groups comprising it—the politicians and the civil servants. It also depends on the working relationship between them. Political leaders usually emerge through the electoral process with no guarantee of the skills and experience for ministerial positions. They may have gone through an internal party process in which the best-qualified person was nominated, but few political parties have democratic procedures for selecting their leaders. The appointed civil servants are usually recruited through open, merit-based competitive processes to attract people with the stipulated qualifications and skills.

In general, the political executive in African governments takes either the presidential or parliamentary form. In presidential systems the president is directly elected by the people and derives authority from a popular democratic mandate. The chief executive appoints ministers who are individually and collectively accountable to him or her, but also subject to parliamentary scrutiny for their performance. In parliamentary systems the president or the prime minister is elected from among the elected members of parliament and is accountable to the legislature. Ministers are also elected members of parliament and serve for a term as stipulated in the constitution.

The ECA country reports suggest that the quality and institutional capacity of the executive has improved in some African countries but needs to improve in others. In Botswana political leaders generally have ample education, skills, experience and integrity. Ministers are generally well educated and experienced in the civil and public services, academia, military and the private sector. Members of parliament are also well qualified, and most are former public servants. In Namibia 89% of civil service managers have university degrees. In Kenya high-ranking civil servants all have degrees or professional qualifications and clear career paths in their schemes of service. In Sierra Leone all persons recruited since the 1990s at the level of assistant secretary have university degrees. In South Africa a 2001 report on qualifications of senior managers in public service revealed that many senior managers obtained their degrees in the liberal arts (49%), followed by science (25%) and commerce (11%) (ECA 2007f). In Tanzania the majority of upper-level civil service personnel have degrees in higher education.

While these examples are encouraging, other countries need to improve. In Burkina Faso vote-catching, patrimonial practices and electoral corruption impede appointment of the most qualified people to public service. In Malawi, despite claims of merit-based appointments of public officials, some ministers and deputy ministers are reported to have questionable qualifications. Most ministers and deputy ministers come from the southern region, where the president is from (ECA 2007b). And in Zambia the structure, composition and quality of both the executive and public service have for a long time been compromised by partisan politics and political expediency.

Merit recruitment in the public service

A competitive recruitment system ensures that the best available people will be selected for the public service. African countries have enacted legislation to regulate and protect the principles of merit and integrity in their recruitment systems. But a transparent and merit-based recruitment system is not always applied.

The weakness in the civil service system stems partly from how the African state developed after independence under the control of strong political leaders and their supportive elites. The postcolonial African state did not conform to the classical Weberian ideal of an institution separate from the personal interests and pursuits of those managing it. Instead, the African notion of patrimony characterized the postcolonial period of state consolidation and nation building. Today recruitment and career prospects in the public services continue to be greatly influenced by ethnic, cultural and social realities rather than by principles of objectivity, equity and transparency. In many African countries ethnic, linguistic, religious and regional affiliations continue to be major factors in the recruitment of public servants.

> ' The quality and institutional capacity of the executive has improved in some African countries but needs to improve in others

In Botswana the selection and promotion of civil servants are based on merit. Vacancies are usually publicly advertised, and a candidate must satisfy the scheme of service that lays down the qualification for the office. But promotions are based on long service, not merit or performance. In Kenya the Public Service Commission enjoys independence in the selection, promotion and evaluation of civil servants on merit. Promotion in the civil service depends on the availability of posts, minimum number of years in the job and professional qualifications acquired that are consistent with the scheme of the service.

In some countries progress towards merit-based recruitment has been slow. In Burkina Faso, despite the regulations prescribing a merit-based recruitment in the civil service, most senior officials are perceived to have strong links with the ruling party. Access to higher bureaucratic positions often depends on a declared or implicit membership in the ruling party. In Zambia the ruling party heavily influences the public service. In Sierra Leone recruitment to the civil service is ostensibly based on merit; perceptions persist, however, that individuals benefit from political patronage. In Senegal merit-based selection, promotion and evaluation were applied rather belatedly to the public service. Civil servants' promotion tends to be based largely on length of service rather than on strict merit. Nigeria has a federal system, and the public service is constitutionally obliged to consider the ethnically plural character of the country in its composition and to

consider, particularly at the federal level, promoting unity in diversity, which means balancing an ethnic quota system with merit, a practice that sometimes generates tension in the country.

Institutionalization of a merit-based public service is still problematic, even in South Africa and Ghana, which have done reasonably well in other areas of governance. South Africa has to grapple with the post-apartheid situation; rectifying the racial imbalances in the public services, ensuring appropriate representation of black South Africans and other historically disadvantaged groups. Obviously, failure to adhere to the principles of merit, qualifications and performance criteria are bound to have negative impacts on the quality and thus capacity of the public service. It may also generate ethnic tensions and suspicions in the governance system, weakening its capacity and undermining the trust and credibility of the executive.

The consulted experts indicated that merit-based recruitment continues to be elusive in many African countries. Most think that civil service appointments continue to be influenced by political, kinship and religious ties and that many countries fared poorly in institutionalizing merit as the governing principle in the public services. A significant majority of the consulted experts in Chad, Niger, Republic of Congo, Togo, Cameroon, Gabon and Egypt opined that the public services were rarely or not at all governed by merit principles (figure 5.1). Only in Malawi, Morocco and Burkina Faso

> *Merit-based recruitment continues to be elusive in many African countries. Civil service appointments continue to be influenced by political, kinship and religious ties*

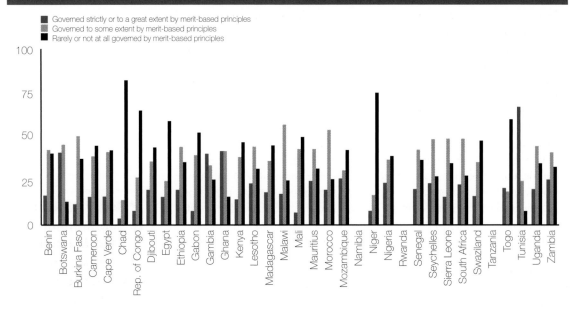

Figure 5.1 Expert opinion on the extent to which recruitment into the public service is governed by merit-based principles

Share of experts surveyed, by country (%)

- Governed strictly or to a great extent by merit-based principles
- Governed to some extent by merit-based principles
- Rarely or not at all governed by merit-based principles

Source: ECA survey of experts 2007.

did a majority think that merit was the guiding principle to some extent, while only 42% in Ghana and 41% in Botswana stated that civil service management was strictly governed by merit-based principles. The notable exception is Tunisia, where 67% of the experts supported the judgment that the civil service was strictly governed by merit.

Popular acceptance of the public sector

Ethnic, religious and regional diversity is an enduring African reality. A public sector that reflects societal diversity is likely to be perceived as legitimate because it represents all of the elements of society, responds to the needs, requests and aspirations

of the people and is accountable to the various ethnic, cultural and minority groups.

Representation of the diversities, minorities and disadvantaged people within the public services renders the public sector more inclusive, broadens its popularity and strengthens its effectiveness. Where diversities are widely dispersed within a country it is less difficult to proportionally incorporate them into the public services. Where diversities are concentrated in regions it is imperative to ensure that they are represented not only within the public service but also acknowledged and protected within the entire governance system. This is usually accommodated by the principles of federalism or the devolution of powers to regional or local governments.

Where social diversities are largely contained in geographical regions, such as Ethiopia and Nigeria, or in countries that have been under different political regimes—South Africa under apartheid, for example, or Tanzania, today a union of two previously independent countries, Tanganyika and Zanzibar—constitutional arrangements for federalism or devolution were undertaken to ensure equitable representation of the different sectional and regional populations. Nigeria and Ethiopia adopted federalism to accommodate their ethnic and regional diversities. South Africa evolved a unique system of devolution in which the national, provincial and municipal spheres of government are each endowed with their own constitutional responsibilities but are obliged to cooperate, reinforce and support each others' responsibilities. And Tanzania opted for a union government, with specific devolved powers to Zanzibar to ensure the preservation of its cultural diversity. There is thus one sovereign state of the United Republic of Tanzania, one major public sector for the entire governance system and one devolved regional public sector for Zanzibar. Tanganyika, the other part of the union, is under the Union government, without its own regional government. The Union public sector does, however, represent the diversities within Tanganyika.

Apart from granting considerable authority for regional self-rule,

federalism, or devolution of powers coupled with the appropriate functions, may allay fears of domination by one ethnic or regional group. In Nigeria minority states take roughly 40% of the federal civil service posts from grade levels 15 and above. In Ethiopia the constitution provides for a bicameral parliament in which each ethnic group is guaranteed proportional representation in the House of Federation on the basis of its population.

Many African countries do not have balanced and proportional representation of their different sectional interests in senior appointments in the public services. Only in Tunisia and Botswana did a majority of the respondents feel that the composition of senior appointees reflected fully or largely a cross-section of society. The respondents replied that appointments reflected a cross-section of society to some limited extent in Benin, Burkina Faso, Cape Verde, Malawi and Senegal. On the other hand, at least half of the respondents in Chad, Togo, Madagascar, Egypt, Republic of Congo and Kenya indicated that the composition hardly or did not at all reflect a cross-section of society at large.

Women in the public service

In many African countries women make up at least half of the population. Their full and effective participation is critical to both development and democratization. Equitable representation of women in the public services is not only a human rights issue. It also utilizes all available human resources for development. Empowerment of women has

> *Many African countries do not have balanced and proportional representation of their different sectional interests in senior appointments in the public services*

been recognized and acknowledged by African governments, and many countries have adopted the Convention on the Elimination of Discrimination against Women. The summit of heads of state and government in Lusaka in August 2007 resolved to raise the percentage of women in decision-making positions from 30% to 50%. But many African governments have not been able to meet that goal.

In Cape Verde women constitute 61% of the public service. Five (of 14) ministers and 2 (of 7) secretaries of state are women. The percentage of women appointed is 18%. But in local government only one woman is among the 17 elected presidents of the municipalities, and women occupy 16% of the executive positions. In Rwanda the government's most notable achievement in promoting gender equality was a policy reform to enhance the participation of women, causing a dramatic leap in women's participation in the parliament. And by 2004 the number of female state ministers had surpassed that of males. In the other offices the progress in Rwanda has not been that dramatic. The 18-member cabinet includes 4 women, and 5 of the 11 ministers of state are women. Following the election of March 2001 women made up 26.0% of the district councils, 24.0% of the district steering committees and 6.7% of the mayors (Rwanda National Election Commission 2006). Following the 2006 election for local administration, 2 of the 30 mayors, 32 of the 60 vice-mayors and 21 of 30 secretaries of district councils were women (AfDB 2007).

In Botswana, despite an enabling policy and institutional framework for the promotion of women's interest, men still tend to dominate in higher positions. The proportion of women in the cabinet is 15%; they held 40% of the top civil service positions in the early 2000s. In Congo women constitute only 1.3% of senior officials in the public service. In Burkina Faso women make up 20% of the total number of public servants, and they occupy 25% of the positions of state responsibility.

Minorities in the public sector
Namibia has made efforts to ensure that the San minority is included in mainstream activities by teaching them skills that will enable them to be entrepreneurs. Though no data provide an overall picture of San representation in the public service, it is reported that the prime minister has recently employed two San individuals. In Rwanda the Twa people, who constitute about 1% of the population, are not represented in the public service. In Botswana the Baswara minority group is not adequately represented in the civil service. In the Republic of Congo, although the pygmies constitute 6% of the population, there is not yet a senior official, magistrate or public officer who is a pygmy. In Rwanda the Federation of the Associations of the Disabled is allowed one seat in the Chamber of Deputies (AfDB 2007).

Remuneration, training and facilities in the public sector
Decent wages will attract the best recruits into the public service if it also includes an amiable working

> *Empowerment of women has been recognized and acknowledged by African governments, and many countries have adopted the Convention on the Elimination of Discrimination against Women*

environment, good career prospects, training facilities, and reliable retirement benefit.

Remuneration

If they can maintain a decent living standard from their income, public servants are unlikely to be tempted into corrupt practices or seek additional employment. Remuneration commensurate with the professional and social status of the civil servant has been a critical factor in sustaining the quality and integrity of the public sector of African countries.

After years of erosion, civil service salaries in Africa have begun to show some signs of improvement. In Seychelles earnings in the public sector are comparable to those in the private sector, in some cases even higher. The government is aware of the problem of brain drain and announced an automatic increment for all public-sector employees in 2006. A new remuneration package for university graduates employed in the public sector also became effective in 2006. In 2007 the Ethiopian government increased the salaries of government employees in response to rising inflation.

In Botswana the working environment and remuneration for public servants are considered unattractive, and there has been considerable turnover of staff, particularly among nurses and police officers. But salaries in the public sector provide a living wage because government always considers inflation when increasing employees' remuneration. Typically, there is an across-the-board salary increment for the public

sector every two to three years. In Mauritius the Pay Research Bureau formulates policies and makes recommendations after reviewing pay levels and conditions of service in the civil service, parastatal bodies, local authorities and private secondary school. The Bureau normally publishes its reviews at five-year intervals.

Still, the state of remuneration in many African countries leaves much to be desired. Salaries in Tanzania do not provide a living wage for most employees. But the average pay of public servants has continued to rise steadily: from September 2000 to July 2006 gross wages increased by an average annual rate of 19.6%. In Burkina Faso wages of the civil service do not allow for decent living (although they are regularly paid and on time), making it difficult for the public sector to retain the best employees. In Egypt a uniform wage structure has been in force since the 1960s in both government and public enterprises. The government salary scales are maintained at levels far below rates of inflation, causing pay in the public service to decline in real value.

Training

Recognizing the importance of training, African governments have taken a number of initiatives. In Ghana newly recruited officers in the civil service are given orientation and induction in the principles and procedures of the service. A training school for local government officials caters to civil service recruits and existing staff to enhance their knowledge and share experiences.

> ❛ The state of remuneration in the public service in many African countries leaves much to be desired

Every year in Tanzania each government agency must prepare a training programme, elaborating training gaps for each staff and recommending training with estimated costs. But implementation has been very difficult due to budgetary constraints.

Several legislative acts and white papers have committed the South African government to public service training and development. In Congo civil servants regularly follow training programmes and are paid allowances when they attend training. In Malawi most top public servants go to the Malawi Institute of Management to upgrade their skills; staff of lower categories attend the Mpemba Staff Development Institute. In Togo high-level public servants are trained abroad as well as at the National School of Public Administration.

Facilities
In many African countries the public service faces considerable disabilities in lack of information technology and equipment and the availability of basic supplies of stationery. These shortages stem largely from revenue shortfalls. Proposed budgets of the ministries, departments and agencies are often reduced, especially when donor inflows, which constitute a large part of government revenue, do not come in as expected. In Congo lack of buildings, office furniture and computers is common. In Ghana the public service faces a lack of facilities stemming from government's inability to meet demands from various sector ministries. In Malawi information technology in the civil service is poorly developed, and most government information is recorded manually. The Nigeria government lacks vital data processing equipment such as computers and other facilities in most departments of statistics, though recently there has been significant improvement in federal government support to the Federal Bureau of Statistics.

Civil service reform

Efficiency and productivity in the public services have become the overriding objectives of public-sector reforms in most African countries. To this end, many governments have embarked upon civil service reforms focused on the following:

- Public-sector management reforms, including performance and monitoring standards for services that the public can reasonably expect. Providing information about public services in a straightforward and understandable manner. Providing courteous and prompt services to their clients.

- Accountability and responsiveness in public services, including effective accounting and auditing, and making public officials responsible for their actions and responsive to consumers.

- Availability of information and transparency to enhance policy analysis, promote public debate and reduce the risk of corruption.

In the late 1980s the government of Ghana acknowledged major shortcomings in the efficiency and

> *Efficiency and productivity in the public services have become the overriding objectives of public-sector reforms in most African countries*

effectiveness of the country's public sector, shown by unnecessarily high numbers of employees, a correspondingly high wage bill and low morale and poor performance by civil servants. Recognizing the need to sustain and preserve the effectiveness of the civil service, Ghana implemented a civil service reform program from 1987 to 1993. Costs of the civil service had outrun the country's capacity to meet them, so the reform aimed at reducing the size and cost of the civil service and improving its management. The reforms have had a positive impact by reducing the size and promoting efficiency in the civil service in Ghana.

Ethiopia, Ghana, Mauritius, Senegal, Tanzania and Uganda have embarked on comprehensive reforms to establish efficient and effective public services. In Egypt the Ministry for Administrative Development has put in place a program to enhance the efficiency of Egypt's administrative agencies. This programme is expected to focus on improving the performance of government workers, introducing a system of modern management and developing the organisational structure of governmental agencies.

Local governments

In Africa local governments—and in some instances the recognized traditional authorities—are the main suppliers of social services, and to some extent they maintain law and order in the rural areas. Local governments are largely the products of decentralized or devolutionary powers, constitutionally provided

or legislatively enacted. In Uganda, Nigeria and South Africa the powers of the local governments are entrenched in the constitution. In the rest of the African countries under review the constitution either directs the legislature to enact appropriate laws creating local governments, as in Ghana, or such legislation already exists.

Decentralization enables the central government's executive branch to perform its core functions of maintaining peace and security, promoting an enabling environment for businesses and delivering goods and services as promised in the electoral mandate. It can also help to modernize and democratize the traditional local governance institutions, promote greater popular participation at the grass roots level and encourage local ownership of the conduct of affairs directly relevant to the people.

Local governments are primarily responsible for delivering education, health, sanitation, environment and roads maintenance, and generally for maintaining law and order in their jurisdictions. There are, however, serious shortfalls in skilled and experienced personnel, management and funding in local governments.

Independence and financial autonomy

In Botswana local authorities are not independent of the central government. The Ministry of Local Government exercises considerable control over them through financial administration and human resource management. Although the ministry

In Africa local governments are the main suppliers of social services, and to some extent they maintain law and order in the rural areas

was allocated 16% of the 2007 national budget, the authority of local officials to determine their own priorities for spending is limited. Because local governments raise an insignificant proportion of their own revenue, local authorities are largely dependent on the central government for their development budget. The land boards and district councils rely on the central government for up to 95% of their recurrent requirements, the urban councils for up to 70%.

In Seychelles all district administrators get their revenue from the central government. As a result, they are subjected to regular instructions from the central government on how they should function. In Kenya local authorities are neither independent nor autonomous; the minister of local government must approve every aspect of their operations, including budgets. Although the local authorities are elected, they are not accountable to their respective electorate but to the minister of local government through the town clerks and chief officers. Local government expenditure constitutes 7% of the total national budget. But the local authorities are not permitted to raise their own revenue—this is the mandate of the minister of local government, who in turn must seek the approval of parliament by presenting the ministry's national budget.

In Malawi previous provisions entitling district councils to hire their own staff have been withdrawn for fear that the appointments might be influenced by nepotism. The decentralization policy stipulates that at least 5% of net government revenues,

excluding debt service, be transferred to local assemblies as unconditional grants for development purposes. Due to demands on the government to provide additional services, however, the funding of assemblies has always been far below 5% of net national revenue (Chiweza 2007). In the 2004/05 budget the assemblies were allocated 0.79% of the stipulated net national revenue (Malawi 2005).

In Egypt local government spending constitutes 13% to 15% of total government spending. Egypt has recently been moving toward allocating more powers to local units, encouraging popular participation and motivating community participation instead of dependence on central government, all of which is aimed at giving the local governments more autonomy and space for independent actions, including on the mobilisation of resources.

In Ghana the decentralization programme has almost stalled, and civil society, donor partners and some state actors have been critical of its general performance. As a result, the government is planning to revamp the entire decentralization policy. The municipal and district assemblies are now able to raise and spend their own revenues. But this independence is limited due to the low levels of revenue that can be raised locally; few districts generate as much as 30% of their revenue locally. Parliament has allocated 5% of the total national revenues to local governments, and that amount was raised to 7.5% in July 2007. Local governments cannot borrow more than 20 million cedis (US$2,000), limiting them from promoting innovation in their development.

Equitability in resource allocation to local governments

Lack of human and material capacity is an enduring problem for local governments in Africa. It has created an enormous inequality between the big cities and the rural areas and small towns. It has also bred a sense of neglect in outlying areas, especially when the incumbent central government executive is identified with a particular political party, region or ethnic group. When resources are distributed unevenly and disproportionately among local governments based on nonobjective criteria, the consequence is imbalanced development among the local authorities, which sometimes fuels tension and conflict between them.

Similarly, appropriately allocating funds by local governments (to their local communities and rural areas) and responding to local community needs can promote local economic growth and development, generating wealth and employment, reducing migration to urban areas and thus relieving the pressure for service deliveries in the cities. Local governments need to allocate resources according to the objective development needs of their local communities and constituencies, rather than on the basis of party support and loyalty or political patronage.

The panel of experts felt that in Chad, Zambia, Nigeria and Madagascar there was rarely or no equitable resource allocation for services by local governments. In Cape Verde, Ghana and South Africa the experts reported fair and equitable distribution of resources. Only in Tunisia, Seychelles, Botswana and Gambia did the majority of experts express the view that local authorities in those countries fully or moderately distribute resources equitably at the local level.

Managing decentralized services

Public policymaking in many cases has been the responsibility of the national executive in Africa. Local governments in many countries are not constitutionally empowered to play major roles in national policymaking, although they might be consulted at the discretion of the relevant ministers. Local governments are, in general, implementers of central government policies, delivering the identified public goods and services to improve the welfare of the people. In most cases they cannot set standards or independently establish agencies to improve existing services or create new ones without permission from central authorities. The exception is only in countries where there is meaningful devolution of powers to local governments, where local governments constitute the bedrock of national governance and form a recognized tier of government in the country—a situation that is lacking in many African countries.

Inadequate capacity and poor management have been the major problems confronting decentralized governance in Africa. Many local authorities in Africa have failed to provide clean and safe water, maintain adequate standards of sanitation, provide street lighting, collect

> *Lack of human and material capacity is an enduring problem for local governments in Africa. It has created an enormous inequality between the big cities and the rural areas and small towns*

garbage, enforce planning laws, repair or new build roads, run markets in an efficient manner, provide amusement parks or regulate businesses in accordance with trading and business laws.

Only in Tunisia, Seychelles, Botswana, Cape Verde, Ghana and Mauritius did the majority of consulted experts perceive the local governments to have either adequate or some capacity to manage decentralized services. Experts from Chad, Republic of Congo, Djibouti, Egypt, Gabon and Togo responded that local governments have poor or no capacity to manage decentralized services. Similarly, from among the nine countries where the household survey was conducted, it was only in Rwanda that a majority of the people responded that local government performance was very good or good. The bleak assessment of the capacity of African local governments has not improved much since AGR I.

Recognizing the need to boost capacity of local government, the government of South Africa has created Project Consolidate, an initiative in which a municipality unable to deliver services is provided with hands-on technical, logistical and financial support by the national and provincial governments. While the initiative appears practical in solving local government service delivery problems, there is a risk that if no opportunities are provided for the municipalities to learn from their mistakes and develop the appropriate capacities, Project Consolidate might contribute to their long-term dependency on the central or provincial governments.

Local government competitiveness
Whether local governments are constituted through competitive elections is a major indication of their trust and popular legitimacy. An overwhelming majority of the consulted experts indicated that regional, provincial and state councils and local and district assemblies were constituted on a competitive basis. In Cape Verde, Malawi, Zambia, Mauritius and Ghana the experts were unanimous in confirming that assertion. In the rest of the countries, between 65% and 80% of expert respondents thought local councils were constituted on a competitive basis.

Mechanisms for community participation
By virtue of their proximity to the grass roots, local governments are generally expected to deliver services effectively. And because they are situated within communities, where the people can make their voices heard, they are expected to be responsive to the needs of the people. But the reality is not encouraging. Only 45% of the consulted experts in Cape Verde felt there were effective or moderately effective mechanisms for community participation, while 70% in Egypt, 66% in Gabon, 66% in Kenya, 69% in Nigeria, 62% in Togo and 67% in Zambia reported that an inadequate mechanism existed or none at all.

Role of traditional structures in government
The post-independence generation of African political and military leaders feared the impact of the chieftaincies and traditional institutions of governance on unity and

> **'Inadequate capacity has been a major problem for decentralized governance in Africa. Many local authorities have failed to provide basic services**

nation building. These leaders could not tolerate other sources of power or influence in the post-colonial state. In some countries traditional institutions were wished away, and in others abolished or severely controlled. They were regarded as anachronistic and unable to cope with the exigencies of the modern state, the challenges of nation building and economic development.

None of the measures to contain or marginalize ethnic or societal diversities have really succeeded. Diversity continues to characterize the African political landscape. And although they have lost their ancient prominence in the governance systems, traditional governance institutions are still respected and continue to provide important services to their people.

In Botswana, Ghana, Namibia and South Africa traditional institutions are entrenched in the constitution, with assigned roles and responsibilities in governance. In Botswana traditional chiefs are officially recognized by law and remunerated by the state. Paramount chiefs are members of the House of Chiefs, an advisory body that complements the elected national assembly. They are significant providers of judicial services and help to resolve local civil and minor criminal cases. These institutions are regarded highly for the preservation of customary culture, and the political cohesion and stability of Botswana is greatly enhanced by the role that traditional leaders play.

In Ghana the constitution recognizes the regional and national houses

of chiefs, which render advice on matters affecting chieftaincy and provide a channel of investigation and appeal for resolving conflicts concerning traditional matters. They are the primary agencies for managing chieftaincy and land disputes in Ghana and are the first point of call in resolving local conflicts. In Egypt the state accepts the customary systems of law as a useful and important means of alleviating the work of an overburdened judiciary system. In those areas where they are recognized and their roles acknowledged, traditional governance structures perform the administration of justice through customary courts with the added advantage of alleviating the work of an overburdened and poorly staffed judiciary system. They settle religious, chieftaincy or Emirate disputes and cultural matters in areas where they are located; and some are often consulted on development and governance issues. They thus provide affordable and easily understood justice to the community. Respected traditional institutions facilitate the peaceful settlement of disputes and conflicts in the remote rural communities that could otherwise degenerate into violence, insecurity and instability. The government sees the non-state arbitrators as efficient tools to deal with violent conflict that could erupt in the villages of the Nile valley and the poorer quarters of the larger cities.

In Togo the traditional leaders in the canton and villages constitute the basic domain of the decentralization of the central administration. They perform key social functions like administering weddings; and

> ' *Diversity continues to characterize the African political landscape, and traditional governance institutions are still respected and continue to provide important services to their people*

serve as a communication channel between the general administration and the citizens they manage. They are responsible for mobilizing the people and facilitating such major undertakings as vaccination and construction of public works. Traditional leaders play a major role in the conduct of traditional justice and the maintenance of peace and security in their respective localities. In Malawi traditional leaders mobilize the people in their areas for development activities, as well as act as custodians of cultural and traditional values. They help in maintaining peace, law and order by performing quasi-judicial activities; they resolve local disputes such as those involving inheritance and family affairs. But the government in power, to serve its political interests, sometimes manipulates them. In South Africa the role of traditional structures in government is largely to perform an advisory function on issues specifically related to traditional leadership and customary law. Traditional courts may administer customary law in recognized traditional communities. They are described as providing services which are generally simple, affordable and easily accessible. Under the Traditional Leadership Governance and Framework Act, traditional authorities are also expected to play a more active role in the administration of traditional communities, decision making and advising local governments.

Rwanda is using traditional structures to promote decentralization. Several structural arrangements have been put in place to facilitate grass roots involvement in planning, implementation, monitoring and evaluation of delivery of services. Among such structures are the *umudugudu*, the *ubudehe* and the *imihigo* (box 5.1).

Although many African governments have recognized the positive role of traditional authorities in promoting good governance, much remains to be done to overcome structural and organisational constraints affecting their efficacy. Chief among these constraints is financial shortages, which are exacerbated by loss of traditional sources of revenue; many central governments have provided little financial and institutional support to make up

---

Box 5.1 Using traditional structures to promote decentralization in Rwanda

Umudugudu is a village-level structure made up of 100 households where all adult residents constitute a village meeting to discuss matters affecting their neighbourhood and pass it over to the local authority for appropriate response. In Rwanda the *ubudehe* programme involves the participatory planning and funding of a project in every local area in the country. In this programme communities design and implement a project of their choice with a great and broad impact against poverty. The output of such a process is expected to be the basis of district strategic plans, annual plans and the national medium-term expenditure frameworks.

Another innovation at the district level is the *imihigo*, a performance contract between the president and district mayors. The *imihigo* is a performance-management tool embedded in the country's tradition but blended with the modern concept of results-based management. The engagement is recorded publicly in a written contract that presents development targets backed by specific performance indicators over a period of one year. The contract is the outcome of several consultations and agreements of the different levels of the district and submitted to the president as a commitment to deliver. Donors and government support some of the activities stipulated in the contract.

Source: AfDB 2007.

for the deficit. Lack of capacity to enforce customary law rulings is also a major impediment, stemming from the abolition of the coercive policing infrastructure of the traditional tribal authorities.

Accountability and transparency

Accountability is a reciprocal relationship between those who have been entrusted with certain functions and those who expect those functions to be performed. Accountability ensures that there will be trust and confidence in those assigned with the responsibilities.

Transparency provides the public with access to information and knowledge to enable them to scrutinize government policies. The bottom line of transparency is openness in the conduct of public affairs at all levels of governance. Openness stunts the temptation of corruption. It is also critical to the promotion of trust in government and state legitimacy.

Accountability

Responsibilities are assigned to individuals or institutions. Since institutions are run and managed by individuals, it is the individual who assumes the responsibility. What constitutes accountability and the manner in which it is exercised ultimately depends on the constitutional provisions, cultures, morals and traditions of a society. In a democratic system of governance accountability obliges incumbent political leaders and bureaucrats to be responsible for their decisions and actions and to explain them in a manner understandable to the people. Accountability requires that public officials, elected or appointed, respond to the requests and demands of the citizens without discrimination.

In Botswana, in addition to being subjected to the regular intervals of election, the president has to account to parliament. Public funds cannot be spent without parliamentary approval. Parliamentary question time and annual reports of the state ministries, departments and other agencies ensure that the executive is responsible and accountable. Botswana has a strict financial accountability system, and all public funds must be approved by parliament before being spent by the executive.

In Mauritius the elected executive is rendered highly accountable through scrutiny by parliament, the report of the director of audit and media reporting. As part of the administrative reform and discipline of financial management, a medium-term expenditure framework was implemented in a few high-spending ministries. The framework has proven to be an efficient instrument for monitoring expenditure. In 1994 each ministry became responsible for setting up its own standards for the assessment of effectiveness.

In Ghana the president's powers are so extensive that accountability appears limited. The president appoints top executives and judges of the Supreme Court, creating an opportunity for patronage and weak accountability. Because the parliament submits its budget for

> ❛ **Accountability ensures that there will be trust and confidence in those assigned with responsibilities, and transparency stunts the temptation of corruption**

executive approval and is dependent on the executive for its functioning, it is not in a position to scrutinize the executive. In Togo accountability of the executive is not always enforced even when mandated by the law.

In South Africa ministries submit annual reports to the relevant parliamentary oversight committees. The Public Finance Management Act and the Local Government Finance Management Act set out the detailed requirements for monitoring and reporting on the utilisation of public resources. Departments perform internal audits, and the annual departmental reports are made available to the public.

Opinions of the consulted experts provide a somewhat mixed profile on executive accountability. In Tunisia (77%), Botswana (62%) and Cape Verde (71%), strong majorities believed that government always or

mostly acts in a publicly accountable manner. In South Africa, Ghana, Senegal and Cameroon the respondents opined that the governments sometimes acted in a publicly accountable manner. In Chad, Republic of Congo, Egypt, Gabon, Nigeria and Uganda most respondents felt that the government rarely or never acted in an accountable way.

The mixed assessment of executive accountability in 2007 sharply contrasts with the result in AGR I, when the governance index on civil service transparency and accountability across project countries indicated an average of less than 50 on a scale of 1 to 100. In Ghana only 31% of the experts surveyed (as against 59% in 2002) said government is always or mostly accountable to the public, suggesting that Africa has a long way to go to make the executive accountable and transparent in the conduct of public affairs.

Accountability of local government
Although local governments are the major providers of social services in the African countries, they do not make decisions on the supply, quality and availability of those services.

Very few countries have put in place accountability mechanisms for service delivery. And even where the mechanisms do exist, their performance has not been very good. The accountability mechanisms in Ghana are considered weak. The Local Authorities Public Accounts Committee is responsible for ensuring performance in the implementation of projects and programs, submission of monthly financial

---

Box 5.2 Accountability in South Africa and Ghana

South African presidential imbizo. The president, ministers, premiers, members of the executive council, mayors and local councilors visit communities to see some of the challenges the people are faced with. People can air their concerns, grievances, suggestions and aspirations directly to the president and other elected leaders. The president and the relevant officials are obliged to provide answers, thus acknowledging and honoring his accountability to the people.

Ghana. The People's Assembly is an annual, unstructured interaction between the president and the people. Ghanaians from all walks of life pose questions about governance, unfulfilled promises, service deliveries and the behavior of the ministers and the civil servants.

Source: APRM 2005, 15; APRM 2007, 89, 107.

and management statements, and final accounts of the local authorities. Due to inadequate capacity, however, local authorities often lag in producing up-to-date financial accounts. In Kenya the local authorities are controlled by the ministry and therefore accountable to the minister of local government, not the electorate that put them in office. In Malawi local assemblies are accountable to the central government through the National Local Government Finance Committee, an oversight body intended to promote financial accountability, effective resource mobilization and allocation of financial resources to local government authorities. The assemblies cannot spend money until the committee approves the estimate. The auditor general audits local government accounts, but due to limited staff in the auditor-general's office, some assemblies have not been audited for five years. Apart from rendering accountability meaningless, it has created temptations for corruption and poor resource management in assemblies.

In Sierra Leone every local council is required to have internal audit departments and to post monthly statements of financial accounts, annual income and expenditure statements, inventories of assets, minutes of council meetings, development plans, bye-laws and notices relating to tax rates and fees. But not all councils adhere to these requirements. The experts in 18 of the 32 countries felt that the local government mechanisms for accountability were rarely effective or not effective and efficient (figure 5.2).

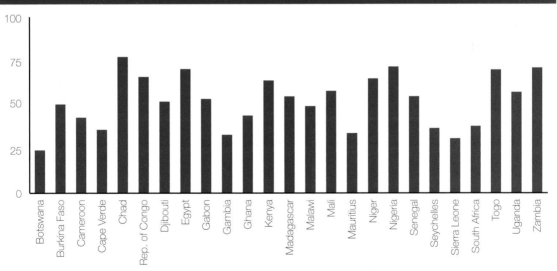

Figure 5.2 Expert opinion on effectiveness of local government accountability

Rarely effective or not effective or efficient (share of experts surveyed, by country, %)

Source: ECA survey of experts 2007.

Transparency

Transparency facilitates the rendering of accountability. Transparency and accountability oblige public officials, both political and bureaucratic, to respond to questions and explain their decisions and actions. Accountability and transparency lead to predictability in the behavior of the executive, which enables people to organize their activities with confidence. For example, predictability in economic regulation facilitates future planning by entrepreneurs or investors.

A unique feature in South African governance is *Batho Pele*, a citizens charter based on a traditional Sesotho adage meaning "people first". The objectives of *Batho Pele* are to ensure that the people are informed about the government and about their own entitlements and obligations as citizens. In light of South Africa's previous system of governance and experience of legalized racism, *Batho Pele* is a deliberate measure to empower all the people to participate effectively in public affairs and enjoy the benefits of citizenship (APRM 2007).

In Zambia most government operations are shrouded in secrecy under the State Security Act, which severely curtails access to information about government operations. It is illegal to receive or communicate classified information. Penalties for infringing the act range from 15 to 25 years imprisonment. Because the act is so broad, almost all information in government hands can be considered top secret by the relevant minister.

In Madagascar each ministry is supposed to have its own web site for posting important information, but the information tends to be inadequate, and the sites suffer from technical problems. The government's reports to parliament on its budget implementation and programmes are published in the official journal, but its circulation is limited.

The lack of transparency in many African countries is evident from the responses of the surveyed experts. While in Mozambique, Tunisia and Gambia the majority of experts responded that information was freely available and accessible or accessible at some cost, the overwhelming majority of the experts in most of the 32 countries believed that information was available but not accessible. In Egypt, Gabon, Senegal and Togo the respondents replied that it was inaccessible or unavailable.

Role of civil society organisations in promoting accountability and transparency

Civil society organisations and the media play important roles in governance by providing voice for the people, identifying abuses of power and agitating for their rectification. They provide knowledge, information and analysis on public affairs, empowering people to be well-informed participants in the democratization of their countries. And they contribute to the promotion of accountability and transparency.

But the reality is that in much of Africa civil society organisations have not been as effective as expected. This is due partly to inadequate capacity, partly to the hostile environment in which these non-state actors operate—rules and regulations and intimidation by governments—and partly to governments' inadequate appreciation of how much civil society contributes to democracy and good governance. Many African governments view non-state actors with hostility rather than as partners in development and democratization.

Although civil society organisations still face many challenges across African countries to promote accountability and transparency in government, on average across countries a sizeable proportion of the experts (40%) felt that CSOs contribute effectively or moderately to the promotion of accountability and transparency in government. But notable exceptions were Egypt, Gabon, Ethiopia, Djibouti and Togo, where over 40% of the experts thought that civil society organisations contributed rarely or not at all to the promotion of transparency and accountability in government.

Coherence in policymaking

A governance system has various actors involved in policymaking: the legislature debates the enactment of legislation, and the judiciary ensures the constitutionality of laws and regulations. Business interests or ethnic, religious and regional groups may also influence policymaking through lobbying. External actors such as development partners and international development institutions—bilateral donors, the World Bank, the International Monetary Fund—are also likely to influence policymakers by attaching

certain conditions or persuasive suggestions to their development assistance or lending.

Given the commitment of African countries to alleviate poverty and achieve the Millennium Development Goals, partnerships between the public and private sectors are clearly important. As a major contributor to employment and taxable revenue, the private sector is a critical factor in the promotion of human development. Low revenue collection might force a reduction of public services. If revenue shortfalls persist, they may generate distrust in the economic system and ultimately undermine the governance system.

Formulation, implementation and evaluation

Policy formulation is a complex and dynamic process involving many people, each playing a particular role that requires specific information, knowledge and experience. It requires strong executive leadership. But the executive consists of several ministries led and managed by senior politicians and ranking civil servants. Coherence among them is critical, or fragmentation and inefficiency will undermine the effectiveness of the executive.

In many African countries formulation of national polices is performed by the executive through the respective cabinet offices. Policy initiatives are usually generated by ministries, which submit their proposals to the cabinet for comments, collective consultation and ultimate decisions. When issues cut across ministry lines, such as gender, corruption, environment or HIV/AIDS, affected

> **Given the commitment of African countries to alleviate poverty and achieve the Millennium Development Goals, partnerships between the public and private sectors are clearly important**

Box 5.3 Support services for policy coordination in South Africa

The new democratic constitution of 1996 created the Office of the President, known today as the Presidency. The Presidency provides support services to the cabinet and its substructures, ensures the implementation of decisions, monitors and coordinates government policy and manages programmes on gender equity, rights of children and disabled persons. These objectives are realised through five programmes, such as administration, that provides the Presidency with strategic leadership, financial and human resources and other support services and manages official households. The Presidency also provides legal advice, protocol and ceremonial services, and communication. The cabinet office programme provides a cabinet secretariat. The policy coordination unit is responsible for the coordination of policy development and implementation and development of programmes to promote gender equality and the rights of disabled persons and children. The National Youth Commission develops and implements programmes to promote the socioeconomic development of young people, particularly from disadvantaged communities.

Source: ECA 2007f.

ministries form an inter-ministerial committee of officials to work jointly on the proposed policy. When submitting a proposed policy, the generating ministry generally circulates memoranda to fellow cabinet ministers for comments.

African governments are also establishing departments and units to ensure effective implementation of public policies. In Namibia the cabinet is responsible not only for initiating and adopting policies but also their implementation and evaluation. A policy analysis department provides professional and technical assistance to the cabinet and its committees, evaluates and monitors the implementation of cabinet decisions, analyzes policy and conducts research on issues being addressed by the cabinet. Cabinet committees

play a crucial role in policymaking. Issues are referred to the cabinet once the relevant cabinet committees have carefully examined them and recommended the best policy. Each cabinet committee monitors development in its area of specialization and recommends the best course of action. As a result, the decision-making process has improved considerably.

In Botswana and Ghana all government ministries must have monitoring and evaluation units. These units, referred to as policy planning, monitoring and evaluation departments, collect and coordinate data within a ministry and plan and coordinate the preparation of budget bids from the various parts of the ministry. A World Bank study concluded, however, that it is unclear whether good use is made of these data or whether a sectorwide approach is taken (World Bank 2000b).

In Kenya many of the ministries have research units, but they are relatively weak and are guided by the dominant economic thought of the two Bretton Woods institutions, the IMF and the World Bank. In Senegal ministries have policy and research units, but the institutional framework for monitoring policies remains weak and ineffective. Reports are rarely published, and when published they are in a technical language hardly comprehensible to the public. In Zambia policy proposals are generated by each ministry, which undertakes due stakeholder consultation on the particular issue. For cross-cutting issues, affected ministries form an inter-ministerial committee of officials. The draft policy is circulated to cabinet ministers, and comments from 75% of the ministries are required before submission to cabinet discussion.

Stakeholder participation

In a democracy policymaking requires input from a range of interests and stakeholders: executive, legislature, civil service, civil society and the business community. With respect to stakeholders' participation in policymaking, the overall picture in Africa is quite discouraging. National policymaking has long been the domain of the central government. While local governments are generally responsible for service delivery, they are not usually involved in an important way in formulating national policy or setting standards for performance (though they might be consulted at the discretion of the ministry).

Although in Sierra Leone there are no formulated or predictable procedures by which civil society can be engaged in policy discourse, the government has shown some willingness to access citizens' opinion on policy issues through such initiatives as the poverty reduction strategy paper (PRSP) sectoral committees, the National Youth Council and the Anti-Corruption Commission. A public forum exists through which citizens at local levels take part in annual budget preparation in discussions with government ministries and departments. Local governments use ward committees to solicit citizen's views on local council discussions. In Botswana, the

government consults with the private sector, local communities, traditional chiefs and non-state actors. But many governments make the consultation simply a matter of informing the various non-state actors about government policies rather than seeking bottom-up inputs into decision making.

In Zambia consultation has, in some instances, been extended to members of the civil society and the general public through dedicated forums, usually when policy proposals generate public interest or are controversial. The Zambian policymaking process is quite elaborate, but it suffers from weaknesses in implementation, monitoring and evaluation of approved policies. The cabinet has weak institutional capacity to monitor and evaluate national policy despite having its own policy analysis and coordination division. In Malawi, prebudget consultations were introduced in the 2000/01 fiscal year, but they have tended to be ad hoc. Since many CSOs did not have expertise in issues of economic governance and accountability, few were involved in budget consultations. In Senegal there is little dialogue or exchange of views between the government and stakeholders.

Law enforcement agencies

The promotion of human development, good governance and democracy is most likely to be sustained in an environment in which the rule of law, due process of law and protection of life and property are observed. The police and other law enforcement agencies are mandated to maintain law and order. They are

> *With respect to stakeholders' participation in policymaking, the picture in Africa is discouraging. National policymaking has long been the domain of the central government*

also expected to protect citizens' lives and property and respect the basic rights of the people. Indeed, the constitutions of all African countries provide for the rule of law and due process of law, protection and promotion of human rights and citizenship entitlements. But the quality of training, equipment and discipline of law enforcement agencies is a matter of great concern.

Across Africa the ratio of police officers to population is rather high. Only Namibia, Botswana, Senegal and Egypt, where the police–population ratio is 1:180, 1:269, 1:300 and 1:205 respectively, are below the recommended international standard of 1:500. In Malawi the police force is small, with a ratio of one policeman to 1,470 citizens, which is the general pattern in most African countries. The challenge of policing is therefore made arduous as there is an inadequate number of police officers to protect lives and property, prevent crime, and maintain internal security in most countries.

The consulted experts were asked whether the police forces represented a cross-section of society in their country. A majority responded largely in the positive (figure 5.3). In Botswana a substantial majority (86%) indicated that the composition of the police services did reflect a cross-section of society. In Ghana the perception has improved since AGR I: in 2006, 70% of the experts, compared with 63% in

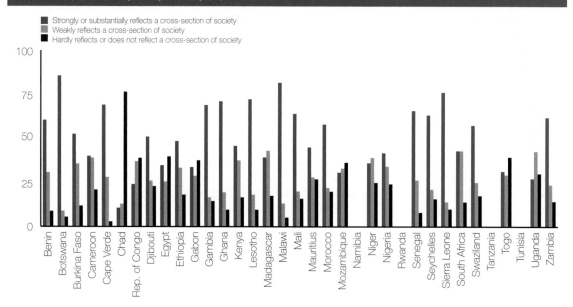

Figure 5.3 Expert opinion on police force composition

Share of experts surveyed, by country (%)

- Strongly or substantially reflects a cross-section of society
- Weakly reflects a cross-section of society
- Hardly reflects or does not reflect a cross-section of society

Source: ECA survey of experts 2007.

2002, believed the composition of the police services strongly or substantially reflects a cross-section of society.

The effectiveness of policing leaves much to be desired in many African countries. In Nigeria the police tend to conduct prosecutions in an unprofessional manner. Given the immensity and complexity of maintaining law and order, preventing crimes, apprehending and conducting prosecutions in the entire country, the Nigeria police services are generally perceived to be inadequately trained, equipped and remunerated and lacking in the professionalism and dedication needed to confront such tasks.

Police pay varies considerably from country to country. Salaries are generally low across the continent, and the force is poorly equipped. In Ghana, Nigeria and Senegal remuneration and pay in the police services are generally low; in Botswana and Seychelles police pay is competitive and comparable to public officers in those countries.

In most African countries the courts are overstretched as they struggle to deal with a backlog of cases, resulting in delayed justice and overcrowded prisons. South African prisons have the capacity to accommodate 116,266 prisoners, but the national prison population is 160,072 (ECA 2007f). Built in 1919 for a population of 1,000 prisoners, the Zomba prison in Malawi now accommodates 2,000 prisoners; Chichiri prison, built in 1960 for 1,000 prisoners, now houses 800 more than its capacity. In Sierra Leone the prisons are filled to 113% of their capacity. Human rights organisations have shown that these prisons have deplorable conditions: inadequate and poor food, poor sanitation and medical care, improper sleeping facilities and lack of recreation.

Asked if they had any confidence in the law enforcement agencies to protect citizens from theft or other types of crime, a majority of the consulted experts (68%) of the countries surveyed responded in the negative. Large majorities in Chad (92%), Mozambique (80%), Kenya (76%), Mali (65%) and South Africa (66%) responded that they had little or no confidence.

Still, improvements in law enforcement agencies and the delivery of police services have been reported in some African countries. Ghana has recently improved the operational efficiency of the police force by increasing its number of vehicles. It has also established the Police Intelligence and Professional Standards Unit to receive complaints from the public, help combat corruption and investigate reports of human rights abuses and police brutality.

To enhance the competence and integrity of its law enforcement agencies, Seychelles has created a special unit to maintain and promote professionalism, integrity and a strict code of ethical standards in the police force. The unit also deals with citizen complaints and investigates allegations of police corruption. Seychelles has adopted a community policing system that plays the

> *Improvements in law enforcement agencies and the delivery of police services have been reported in some African countries*

traditional constabulary role of preserving life and property, preventing and detecting crime and ensuring and keeping peace. It has also created a police academy to train new recruits in legal procedures, constitutionalism, human rights and searches.

In Sierra Leone a police partnership board with community representatives addresses areas of friction between police and the community. In Botswana the system of policing is effective but under strain from the increased policing needed because of the influx of immigrants from neighbouring countries, especially Zimbabwe, and also rising crime levels. But it is responsive to the needs of society. Local community needs are fulfilled through increased coverage of patrol services. Special constables who are not full police officers complement the work of the officers.

The manner in which the police conduct themselves has created concerns and fears in the citizens of

many African countries. In many African countries the presence of the police invariably inspires fear and suspicion rather than tranquility and a sense of protection. In the eyes of many citizens the police are looking for victims to extract bribes from, and they fear harassment or wrongful incarceration should they refuse to comply with police demands.

In Kenya the police are not accountable to local communities, so there is little mutual trust between them. There are no effective procedures for holding police accountable or for addressing civilians' complaints against them. Consequently, there is little confidence in the law enforcement agencies. The police force is also perceived to be riddled with corruption. Moreover, because the integrity of prosecutors is also in doubt, accountability of the police force to the community where it operates is virtually zero. Accountability of the police is mostly to the incumbent executive.

Botswana, Sierra Leone and Seychelles have created internal and external mechanisms to ensure police accountability and to check police behavior and protect human rights. Ghana has established the Police Intelligence and Professional Standards Unit to receive complaints from the public, help combat corruption and investigate reports of human rights abuses and police brutality. In Botswana accountability is enforced through an appointed police commissioner, internal codes of conduct and recourse to the law. Disciplinary measures deter and punish police brutality, misconduct

Box 5.4 Rights in Ghana

The 1992 constitution of Ghana contains the unique Directive Principles of State Policy, stipulating the country's fundamental social, economic, political, education and cultural objectives, and the rights of all Ghanaians. The constitution includes economic rights, education rights, women's rights, children's rights and rights of the sick and disabled. These rights constitute the obligations of those in authority, making the leaders accountable to the people. Moreover, as the chief executive the president is constitutionally obliged to issue, at least once a year, a report on actions taken by the government in pursuit of basic human rights, the health of the economy, the right to work, health care and education. It is also incumbent upon the president to ensure that the national economy is managed in a manner that maximizes the rate of growth and development, thus securing the promotion of human development.

and corruption, and there are a number of watchdog organisations to safeguard the public interest.

Delivery of public services: accessibility, affordability and quality

The accessibility, reliability and affordability of public services are major indicators of a country's quality of life and welfare. Good health is conducive to creative and productive activities. It also ensures a continuous supply of labour to the private sector. Poor health reduces consumers' purchasing power, affecting the health of the economy.

Education inculcates children with the values, mores and traditions of their society, enabling them to grow and live in peace and harmony with other people. It also empowers people with knowledge and information, enabling them to earn their living and support their families. Education empowers people to participate in economic and social development and in democracy. A government that fails to deliver the expected public services generates frustration and disillusionment and loses the trust of the people. The public is more likely to feel confident in the government if their expectations for quality and affordable public services are met.

The anti-colonial struggle in Africa was an attempt to improve the welfare of the African people. Accordingly, postcolonial leaders built schools, colleges and universities where none existed before and substantially improved the standards of those that existed. They built hospitals, clinics and dispensaries, established health stations in rural areas, trained doctors and nurses and provided hospital support. They raised the levels of adult literacy and gave pride and self-respect to those who for the first time could read newspapers. The new African leaders brought piped water to isolated towns and improved the quality of drinking water to villages. They extended the reach of electric power and improved the transport and communication network, connecting the areas to the urban centers and bringing villages closer to each other. And postcolonial governments moved into manufacturing and the supply of basic consumer goods. The first decades of independence were truly exciting, productive, and full of hopes for the future for many people.

But the post-colonial state became overextended by trying to cope with the demands of the growing population. Undisciplined expansion and politicization of the public sector caused the quality and delivery of public services to deteriorate. Moreover, the dominance of the executive, and in particular the cult of the "Big Man", in the allocation of public service created a discriminatory system of public service delivery. The situation was worsened by the economic crisis of the early 1980s and the imposition of structural adjustment programs by international lenders, which changed the paradigm from economic development led by the public sector to an economy of free enterprise and a government-regulated private sector.

> ❛ The anti-colonial struggle in Africa was an attempt to improve the welfare of the African people, but the post-colonial state became overextended

The minimal government advocated by the structural adjustment programs entailed retrenchment of civil servants and drastic reduction of public services, some of which were privatized. While the liberalization of the economy provided some potential for empowering citizens to participate in the economy, it was done at the expense of governments' capacities to produce and deliver essential public goods. There are now three providers of services to the people: the private sector, non-profit citizens organisations and the public sector. The delivery of services in the private sector is based on the market principles of profits and the ability of consumers to pay for the services. Those delivered by civil society organisations are nonprofit or heavily subsidized. And those delivered by the public sector— mainly local government agencies— are expected to be free or at a minimal cost. The role of the executive has primarily become one of providing the regulatory framework within which all the providers of services are expected to conduct their activities, to ensure sustained quality of services delivered and when necessary to rectify deficiencies in services delivered to poor or disadvantaged people.

The delivery of services in many African countries is far from satisfactory. Water sanitation is poor in Ghana, where low remuneration, inadequate resources and political interferences hamper service delivery. In a 2005 survey conducted by Afrobarometer, 52% of the respondents stated that there were major difficulties in obtaining household amenities such as power, water and telephone services. Public health clinics are expensive for the average Ghanaian. In the same vein, AGR I reported that 52% of the consulted experts stated that access to services was limited or difficult; that figure rose to 61% in 2007. In Sierra Leone social services are grossly inadequate. The business community is compelled to provide its own electricity, and there are no publicly announced service delivery targets. The consulted experts affirmed that there is very limited access to services (ECA 2007e).

In general the quality of services in the health sector remains poor. The sector has critical shortages of trained and qualified health personnel, particularly in rural communities. Hospitals and clinics are overcrowded and operate at less than capacity. In Zambia the doctor–population ratio is as high as 1:69,000, well above the World Health Organization's recommended ratio of 1:15,000.

A marked decline in education infrastructure and the supply of basic equipment, books and other educational materials plagues educational services. Student–teacher ratios are exceedingly high, contributing to the poor quality of education in many countries. In Gambia's secondary schools more than half of the teachers are unqualified or untrained. Access to education for marginalized groups and those with special needs trails behind the general increase in enrollment in many African countries (ECA 2007a).

> *Liberalising the economy enabled citizens to participate in the economy, but it was at the expense of governments' capacities to deliver essential public goods*

Despite improvements in recent years, Africa still has some distance to travel to provide access to universal education for all eligible children. According to UNICEF (2008, 18), "low levels of education particularly among women and girls represent a major obstacle to child and maternal survival throughout much of Sub-Saharan Africa". The percentage of net primary school attendance between 2000–2006 for Sub-Saharan Africa for male is 64% and female 60%. Net secondary enrolment for the same period is 25% for male and 22% for female (UNICEF 2008). These data suggest a serious gap in the transition from primary to secondary education in Sub-Saharan Africa in which a large proportion of children drop out of school after primary education and in which there is a poor rate of secondary school enrolment and attendance in the region.

But there are notable exceptions in Mauritius, Botswana, Cape Verde and Seychelles. In Mauritius delivery of domestic water, health, education and power is the highest in Africa (ECA 2007c). Health services, both preventive and curative, are accessible and free to all citizens, and education is free up to the tertiary level. In Botswana public services are accessible, reliable and generally affordable. There are also a number of health facilities, ranging from mobile clinics to appropriately equipped hospitals. By 2005 Cape Verde had achieved most of the MDGs for education, health and water. Seychelles has been able to provide total welfare for the very young and the elderly: free education

for children and adolescents up to 19 years of age, free day care for children under five years, and primary school enrolment for almost all children between the ages of five and nine. And there is a social welfare policy for all elderly citizens.

The alleviation and eventual elimination of poverty continues to be a popular electoral issue in Africa. The groups most vulnerable to poverty are the very young and the very old. Given the breakdown of the traditional African cultures in which the elderly were respected and protected and the impact of the HIV/AIDS pandemic that has created many orphans to be cared for by surviving grandparents, the plight of the elderly in Africa is a major issue. In this regard one African country, Seychelles, has a policy for the elderly that should be emulated by others (box 5.5).

Delivery of public services: AGR II update

AGR I was based on the findings of 27 country surveys, including surveys of household respondents. The

---

Box 5.5 Care for the elderly in Seychelles

Social policies geared towards the elderly ensure that those who are independent have self-catering facilities provided by government in district homes. Those who prefer to remain in the family have the assistance of home carers who cater to their daily needs, and the dependent ones are cared for at a residence for the elderly recently opened at North East Point. *The Ministry of Employment and Social Affairs has made provisions to ensure that the senior citizens remain prominent in the family and with financial support and caring facilities; they spend the rest of their days in comfort and dignity.*

Source: ECA 2007d, 107 (emphasis added).

present report is based on 35 country reviews, but only 8 of the additional countries have undergone household surveys. Following is a summary of survey responses on the state of public service delivery in these countries, especially from the household survey. The main message from AGR II is that the access, quality and affordability of social services are inadequate in many of the new project countries.

Health

Accessibility. Asked how accessible health clinics are, 51% of the households in Cape Verde, 51% in Republic of Congo, 63% in Djibouti, 90% in Seychelles and 57% in Togo responded that access was very easy or easy. On the other hand, 38% Madagascar and 33% in Sierra Leone replied that it was difficult or very difficult. On the quality of health services, 55% in Djibouti, 55% in Madagascar and 72% in Seychelles responded that the quality was very good or good, while 56% in Republic of Congo, 36% In Sierra Leone and 32% in Togo reported that the quality was poor or very poor.

Costs. With regard to costs, 66% in Cape Verde, 84% in Republic of Congo, 73% in Rwanda, 55% in Sierra Leone and 72% in Togo found medical expenses costly or very costly. Seychelles is the only country where medical care is free. Asked if medical service was denied to any member of a family on account of inability to pay, 62% in Republic of Congo, 83% in Rwanda and 49% in Togo responded affirmatively.

Quality. In Rwanda, Madagascar, Seychelles and Djibouti large

majorities of the household respondents felt that the quality of health care was good or very good. In most of the other surveyed countries only a small proportion of experts felt that quality was poor or very poor.

Education

Accessibility at primary schools. Respondents were asked about access to primary public schools. With the exception of Sierra Leone, where 48% found it difficult or very difficult, in the remaining eight countries, the overwhelming majority—in Cape Verde 79%, Republic of Congo 77%, Djibouti 75%, Madagascar 85%, Rwanda 88% and Seychelles 89%—affirmed that access was very easy or easy.

Accessibility at secondary schools. Regarding access to public secondary schools, 60.8% of the respondents in the Republic of Congo, 55% in Djibouti and 85% in Seychelles reported that access was easy, while 57% in Cape Verde, 51% in Madagascar, 55% in Rwanda and 77% in Togo found access not easy or difficult or very difficult.

Affordability. Asked if any member of the family had been denied access to school due to inability to pay, with the exception of Rwanda, where 43% responded yes, the majority of the respondents in the remaining eight countries stated that it did not occur.

Quality. The quality of education was considered very good or good in Djibouti (64%), Madagascar (52%), Rwanda (90%) and Seychelles (75%), while 46% of the respondents in

> ' **The main message from AGR II is that the access, quality and affordability of social services are inadequate in many of the new project countries**

Republic of Congo and 41% in Togo judged that the quality of education was poor or very poor.

Asked about the adequacy of public school buildings, 63% of the respondents in Djibouti, 55% in Rwanda and 73% in Seychelles found public school buildings good or very good, while 44% in Cape Verde, 44% in Republic of Congo, 51% in Sierra Leone and 42% in Togo found the buildings fairly adequate.

On the adequacy of teaching, 55% of respondents in Cape Verde, 53% in Djibouti, 52% in Madagascar, 80% in Rwanda and 76% in Seychelles found it very good or good. In Republic of Congo 49%, in Sierra Leone 49% and in Togo 44% found teaching only fairly adequate. Asked about the adequacy of educational materials, with the exception of Djibouti (49%) and Seychelles (63%), where respondents found them good or very good, majorities in Republic of Congo (56%) and Togo (60%) found the educational materials poor or very poor.

Access to services

Water. Respondents in Cape Verde (66%), Djibouti (69%), Madagascar (50%) and Seychelles (94%) responded that they had access to clean water; while 81% of the respondents in Republic of Congo, 64% in Rwanda, 55% in Sierra Leone and 63% in Togo replied that they had no access to clean water.

Electricity. On electricity, 66% in Cape Verde, 53% in Djibouti and 99% in Seychelles affirmed that

they had access to it, while 85% in Republic of Congo, 95% in Rwanda, 58% in Sierra Leone and 79% in Togo responded that they had no access.

Land. Only 53% of the respondents in Seychelles replied they had access to land, while 50% in Cape Verde, 51% in Madagascar, 66% in Rwanda and 49% in Togo responded that they had no access to land.

Housing. In Seychelles 59% replied that they had access to affordable housing, while 68% in Cape Verde, 53% in Republic of Congo, 58% in Djibouti, 53% in Madagascar, 60% in Rwanda, 52% in Sierras Leone and 54% in Togo responded that they had no access to affordable housing.

Agricultural extension. Respondents stated that they had no access to extension services in the following percentages: 74% in Cape Verde, 65% in Rwanda, 68% in Sierra Leone and 60% in Togo.

Credit. In regard to credit access, 68% in Cape Verde, 95% in Rwanda, 84% in Sierra Leone and 70% in Togo responded that they did not have access to credit.

Irrigation. On irrigation services 67% in Cape Verde, 92% in Rwanda, 65% in Sierra Leone and 73% in Togo replied that they had no access to irrigation services. In some countries the question was not regarded as relevant.

Infrastructure. Only in Seychelles did a sizeable majority of households

(86%) say they had access to waste disposal, as opposed to 69% in Rwanda, and 51% in Djibouti. And 69% in Madagascar, 72% in Sierra Leone and 93% in Togo said they had no access.

Road availability was considered good by 46% of the respondents in Djibouti and 56% in Seychelles. But 86% of the respondents in Republic of Congo, 53% in Rwanda, 64% in Sierra Leone and 92% in Togo replied that the availability of roads was poor or very poor.

On transport services only 54% of the respondents in Djibouti and 52% in Seychelles considered the services very good or good, while 67% of the respondents in Republic of Congo, 54% in Madagascar, 61% in Rwanda, 59% in Sierra Leone and 88% in Togo found the service poor or very poor.

Addressing poverty with social services

Nearly half the population of Sub-Saharan Africa, approximately 300 million people, lives below the international poverty line of US$1 a day. In the 1990s the number of poor in the region increased by a quarter. The number of impoverished people in Sub-Saharan Africa is expected to rise to 404 million by 2015. If current trends continue, Africa will be the only region where the number of poor people in 2015 will be higher than in 1990.

Poverty in Sub-Saharan Africa is pervasive in some places. Apart from the severity for those gravely affected by its burden, the incidence of

poverty is increasing faster than in any other region of the world. If the Millennium Development Goals are met, 500 million will escape poverty by 2015, 250 million will be spared from hunger and 30 million children who would not have lived past their fifth birthday will do so. But at its current rate of progress Sub-Saharan Africa will not meet any of these targets.

Given the grim situation, it is no wonder that poverty and the problem of unemployment were identified in the household survey as the most serious problems confronting the region. In Rwanda 71% and in Madagascar 45% of the households identified poverty as their number one problem. In Djibouti (41.8%) and Republic of Congo (39.6%) unemployment was rated as the most serious problem demanding action.

The overwhelming majority of the consulted experts expressed the view that governments have not been successful in addressing the service needs of the poor (figure 5.4). Across the surveyed countries a majority of the panel of experts in Benin, Chad, Republic of Congo, Egypt, Ethiopia, Gabon, Niger, Nigeria, Togo, Uganda and Zambia believed that government services rarely or do not address the basic needs of the communities and the poor.

Asked if the government was responsive to the basic needs of the people, the consulted experts responded as follows: 55% in Botswana, 53% in Burkina Faso, 64% in Cape Verde, 52% in Mali and 55% in Nigeria felt that government

> **If current trends continue, Africa will be the only region where the number of poor people in 2015 will be higher than in 1990**

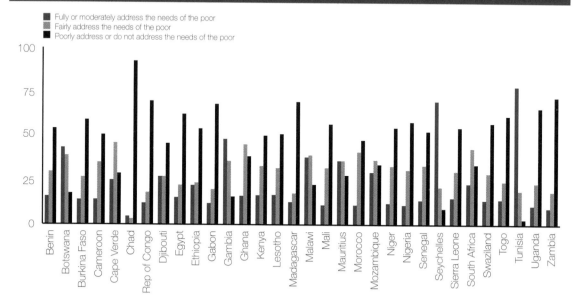

Figure 5.4 Expert opinion on how well government services address the needs of the poor

Share of experts surveyed, by country (%)

- Fully or moderately address the needs of the poor
- Fairly address the needs of the poor
- Poorly address or do not address the needs of the poor

Source: ECA survey of experts 2007.

services responded fairly well to their basic needs. But sizeable numbers in other countries—87% in Chad, 62% in Djibouti, 61% in Gabon, 61% in Ghana, 62% in Madagascar, 63% in Senegal, 52% in Uganda and 66% in Zambia—responded that it rarely or never responded to their basic needs.

On accessibility of government services to the poor, 81% of the consulted experts in Seychelles, 76% in Botswana and 71% in Mauritius responded that people had ready or mostly ready access to government services, while 49% in Niger, 46% in Sierra Leone, 45% in South Africa, 43% in Uganda and 42% in Zambia responded that access was limited. In Chad 68%, in Republic of Congo

47% and in Mozambique 44% responded that there was very little access or access was difficult.

With regard to the services provided for women, 88% of the consulted experts in Tunisia and 72% in Seychelles believed that government services adequately or moderately addressed the needs of women. And 82% in Chad, 46% in Gabon, 47% in Kenya and 47% in Togo responded that government services addressed women's needs poorly or not at all.

The HIV/AIDS pandemic in Africa

Although the 2007 UNAIDS report showed a slight decline in

HIV/AIDS worldwide, the numbers for Africa are still worrisome. Sub-Saharan Africa remains the most affected region in the world with 68% of all HIV-positive people and over 76% of deaths from AIDS in 2007. Unlike in other regions, 61% of the people living with HIV in Africa are women (UNAIDS 2007). In many Sub-Saharan African countries AIDS is erasing decades of progress in extending life expectancy. Millions of adults are dying from AIDS while still young or in early middle age. Average life expectancy in Sub-Saharan Africa is now 47 years (it had been projected to be 62 years without AIDS). HIV is also responsible for the deterioration of other indicators that had once been improving in Africa—in education, for example, enrollment and literacy have been weakened by the high morbidity and mortality of skilled personnel.

Different epidemics

There are large variations in the patterns of the AIDS epidemic in African countries. It is important to understand this diversity to plan appropriate policies for treatment and prevention for each of its geographical, structural and societal variations.

In East Africa the trend of stabilizing or declining HIV prevalence appears to be continuing. In West and Central Africa national adult HIV prevalence continues to be lower than other parts of the continent. There are no signs of declining HIV prevalence in Southern Africa, especially in Botswana, Namibia and Swaziland, where exceptionally high

infection levels continue. Nor does South Africa's AIDS epidemic show any evidence of appreciable decline. An estimated 5.5 million, or 18.8% of adults 15–49 years old, were living with AIDS there in 2005.

The challenge of HIV for governance

The pandemic diverts resources from prevention programmes to treatment and caring for the sick and the orphans. It also undermines capital formation and economic growth. And the dislocation of families caused by the high number of deaths deepens other social crises and increases the threat to national security.

The ECA Commission on HIV/AIDS and Governance in Africa concluded that HIV/AIDS was undermining the pillars of governance in high-prevalence countries by reducing the state's capacity to implement public policies and by undermining the countries' workforce and work duration (ECA 2008). The magnitude of HIV/AIDS in the continent affects democratic processes and ultimately risks political stability. Patterns of participation in elections have been reshaped, and the support for political parties has weakened. Women and youth, who are particularly affected by the epidemic in Sub-Saharan Africa, will not only lose electoral power but also their ability to be represented in government. The overall effect will be greater political alienation and tenuous electoral support for governments.

The impact of HIV/AIDS on public service delivery is even more evident,

> ' **Although the 2007 UNAIDS report showed a slight decline in HIV/AIDS worldwide, the numbers for Africa are still worrisome**

with a reduced work force, loss of specialized skills and deteriorating morale. The overall consequence is a reduced capacity to design, formulate and implement the appropriate policies for the affected African countries. The pandemic has, as it were, precipitated a vicious circle of decline in service delivery. It has reduced skilled human resources, lowering levels of capacity for service deliveries while at the same time creating a greater need for services for those affected by the disease.

Government responses to the epidemic

Many African countries have launched sustained prevention and care efforts to combat the HIV/AIDS pandemic. In Senegal effective prevention campaigns are reflected in the relatively low adult HIV prevalence rate of 0.9%. The experience of Uganda shows that an epidemic can be brought under control. The HIV general prevalence in Uganda fell from around 15% in the early 1990s to around 5% by 2001. This change is attributed to HIV prevention campaigns.

In Rwanda and Namibia more than 70% of people in need of an antiretroviral drug (ARV) are receiving it. In Cameroon, Côte d'Ivoire, Kenya, Malawi and Zambia between 25% and 45% of people requiring ARVs were receiving them in December 2006. Although South Africa is the richest nation in Sub-Saharan Africa and should lead the way in ARV distribution, its government has been slow to act. To date only 33% of those in need of treatment in South Africa are receiving it. In Ghana,

---

Box 5.6 Lessons learned on HIV/AIDS: Senegal and Uganda

Senegal has managed to keep its HIV/AIDS prevalence very low, and in four years Uganda has succeeded in reversing the trend from almost 30% infection rate in some areas to 8%. For both countries success lies in a combination of political, social and behavioural initiatives. The lessons learned are:

- Provide early response by the national leadership.
- Build on national systems of communication and collaboration.
- Actively involve communities.
- Reinforce positive sexual norms by regular prevention messages.
- Maintain prevention services.
- Enhance the position of women in society.

Source: ECA 2008.

Mozambique, Nigeria, Tanzania and Zimbabwe the figure is less than 20%. The commitments of the Abuja Declaration are still not being realised in some countries. African governments still have a long way to go in fighting the pandemic and preventing its devastating effects on governance.

Concluding remarks

The executive plays a major role in African governance. While the quality and effectiveness of the executive have improved in some countries, more still needs to be done. Lack of competitive intra-party democratic electoral processes in many African countries impedes the emergence of competent and committed leaders.

Implementation of competition and meritocracy in the recruitment of civil servants has been slow in some countries, neglected for political and ethnic reasons in others and affirmed in only a few. In countries

with visible and pronounced societal diversities and minorities there is
likely to be tension between the principles of meritocracy and those of
equity and inclusivity. These issues
need to be addressed to ensure a
wider understanding of their importance in promoting good governance,
democratization and development.

Adequate remuneration, a good
working environment and training are lacking in the public sector
of many African countries. Only in
a few countries have salaries been
raised to match the cost of living,
while in many others public salaries do not provide a decent living,
especially for the lower ranks of the
service. While training facilities
are available in almost all the countries under review, the conditions
under which the training is provided
leave much to be desired. Similarly,

with the exception of a few countries, public service reforms have not
achieved their intended objectives.

With only a few exceptions, the
executives of African countries
are not serious about improving
accountability and transparency.
The problem is even more acute at
the local government level. Accountability and transparency are critical to the viability and vibrancy of a
democracy as well as the legitimacy,
trust and popularity of the executive. The role of civil society organisations in advancing human rights,
accountability and transparency
should be constitutionally protected. And the electoral mechanisms
and processes to ensure free and fair
elections should be strengthened.

Delivery of public services is still
a major problem in many African
countries, due partly to constraints
on utilizing human and material
resources. Lack of accountability and
responsiveness to stakeholders, especially at the local levels, reinforces
the tendency to ignore or perpetually delay fulfillment of such responsibilities. A few countries, however,
have been able to provide comprehensive welfare for their very young
and elderly citizens.

Although many countries have taken
steps to facilitate collection, circulation and analysis of information and
knowledge to ensure integrity in the
policy processes, there is still more to
be done. Given the impact of globalization and the exigencies of public-private partnerships, governments
in Africa need more specialized
information and knowledge, better

coordination within the governance system and closer cooperation and consultation with the private sector and civil society. Because local governments are major players in service delivery at the grassroots level, they too should be part of such consultations and cooperation.

Law enforcement agencies should inspire confidence, tranquility and hope of assistance. Unfortunately, in most countries more must be done to ensure that the law enforcement agents perform their functions as required by the rule of law, their own codes of conduct or the expectations of citizens.

The HIV/AIDS pandemic has not declined, though its expansion has been contained in some countries and reduced in a few others. But the pandemic is still a devastating threat to the economies, societies and governance systems in Africa. A comprehensive approach is needed to combat it. The medical and technological components to combat the pandemic must be in place and updated as medical and technical knowledge improves. But in the last analysis the most critical factor is the people and what they can and must do to confront, contain, moderate and eventually eliminate HIV/AIDS. Through sustained dissemination of information and public services they must better understand the pandemic and its impact on their lives and livelihoods.

References

AfDB (African Development Bank). 2007. *Governance in Rwanda*. Abidjan.

APRM (African Peer Review Mechanism). 2005. *Ghana Self-Assessment Report*. Abidjan.

———. 2007. *South Africa Country Review Report No. 5.* Abidjan.

Chang, Ha-Joon. 2004. *Globalization, Economic Development and the Role of the State*. London: Zed Books.

Chiweza, A.L. 2007. "Local government." In Nandini Patel and Lars Svåsand, eds., *Government and Politics in Malawi*. Zomba: Kachere Series.

ECA (Economic Commission for Africa). 2007a. Gambia country report. Addis Ababa.

———. 2007b. Malawi country report. Addis Ababa.

———. 2007c. Mauritius country report. Addis Ababa.

———. 2007d. Seychelles country report. Addis Ababa.

———. 2007e. Sierra Leone country report. Addis Ababa.

———. 2007f. South Africa country report. Addis Ababa.

———. 2008. *Securing our Future. Report of the Commission on HIV/AIDS and Governance in Africa*. Addis Ababa.

Kaldor, Mary. 2002. "Civil Society and Accountability." Background paper for *Human Development Report*, United Nations Development Programme, Human Development Office. New York.

Malawi, Government of. 2005. National Local Government Finance Committee. "Malawi Local Government Authorities: 2004/05 Revised and 2005/06 Budget Estimates."

Mohiddin, Ahmed. 2007. "Towards the Capable State in Africa: Issues Paper for African Governance Forum V11." In *The Challenge of Good Governance in Africa: Democratization and the Promotion of Human Development*. United

> The HIV/AIDS pandemic has been contained in some countries and reduced in a few others. But it is still a devastating threat to the economies of Africa

Nations Development Programme. Conference papers.

Rondinelli, Denis A., and G. Shabbir Cheema. 2003. *Reinventing Government for the Twenty-First Century: State Capacity in a Globalizing Society.* Sterling, VA: Kumarian Press.

Rwanda National Election Commission. 2006. "Report on elections of authorities of local administration and specialized structures." Kigali.

UNAIDS (Joint United Nations Programme on HIV/AIDS). *2007 AIDS Epidemic Update.* Geneva: UNAIDS.

UNICEF (United Nations Children's Fund). 2008. *The State of Africa's Children, 2008.* New York: UNICEF.

World Bank. 2000a. *Can Africa Claim the 21st Century?* Washington, D.C.

———. 2000b. "Monitoring and Evaluation Action Plan." World Bank: Washington, D.C.

———. 2004. *Building Effective States, Forging Engaged Societies.* Report of the World Bank Task Force on Capacity Development in Africa. Washington, D.C.

Protection of human rights and support for the rule of law are the very essence of good governance. African countries have overwhelmingly ratified or acceded to the primary international human rights instruments. And Africa has a strong regional human rights framework that in some instances far exceeds the international instruments in their scope and progressive positions.

But these progressive developments also mask a wide gap between the rhetoric about human rights and their realization on the ground. Most countries have not fulfilled the obligations they assumed in ratifying human rights treaties by incorporating those treaties into domestic law, thereby leaving in place a discriminatory and sometimes repressive legal framework. They have not adopted laws and policies to redress discriminatory practices against women and have limited access to justice for their citizens. They have not done enough to support the institutions that they themselves have created to protect human rights—in fact, all too frequently they have actually undermined the institutions. And governments have not cooperated sufficiently with the international and regional human rights systems in addressing human rights challenges. In sum, there is uncertainty and equivocation about human rights in Africa.

Many countries have taken important steps towards democratization and the opening of political space and have improved the overall human rights situation. But these governments are too few and are often overshadowed by very public setbacks. The ECA country reports show that an increasingly aware and engaged public acknowledges progress in their societies but is exasperated by the slow pace of change.

For most Africans human rights remain only lofty promises 60 years after adoption of the Universal Declaration of Human Rights. The gap between the aspirations of major international and regional treaties by African states and the experience of households, children, women, the elderly, workers and ordinary citizens has not significantly narrowed since AGR I. Officially, the centrality of human rights in the work of intergovernmental, governmental and nongovernmental organisations is affirmed. The human rights approach to programming is increasingly acknowledged as a working method by a variety of actors, including those working on climate change, HIV and AIDS, malaria, tuberculosis and poverty. But the reality is that very few have understood and attempted to apply the human-rights-based approach in their work. There is still a huge knowledge gap that must be addressed before human rights can be mainstreamed in development work.

The equal access of men and women to the spheres of decision making has advanced significantly. The best illustration of the advancement of women's growing participation in decision making is the Rwandan parliament, where women hold over half of the seats, the highest rate in the world. Still, ordinary women and girls have continued to suffer from diverse forms of gender-based violence. There are fewer coups d'état in Africa, but armed conflicts continue to force millions to flee in search of safety as refugees, migrants or internally displaced persons.

On a positive note, the use of the death penalty is on the decline in Africa despite the fact that many prisoners remain under the death sentence in several countries. In Tanzania the authorities commuted all death sentences in 2006. The Democratic Republic of Congo deleted references to the death penalty in the constitution and criminal code. Rwanda abolished the death penalty in June 2007, a year after some 600 were sentenced to death. This was followed by the announcement by the government of Gabon that it would abolish the death penalty, which had not been used for about 20 years. And South Africa confirmed its resolve not to reintroduce the death sentence, even in the face of many calls in its favour as a solution to the growing crime rate in the country.

Many Africans are skeptical that the modern judicial and law enforcement systems can deal with everyday human rights concerns. For example, serious crimes such as the illegal trade of minerals of war-torn countries and the phenomenon of "blood diamonds" remain poorly investigated or condoned by unwilling domestic and international legal regimes. Indigenous justice systems such as the *Gacaca* in Rwanda, which appear

more accessible to the majority, especially among rural populations, fall short of international standards for fair trial and are vulnerable to political and ethnic manipulations. And in several countries, the nexus of corruption and impunity tarnishes the image of the judiciary.

The African Court on Human and Peoples' Rights has taken seat in Arusha, Tanzania, and will have jurisdiction over the full range of rights enshrined in all human rights treaties in force on the African continent. The Pan African Parliament based in Midrand, South Africa, is striving to harmonise African domestic laws in a variety of fields while the Committee of Experts on the Rights and Welfare of the Child has become more visible than it was a few years back. These mechanisms set up by African states to monitor compliance with African human rights treaties lack the required authority, resources, recognition and capacity to discharge their full mandate and to enforce their decisions. The African Union (AU) has continued its efforts to adopt a number of forward-looking treaties, declarations and resolutions that emphasise the centrality of human rights to peace, security and development in Africa. The AU has consistently applied the Lomé Declaration and the provisions of the AU Constitutive Act to unconstitutional changes of government by suspending countries whose governments have come to power through coup d'état.[1] At the same time, the AU seems reluctant to publicly denounce human rights violations in some of its member states such as Zimbabwe and in the Darfur region of Sudan.

> *The human rights instruments signed by African governments mask a wide gap between the rhetoric about human rights and their realization on the ground*

The cooperation between the United Nations and the African Union was given an impetus with the signing in November 2006 of a joint declaration for a decade-long capacity-building programme for Africa in strategic areas, including human rights, the rule of law, justice and reconciliation. This declaration was backed in 2007 by a UN General Assembly resolution calling for a comprehensive strategy to address human rights from an inclusive and global perspective.

Overall, there has been progress on human rights in Africa since AGR I. The aggregate data on human rights from ECA surveys showed an increase of 2 percentage points and a marginal increase of 3 percentage points on respect for the rule of law. But this progress is marginal. Sustained efforts by all human rights stakeholders are required to ensure substantial improvement in the promotion and protection of the rights of the average African citizen.

Legal framework for the protection of human rights

Almost all of the countries surveyed have ratified or acceded to the major international human rights treaties.[2] Only the recently adopted Convention on the Rights of Persons with Disabilities has not received a substantial number of signatures or ratifications. Twenty-nine African countries have signed the convention, but only four—Gabon, Guinea, Namibia and South Africa—have ratified it.[3]

This impressive record of ratifications by African countries is countered by the failure of many countries to take necessary action to give effect to these treaties as legally binding instruments at the domestic level. In only a small minority of countries do international treaties become law upon ratification. The preamble to the 2001 Senegalese constitution provides for the incorporation of several human rights protective instruments once they are ratified by the country and vested with constitutional and legal value. But in Senegal and some other African countries the fact of ratification is enough for the treaty to have legal effect and to be invoked as the basis for legal action.

In most African countries international treaties are not self-executing but require implementing legislation to be incorporated into national law (the process of domestication). In Burkina Faso a duly ratified treaty must be published in the *Official Journal* for it to take effect. Despite Burkina Faso's otherwise good record, this has not been done. As a result, citizens are not sufficiently informed or empowered to invoke those treaties in court.

The major human rights treaties have committees to implement and monitor their provisions. But the committees charged with the monitoring of the implementation of those treaties—the Human Rights Committee, the Committee on the Elimination of Racial Descrimination, the Committee on Economic, Social and Cultural Rights, the Committee Against Torture and the committee for the Convention on the Elimination of all Forms of Discrimination Against Women—have told Zambia that it has not fully incorporated

'**Overall, there has been progress on human rights in Africa since AGR I, but this progress is marginal**

the Convention Against Torture and other Cruel, Inhuman, or Degrading Treatment or Punishment, the International Convention on the Elimination of All Forms of Racial Descrimination, the International Convention on Economic, Social and Cultural Rights and the International Covenant on Civil and Political Rights into its domestic laws. Botswana, Burkina Faso, Kenya, Malawi and Uganda, among others, are in a similar situation.

For all practical purposes, therefore, the human rights treaties have no effect at the national level and cannot be invoked in courts of law, even though the state party remains bound internationally as required by international law. In Madagascar, which has ratified most of the international treaties, the judiciary often ignores these treaties.

Most of the countries covered in this report have also ratified or acceded to the African regional human rights instruments. All 53 countries have ratified the African Charter on Human and Peoples' Rights. The legal status of regional human rights instruments raises the same problems as those of the international treaties. Despite widespread ratification, the African Charter does not enjoy automatic applicability in African countries.

Mechanisms for promoting and protecting human rights

Mechanisms are available at the international, regional and national levels to effect the goals of human rights treaties.

> *Mechanisms are available at the international, regional and national levels to effect the goals of human rights treaties*

International mechanisms

Each international treaty has a committee that parties are obligated to report to periodically to describe their progress in implementing the treaty. Some treaties also have a complaint procedure whereby individuals can bring cases before the respective committees, which then give their findings and recommendations to the state party concerned. The UN Human Rights Council also has a system of independent experts and bodies (called special rapporteurs, independent experts or special representatives of the Secretary-General) who are given a mandate to monitor human rights in their respective areas. The universal periodic review (UPR) mechanism of the newly established Human Rights Council offers an opportunity to promote and protect human rights (box 6.1). Algeria, Benin, Gabon, Ghana, Mali, Morocco, South Africa, Tunisia and Zimbabwe have already been reviewed through the UPR; Botswana, Burkina Faso, Burundi and Cape Verde will submit to the review in December 2008. The UPR has the potential to become an important tool for accountability and could contribute to protecting human rights at the national level if it has appropriate government commitment and full involvement of civil society and other stakeholders.

Many African countries have a weak record of reporting to the UN treaty bodies; many have outstanding reports from several years. Equally, cooperation with the UN special rapporteurs has not been very positive. Uganda, for example, has submitted only a few reports to relevant international bodies, and many reports are still overdue (UNICEF 2003; 2004). Uganda has also failed to take action or respond to comments and recommendations made by several treaty bodies since 1997 (UNICEF 2003; 2004). The Uganda report attributes this tardiness to insufficient manpower in key ministries to do the reporting, lack of awareness in responsible ministries of their reporting obligations and lack of overall coordination (UNICEF 2003; 2004).

African regional human rights mechanisms

The African Commission on Human and Peoples' Rights has a broad mandate to monitor states' compliance with the African Charter on Human and Peoples' Rights. Its mandate includes receiving periodic reports from states on their progress in the implementation of the Charter and to receive complaints from individuals and nongovernmental organisations (NGOs). The Committee of the Experts on the Rights of the Child was established under the African Charter on the Rights and the Welfare of the Child with a broad mandate to monitor its implementation. But its secretariat has only one staff person.

It is hoped that the African Court of Justice and Human Rights, which will be established soon to replace both the African Court on Human and Peoples' Rights and the Court of Justice of the African Union, will receive adequate funding and support from member states to enable

---

Box 6.1 The universal periodic review

The universal periodic review (UPR) is an innovative feature of the Human Rights Council, which was created by the UN General Assembly in June 2006 to replace the Commission on Human Rights. The Council's mandate is to "undertake a universal periodic review, based on objective and reliable information, of the fulfillment by each state of its human rights obligations and commitments" (General Assembly Resolution 60/251, para. 5(e)). The objectives of the UPR include the improvement of human rights in a country, fulfillment of a state's human rights obligations and assessment of positive developments and challenges. It also seeks to enhance a state's capacity. Each country is to be reviewed once every four years based on three documents: a report prepared by the state and two reports prepared by the Office of the High Commissioner for Human Rights (one a compilation of UN information, the other a summary of inputs provided by other stakeholders).

---

it to discharge its responsibilities on human rights protection and adjudication. The Protocol on the Statute of the African Court of Justice and Human Rights was adopted in July 2008. The perception of the surveyed experts was that the reporting mechanism in their countries is either rarely effective or ineffective.

National human rights bodies

National human rights institutions are to be governed by the Paris Principles, which stipulate the criteria for their establishment, tenure for members, remuneration and operational autonomy.[4] A system of accreditation has been developed by the International Coordinating Committee of the National Human Rights Institutions to classify institutions according to their compliance with the Paris Principles and to advocate for their independence. Several national human rights institutions in Africa have attained "A" status through accreditation with the Coordinating Committee, signalling their compliance with the Paris Principles.[5]

The South African Human Rights Commission, also awarded an "A" by the Coordinating Committee, has a general mandate to "promote, protect and monitor the advancement of human rights in the Republic", and under section 184(3) of the constitution has a specific duty to monitor government measures for realizing socioeconomic rights, including the rights to housing, health, food, water, social security, education and a healthy environment. The Commission has the power to investigate and report on the observance of human rights, to take steps to secure appropriate redress where human rights have been violated, to educate, and to make recommendations to all levels of government.

Burkina Faso, Cameroon and Nigeria are rated "B" by the Coordinating Committee, indicating that they have observer status, and the national human rights institution of Madagascar has "C" status, indicating that it has not complied with the Paris Principles.

In addition to a national human rights institution, some countries have established bodies to deal with specific issues—for example, the Commission on Equality in South Africa. In Kenya the Office of the Ombudsman, the Kenya Anti-Corruption Commission (KACC) and the Standing Committee on Human Rights (SCHR) complement the Kenya National Commission on Human Rights (KNCHR). Senegal has established the *Médiateur*

de la République, and the Senegalese Human Rights Committee annually reports on human rights in the country.

There have been cases of executive interference in the functioning of the human rights institutions, and many of the bodies confront funding and capacity constraints. In Nigeria the chairperson of the Human Rights Commission was recently dismissed because the government was not happy with a position that he took.[6]

Perception of the effectiveness of human rights watchdog bodies varies from positive to very negative across project countries. In a few countries, such as Benin, Botswana, Malawi and Tunisia, a majority of the consulted experts rated the watchdog institutions in their countries as fully or largely effective in promoting human rights (figure 6.1). In fifteen countries—including Burkina Faso, Cape Verde, Gabon, Ghana, Mauritius, Morocco, Mozambique, Senegal, Seychelles, Sierra Leone, South Africa, Uganda and Zambia—the majority view of the experts was that watchdog institutions are sometimes effective in promoting and protecting human rights. In Chad, Democratic Republic of the Congo, Ethiopia, Madagascar, Nigeria, Swaziland and Togo the majority of experts felt the watchdog institutions were rarely effective or ineffective.

The judiciary and human rights protection

Charged with protecting persons and personal property against damages or wrongs, the courts have an

> *It is hoped that the African Court of Justice and Human Rights will receive adequate support from member states to enable it to discharge its responsibilities*

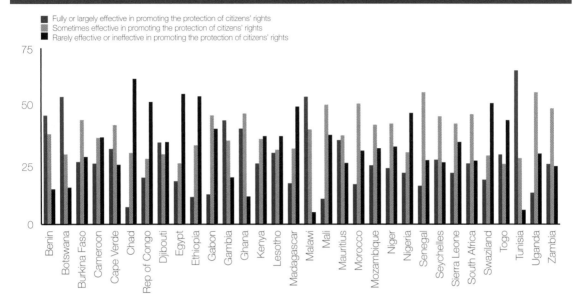

Figure 6.1 Expert opinion on effectiveness of watchdog organisations

Share of experts surveyed, by country (%)

■ Fully or largely effective in promoting the protection of citizens' rights
■ Sometimes effective in promoting the protection of citizens' rights
■ Rarely effective or ineffective in promoting the protection of citizens' rights

Source: ECA survey of experts 2007.

important role to play in protecting human and peoples' rights. The effectiveness of the judiciary can only be ensured through transparent appointment and removal of judges and magistrates, sufficient funding, development of satisfactory conditions of service and the creation of accountability systems.

Because of Africa's strong sense of communalism, it is important that the judiciary combine two aims: adjudicating cases on the basis of the positive law and reconciling parties to various disputes in amicable ways. This would be a uniquely African way of providing justice and peace. But the judiciary is perceived by most Africans as unable to deliver impartial justice and reconcile

people. This perception reflects the acute shortage of trained professionals, the cumbersome and costly judicial procedures, the elitist nature of the judiciary and the incidence of corruption in the judicial system. In other words, modern courts are not easily accessible to most Africans, and they are a weak institution for promoting and protecting human and peoples' rights.

There is a worrisome double standard in applying human rights principles at the international level. When states and leaders expected to be role models in the observance of human rights commit abuses and go free, the task of demanding respect for values of human rights becomes more complicated. The lack of an effective redress system at the international level weakens human rights protection globally.

Poorer countries in Africa are increasingly perceiving the system to be skewed against them in the dispensation of justice at the global level. The trial of Charles Taylor, the former president of Liberia, and the indictment of the current president of Sudan by the International Criminal Court for war crimes have generated serious controversy in Africa about the universality of international criminal law. While rights violations are condemnable criminal offences, critics point to several cases of rights violations committed by powerful countries and their leaders that are not addressed or sanctioned. For international law to be meaningful and its judicial system credible, it has to be global and universal in nature and application.

Implementation of specific rights

A report card on how well African countries implement their human rights commitments would be mixed.

Equality and nondiscrimination
The principles of equality and nondiscrimination are considered fundamental to the human rights regime and are contained in all the major human rights instruments.[7] The International Covenant on Civil and Political Rights and the International Covenant on Economic Social and Cultural Rights, among others, guarantee equality of all human beings without discrimniation.[8]

The African Charter on Human and Peoples' Rights contains a nondiscrimination provision covering sex, equal protection before the law and, most importantly, the injunction that the state shall ensure "the elimination of *every* discrimination against women" (emphasis added). In *Legal Resources Foundation v. Zambia* the African Commission adopted the definition of discrimination from the Human Rights Committee, noting that the "right to equality is very important. It means that persons under the jurisdiction of a state should expect to be treated fairly and justly within the legal system and be assured of equal treatment before the law and equal enjoyment of the rights available to other individuals" (UNHRC 1989).

Almost all African countries reviewed for this report have constitutional provisions that prohibit discrimination. Still, structural, systemic and informal discrimination take place in many of those countries in Africa. Claims of discrimination, exclusion, unequal treatment and marginalization are behind many of the woes in Africa, including conflicts. Many forms of de jure and de facto discrimination—on the basis of gender, ethnicity, religion, class, race, political affiliation, geography and health—are common in the continent and have been behind some of the intractable conflicts of the last two decades.

Despite the commitments made to international and regional bodies and the inclusion of nondiscrimination clauses in constitutions, most countries reviewed for this report

> **Almost all African countries have constitutional provisions that prohibit discrimination. Still, discrimination takes place in many of those countries**

seem reluctant to place priority on discrimination and equal protection in policymaking. Namibia and South Africa are among a few countries that explicitly address equality and discrimination as human rights issues and have programs in place to protect minority rights.

There is a strong belief that acknowledging minority rights and issues of discrimination would have a negative impact on national unity. In Botswana the government's response to the claim of the Baswara for the recognition of their separate identity was that all the people of Botswana are Batswana and are all indigenous to Botswana, that all people are the same and equal under the constitution and that recognition of distinct identities would undermine the unity of the country.[9] This policy of ethnic and racial neutrality does not reflect the diversity of the Botswana population, which in addition to the Tswana majority comprises other tribes such as the San, Yei, Ikalanga and Ovahero and people of European, Asian and mixed ancestry (ISS 2008). It should be noted that in September 2007 Botswana voted in favour of the UN Declaration on the Rights of Indigenous Peoples, which provides a set of principles for treatment of indigenous peoples. This may be an indication of a policy change in the country.

Right to life, liberty and security of persons

Although international human rights law does not prohibit the death penalty as such, there is a strong global movement for abolishing capital punishment. In 2007 the UN General Assembly adopted a resolution calling for a moratorium on the death penalty, and many African countries have now abolished it outright or have frozen executions.

Human rights law also prohibits the use of torture and other cruel and inhumane treatments.[10] But almost all of the ECA country reports include allegations of torture and other abuses, particularly by law enforcement officials. They also report that perpetrators of torture often enjoy immunity and are not punished for their conduct.

The country reports cite arbitrary arrests and detention, poor and overcrowded prisons and a significant percentage of detainees who have never been charged with any offences or tried and convicted. In Mauritius, despite a generally favourable perception about the state of human rights, there were reports of abuse of power by the police.

The ECA Kenya country report highlights congestion and poor health conditions in prison facilities as the cause of 631 deaths in 1997 and 563 deaths in 1998 (ECA 2007b). The report notes that while magistrates and judges have the power to visit and inspect prisons at any time as part of their duties, they rarely do so. The expert panel addressed the question of police respect for life and political rights. While 1% of the experts on the panel said that the police always respect these rights, 17% held the view that they usually respect the rights, 41% stated they sometimes

There is a strong belief that acknowledging minority rights and issues of discrimination would have a negative impact on national unity

respect the rights, 33% claimed the police rarely respect the rights and 8% were categorical that they never respected these rights.

Kenyan law provides for the protection of suspects or prisoners from abuse and requires that investigations of allegations made against police officers and that findings of abuse be submitted to the attorney general. The Kenya National Human Rights Commission has taken steps to raise human rights awareness in the police and other law enforcement institutions. The Commission is also facilitating forums that engage police, civil society and citizens on human rights issues. And it has put posters in police stations listing the human rights of the suspects. The Prisons Department is similarly opening up by allowing relatives and lawyers access to prisoners and allowing the media to talk to prisoners. Finally, attempts are being made to improve the integrity, competence and effectiveness of prosecutors.

In South Africa the Independent Complaints Directorate, established within the Department of Safety and Security and specifically mandated to promote "proper police conduct", received a total of 5,119 complaints of police misconduct in 2005/06, of which 621 were deaths. Of all the cases reported during this period, 93% were resolved. Of the criminal offences reported, 43% related to assaults on suspects.

In Senegal at the end of 2003, 5,887 prisoners were incarcerated in a facility meant for 2,972 persons—a 98% overcrowding rate. There was

one mattress for five people, one hospital bed for 249 prisoners and no statistics on prison mortality. In Namibia the prison system is characterized by unlawful killings, torture, beatings and abuse of criminal suspects by the security forces. The report also cites overcrowding in the prisons, prolonged pretrial detentions and long delays in trials.

The majority of complaints registered by the Uganda Human Rights Commission involved the police, the army or intelligence organisations. Others were against individuals, companies and local governments. The majority of violations were torture and cruel and inhuman treatment. Of the cases reported to the Commission in 2004, 78.3% of the charges of torture were proved true. Torture by state agents included intelligence bodies such as the Internal Security Organisation (ISO) and the Office of the Chief of Military Intelligence (CMI), but the army was the biggest culprit. Between 2000 and 2004 there was an increase in cases of torture reported to the UNHRC from 7.9% to 21.2%. The report claims that during elections the police, army and intelligence openly sided with the ruling party (UNICEF 2003; 2004).

Only in five countries—Benin, Botswana, Cape Verde, Djibouti and Mauritius—did most of the consulted experts regard their police services positively as always or usually respecting human rights. The situation is quite bleak in other countries (figure 6.2).

In most countries the monitoring and reporting of human rights violations

> In 2007 the UN General Assembly adopted a resolution calling for a moratorium on the death penalty, and many African countries have now abolished it outright or have frozen executions

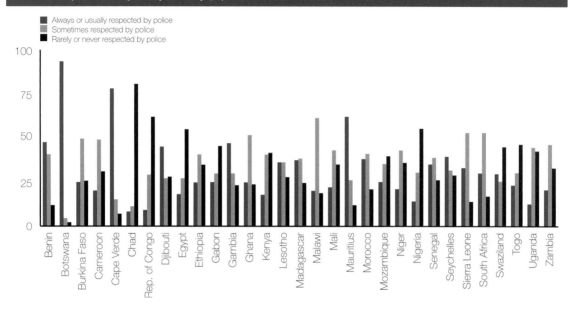

Figure 6.2 Expert opinion on police respect for human rights

Share of experts surveyed, by country (%)

Legend:
- Always or usually respected by police
- Sometimes respected by police
- Rarely or never respected by police

Source: ECA survey of experts 2007.

by civil society organisations (CSOs) is very poor, due partly to the limited space provided for CSOs to perform this function. Human rights monitoring is a sensitive area for most governments, and they prefer to shield civil society from the information. Further, CSOs lack the capacity to monitor and report rights' violations. Only in Botswana, Cape Verde, Senegal and Sierra Leone did most of the experts agree that CSOs regularly monitor and report human rights violations. In a majority of the project countries most of the experts believed that CSOs rarely or never monitor and report human rights violations, especially those by the police.

Dealing with the police in Africa is perceived as risky. There are profound reasons why the average person keeps a distance from the police. The legacy of the police as a tool for colonial repression has not faded, and the police force is still largely perceived as a tool for repression. Structurally, the services of police are closely linked to the governance style in the country: the more democratic a country is, the more people-centered the police are. African countries have laws that on their face convey the police as an institution to protect citizens and their property, and some countries are making bold efforts to translate that vision into reality and end human rights violations. In other countries the police still act brutally, sustaining fear rather than alleviating it. Police officers in some

African countries have continued to commit human rights violations—unlawful killings, torture or other ill treatments—with impunity. As a consequence, the police still have a negative public profile in many countries.

Freedom of religion and belief, expression, association and peaceful assembly

The right of freedom of opinion and expression and the related rights of freedom of association and assembly are fundamental human rights. They contribute to the accountability of government, effective policies and participation in decision making. Limiting them undermines democracy and good governance. The constitutions of most African countries contain guarantees of freedom of association, echoing the African Charter on Human and Peoples' Rights, which provides for freedom of expression and opinion, freedom of association, the right of assembly and the right to participate in political life.

Direct and indirect censorship is one way to interfere with freedom of expression and opinion (Human Rights Council 2008). Administrative regulations such as media licensing and taxation can be used to create an environment of self-censorship in which the media shuns criticism of the authorities. In some cases the renewal of licenses has been used to wield power over editorial content, often with the threat of being shut down.

The media also faces physical threats. Worldwide between 2002 and 2007 there were 67 reported kidnappings of journalists, over 1,500 physical attacks and nearly 80 killings (Reporters Without Borders 2008). The danger to the media is particularly heightened during armed conflicts. United Nations Security Council Resolution 1738 (2006) expressed deep concern "at the frequency of acts of violence in many parts of the world against journalists, media professionals and associated personnel in armed conflict". It is especially during elections, public crises and states of emergency that acts of state brutality are perpetrated against media workers.

Prosecution of media professionals or ordinary citizens on charges of defamation, libel or slander is another form of control and harassment. The purpose of defamation laws is to protect a person against a false statement that could damage one's reputation (UN 1948). But the defamation laws are strictly limited to situations clearly established by law and for aims that are recognized as lawful, and their use must be proportional to the nature of the offending statement.

Counter-terrorism laws have been used to restrict freedom of expression and opinion and the right to peaceful assembly and freedom of association. The UN Security Council has stated that restrictions on freedom of expression must be in accordance with article 19(3)(b) of the ICCPR, provided by law and must be necessary "for the protection of national security and public order" (United Nations Security Council 2005).

> **The constitutions of most African countries contain guarantees of freedom of association, echoing the African Charter on Human and Peoples' Rights**

The country reports show both progress and setbacks on political rights, dissent and freedom of association. In several countries political space has increased, with political parties enjoying significantly more freedom. The reports also indicate that there is greater freedom of speech and association. But there have been incidences when demonstrations have been violently dispersed and organisers beaten and arrested. Freedom of association is guaranteed in most constitutions, but it is constrained and severely limited in the context of political campaigns.

In Uganda press laws have been made less repressive through constant challenges in the Constitutional Court. But the state maintains control of journalists through other means—by closing down newspapers and radio stations, usually illegally, and refusing or withdrawing advertisements from newspapers and radio and TV stations to express its displeasure over critical reports. Uganda operates within an environment where media rights are frequently violated by the government or ruling party but with some protection from the courts or in an environment where freedom of expression is under constant threat by the government's oppressive and restrictive press laws (ECA 2007d).

Namibia has one of the most favourable, media-friendly constitutions in the region. But in Seychelles the government holds a near monopoly of the media and uses license fees, registration requirements and libel laws to restrict freedom of the press.

Malawi has seen cases of executive interference with freedom of the press: the Malawi Communications Authority seized transmission equipment, threatened to revoke licenses and harassed journalists (Media Institute of South Africa 2006). In Nigeria a journalist, Mike Gbenga Aruleba, was arrested after hosting a discussion critical of the purchase of a new presidential jet. Incidences of the executive using security forces and other instruments of state against those considered defiant are still rampant in many African countries.

Economic, social and cultural rights

In 1981 the African Charter on Human and Peoples' Rights (OAU 1981) adopted an integrated vision of human rights that gives equal eminence to economic, social and cultural rights and civil and political rights.[11] The interdependence and indivisibility of human rights have been repeatedly reaffirmed by the international community since the end of the Cold War, most notably at the Vienna World Conference in 1993 and at the 2000 and 2005 Summits of Heads of State and Government.[12]

Many governments are reluctant to acknowledge economic, cultural and social rights, refusing to promote and protect them or provide remedies for their violations. One exception to the rule is South Africa, where the Constitutional Court has adopted a progressive approach to the advancement of social and economic rights litigation. The Committee on Economic,

> **Many governments are reluctant to acknowledge economic, cultural and social rights, refusing to promote and protect them or provide remedies for their violations**

Social and Cultural Rights has noted that the full achievement of human rights cannot be realised as a mere byproduct, or fortuitous consequence, of some other developments, no matter how positive. Ensuring respect for those rights requires targeted policies and vigilance. In a statement to the World Conference on Human Rights, the Committee on Economic, Social and Cultural Rights stated:

> [J]ust as carefully targeted policies and unremitting vigilance are necessary to ensure that respect for civil and political rights will follow from, for example, the holding of free and fair elections or from the introduction or restoration of an essentially democratic system of government, so too is it essential that specific policies and programmes be devised and implemented by

any government which aims to ensure the respect of economic, social and cultural rights of its citizens (UNDP 2000).

The enjoyment of social, economic and cultural rights—the right to health, education, a clean environment, food, water and development—is still a distant dream for most Africans, the majority of whom remain under the poverty line despite the universal endorsement of the Millennium Development Goals and other development plans such as New Partnership for Africa's Development (NEPAD). Most African countries still do not consider social, economic and cultural rights as justiciable, even though they are parties to the African Charter on Human and Peoples' Rights, which makes these rights justiciable. Constitutional provisions of socioeconomic rights in Nigeria, Zambia, Gambia and Ghana are contained in the Directive Principles of State Policy, which makes those rights nonjusticable. On the contrary, South Africa, Senegal, Egypt and Malawi have made progress by making the rights to health, food, education and clean water justiciable.

Unequal access to natural resources, including land, undermines socioeconomic and cultural rights in Africa. Access to natural resources is also a root cause of most conflicts on the continent. The alarming scale of corruption and the low level of investment in social services in many African countries are further impediments to the enjoyment of socioeconomic and cultural rights.

Box 6.2 Political and civil rights versus economic, social and cultural rights

The unnatural cleavage that took place decades ago when the full, interconnected span of rights set out in the Universal Declaration of Human Rights were split into supposedly separate collections of civil and political rights, on the one hand, and economic, social and cultural rights, on the other, has done great damage in erecting quite false perceptions of hierarchies of rights. In the area of justiciability of rights, particularly, the notion of economic, social and cultural rights as essentially aspirational, in contrast to the "hard law" civil and political rights, has proven especially difficult to undo. At the national level, some judiciaries have been bolder than others in this area, while at the international level, discussions continue to proceed slowly on the elaboration of an Optional Protocol permitting individual complaints for violations of the International Covenant on Economic, Social and Cultural Rights.

Source: Arbour 2008.

The measures a state can take to promote economic, social and cultural rights may not require as many resources as once feared. The justiciability of these rights is not as serious a problem as many governments report. It is a social demand that places responsibility on the state to allocate its scarce resources judiciously and cater to its own citizens for the overall goal of national development.

Beyond the challenges of recognizing economic, social and cultural rights as legally enforceable, many countries have not created frameworks to advance socioeconomic rights. Deepening poverty and a widening gap between the rich and poor make the realization of economic, social and cultural rights more daunting.

Gender equality and human rights
The normative framework for women's rights in Africa is defined in the International Convention on the Elimination of all Forms of Discrimination Against Women (CEDAW) and the Protocol to the African Charter on Human and People's Rights on the Rights of Women in Africa (ACHPR 2003). Dubbed the "African CEDAW", the Protocol is modeled on the Convention and adopts a progressive position on many women's rights issues and goes even further than CEDAW in addressing the problem of violence against women. Article 14 on reproductive rights, which recognizes a woman's right to control her own fertility and to decide on the number and spacing of children, is another progressive, albeit controversial, provision.

The Protocol also provides, for the first time in human rights law, a limited right to abortion in cases of sexual assault, rape, incest and where the continuation of the pregnancy would endanger the health of the mother or the foetus. In a continent where it is estimated that more than 4 million illegal abortions are carried out annually, African states have recognized that eliminating discrimination against women may involve providing services needed only by women.

Like CEDAW and the other African human rights instruments, the Protocol covers civil and political as well as economic, social and cultural rights. In addition to the Protocol, the Constitutive Act of the African Union also evidences a commitment to gender equality (African Union 2002). But as the CEDAW Committee has observed, a "purely formal legal or programmatic approach is not sufficient to achieve women's *de facto* equality with men". In addition, the Convention requires that women be given an equal start and that they be empowered by an enabling environment to achieve equality of results. It is not enough to guarantee treatment that is identical to that of men. Rather, biological as well as socially and culturally constructed differences between men and women must be taken into account. Under certain circumstances, nonidentical treatment of women and men will be required in order to address such differences. Pursuit of the goal of substantive equality also calls for an effective strategy aimed at overcoming underrepresentation of women and a redistribution of

> *African states have recognized that eliminating discrimination against women may involve providing services needed only by women*

resources and power between men and women.

While the Protocol has generally been welcomed as a progressive instrument, critics point to a number of areas where it falls short of, and even reverses, international trends. Its broad definition of discrimination as well as article 8 take the unequivocal position that "men and women are equal before the law and shall have the right to equal protection and benefit of the law". State parties are expected to strive for equality of opportunity as well as achieve the result (substantive equality). Yet this understanding of equality is not found throughout the Protocol. With respect to women's right to property upon death or divorce, for instance, articles 7 and 21 of the Protocol provide for an "equitable sharing" of marital or inheritance property, respectively. Equitable can be a lower standard and requirement than equality.

Article 6(h) on the nationality of children has been criticized for watering down international standards. It provides that "a woman and a man shall have equal rights with respect to the nationality of their children *except where this is contrary to a provision in national legislation or is contrary to national security interests*" (emphasis added). This provision is not consistent with the notion of nondiscrimination as defined in the Protocol and CEDAW, nor does it deal with polygamy.

Many countries place a premium on redressing gender inequality. The Solemn Declaration on Gender

> **Many countries place a premium on redressing gender inequality. The Solemn Declaration on Gender Equality adopted by the African Union in 2004 underscores this goal**

Equality adopted by the African Union in 2004 underscores this goal. The African Union's example of allocating 50% of senior positions in the AU Commission to women has been replicated in several countries.

Most of the countries covered in this report have ratified the Protocol to the African Charter. Several have entered reservations to critical provisions of the Protocol almost parallel to those in CEDAW. The Committee on the Elimination of Discrimination against women has on several occasions stated that the most common reservations—to articles 2 (state obligations), 9 (nationality), 15 (equality and freedom of movement) and 16 (marriage and family relations)—are contrary to the object and purpose of the Convention and therefore impermissible. The committee has also spoken out against broad and imprecise reservations.

The constitutions of Ethiopia, Ghana, Nigeria and South Africa contain explicit provisions that outlaw discrimination on grounds of sex or gender. These constitutions also place nondiscrimination above custom, culture or religion. The constitutions of Ethiopia and Ghana also have provisions on a woman's right to be free from discrimination and other gender-related harmful practices. A few constitutions, while guaranteeing equality before the law, are silent on the relation between potentially discriminatory customary or religious laws and the nondiscrimination provision (Nzegwu 2001).

On the other hand, the Constitutions of Botswana, Zambia and

Zimbabwe[13] exclude customary personal laws from the reach of the nondiscrimination provision, meaning in effect that discrimination against women on matters of personal status law is permitted.[14] In Kenya the constitution was amended in 1997 to outlaw discrimination on the basis of sex, but section 82(4) still permits discrimination with respect to adoption, marriage, divorce, burial and devolution of property.

On the issue of polygamy, the Protocol provides that "[m]onogamy is encouraged as the preferred form of marriage and that the rights of women in marriage and family, including in polygamous marital relationships are promoted and protected".[15] In its general comment 28 on equality between men and women, the Human Rights Committee stated: "Polygamy violates the dignity of women. It is an inadmissible discrimination against women. Consequently, it should be definitely abolished wherever it continues to exist" (Human Rights Committee 2000). But the regional systems are less clear, and many states in Africa, Asia and the Arab region continue to recognise polygamy, and some lodged reservations to CEDAW in order to retain personal laws sanctioning polygamy.

The Protocol acknowledges the need to tackle both de jure and de facto discrimination and to challenge gender stereotypes. It defines discrimination against women as "any distinction, exclusion or restriction or any differential treatment based on sex and whose objectives or effects compromise or destroy the recognition, enjoyment or the exercise by women, regardless of their marital status, of human rights and fundamental freedoms in all spheres of life" (AU 2003, article 1(f)).

The Protocol acknowledges that "women in Africa still continue to be victims of discrimination and harmful practices," despite the widespread ratification of the African Charter and several international human rights instruments. Although CEDAW obliges state parties to abolish existing laws, regulations and customs and practices that constitute discrimination against women, many countries still have laws that directly discriminate (AU 2003). In its concluding observations to Uganda's report, for example, CEDAW noted that although article 33(5) of the Constitution "prohibits laws, customs, or traditions which are against the dignity, welfare or interest of women, there were still legislations, customary laws and practices on inheritance, land ownership, widow inheritance, polygamy, forced marriage, bride price, guardianship of children and the definition of adultery that discriminate against women and conflict with the Constitution and the Convention."

According to CEDAW country reports, de jure discrimination against women remains in many areas. In some countries pregnant girls are excluded from school while the boys responsible are not affected, thus unfairly curtaining the girl's right to education and reducing her life chances (CEDAW 2006). In

‘ *De jure discrimination against women remains in many areas*

Madagascar the lawful age of marriage is 17 for men and 14 for girls, presumably because women mature earlier. In Burkina Faso the minimum age of marriage for a girl is 17, and 20 for boys. Early marriage generally curtails education, which in turn hampers other opportunities and might also have health consequences for girls. It also raises issues about the girl's legal capacity to give consent. The UN treaty bodies have identified early marriage as a human rights violation and have urged governments to amend their laws to raise the minimum age of marriage to 18 years for both boys and girls.

Kenya and Nigeria restrict a woman's right to pass her nationality to her spouse and children. Section 26 of the Nigerian 1999 Constitution stipulates that a foreign man who marries a Nigerian woman does not automatically acquire Nigerian citizenship. In Egypt a woman needs her husband's permission to obtain a passport and travel. In Cameroon a husband has the right to determine whether his wife works, what she may study and what type of work she can do.

In South Africa the constitution guarantees the rights of women. While it allows the option of applying customary law, customary law does not supercede constitutional rights. South Africa reports one of the better indicators for addressing gender equality: a high number of women hold important political positions. Women hold 12 of 28 cabinet positions, the vice-presidency and 131 seats in the national assembly. Strong women's organisations have consistently challenged

patriarchal attitudes, and creation of the constitutionally mandated Commission on Gender Equality has been an important step. But the country report also cites de facto discrimination on issues surrounding marriage, divorce, inheritance, violence and property rights.

Violence against women is a growing problem in Africa. There are many reported cases of violence in the home, including wife beating and what amounts to rape. The legal systems of Kenya, Ghana, Ethiopia and Nigeria permit nonconsensual sex in marriage. South Africa has one of the highest rates of sexual abuse, and the government has acknowledged that domestic violence and rape, both criminal offences, are serious problems. But cases are mostly underreported, and police response is inadequate. The Sexual Offences and Related Matters Amendment Bill of 2007 acknowledges the high incidence of sexual offenses and broadens the definition of rape, and 52 specialized courts for sexual offenses have been established.

The Namibian government has taken a strong stand against rampant cases of violence against women and children. Domestic violence, characterized by widespread beatings and rape, is one of the most serious violations of women's rights. The country's Combating of Rape Act is one of the most advanced in the world. It adopts a gender-neutral definition of rape, is sensitive to the needs of rape victims, provides greater protection of privacy and has procedures to facilitate testimony of victims without compromising their privacy.

‘ *Violence against women is a growing problem in Africa*

In Uganda female applicants to Makerere University are given an additional 1.5 points to their scores to enable them to have a slight edge in admission. Uganda also has set aside seats for women in the national parliament. Such affirmative actions are consistent with CEDAW, which in article 9 calls on states to take "specific positive action . . . through affirmative action, enabling legislation and other measures" to ensure that women can participate without discrimination in elections and public life (Tamale 1995). Women in Uganda have also been granted the right of consent to land sales and to the transfer of matrimonial homes.

But the ECA Uganda country report indicates that there are no programmes to specifically address the rights of women. Although the country's Poverty Elimination Action Plan (the name given to Uganda's Poverty Reduction Strategy Paper) and Program for the Modernisation of Agriculture refer to the problem of gender inequality, both view it primarily through the perspective of economic growth and efficiency in production rather than as a right of development. None of these programmes fundamentally challenge the traditional patriarchal relations.

The Protocol to the African Charter on Human and People's Rights on the Rights of Women in Africa requires states to report to the African Union in the first year of its entry into force, then every four years. Only eight states have so far reported. In its 21-year history the African Commission on Human

Rights, mandated to entertain individual complaints and investigate "grave and systematic" breaches of human rights, has not heard a complaint related to discrimination against women.

Overall, public perception in the surveyed countries indicates fairly low confidence in the institutional mechanisms for reporting women's rights. In Kenya 8% of the respondents said the system was effective, 34% were of the view that it is sometimes effective, 36% noted it is rarely effective, and 21% indicated that it was ineffective. In regard to violence against women, 1% said reported cases are always acted upon, 10% noted they were usually acted upon, 36% held the view they were sometimes acted upon, 47% said they are acted upon promptly only in high-profile cases, and 5% were categorical that they are never acted upon. The trend is similar in most of the countries covered by this report.

Rights of the child

The 1990 African Charter on the Rights and Welfare of the Child has been ratified by 19 countries out of the 35 covered in this report (OAU 1990). The Charter provisions parallel those of the UN Convention on the Rights of the Child, which has been ratified by 193 states and is the most widely ratified international human rights treaty. Only the United States and Somalia have not ratified the UN Convention (the United States signed in 1995, Somalia in 2002). The Charter emphasizes the principles of nondiscrimination and equal protection before the law and highlights the harmful social and

> ' *There is fairly low confidence in the institutional mechanisms for reporting women's rights*

cultural practices that prevent children from enjoying their rights, in particular discrimination experienced by girls. It requires states to take appropriate steps to eliminate customary practices that discriminate on grounds of gender. In particular, it proscribes child marriage and sets the minimum age of marriage at 18 years for both sexes.

But many shortcomings remain in realizing the rights of the child. In many countries provisions governing children's rights are scattered under different laws, from penal codes to legislation on adoption, education, social welfare and divorce and separation proceedings (Doek 2007). This, together with the pluralist nature of legal systems in the region where common and civil law coexist with customary and religious law, has a negative impact on implementing children's rights. Nine of the 13 countries surveyed—Botswana, Kenya, Lesotho, Madagascar, Malawi, Mozambique, Namibia, South Africa and Uganda—have undertaken comprehensive reviews of their legal systems and have either enacted or drafted a comprehensive act for children's rights or grouped their rights into thematic legislation, such as child justice and child welfare (Doek 2007). This is a significant development, but needs to be viewed as an ongoing process that continually addresses new or emerging issues and gaps in law and practice.

Under the African Charter and the UN Convention a child is anyone under age 18. But some countries are inconsistent in setting minimum legal ages, varying them for criminal responsibility, sexual consent and marriage. As a result, children continue to suffer from inconsistent and ineffective legal protection. Nine of the 13 surveyed countries—Angola, Burundi, Ethiopia, Mozambique, Namibia, Swaziland, Tanzania and Zimbabwe—have no official definition of a child in their legislation or constitution.

In most cases countries have both constitutional and legislative provisions that formally protect children from torture or inhuman and degrading treatment. They also prohibit harmful traditional practices, such as female genital mutilation and early marriage. But this formal protection is contradicted by the fact that none of the countries in this review prohibits corporal punishment in the home, schools or other institutions. In fact, many countries have provisions in their law that recognize corporal punishment as an acceptable form of discipline. Some countries do prohibit corporal punishment in schools or other institutions, or as a penal sanction, but none prohibit its use in the home. South Africa's proposed amendment to the Children's Act would be the first in the region to specifically prohibit the use of corporal punishment on children in any setting.

The United Nations Study on Violence against Children recommended that states prohibit all forms of violence against children, including early and forced marriages. In Ethiopia, Mozambique and Uganda half of all women married are below the age of 18. The legal age of marriage

> **Nine of the 13 countries surveyed have either enacted or drafted a comprehensive act for children's rights or grouped their rights into thematic legislation**

is 16 in Zimbabwe and 15 in Tanzania and South Africa.

All countries in Africa have provisions in their constitution or in legislation to protect children from economic exploitation and work that is hazardous or likely to impede their education. All of the countries in this study have ratified the International Labour Organisation's Convention on the Worst Forms of Child Labour. But not all of them apply the recommended minimum age of 15 years for employment of children, nor do they all have rules on the kind of work children can participate in or conditions for their employment. Even where there are standards for children's work, there is inadequate monitoring to ensure implementation of these standards. Zimbabwe has the lowest minimum age for employment, at 12 years, and Zambia the highest, at 18. Botswana's constitution leaves open the possibility of employing children under the age of 12 in certain industries and does not outlaw their employment even if it is proved to be hazardous to them.

The African Committee on the Rights and the Welfare of the Child has indicated that the age at which compulsory education ends should be the age for access to full-time employment. Only in Namibia is the minimum age for employment the same as the age at which children complete their basic education. In six of the countries reviewed there is a gap of one to four years. In Burundi and Rwanda the gap is four years. It is three years in Madagascar, two years in Kenya and Tanzania and one year in Comoros.

There is a clear disparity between legal and policy provisions and the situation on the ground. In its second report to the Committee on the Rights of the Child Ethiopia stated that 83% of children ages 5–14 years are engaged in a productive activity (including paid work and unpaid domestic labour on farms) or the performance of household chores. In the 15–17 year cohort the proportion rises to 97%. More worrying is that 62% of children ages 10–14 and 39% of children ages 5–9 are engaged in at least one type of employment besides household chores. Such disconnection between formal protection and the reality on the ground can be attributed primarily to poverty exacerbated by user fees for basic health and education services. Poverty means that children need to work, either because they are fending for themselves or to contribute to a meagre family income.

In 2006 the UN estimated that worldwide more than 250,000 children were involved in armed conflict in government armed forces, government militias or armed opposition groups; 120,000 of these children were in Africa. The most affected African countries are Angola, Burundi, Mozambique, Rwanda and Uganda. The CRC requires states to ensure that children under 15 years of age do not take a direct part in hostilities and to give priority to recruiting the oldest among those between 15 and 18. The African Charter is more comprehensive in prohibiting involvement of children under age 18 in armed conflict. In 2000 the Optional Protocol to the Convention on the Rights of the Child on the

> ❛ *All countries in Africa have provisions to protect children from economic exploitation and work that is hazardous or likely to impede their education*

Involvement of Children in Armed Conflict was adopted, seeking to strengthen standards, including raising the age for conscription to 18.[16]

A major obstacle to enforcing minimum ages for conscription is one that spans all other protective ages for children—lack of birth registration. Without formal birth registration it is difficult to ascertain the age of children. The CRC expressed concern, for example, about possible gaps in Uganda's recruitment process due to lack of birth registration. A similar concern has been expressed about Zambia's apparent age for voluntary recruitment, noting that "less than 10% of children were registered at birth in 1999, even less in rural areas" (CRC 2003). The lack of universal and compulsory birth registration plagues many countries in this review.

The African Charter on the Rights and the Welfare of the Child and the CRC have committees to monitor their implementation by examining state party reports. The African Committee of Experts on the Rights and Welfare of the Child began meeting in 2001, but to date it has received only four state reports. Rwanda is the only country in this review to have submitted regular reports. The African Committee can entertain a complaint from anyone in matters relating to the Charter. For this reason it is stronger than its CRC counterpart. Nonetheless, a critical flaw of the African Committee is that its reports can only be published upon the approval and scrutiny of member states, which undermines the independent monitoring role it is supposed to play.

Without widespread dissemination and publication of CRC reports and the concluding observations of the Committee on the Rights of the Child, there can only be limited feedback from citizens. For most countries in this review, alternative reports were submitted by NGOs, as provided for under article 45 of the CRC. These reports supplement state reports and shed light on gaps, inconsistencies and other issues that governments have avoided. Most states in this review have not yet submitted a second or subsequent report that addresses specific issues raised by the CRC Committee in their concluding observations, such as recommendations for changes in law and policy.

At the national level mechanisms for monitoring and reporting are either lacking or insufficient. In Tanzania the Child Labour Unit was established to inspect and prosecute cases, but it is underfunded and understaffed. Despite rampant child labour problems, it has only managed a few prosecutions and has been ineffective in coordinating with other stakeholders to combat child labour. The problem is exacerbated by lack of clarity about where institutional responsibility lies: the Ministry for Women and Children's Affairs deals with children's rights, but monitoring and implementation of child labour legislation lies with the Ministry for Labour and Youth.

Human rights and the global security order

Human rights law has sought to strike a balance between the public interest in security and stability, on the one hand, and fundamental rights and freedoms on the other. Article 51 of the International Covenant on Civil and Political Rights and article 27(2) of the African Charter on Human and Peoples' Rights acknowledge that human rights advocates should be cognizant of legitimate security interests. According to article 27(2) of the African Charter, its rights "shall be exercised with due regard to the rights of others, collective security, morality and common interest".

Recent efforts at tackling terrorist threats have challenged this balance. Among the countries examined in this report there are cases in which the pursuit of counter-terrorism has degraded human rights. A key challenge is to define terrorism. In Egypt it is defined by the penal code as:

> any use of force or violence or threat or intimidation to which the perpetrator resorts in order to carry out an individual or collective criminal plan aimed at disturbing the peace or jeopardizing the safety and security of society and which is of such a nature as to create harm or create fear in persons or imperil lives, freedom or security; harm the environment; damage or take possession of communications; prevent or impede public authorities in the performance of their work; or thwart the application of the Constitution or of laws and regulations (EIPR 2006).

The Human Rights Committee has questioned this broad definition, which clearly seems to cover all kinds of activities and potential offenses (UN Human Rights Committee 2007).

Counterterrorism efforts often encompass far-reaching restrictions on civil liberties, crackdowns against political opponents, pervasive secrecy, arbitrary arrest and detention for extended periods. Some governments have used incommunicado detention, abused state of emergency laws, restricted due process rights and used the death penalty and torture (Scheinin 2007). A debate has been going on in the United States about whether waterboarding is a legal tool or illegal torture.

Such extreme measures have been justified by the threat terrorism poses to global peace and security. Some have equated the threat of terrorism to national emergencies that can trigger wide-ranging government powers and restrictions on fundamental rights and freedoms. Article 4 of the ICCPR allows for derogation of certain human rights during states of emergency. The African Charter, on the other hand, does not provide for derogations. Yet certain rights—the right to life; freedom of thought, conscience and religion; freedom from torture and cruel, inhuman or degrading treatment or punishment—cannot be derogated under any circumstances according to the ICCPR. In addition to the nonderogable rights in article 4 of the ICCPR, international law imposes very strict requirements that must be met if individual rights are to be restricted during a state of emergency: individuals must always be treated with respect and

Recent efforts at tackling terrorist threats have challenged the balance between rights and security

dignity, abductions and unacknowledged detentions are strictly prohibited and the right to a fair trial must be preserved (UN Human Rights Committee 2001).

The African Commission on Human and Peoples' Rights has also developed detailed principles for states of emergency. In several cases from Nigeria involving the detention of individuals under the state security laws and their trials by special tribunals, the Commission held that the authorities committed serious human rights violations (ACHPR 1998b). All the victims were arrested and kept in detention for a lengthy period under the State Security (Detention of Persons) Act of 1984 and State Security (Detention of Persons) Amended Decree No. 14 (1994), which stipulate that the government can detain people without charge for as long as three months in the first instance without the right to judicial recourse. The Commission found that decree to be a prima facie violation of the right not to be arbitrarily arrested or detained found in article 6 of the African Charter on Human and Peoples' Rights (ACHPR 1998a).

Among the countries reviewed for this report, Egypt has had the longest state of emergency, lasting since 1981.[17] Measures under the state of emergency in Egypt have intensified since 9/11 to include arrest and detention at will without trial for extended periods; prosecution of civilians in military or exceptional state security courts; prohibition of strikes, demonstrations and public meetings; censorship of newspapers

and shutting down of publishing houses. A new antiterrorism law proposed since 2006 seeks to amend the constitution to suspend constitutional protections against detention, house and body searches or invasion of private communication. And it would allow cases to be sent to military courts and other exceptional tribunals.

Many African countries have enacted draconian antiterrorism laws. In view of the fragility of democracy and human rights in many of the countries, this is a dangerous trend that can erode the tentative gains of the last decade. Individual liberties need not be sacrificed to attain security. On the contrary, violations of human rights themselves can contribute to insecurity and instability. The fight against terrorism cannot become an excuse to promote autocracy and dictatorship and undermine peoples' rights and freedoms.

Perceptions of the state of human rights and the rule of law

Perceptions vary among the public and experts about the state of human rights in Africa. The ECA country reports are consistent in showing some progress but with setbacks. The Kenya country report described significant improvements in the human rights situation in the country with the advent of the National Rainbow Coalition (NARC) government—improvements in voter registration, freer and more robust media and increased political participation (ECA 2007b). But elections at the end of 2007 were marred by violence.

'*Perceptions vary among the public and experts about the state of human rights in Africa. The ECA country reports are consistent in showing some progress but with setbacks*

Across project countries the general perception is that the government doesn't usually take prompt and effective actions against human rights violations and in some cases the government itself is culpable in rights violations of its citizens. Only in Botswana and Seychelles did a majority of the experts credit the government with always or usually taking prompt actions against human rights violations. In Cape Verde, Ghana, Malawi, Mauritius, Morocco, South Africa and Zambia the experts agreed that the government sometimes takes prompt actions. The poor performers according to the experts surveyed were Burkina Faso, Cameroon, Djibouti, Egypt, Kenya, Lesotho, Madagascar, Mali, Niger, Nigeria,

Senegal, Sierra Leone, Swaziland, Togo and Uganda, where the experts rated their governments as rarely or never taking prompt action on human rights violations.

In Burkina Faso, Chad, Republic of Congo, Egypt, Ethiopia, Madagascar, Mali, Niger, Nigeria, Togo and Uganda more than 50% of the expert respondents were of the view that human rights violations are either rarely or never promptly acted upon by state institutions.

While government respect for human rights may have improved, the experts perceive that there are still serious gaps and more needs to be done by the state (figure 6.3). Only in Benin, Botswana, Cape

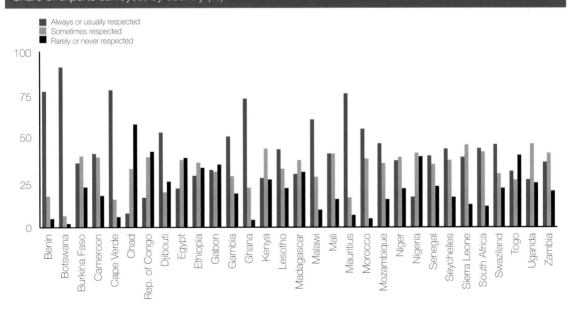

Figure 6.3 Expert opinion on government respect for human rights

Share of experts surveyed, by country (%)

Legend:
- Always or usually respected
- Sometimes respected
- Rarely or never respected

Source: ECA survey of experts 2007.

Verde, Ghana, Mali, Morocco, Mozambique and Seychelles did over half of the expert panel respondents hold the opinion that the government always or usually respects human rights. The opinion was highly negative in Chad, Egypt, Togo, Madagascar, Ethiopia and Republic of Congo.

Conclusion: closing implementation gaps and using indigenous knowledge

In Africa there are many recommendations and normative frameworks for protecting human rights and the rule of law. The challenge confronting African countries is to translate its pledges to protect human rights into realities for the ordinary African. In the field of human rights, numerous recommendations await implementation. Among them:

- The recommendations in chapter 6, "Human rights and rule of law," in *African Governance Report 2005* (UNECA 2005).

- The 2003 Kigali Declaration on the protection and promotion of human and peoples' rights.

- The outcome document of the 2005 UN World Summit and the 2006 declaration jointly signed by the UN Secretary-General and the chairperson of the AU Commission on cooperation between the two institutions.

The first challenge is to retrieve those recommendations and implement them.

African countries must build justice systems that reconcile people instead of deepening social barriers. There should be cross-fertilization between modern and traditional justice systems. Judges and their auxiliaries need to be trained to handle violence against women and children and to adjudicate human rights cases promptly, for justice delayed is justice denied.

In the field of human rights, several gaps must be filled:

Reporting gaps. State human rights reports provide an assessment of both progress and shortfalls in realizing the rights enshrined in treaties that states have signed. State reports are the starting point for observations and recommendations by UN and African regional bodies. Those observations and recommendations are helpful to states. However, the record of many African countries in preparing their human rights reports has been very poor. Only a few do so. African countries must be encouraged to produce and submit human rights reports regularly to the treaty bodies, which will allow those bodies to know the issues, problems and challenges those countries are facing and how to assist them.

Knowledge gaps. Human rights advocates still tend to focus on civil and political rights and on the state as the sole bearer of responsibility. So long as this perception remains, the value of human rights to Africa's political progress will be limited. It is imperative at the domestic level to promote synergy between various categories of rights and how

> **' The challenge confronting African countries is to translate its pledges to protect human rights into realities for the ordinary African**

indigenous and modern mechanisms for conflict resolution can be complementary. It is equally important to operationalize the right to sustainable development, the right to peace and the right to security.

Enhanced role for CSOs in human rights promotion and protection in Africa. The government must open space for civil society organisations to promote and protect human rights in their countries, including rights of children, women and the physically challenged. An open and democratic environment is essential for the CSOs to perform this function. On their part, CSOs have to strengthen their capacity for investigation, research, analysis and advocacy on human rights issues beyond a purely confrontational approach.

Security gaps, especially in countries in or emerging from armed conflicts. In countries in conflict or just out of conflict, peace and security are often fragile, and personal security and property are threatened. Citizens need protective responses from the state. By bringing the cycle of violence and revenge to an end, closing security gaps can greatly contribute to durable peace and pave the way to sustainable development. The promotion and protection of human rights is a major step toward ensuring durable peace and stability in those countries.

Shortage of resources for national and regional human rights mechanisms. The efficacy of the African human rights system depends largely on the existence of independent and well-funded national and regional bodies.

The African Union and its multilateral and bilateral partners need to allocate adequate resources and give more political support to the African Commission on Human and Peoples' Rights, the African Committee of Experts on the Rights and Welfare of the Child and the upcoming African Court of Justice and Human Rights. Similar support should be given to mechanisms established by regional economic communities to promote and protect human rights. When states ratify human rights treaties, they assume the obligation to implement them.

Notes

1. In 2005, for example, the African Union suspended Mauritania over the military coup that took place in the country.

2. For updated information on ratifications of treaties by countries, see http://untreaty.un.org/English/access.asp.

3. Countries that have signed but not ratified the Convention are Algeria, Benin, Burkina Faso, Burundi, Cape Verde, Central African Republic, Republic of Congo, Côte d'Ivoire, Egypt, Ethiopia, Ghana, Kenya, Liberia, Madagascar, Malawi, Mali, Mauritius, Morocco, Mozambique, Niger, Nigeria, Senegal, Sierra Leone, Sudan and Swaziland.

4. The Paris Principles were defined at the first International Workshop on National Institutions for the Promotion and Protection of Human Rights in Paris 7–9 October 1991 and adopted by Human Rights Commission Resolution 1992/54, 1992, and General Assembly Resolution 48/134, 1993.

'**When states ratify human rights treaties, they assume the obligation to implement them**

5. These include the national human rights institutions of Egypt, Ghana, Kenya, Malawi, Mauritius, Namibia, South Africa, Togo, Uganda and Zambia. The ICC accreditation standards are available at www.nhri.net/htm.

6. Buhari Bello was removed from office by the Obasanjo administration in Nigeria under the pretense that he was being redeployed as a civil servant. Many believed that he was removed because of his critical views on the human rights situation in Africa.

7. The Universal Declaration of Human Rights, from which the core international human rights treaties are drawn and which forms the basis of the bills of rights of many national constitutions, was equally clear, providing in article 1 that, "[a]ll human beings are born free and equal in dignity and rights". Article 2 speaks of the entitlement of all persons to the enjoyment of the rights contained within the Declaration "without distinction of any kind, such as race, colour, sex, language, religion, political or other opinion, national or social origin, property, birth or other status".

8. The 1967 Declaration on the Elimination of All Forms of Discrimination against Women, the Convention on the Elimination of All Forms of Discrimination against Women (1979), the Convention on the Rights of the Child (1989), the Migrant Workers Convention (1990) and the Convention on the Rights of Persons with Disabilities (2006) deal with discrimination in specific contexts.

9. In 2005 the Basarwa successfully challenged the government's 1986 policy of relocating them from the Central Kalahari Game Reserve (CKGR) to settlements outside the reserve. The government accepted and respected the decision of the court, showing government commitment to the rule of law, upholding of human rights and respect for the separation of powers and the integrity of the judiciary. See, in this regard, ECA Botswana Country report 2007, 112.

10. See the UN Convention Against Torture and relevant provisions in the International Covenant on Civil and Political Rights and the African Commission on Human and Peoples' Rights.

11. The preamble to the Charter provides: "Convinced that it is henceforth essential to pay particular attention to the right to development and that civil and political rights cannot be dissociated from economic, social and cultural rights in their conception as well as universality and that the satisfaction of economic, social and cultural rights is a guarantee for the enjoyment of civil and political rights"; and goes on in Part I to enumerate civil, political, economic, social and cultural rights and duties in equal measure.

12. This vision goes back to U.S. President Roosevelt's statement in 1941 about the four interrelated freedoms—freedom of speech and expression, freedom of religious worship, freedom from want, and freedom from fear—necessary to sustain peace in a post–World War II context. See Roosevelt (1941). World conference on Human Rights, June 14–25 1993, Vienna Declaration and Programme of Action, U.N. Doc A/CONF.157/23 (July 12, 1993).

13. Constitution of Botswana, 30 September 1966, s. 15 (4); Constitution of Zambia, 1991 (Act No.1 of 1991), s. 23 94 (c); Constitution of Zimbabwe, 1979 as amended (Zimbabwe Constitution Order SI 1979/1600 of the United Kingdom), art. 23 (3).

14. Note that under the 1969 Vienna Convention on the Law of Treaties "a party may not invoke the provisions of its 101. See CEDAW, "General Recommendation No. 21," (1994) paras. 41, 43, 44 and 48; and CEDAW, "Statement on Reservations," (2000) identifies articles 2 and 16 as the core provisions. See para. 6, Arab Development Report (2006), 191 *et seq.*

15. This was apparently a compromise position agreed to after a long and contested discussion between those opposed to polygamy and others who sought to protect it as an aspect of African tradition.

16. As of 2008, 21 of the 35 African nations have ratified the Optional Protocol.

17. Emergency Law no. 162 of 1958; Law No. 97 of 1992.

References

ACHPR (African Commission on Human and Peoples' Rights). 1981. "African Charter on Human and Peoples' Rights." OAU Doc. CAB/LEG/67/3.

———. 1995. Media Rights Agenda and Constitutional Rights Project Case v. Nigeria. Communication No. 105/93, 128/94, 130/94, 152/96. In *12th Annual Activity Report of the African Commission on Human and Peoples' Rights 1998–1999*. Banjul.

———. 1998a. "Protocol to the African Charter on Human and Peoples' Rights on the Establishment of an African Court on Human Rights and Peoples' Rights." OAU/LEG/AFCHPR/Prot (III)."

———. 1998b. *12th Annual Activity Report of the African Commission on Human and Peoples' Rights 1998-1999*. Banjul.

———. 2003. "Protocol to the African Charter on Human and Peoples' Rights on the Establishment of an African Court on Human Rights and Peoples' Rights on the Rights of Women in Africa." Assembly/AU/Dec 14 (II).

———. 2008. African Commission on Human and Peoples' Rights. www.achpr.org.

African Union. 2002. "Constitutive Act of the African Union." OAU Doc. CAB/LEG/23.25.

———. 2006. "Draft Protocol on the Statute of the African Court of Justice and Human Rights." AU Doc. EX.CL/253 (IX).

Arbour, Louise (UN High Commissioner for Human Rights). 2008. Speech at the Opening of the Judicial Year of the European Court of Human Rights, Strasbourg, January 2008.

Committee on the Elimination of Racial Discrimination. 2005. "Concluding Observations of the Committee on the Elimination of Racial Discrimination." CERD/C/ZMB/CO/16. Geneva: CERD.

CRC (Committee on the Rights of the Child). 2003. "Concluding Observations of the Committee on the Rights of the Child." CRC/C/15/Add.206. Geneva: CRC.

Convention on the Elimination of All Forms of Discrimination against Women. 2000a. "General Recommendations No. 21." New York: CEDAW.

———. 2000b. "Statement on Reservations." New York: CEDAW.

———. 2006. "Concluding Observations: Togo, CEDAW/C/TGO/CO/3." New York: CEDAW.

Council of Europe. 2002. "Guidelines on Human Rights and the Fight Against Terrorism." Strasbourg: Council of Europe Publishing.

Doek, Jaap E. 2007. "In the Best Interests of the Child—Harmonisation of National Laws with the Convention on the Rights of the Child: Some Observations and Suggestions." Addis Ababa: ACPF/UNICEF.

ECA (Economic Commission for Africa). 2007a. Botswana country report.

———. 2007b. Kenya country report.

———. 2007c. South Africa country report.

———. 2007d. Uganda country report.

Egypt. 1992. Emergency Law, No. 97.

———. 1952. Emergency Law, No. 162.

EIPR (Egyptian Initiative for Personal Rights). 2006. *Egypt's New Anti-Terrorism Law: A Human Rights Risk Analysis.* www.eipr.org/en/reports/anti%20terrorism%2007/anti_terrorism_report_eng.pdf.

Evans, Malcolm D., and Rachel Murray. 2002. "The Special Rapporteurs in the African System." In Malcolm Evans and Rachel Murray, eds., *The African Charter on Human and Peoples' Rights: The System at Work.* Cambridge: Cambridge University Press.

Human Rights Council. 2008. *Report of the Special Rapporteur on the Right to Freedom of Opinion and Expression to the 7th Session of the Human Rights Council.* A/HRC/7/14. Geneva.

ISS (Institute for Security Studies). 2008. Botswana: Fact File. www.issafrica.org/index.php?link_id=14&slink_id=3388&link_type=12&slink_type=12&tmpl_id=3.

Media Institute of South Africa. 2006. "So This is Democracy: State of Media Freedom in Southern Africa." Windhoek: MISA.

National Human Rights Institutions. 2008. "International Coordinating Committee Accreditation." www.nhri.net/html.

Nzegwu, Nkiru. "Gender Equality in Dual-Sex System: The Case of Onitsha." In *Jenda: A Journal of Culture and African Women's Studies,* 1(1). www.jendajournal.com.

OAU (Organization of African Unity). 1981. "African Charter on Human and Peoples' Rights." OAU Doc. CAB/LEG/67/3.

———. 1990. "African Charter on the Rights and Welfare of the Child." OAU Doc. CAB/LEG/24.9/49. Maputo.

———. 1996. "Special Rapporteur on the Rights of Women in Africa." DOC/OS/34c (XXIII), Annex II. Maputo.

Reporters Without Borders. 2008. "Press Freedom Round-Up 2007." 2 Jan 2008 www.rsf.org/article.php3?id_article=24909.

Roosevelt, Franklin D. 1941. "Annual Message to Congress." Washington, D.C. www.ourdocuments.gov/doc.php?doc=70.

Scheinin, Martin. 2007. "Report of Special Rapporteur on the Promotion of Human Rights and Fundamental Freedoms While Countering Terrorism." UN Doc. A/HRC/4/26. Geneva: United Nations. www.ohchr.org/english/isssues/terrorism/rapporteur/reports.htm.

Tamale, Sylvia. 1999. "Towards Legitimate Governance in Africa: The Case of Affirmative Action and Parliamentary Politics in Uganda." In Edward Kofi Quashigah and Obiora Chinedu

Okafor, eds., *Legitimate Governance in Africa.* Hague: Kluwer International.

UN (United Nations). 1948. "Universal Declaration of Human Rights." New York.

———. 1969. "Vienna Convention on the Law of Treaties." Vienna.

———. 1976. "International Covenant on Civil and Political Rights." New York.

———. 1985. "Convention Against Torture and Other Cruel, Inhuman or Degrading Treatment or Punishment." New York.

———. 1992. "Human Rights Commission Resolution 1992/54." Geneva.

———. 2002. "International Experts Urge States to Take Immediate Action to End Immunity for Violations of Women's Rights." Press Release WOM/1330. New York.

———. 2008. "Universal Human Rights Index of United Nations Documents." 1 June. www.universalhumanrightsindex.org.

UNICEF (United Nations Children's Fund). 2003. *2003 Annual Report of the Uganda Human Rights Commission.*

———. 2004. *2004 Annual Report of the Uganda Human Rights Commission.*

UNDP (United Nations Development Programme). 2000. *Human Development Report 2000: Human Rights and Human Development*. New York. http://hdr.undp.org/reports/global/2000/en.

———. 2006. *2006 Arab Development Report*. New York.

United Nations General Assembly. 1993a. "General Assembly Resolution 48/134." New York.

———. 1993b. "Status of Preparation of Publications, Studies and Documents for the World Conference." In *World Conference on Human Rights*, A/CONF.157/PC/4. Geneva: United Nations.

———. 1993c. "Vienna Declaration and Programme of Action." In *World Conference on Human Rights*, A/CONF.157/23. Vienna: United Nations.

United Nations High Commissioner for Human Rights. 1993. "Status of Preparation of Publications, Studies, and Documents for the World Conference." 4 UN Doc. A/CONF.157/PC/62/Add.5.

UNHRC (United Nations Human Rights Committee). 1989. "General Comment 18: Non-Discrimination." UN Doc. A/45/40. In *Report of the Human Rights Committee*, Vol. I. Geneva.

———. 2000. General Comment 28: "Equality of rights between men and women (article 3)." U.N. Doc. CCPR/C/21/Rev.1/Add.10 (2000).

———. 2001. "General Comment 29: States of Emergency." CCPR/C/21/Rev.1/Add.11. Geneva.

———. 2007. "Concluding Observations of the Human Rights Committee." CCPR/C/ZMB/CO/3. Geneva: CCPR.

United Nations Security Council. 2005. "Threats to International Peace and Security." UN Doc. S/RES/1624.

Uganda Human Rights Commission. 2003. *2003 Annual Report*. Kampala 2003.

———2004. *2004 Annual Report*. Kampala.

Corruption is a major challenge to governance and development in Africa. It erodes the capacity of the state to deliver services efficiently, provide security and maintain peace, order and social stability. When deepseated, corruption generates poverty and turns resource-rich countries into low-income, backward societies. Many African countries are trapped in this cycle of corruption, poverty and underdevelopment.

Corruption is especially debilitating for Africa, the poorest continent. It undermines the ability to achieve the Millennium Development Goals because resources meant for education, health, rural roads and electricity are diverted for personal use. It also increases the cost of doing business and is a disincentive for foreign direct investment.

The pervasiveness of corruption, especially in the developing world, has generated momentum to address the problem. The United Nations designed the UN Convention against Corruption (UN Convention). In Africa continent-wide and regional instruments have emerged to tackle the problem: the African Union Convention on Preventing and Combating Corruption (AU Convention) was formulated in 2003, and the Economic Community for West African States and the Southern Africa Development Community have developed regional frameworks. And many African states have formulated anti-corruption laws and institutions.

To eliminate corruption, purposeful leadership and the rule of law are indispensable. Building a critical anti-corruption constituency—in the executive, legislative and judicial branches of government and in the media and civil society—is critical. And addressing the problem of low wages and poor remuneration, especially in the public service, is vital to discouraging petty stealing as well as large-scale bribery in public bureaucracies.

Phenomenon of corruption

Corruption is a complex and multifaceted phenomenon that affects all countries in various degrees, including developed countries. The 2007 Global Integrity Report affirmed that developed countries are still mired in corruption, contrary to the general perception that the wealthier countries are less corrupt because they have reached appreciable levels of development (Global Integrity 2007).

Former United Nations Secretary-General Kofi Annan has pointed out that corruption causes enormous harm by impoverishing national economies, threatening democratic institutions, undermining the rule of law and facilitating terrorism (Webb 2005). This awareness is reflected in the preamble to the AU Convention, which states that corruption "undermines accountability and transparency in the management of public affairs as well as socioeconomic development".

Being a multifaceted phenomenon, corruption is hard to define in a succinct manner. Instead, both the UN Convention and the AU Convention provide a catalogue of acts that are criminalized under several national penal laws and now form part of the international and regional legal framework for combating corruption. In the UN Convention the acts in question include:

> '*To eliminate corruption, purposeful leadership and the rule of law are indispensable. Building a critical anti-corruption constituency is critical*

- Bribery of national public officials;

- Bribery of foreign public officials and officials of public international organisations;

- Embezzlement, misappropriation or other diversion of property by a public official;

- Trading in influence;

- Abuse of function or position;

- Illicit enrichment—a significant increase in the assets of a public official that he or she cannot reasonably explain in relation to his or her lawful income;

- Bribery in the private sector;

- Embezzlement of property in the private sector;

- Laundering of the proceeds of crime;

- Concealment;

- Obstruction of justice.

The common denominator of such acts is that they consist of obtaining undue advantage from public officials or private entities for private or personal gain.

The approach of the AU Convention is similar. It identifies the following acts:

a. the solicitation or acceptance . . . in exchange for any act or omission in the performance of . . . public functions;

b. the offering or granting . . . in exchange for any act or omission, in the performance . . . of public functions;

c. any act or omission . . . for the purpose of illicitly obtaining benefits for [oneself] or for a third party;

d. the diversion . . . for purposes unrelated to those for which they were intended . . . of any property belonging to the State or its agencies, to an independent agency, or to an individual . . . by virtue of his or her position;

e. offering or giving, promising, solicitation or acceptance . . . of any undue advantage . . . in any capacity, a private sector entity . . . in breach of his or her duties;

f. offering, giving, solicitation or acceptance . . . or promising of any undue advantage . . . by exert[ing] any improper influence . . . in the public or private sector in consideration thereof, whether the undue advantage is for himself or herself or for anyone else;

g. illicit enrichment;

h. the use or concealment of proceeds derived from any of the acts referred to in this Article (African Union 2003).

Because it is difficult to give a conclusive definition of corruption, the AU Convention contains an open-ended clause in article 4.2 making any other act or related offence illegal if two or more parties to the Convention agree that such an act constitutes corruption.

International and regional anti-corruption frameworks

The UN Convention, adopted in 2004 following a long process of negotiation, provides a comprehensive framework for preventing as well as criminalising corruption. It covers prevention, criminalisation and law enforcement, international cooperation, technical assistance, information exchange and mechanisms for implementation (Webb 2005).

The AU Convention, adopted in 2003, is a binding legal instrument that covers various anti-corruption actions. In addition to calling upon states to make certain acts of corruption criminal offences in their domestic law, it addresses the jurisdiction of states over corruption and related offences (article 13), minimum fair trial guarantees (article 14), extradition (article 15), confiscation and seizure of the proceeds of corruption including their repatriation (article 16), bank secrecy (article 17), cooperation and mutual legal assistance (article 18), international cooperation (article 19), national authorities (article 20) and follow-up actions (article 22).

While the UN Convention is regarded as the more comprehensive instrument for fighting corruption, it has several similarities to the African Union Convention (Webb 2005). For example, some offenses are found in both conventions. Despite minor differences in wording, passive corruption committed by a public official is dealt with in the same manner by both conventions. Other similarities include bribery of public officials and laundering the proceeds of corruption.

Both conventions provide for national anti-corruption bodies with dedicated responsibilities for fighting corruption. Article 6 of the UN Convention tasks a national anti-corruption institution with developing, implementing and coordinating anti-corruption investigations and policies; promoting the inclusion of civil society organisations in anti-corruption programmes; ensuring proper management of public resources and transparency, accountability and integrity in public management and undertaking regular evaluation of the adequacy of legal and political frameworks in fighting corruption. In its article 20 the AU Convention further mandates national anti-corruption agencies to make and receive requests for assistance and cooperation on corruption cases. Both documents recognise the need for institutional autonomy, both administrative and financial, if anti-corruption bodies are to perform their functions efficiently and effectively.

While the UN Convention Against Corruption is regarded as the more comprehensive instrument for fighting corruption, it has several similarities to the African Union Convention

Box 7.1 President Ellen Sirleaf Johnson declares corruption public enemy no. 1 in Liberia

Following her country's beleaguered history of war and pervasive corruption, President Ellen Sirleaf Johnson has led the Liberian government to adopt a tough stance against corruption. A national anti-corruption strategy has been developed, a national anti-corruption institution established, a code of conduct for civil servants put in place and the country has signed the UN and AU conventions on corruption. Indicted civil servants and political office holders have been removed from their jobs. The fight against corruption has begun to have positive pay-offs for the country. The government's revenue rose from US$80 million in 2004/2005 to US$142 million in 2006/2007 and is projected to be around US$180 million in 2007/2008.

Both conventions have similar provisions on bribery of public officials. They provide that promising, offering or giving a public official an undue advantage to persuade the official to act (or refrain from acting) in a certain way in the exercise of official duties constitutes corruption. Both conventions also determine that the solicitation or acceptance by a public official of such an undue advantage constitutes corruption. The definition of such acts as bribery of public officials is comprehensive and sets a standard for people in official capacities.

Both the UN and AU conventions treat the misuse and embezzlement of public property or resources as serious corrupt acts. The AU Convention calls for outlawing the diversion by a public officer or any other person of property belonging to the state or its agencies, for purposes for which the property is not intended, or for the benefit of the officer or person in question. This form of corruption impedes the realisation of the public interest and retards social and economic development. By outlawing it in such an elaborate manner, both conventions tackle a vicious problem.

On money laundering the two conventions are substantively similar, although the UN Convention is more detailed. Article 23 of the UN convention prohibits the conversion or transfer of property, knowing that such property is the proceeds of crime, for the purpose of concealing or disguising the illicit origin of the property or of helping any person who is involved in the commission of the predicate offence to evade the legal consequences of his or her action as well as the concealment or disguise of the true nature, source, location, disposition, movement or ownership of or rights with respect to property, knowing that such property is the proceeds of crime.

The level of detail and the precision of these provisions on money laundering are meant to inspire national legislators to pass relevant rules and regulations in civil, penal and administrative law. Some have argued that the money-laundering provisions of both conventions are not precise enough by providing that to be guilty of money laundering a person must know that the property in question is the proceeds of a crime. Analysts have recommended that such a requirement should be extended to "persons who ought reasonably to have known" that the property is the proceeds of crime (ISS 2004).

Both conventions recognise that corruption is a societal phenomenon transcending the public sector and public officials by addressing corrupt practices in the non-state and non-public sectors. Article 4(1)(c) of the AU Convention provides that the abuse of position may be committed either by a public official or by "any other person," which has been interpreted to mean that such a provision covers private-sector agents and operators including civil society organisations (ISS 2004). The UN Convention has specific provisions dealing with the private sector.

On the funding of political parties, both documents insist on transparency and accountability in political party management. The AU Convention states that "each state party shall adopt legislative and other measures to (a) proscribe the use of funds acquired through illegal and corrupt practices to finance political parties; and (b) incorporate the principle of transparency into funding of political parties." In this regard the benchmark set by the AU Convention is more precise and legally enforceable.

The issue of sanctions is addressed in the UN Convention's article 30(1), which states that governments shall make the commission of an offence established under the Convention liable to sanctions that take into account the gravity of the fault. The Convention also calls for the removal, suspension or reassignment of officials accused of acts of corruption. The AU Convention is silent on that issue, representing one of its weaknesses.

Asset recovery is a priority of the UN Convention. It compels states to take all necessary measures to ensure that the identity of owners of funds deposited in high-value accounts be made public and to reveal whether they have been entrusted with public functions. The Convention further obliges states to allow other states to initiate judicial proceedings before their courts in order to establish title to or ownership of property acquired through corrupt practices. Additionally, the UN Convention requires governments to ensure that their courts can order payment of compensation or damages to the harmed state and can declare the harmed state's claim as legitimate. Article 57 of the UN Convention provides a framework for the actual return of assets.

The benchmarks provided for by the international and regional conventions on corruption are likely to lead to effective and consensual anti-corruption activities across borders. The way forward in this respect lies in ensuring enforcement and implementation of these international and regional commitments.

Profile of corruption in Africa

According to Transparency International's corruption perceptions index for 2007, corruption and lack of transparency were perceived to be rampant in 36 countries. Namibia, Seychelles, South Africa and Swaziland were rated as having improved in their anti-corruption stance (Transparency International 2007a).

Although many African countries have ratified the UN Convention[1] and the AU Convention,[2] their commitment to those documents remains

> *Although many African countries have ratified the UN Convention and the AU Convention, their commitment to those documents remains more formal than substantive*

more formal than substantive. Few countries have domesticated the conventions' provisions—that is, made them part of domestic law—so the legal framework for combating corruption is weak in many countries. In addition, some political leaders in Africa are reluctant to domesticate and implement international and regional frameworks because they might circumscribe their access to wealth and shut down the conduits to public resources.

But due to the demands of civil society organisations, the efforts of parliaments and sometimes even at the initiative of some members of the executive, progressive anti-corruption laws are being enacted in some African countries. In many cases there are multiple laws addressing corruption. Nigeria has six laws: the Money Laundering Prohibition Act, 2004; Public Procurement Act, 2007; Fiscal Responsibility Act, 2007; Code of Conduct Act, 1989; Independent Corrupt Practices Commission Act, 2000; and the Economic and Financial Commission Act, 2004. The latter two laws establish and empower the two major anti-corruption institutions in the country. Ghana enacted the Financial Administration Act, 2003 (Act 654); the Public Procurement Act, 2003 (Act 663); Internal Audit Agency Act, 2003 Act 658); Audit Service Act, 2000 and the Money Laundering Act, 2007. This is the general trend in Africa. The challenge is to update and harmonise those laws with the UN Convention and the AU Convention and ensure their active implementation in African states.

Executive

Without appropriate checks and institutional controls, the executive is prone to abuse power and engage in corrupt acts. Liberalisation of the political arena and democratisation have provided some checks on the powers of the executive and compelled some measure of transparency in its activities. Political executives are now subjected to periodic elections, and civil society organisations and the media have a freer environment for exposing corruption. Through a more open environment and careful institutional reforms, Botswana has promoted executive responsibility and accountability. The government has enforced relative openness in economic policy-making, priority setting and national development planning. And it has strengthened the constitutional roles of the auditor general, attorney general, the Directorate on Corruption and Economic Crime and an independent judiciary (Kyambalesa2006). South Africa and Madagascar have also adopted some national anti-corruption strategies and have put in place mechanisms to implement, monitor and report on them.

Despite these few positive cases, the general trend in Africa is that the national executive will make arbitrary use of public funds and engage in corruption. Sani Abacha, the former president of Nigeria, was listed as the world's fourth most corrupt leader in recent history by Transparency International in 2004, having appropriated an estimated US$4–5 billion from Nigeria's treasury through embezzlement, fraud, forgery, and money laundering between 1993 and 1998. Abacha and his associates were alleged to have invested most of the monies in accounts in Luxembourg, Switzerland, the United Kingdom and the United States (Shehu 2004). And several panels in Nigeria are investigating contracts in the energy and road sectors awarded by the Obasanjo civilian administration, which governed from 1999 to 2007.

Nigeria is not an isolated case. In Zambia and Malawi former presidents Patrick Chiluba and Baliki Muluzi are on trial on corruption charges.[3] In Kenya John Githongo, the former top anti-corruption official, fled into exile, alleging threats to his life after ostensibly exposing the details of high-level corruption (Holman 2006; Michael 2004). Githongo alleged that at the beginning of 2004 the government of Kenya "had granted a contract worth about $41 million to an entity that did not exist and . . . some of those transactions were conducted by members of the administration to raise money for political financing" (Githongo 2007, 4).

Corruption in the executive is not limited to the elected political leadership or public office holders; other executive organs, including the police services, can be corrupt. In South Africa 222 members of the South African Police Service were suspended on corruption charges in 2006/2007 (Faull 2008). In Nigeria a former inspector general of police was arraigned in court on a 70-count charge of stealing and

money laundering of about 13 billion naira (US$118 million). He was convicted on some of the charges (Amah 2005).

In some countries the law requires public officials to declare their income, assets and liabilities before assuming office and again when they leave office—in Ghana the 1998 Public Office Holders (Declaration of Assets and Disqualification) Act (Act 550), in Tanzania the Leadership Code of Conduct, in Uganda the Leadership Code of Ethics Act (No.13) and in Nigeria the Code of Conduct Bureau. But in most cases these instruments have not been effective. The declarations of wealth are mostly done in secret, and the public rarely has access to the information. Monitoring and enforcement are weak in many countries, so officials can give a false declaration. And officials have devised means to circumvent this regulation by operating proxy accounts in the name of family members, friends and business allies while in office. The result is that corruption flourishes despite the asset declaration laws.

The perception of the experts in most of the project countries is that the executive is fairly or completely corrupt (figure 7.1). In Congo, Chad, Burkina Faso, Uganda, Mali, Nigeria, Togo, Madagascar, Cameroon, Egypt and Senegal over 50% of the expert respondents considered the executive to be completely or fairly corrupt. Only in Tunisia and Botswana did less than 10% of the experts regard their executive as fairly or completely corrupt.

> *In some countries the law requires public officials to declare their income, assets and liabilities before assuming office and again when they leave office. But in most cases these instruments have not been effective*

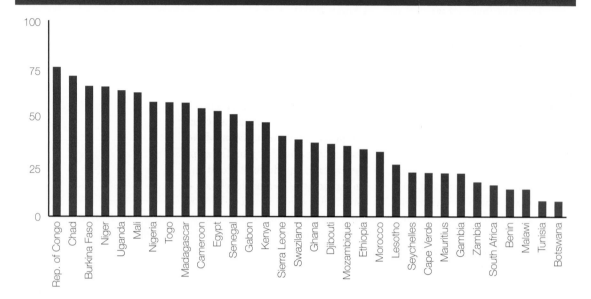

Figure 7.1 Expert opinion on corruption in the executive branch

Fairly or completely corrupt (share of experts surveyed, by country, %)

Source: ECA survey of experts 2007.

Legislature

Well-managed parliaments, chosen through open and competitive elections and provided with significant institutional capacity, can promote accountability and transparency in the public sector and combat corruption (Stapenhurst et al. 2006). A parliament can conduct its anti-corruption agenda through its oversight of public institutions and agencies, public hearings, parliamentary committee investigations and the appropriation of funds for the state.

But in many countries the parliament is weak and rarely serves as a counterpoise to executive power or as an oversight agency. Some lack the expertise to enact anti-corruption legislation, while in others

there is little interest in doing so. In some instances African parliaments are themselves caught in a web of corruption, as some members of parliament win office through vote buying, rigging, bribery and violence. Studies have shown significant vote buying in countries like Cameroon, Kenya, Uganda, Zimbabwe and Nigeria (Stapenhurst et al. 2006). In addition, the huge costs of elections often compel some politicians to use bribery and other illegal tactics to carry out their legislative functions in order to recoup their electoral investments. Thus African legislators "have not effectively, efficiently and honestly used their positions as parliamentarians to fight with their heart and soul against the scourge of corruption" (Stapenhurst et al. 2006, 104). In Nigeria five parliamentary leaders (three presidents of the Senate and two speakers of the House of Representatives) were removed from office on allegations of corruption between 1999 and 2007.

In 11 project countries over 30% of the consulted experts considered the legislature to be largely or completely corrupt (Chad, Republic of Congo, Nigeria, Kenya, Egypt, Togo, Burkina Faso, Swaziland, Madagascar, Uganda and Niger). Only in 6 countries—Mauritius, Ghana, Tunisia, Gambia, Botswana and Cape Verde—did less than 10% of the expert panel regard the legislature to be largely or completely corrupt, depicting a low level of corruption in the parliament of those countries (figure 7.2).

Despite the weakness of the parliament in tackling corruption in many African countries, some efforts are being made. In Kenya the parliament uncovered the Goldenberg scandal, one the biggest cases of official corruption in Sub-Saharan Africa. The government had instituted an export compensation system, seemingly to help earn foreign exchange through the export of gold and diamonds. It turned out that it was a government-sanctioned system to draw off funds from the Central Bank of Kenya. The scandal came to light when the opposition party blew the whistle in parliament. It presented evidence in the House demonstrating that about

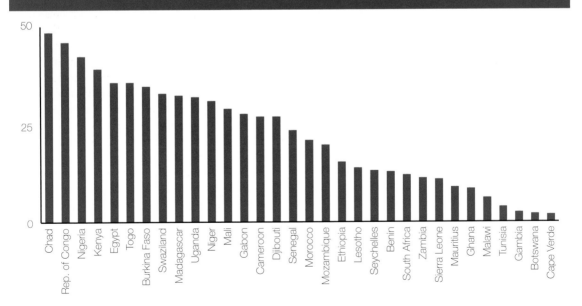

Figure 7.2 Expert opinion on corruption in the legislature

Largely or completely corrupt (share of experts surveyed, by country, %)

Source: ECA survey of experts 2007.

24 billion Kenyan shillings had been transferred to the Exchange Bank, which was owned by Goldenberg International. In this case, parliament was effective in exposing the scandal and thus preventing further looting (Stapenhurst et al. 2006).

In 2005 in Senegal the National Assembly enacted a law on the ratification of the UN Convention against Corruption. The same year, the national unit for the procession of financial information to prevent money laundering and the committee for corruption and nontransparency control started their activities (ECA 2007f). In Nigeria in 2006 the parliament thwarted the ambition of the executive to compromise the constitution and extend its tenure in power. This was a form of high-level corruption, as it constituted an abuse of power and a manipulation of the political and legal processes of the country. In addition, allegations and counter-allegations of bribery of the federal legislators to support the agenda were rife in the public domain. If the attempt had succeeded, it could have been a major political corruption of monumental magnitude in the country (Adejumobi 2007). As the elected representatives of the people, parliamentarians will have to make a culture of ethics and accountability a priority in their conduct of public affairs, and assert their oversight responsibilities. Ethically, members of parliament must justify the confidence the people reposed in them through the electoral system. They must also reinforce the technical capacity of the parliament to carry out its watchdog functions over other arms of government and

public agencies. And they must protect the independence of parliament, especially from executive influence. In a parliamentary system where the ruling party has an overwhelming majority, parliamentary independence is usually compromised and accountability suffers. Even in a presidential system the executive often intimidates members of parliament. Separation of powers is a cardinal element of democratic governance, and it must be respected if the parliament is to play its constitutional role in preventing and combating corruption.

Judiciary

Only in a few African countries has the judiciary demonstrated the will and resilience to address corruption. In Mali a corruption investigation by the public prosecutors of some members of the cabinet has resulted in trials, fines and imprisonment. In Uganda, investigations have been conducted but the courts have made no convictions (USAID 2007).

But in most African countries the judiciary does not exercise real independence, and its ability to fight corruption is weak. The executive appoints key judicial officers, and ruling parties often ensure that they appoint party sympathisers or their political allies to sensitive judicial positions. In addition, poor remuneration of judges exposes them to corrupt influences. Courts in Africa are generally poorly equipped, and trials take a long time, making it possible for the police to manipulate the process and subvert the cause of justice in corruption cases. Consequently, most grand corruption cases usually end up without convictions.

> *In a few African countries the judiciary has demonstrated the will to address corruption. But in most countries the judiciary does not exercise real independence, and its ability to fight corruption is weak*

The results of ECA's expert survey suggest that the judiciary is perceived to be very corrupt in most countries (figure 7.3). In fourteen countries (Mali, Togo, Cameroon, Kenya, Republic of Congo, Madagascar, Morocco, Niger, Sierra Leone, Ghana, Chad, Burkina Faso, Senegal and Ethiopia) 50% to 84% of experts consulted felt that the judiciary was fairly or completely corrupt. Only in Botswana, Cape Verde, Malawi and Tunisia did less than 10% of the experts rate the judiciary as less corrupt.

To be a strategic partner in the anti-corruption effort, the judiciary requires judges who are not subject to the whims and caprices of the executive. Some countries have created a judicial service commission to appoint and discipline judges. Salaries and remuneration of judicial officers should be adequate and the judiciary's financial autonomy protected. Mechanisms of accountability should be established and enforced in the judiciary. And the technical capacity of the judiciary to deal with corruption cases must be enhanced. Special corruption courts could be established to try high-profile corruption cases in order to prevent their manipulation by the executive and the police.

Civil service

Most countries have strict rules to safeguard the civil service from corrupt practices. But corruption exists in the civil service of many

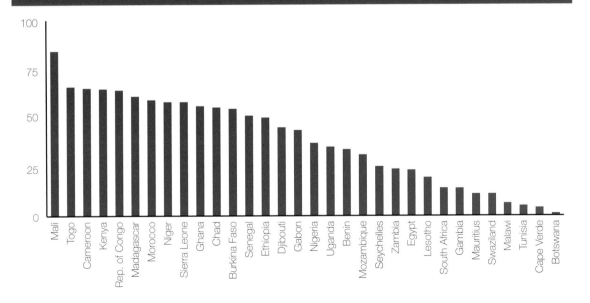

Figure 7.3 Expert opinion on corruption in the judiciary

Largely or completely corrupt (share of experts surveyed, by country, %)

Source: ECA survey of experts 2007.

African countries. In some countries—Benin, Burkina Faso, Rwanda, Senegal, Cameroon, Nigeria, Sierra Leone, South Africa, Uganda and Zambia—the government has established mechanisms to monitor the performance of civil service agencies, but this does not preclude corrupt practices. Only in few countries—Benin, South Africa and Uganda among them—do citizens have a recourse when services fail (Gbadamosi 2005; AfDB 2003; USAID 2007). But service delivery remains poor in many countries, due partly to corruption. In Kenya, for instance, despite the existence of a relatively comprehensive anticorruption system, the cost of corruption in state-controlled enterprises has been estimated as high as US$104.5 million annually (Hope and Chikulo 2000).

Corruption thrives in the allocation of resources and procurement processes in the water sector in Africa. A study noted that "corrupt practices are endemic to many water supply and sanitation (WSS) institutions and transactions in Africa. This corruption varies substantially in size and incidence, but it is clear that significant WSS sector finances are being lost to those charged with making decisions about, and delivering water and sanitation services" (Plummer and Cross 2007, 222). At the level of local water delivery, corrupt officials provide illegal connections, resell utility water, use utility vehicles for private purposes and give preferential treatment for repairs or new services in exchange for bribery (Plummer and Cross 2007). The financial leakage from

> ‘ *Corruption in the civil service is almost a universal problem in Africa. Rescuing the civil service from the abyss of corruption will require reinventing the institution in many countries*

corruption in the water sector in Africa is estimated at about 30% of total expenditure.

The ECA expert survey confirms that corruption in the civil service is almost a universal problem in Africa (figure 7.4). Rescuing the civil service from the abyss of corruption will require reinventing the institution in many countries—a radical overhaul of its compensation system, revival of an ethos of commitment and professionalism and mechanisms to weed out those who are redundant, unproductive or corrupt. Effective service reform must be results-based and include the public interest in the design of performance assessment tools.

Tax system
In many African nations the revenue agency is among the most corrupt public institutions (Le 2007). It is estimated that corruption causes African governments to lose up to 50% of their tax revenue, which in most cases exceeds a country's foreign debt (AfDB 2006). Efforts to improve the tax systems have led to various administrative, structural, operational and legal changes.

Ghana has established the Revenue Agencies Governing Board, and the Tax Audit and Legal Services Division to stem tax evasion, and a separate division of the law courts has been established to speed up the prosecution of tax defaulters. But these and other innovative policies are yet to end tax evasion and corruption. Of the experts surveyed in Ghana, 31% felt that the tax system is sometimes affected by evasion

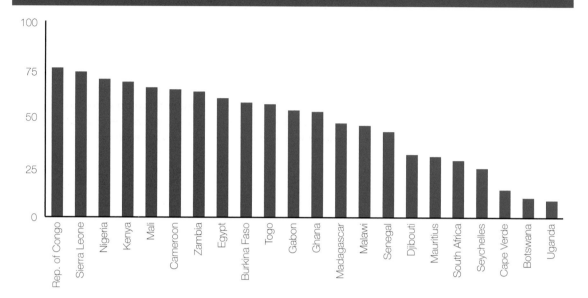

Figure 7.4 Corruption in the civil service

Largely or completely corrupt (share of experts surveyed, by country, %)

Source: ECA survey of experts 2007.

or corruption, while 55% said it is mostly and 10% said it is always affected by evasion or corruption.

Namibia's introduction of a value-added tax improved its tax collection. The country's commissioner of inland revenue in the Ministry of Finance reports that there have been no cases of tax evasion since the introduction of the tax (ECA 2007e). As is the case in most African countries, the Ministry of Finance in Namibia imposes stiff penalties for tax evasion, ranging from fines to jail sentences. The fines can be as high as N$3000 (about US$283) per day as long as the evasion continues, or the offender may have to pay double the amount involved. Tax officers

who contravene the law can be fined as much as N$50,000 (about US$4,730). While tax evasion has not been eradicated, it has been reduced. This improvement is mainly attributed to the intensification of the audit functions within the Ministry of Finance. It is simply more difficult now to evade taxes.

In Djibouti the Penal Code severely punishes corruption and bribery. Article 200 states:

> The fact that a person vested with public authority or in charge of a public service mission, a person with an elected public mandate, a juror, an arbitrator or an expert [who] solicits or accepts, without

the right, directly or indirectly, offers or promises, gifts or presents, or any benefit for carrying out or refraining from any of his functions, or facilitated by its function, is punishable by ten years imprisonment and a fine of 5,000,000 DJF [about US$28,552].

The punishment is even higher if committed by a magistrate:

> [If t]he offence specified in the preceding paragraph has been committed by a magistrate for the benefit or detriment of a person who is the subject of criminal proceedings, the penalty is increased to fifteen years of imprisonment and a fine 7000000 DJF [about US$39,974].

These measures have contributed to a reduction in tax fraud (ECA 2007c). Other steps taken by Djibouti authorities may have contributed—in particular, the ratification in 2005 of the UN Convention against Corruption, which strengthened existing national regulations. And revenue reforms undertaken from 2000 through 2004 had already led to some improvement in the tax system through a more efficient tax department, which has harmonized tax laws and improved the quality of services to taxpayers.

Swaziland and Botswana have well-managed tax systems. In Swaziland 53.3% of the ECA expert respondents felt that the tax system was well managed (ECA 2007g). In

Botswana there are two categories of punishment for tax evasion: penalties imposed by the tax commissioner and those levied by a court. Conviction of tax evasion incurs a fine not exceeding 4000 pula and up to two years imprisonment (ECA 2007b).

Despite these and other success stories, the tax systems of many African countries are still safe havens for evasion. In Tanzania, as in many countries, the wealthy often escape fair tax assessment or avoid paying taxes altogether through bribery and other forms of patronage with tax officials. By the same taken, in many countries officials are notorious for using delays, the threat of high tax assessments or the promise of low assessments to extort funds from individuals and businesses (Stapenhurst et al. 2006). Indeed, within the public sector the tax department and the customs agency are considered to be the most lucrative (a euphemism for corruption) for public servants.

Non-state institutions
Corruption is not restricted to the three branches of government and the civil service. Non-state actors are also actively engaged in the corruption maze—as victims, perpetrators or mobilisers against it.

Civil society organisations
The expansion of political space has fostered the growth of civil society organisations (CSOs) in many African countries. Some CSOs are established as corruption watchdogs—monitoring, reporting and exposing it in their countries.

> ' **Despite some success stories, the tax systems of many African countries are still safe havens for evasion**

Transparency International now has local chapters in many countries, connecting them to a global anti-corruption grid. Anti-corruption civil society networks also exist in some countries. In Liberia, for example, the Coalition against Corruption was formed in 2005 by eleven CSOs to campaign for ratification of both the UN Convention against Corruption and the African Union Convention on Preventing and Combating Corruption. The coalition succeeded in raising public awareness of the content and purposes of the two conventions and increased political pressure on the policy makers to act. Liberia has since ratified both conventions.

Budget tracking has become a specialisation for some CSOs in Africa. Others advocate for a freedom of information law, which would remove obstacles to corruption investigations. Yet others initiate bills and provide technical backstopping for parliamentary committees in investigating public corruption. Sometimes CSOs fight for free, fair and credible elections. And sometimes they serve as whistle blowers.

African CSOs have made remarkable progress, especially in monitoring elections and preventing electoral corruption. In Nigeria the Transition Monitoring Group and the Alliance for Credible Elections played key roles in exposing some of the imperfections and electoral corruption in the April 2007 elections. In the 2007 elections in Sierra Leone civil society organisations constituted themselves into a single national election watch group.

But CSOs are faced with major challenges in their own internal management and corrupt practices. Many CSOs in Africa have a poor funding base, tempting corruption. Most CSOs depend on donor funding to exist. In most cases donor funds are project-based and do not provide funding for staffing and office maintenance. The consequence is that CSOs in Africa sometimes undertake what is referred to in civil society circles as "creative accounting"—shorthand for diversion of project funds to nonproject activities.

Many NGOs are personal entities owned by individuals who control the budget and manage the finances of the organisation, often to their personal advantage. Although those organisations appoint accountants or account officers, real financial powers often lie with the owner of the organisation. Since CSOs are considered to be charity organisations and not taxed in many countries, they have become a conduit for financial misappropriation, especially of donor funds.

In some cases government officials and CSOs collaborate in corrupt acts. CSO leaders are sometimes bribed by public officials to suppress information on corrupt acts by public officials or they are courted to project a positive image. The media is also culpable, and the culture of "brown envelopes" (money slipped to journalists) is quite common in many countries.

The expansion of political space has fostered the growth of civil society organisations in many African countries

The business sector

The private sector in Africa is not immune to corruption. The drive to maximise profit often influences a company's transactions and relations with the government and other companies. Corruption flourishes in the private sector in several ways: bribing public officials to register firms or to influence contracts from the state, listing of public officials as board members in private firms in order to influence government actions and policies in their favour,[4] donating to political parties in anticipation of future benefits, colluding with government officials to evade or underpay tax and committing outright fraud.

Facing bureaucratic red tape, private firms often prefer to bribe public officials to shorten the long procedure of getting a license, securing a work permit or processing a contract bid. The low pay in the public sector makes public servants ready accomplices in such corrupt acts. The Business Anti-Corruption Portal shows that companies frequently encounter corruption in meeting with government authorities in African countries.[5] In Egypt businesses report spending 8% of their earnings on unofficial payments. About one-quarter of companies in Egypt claim that tax inspectors expect gifts and bribes in return for low tax assessments and contracts from government. In Cameroon 18% of the large companies surveyed admitted paying bribes to win contracts and market shares, while 63% thought that approximately one-tenth of their turnover is used to bribe government officials.

Senegal's onerous bureaucracy breeds corruption in the private sector. According to a World Bank enterprise study, 25% of companies in Senegal reported paying bribes to "get things done" (Business Anti-Corruption Portal). Both domestic and foreign firms pay bribes, with 40% and 39% of manufacturing companies and service firms, respectively, saying that corruption is a major or very severe constraint to their operations. South Africa and Nigeria have experienced scandals and instances of unethical and dishonest practices in the business sector (ISS 1997). In Nigeria some companies do not post a sign outside their premises, ostensibly to avoid the solicitation of bribes by state officials, while some firms spend as much as 12% of their annual income for bribery (Business Anti-Corruption Portal).

But in a few countries there is movement in the private sector to combat corruption. The fight against corruption in Malawi has not been left to the government alone. In 1995 the business community established the Business Coalition against Corruption. The group has drawn up a code of conduct and united the business sector to work to uproot corrupt practices. The coalition intends to assist in the drive against corruption within companies (ECA 2007d). In Senegal the penal code provides for sanctions against active and passive corruption of civil servants and staff of private companies, which has not proved quite effective in combating corruption in the country. (ECA 2007f).

Private firms may reap initial gains from corrupt practices, but in the medium to long term it is inimical to their interests. Corruption creates uncertainty and unpredictability for those running private enterprises, especially in their relationships with the state. Corruption makes it difficult to enforce contract laws and compromises corporate integrity. By raising the cost of doing business and distorting competition for public contracts, corruption also chases away foreign and local investors. For this reason, the involvement of the private sector in the battle against corruption will be a win-win situation, because it will help African countries be more conducive to business. Still, in many project countries businesses continue to report a prevalence of corruption when dealing with public officials.

Anti-corruption commissions
Realising the impact of corruption on the national economy and political systems, and under pressure from international development partners, many African countries have established commissions to prevent, investigate and prosecute corruption and to educate the public. Anti-corruption commissions now exist in Botswana, Malawi, Tanzania, Uganda, Zambia, Ethiopia, Nigeria, Kenya, Madagascar, Mali, Mozambique, Senegal, Uganda, Cameroon, Sierra Leone, Swaziland, Lesotho, Benin, Burkina Faso, Mozambique, Mauritius, Namibia, Zimbabwe, Madagascar, Democratic Republic of Congo, Ghana and South Africa (Kofele-Kale 2006; Hansungule 2003; AfDB 2003; Klitgaard 1988; Doig et al. 2005).

The agencies vary in their level of development and performance. The Economic and Financial Crimes Commission in Nigeria has been able to get the country removed from the blacklist of the Financial Action Task Force by prosecuting many high-profile cases, including state governors, ministers, an inspector general of police and senators. The Commission has secured over 200 convictions for corruption, money laundering, bank fraud and advanced fee fraud, and recovered about US$5 billion stolen from the Nigerian treasury by public officials (Akomaye 2007).

In Ghana the Commission for Human Rights and Administrative Justice is a human rights commission, an ombudsman and an anti-corruption agency. It has ten regional offices, 98 district offices and a staff of 787, and it covers the entire country in its operations (Ayamdoo 2007). This commission has handled several high-profile cases of ministers, members of parliament and senior civil servants.

In Uganda the anti-corruption commission is poorly staffed, and turnover is estimated at 20% every year. In Malawi the Anti-Corruption Bureau has only 78 staff members, but with very few lawyers (in 2007 only four) to prosecute mounting corruption cases (AfDB 2003; Doig et al. 2005; USAID 2007). The poor remuneration of the Bureau ensures that once the lawyers acquire some experience they will leave for greener pastures, mostly in the private sector (Madise 2007).

Many of the anti-corruption institutions lack autonomy, face political interference, have poor funding

'*Realising the impact of corruption, many African countries have established commissions to investigate and prosecute it*

and poor institutional capacity and in a few cases are themselves entangled in corruption controversies. In Nigeria and Kenya the heads of anti-corruption agencies have had to leave office in questionable circumstances, which suggests the low level of institutional autonomy enjoyed by those agencies.[6]

Most anti-corruption institutions in Africa are donor-funded, which raises the question of local ownership and agenda setting. It appears that the anti-corruption initiative is virtually a donor-driven agenda in Africa. Even for resource rich countries like Nigeria, donor presence is still ubiquitous in the funding of their anti-corruption agencies, supporting the Economic and Financial Crimes Commission to the tune of $40 million (Guardian [Lagos]).

To make headway in the anti-corruption war African governments must give greater priority to anti-corruption agencies in four critical areas: the law establishing them, which must conform with the minimum standard set by the UN Convention and the AU Convention; the institutional and administrative autonomy they exercise; their funding and the process for appointing and removing heads of the institutions. In turn, anti-corruption bodies have to be accountable to democratic institutions, especially the parliament, and the people through transparency in their own activities.

Other corruption-fighting institutions

Since corruption is a multifaceted phenomenon, an anti-corruption

institution alone is not sufficient to deal with the problem. To fight the different aspects of corruption, many African states have established ombudsmen, auditors general and parliamentary investigative committees to combat misadministration, which encompasses but is not limited to combating corruption. Commissions of inquiry and administrative tribunals are ad hoc bodies established by the executive to investigate cases that may be related to corruption.

Botswana, Uganda, Namibia, Rwanda, Tanzania, Gambia, Zimbabwe, Burkina Faso, Malawi, Lesotho, Senegal, South Africa and Sudan have established ombudsperson offices. But the capacity, autonomy and performance of the offices are uneven. In a few countries—Botswana, Seychelles, Rwanda and Mali among them—the work of the ombudsman is considered credible.[7]

In Botswana the office of the ombudsperson was created in 1995 to complement the Directorate on Corruption and Economic Crime. The ombudsperson is charged with ensuring ethical and fair conduct in the public service, a requisite to an effective war against corruption. The office investigates complaints of injustice in the public service received from the public (including corporate bodies). When such complaints are valid, the office of the ombudsperson makes recommendations to the appropriate authority for compliance. From 1997 to 2004 the ombudsperson received 3,773 complaints, of which 2,501 were resolved (ECA 2007b).

> *To fight the different aspects of corruption, many African states have established ombudsmen, auditors general and parliamentary investigative committees*

In Seychelles the constitution provides that corruption cases be considered by the ombudsperson. To work in the office of the ombudsperson, a citizen of Seychelles must be of proven integrity and impartiality, possess demonstrable competence and experience and not be member of any of the three branches of government. To ensure the independence of the ombudsperson, the office's salaries and other allowances are charged to the consolidated fund rather than the presidency. The ombudsperson is mandated to investigate public authorities when the exercise of their administrative functions results in injustices or harsh, oppressive or unfair actions. The office is also empowered to investigate fraud and corruption allegations against public authorities. The ombudsperson's office is reputed to be performing well in Seychelles.[8]

But in many other countries the office of the ombudsperson is weak and relatively unknown, and has few cases and petitions before it. Where the president or the head of state appoints the office, its autonomy is usually circumscribed. Often the office is poorly funded, and sometimes it has no visibility of its own because it is merged with the national anti-corruption body. The result is that the ombudsperson is either moribund or ineffective.

The office of the auditor general, which exists in many African countries, is an important part of the whistle-blowing mechanism of the state. Although usually regarded as part of the executive, the auditor general is supposed to enjoy relative autonomy and serve as a major counterforce to financial abuses by other arms and agencies of the executive and the state generally. In some countries the office of the auditor general has been active, conducting regular audits of government accounts and making its reports available to the public, thereby exposing financial improprieties by agencies of government. In Nigeria the office has assisted the National Assembly in its public hearings and investigations into cases of financial mismanagement and abuses by government departments. The auditor general has provided valid statistics on distorted accounts of some government departments, greatly facilitating the work of the National Assembly.

In Ghana the auditor general exposed how corrupt government officials embezzled about US$401 million between 1983 and 1992, but no one was charged or prosecuted by the state (Hope and Chikulo 2000). The office has no power to prosecute or bring indicted people to court. In many countries the auditor general is appointed by the president and can be unilaterally removed. Additionally, the office often does not have the qualified personnel to assist in probing and auditing government accounts and is usually subjected to severe political pressure to be silent on cases of financial impropriety by government departments.

Although relatively new to fighting corruption, parliamentary committees are increasingly important in investigating and exposing

> *In some countries the auditor general has conducted regular audits of government accounts and made its reports available to the public, exposing financial improprieties*

corruption cases. In South Africa, Nigeria, Rwanda, Zambia, Tanzania and Uganda parliamentary committees are asserting themselves and conducting useful investigations aimed at curbing mismanagement of public institutions. But many of those committees lack the technical support and resources required to conduct thorough investigations.

Special initiatives against corruption: the extractive industries

The level of corruption in the extractive sector is enormous, with international dimensions. Because the extractive industry is strategically important to developing countries as a major revenue-earning source and to developed countries as a major source of raw materials, it has become a focal point for international anti-corruption initiatives, notably the Kimberley Process, the Extractive Industries Transparency Initiative and the Publish What You Pay Initiative.

The Kimberley Process

The Kimberley Process was launched in May 2000 in Kimberley, South Africa, as "a joint government, industry and civil society initiative aiming to stem the flow of conflicts which are financed through trafficking of rough diamonds by rebel movements for the financing of wars against legitimate governments" (Kimberley Process 2008). Its objective is promote transparency and accountability in the diamond trade, specifically stopping the illicit trade used by rebel movements to fund insurrections in Sierra Leone, Angola and the Democratic Republic of the Congo. The revenue of rebels from conflict diamonds in Sierra Leone and the Democratic Republic of Congo during their wars was estimated to be US$70 million and US$30 million, respectively (Wright 2008; Bone n.d.; Smillie 2005; Smillie 2002; Rogers 2006). In the late 1990s nearly 15% of the world's annual diamond production was categorized as conflict diamonds.

The Kimberley Process Certification Scheme requires member states to certify that diamonds mined within their borders are conflict-free. The scheme is monitored through review visits, annual reports and regular exchanges and analysis of statistical data (Wright 2004; Global Policy Forum 2008; Global Witness 2006).

The Kimberley Process has 48 members, including 17 African countries (among them, Angola, Botswana, the Central African Republic, the Democratic Republic of Congo, Côte d'Ivoire, Namibia, Sierra Leone, South Africa, Tanzania, Togo and Zimbabwe). The countries in the Kimberley Process represent an estimated 99.8% of rough diamond production worldwide. The Process enjoys the United Nations and World Trade Organisation's support (Smillie 2005; Smillie n.d.).

The Kimberley Process has contributed to the cessation of hostilities by draining the funding sources of rebel groups and compelling them to negotiate peace deals. It has also improved the revenues of post-conflict countries. The trade in conflict

> ' **Because the extractive industry is strategically important to developing countries, it has become a focal point for international anti-corruption initiatives**

diamonds declined from 4% of the global diamond trade (amounting to US$255 million) to less than 1%, which, in turn, has enhanced the level of legitimate rough diamond exports for some African states. For example, Sierra Leone exported only US$26 million in diamonds in 2001, but in 2004 the amount increased to US$126 million (Smillie 2005).

Despite the progress, there are still challenges to the initiative. While trade in illegal diamonds has been reduced drastically, it has not stopped. Weak internal control mechanisms, especially in post-conflict countries, allow the illicit diamond trade to still flourish. Corruption of state officials involved in the certification process also thwarts the objectives of the scheme. In Sierra Leone, Angola and the Democratic Republic of Congo illegal foreign and local diamond miners still circumvent the Kimberley Process and use their international networks to place their products in the international market. In Sierra Leone it is estimated that trade in illicit diamonds is about 20% of the country's total diamond production. Global Witness has stated that "a UN group of experts on Côte d'Ivoire has found that poor controls of diamonds are allowing significant volumes of blood diamonds to enter the legitimate trade through Ghana, where they are certified as conflict free and through Mali" (Global Witness 2005, 2).

The Publish What You Pay campaign

The paradox of natural resource wealth is that many of the countries endowed with such resources also have a high level of poverty. This includes Nigeria, Equatorial Guinea, Angola, Sierra Leone, Ghana, South Africa, Democratic Republic of the Congo, Gabon, São Tomé and Príncipe and Chad. Notable exceptions are Libya, Botswana and Algeria.

The Publish What You Pay campaign is an initiative launched in 2002 by Global Witness, the Catholic Agency for Overseas Development, the Open Society Institute, Oxfam, Save the Children UK and Transparency International UK. The campaign aims to improve transparency and accountability for revenues generated by oil, gas and mineral industries. Currently the coalition includes more than 300 nongovernmental organisations. African countries in the campaign are Chad, Republic of Congo, Côte d'Ivoire, Democratic Republic of Congo, Gabon, Guinea, Liberia, Mali, Niger, Nigeria, Sierra Leone and Zambia.

The campaign calls for "the mandatory disclosure of payments made by oil, gas and mining extractive companies to each national government". By encouraging private firms to "publish what they pay" to governments, the initiative enables citizens in resource-rich countries to hold their governments accountable. The Publish What You Pay campaign's proposed monitoring mechanisms include an independent monitoring body and using the IMF (Publish What You Pay; Human Rights Watch 2004).

This initiative was prompted by the lack of transparency that usually

> *The paradox of natural resource wealth is that many of the countries endowed with such resources also have a high level of poverty*

characterises financial transactions between multinational corporations and governments, especially in the extractive sector in the developing world. Citizens barely know how much MNCs pay in rent on natural resources to their governments and where the money ends up.

There has been some progress through the initiative. One study reported that "Angola allowed the publications of some IMF investigations into its account. It also disclosed the details of its deal with the US oil company Chevron Texaco" (CAFOD 1999, 5). But there have been challenges for the initiative. The lack of a freedom-of-information law in many African countries constrains public disclosure; companies in some cases are wary of a backlash from the state on financial payment disclosure and there is no monitoring, sanctions or enforcement regime for the initiative beyond pressure from CSOs and the international development partners.

Extractive Industries Transparency Initiative

Launched in 2002, the Extractive Industries Transparency Initiative (EITI) is "an independent, internationally agreed upon voluntary standard for creating transparency in the extractive industries". A complement to the Publish What You Pay Campaign, the initiative is based on voluntary disclosure of information by governments and therefore is dependant on a country's political will. The objective is "to increase transparency in the payments made by companies and revenues received by governments relating to the

exploitation of extractive resources such as oil, gas and minerals", which should help the public hold governments accountable for the management of extractive resources (World Bank 2008, 1; Publish What You Pay and Revenue Watch Institute 2006).

The EITI is a multi-stakeholder initiative involving multinational and state-owned companies, host governments, business and industry associations, international financial institutions, investors and civil society organisations. The coalition established a permanent secretariat to work with civil society organisations to monitor the implementation of the initiative (Goldwyn 2008). To date sixteen African countries have joined the initiative: Cameroon, Chad, the Democratic Republic of Congo, Equatorial Guinea, Gabon, Ghana, Guinea, Liberia, Madagascar, Mali, Mauritania, Niger, Nigeria, Republic of Congo, São Tomé and Príncipe and Sierra Leone.

Under the initiative the government and private firms are to disclose their financial payments and receipts from the extractive sector. Governments are expected to prepare and present reports disclosing revenues generated from the extractive sector. Five African countries— Cameroon, Gabon, Ghana, Mauritania and Nigeria—have issued reports under the initiative. In Nigeria and Ghana the involvement of the civil society in the process has been remarkable. In Nigeria the process has been domesticated and referred to as the Nigerian Extractive Industry Transparency Initiative. The process

> *Publish What You Pay was prompted by the lack of transparency that usually characterises financial transactions between multinational corporations and governments*

has secured the endorsement of the Nigerian government at the highest level, there is an active engagement of different stakeholders in government, industry and civil society groups and a sustained commitment to the process is shown in the establishment of the National Stakeholders Working Group with a permanent secretariat and a professional staff. In Ghana and the Democratic Republic of the Congo civil society groups have been active in monitoring the implementation of the EITI process (McPherson and MacSearraigh 2007).

The EITI process, though commendable, is still in its infancy in promoting a corruption-free extractive sector in Africa. The sector is still enmeshed in ugly corruption in Africa. There is still a danger that the government and private firms will make false declarations and that civil society organisations can be co-opted through bribes, contracts and other incentives. And developed countries may be unwilling to impose sanctions on the firms not cooperating with the process.

International dimensions of corruption in Africa

For national anti-corruption efforts to be successful, it is necessary to address the international dimension of the problem, particularly asset repatriation and money laundering. Both those who steal funds and assets and the receivers of such items—the money launderers and the receivers of such laundered funds—are equally guilty. In other words, grand corruption in Africa would prove unattractive without

safe haven and receiving banks in the Western world for such stolen funds. If asset repatriation becomes part of international legal culture, the peculation of national funds by leaders and policy makers would be significantly discouraged.

Asset repatriation

Asset repatriation was in the forefront of negotiations for the UN Convention against Corruption because it is "a vital issue for developing countries where cases of grand corruption have exported national wealth to international banking centres and financial havens, and where resources are badly needed for financing for development" (Webb 2005). The UN Convention calls on states to help other states identify, trace, freeze, seize and confiscate assets acquired through corrupt practices.

Several initiatives have been taken in Africa, including calls by Transparency International's representatives in African countries for actions, policies and laws more conducive to the tracing, recovery and repatriation of wealth stolen from Africa.[9] But asset repatriation has proven very complicated and fraught with serious difficulties and challenges.

The difficulty stems from the legal regime in force in some Western countries. It has been rightly argued that the best way to confiscate and return assets is through direct recognition and enforcement of foreign orders, rather than by applying for a domestic order in the requested country (OECD 2008). However, few Western countries agree to do

'If asset repatriation becomes part of international legal culture, the peculation of national funds by leaders and policy makers would be significantly discouraged

it.[10] The current practice does not make the confiscation and return of assets easy. Switzerland and Liechtenstein have asset secrecy laws that make it difficult for third parties to access personal accounts of depositors, even if it is in the national interest of the asset-fleeing country. The political economy of asset recovery is that the proceeds of corruption provide valuable and cheap investment resources for the recipient countries, which they are often reluctant to repatriate back to the originating country. The complicated legal regime in the beneficiary countries serves as formidable obstacles to the process of assets repatriation.

Asset recovery is also expensive, involving very high legal costs and continuous engagement of competent experts. The substantial cost and lengthy time it takes for recovery is a disincentive for asset-fleeing countries to pursue the course.

The international community needs to identify the obstacles a country engaging in asset recovery faces and assist in overcoming those obstacles. The provisions on asset repatriation in the UN Convention must be strictly enforced. And the UN Security Council may need to consider classifying the receipt and harbouring of stolen assets as a global security risk because it threatens the peace, progress and development of many African and developing countries.

Countries that serve as financial havens should be sensitised to the consequences of their policies and urged to work in accordance with the standards provided in the relevant instruments. The civil society of these countries should also be involved and be aware that "it is morally reprehensible, unjust, and unfair and against all established human values to engage in actions that actually encourage corruption in poor nations to fatten [their] own countries. . . . The thief and the receiver are guilty of the same offence" (Scher 2005).

Laundering the proceeds of corruption

There is an international consensus that laundering the proceeds of corruption should be illegal.[11] Laundering refers to activities that conceal or disguise the illicit origin of property or help persons involved in corrupt activities escape the legal consequences of their acts. Money laundering is done through three steps: placement, which is putting the proceeds of corruption into the financial system; layering, which consists in breaking the linkages between the goods and their criminal origins through highly complex transactions, conversions and transfers and integration, which is placing the proceeds of crime into the economy in an apparently legitimate source.

Money laundering supports complex corrupt practices that in turn facilitate the commission of crime (Moshi 2007). It promotes illegitimate enrichment, threatens the effectiveness of the state, undermines the rule of law and has the potential to destroy public confidence in state institutions.

> ' The international community needs to identify the obstacles a country engaging in asset recovery faces and assist in overcoming those obstacles

Due to the clandestine character of the practice, it is difficult to estimate the amount of money being laundered in Africa. But "there is no country where the amount of illicit money generated is believed to be negligible" (Moshi 2007). The prevalence of money laundering in the continent is disturbing, especially in relation to the extractive industries and the illegal drug trade. Money laundering flourishes where financial systems are fragile and the capacity of law enforcement agencies is weak. The capacity to investigate and prosecute corrupt officials and corporations in money laundering cases is often inadequate in many African countries, given the legal technicalities and logistics involved (Standing 2007).

Despite the difficulty involved in prosecuting money laundering, there are a few encouraging examples where some African countries have managed to trace and confiscate assets and punish those involved. In Lesotho the World Bank was funding the construction of a dam and tunnel system meant to provide water to South Africa and electricity to Lesotho. The Lesotho Highlands Development Authority was managing this project. It appeared that transnational companies, to secure contracts, had paid bribes to high-level officials through Switzerland-based bank accounts of intermediaries. A large part of the money paid to such intermediaries was paid to the chief executive officer of the development authority (Levi et al. 2007).

Several initiatives have been taken at the global and regional levels to combat money laundering, including in connection to financing for terrorism. The Anti-Money Laundering/Combating the Financing of Terrorism (AML/CFT) framework requires financial institutions worldwide to monitor, investigate and report suspicious transactions. Under this framework, states have several obligations that depend somewhat on their ratification or accession to various other conventions. The Financial Action Task Force, put in place in 1987 by the G7 industrial countries to address money laundering, sets the AML standards. Given the complexity of action required under the AML/CFT standards, Africa needs assistance in implementing its obligations; the IMF has committed itself to this end (Levi et al. 2007).

Other regional initiatives include the Inter-Governmental Action Group against Money Laundering in West Africa (GIABA) established by the Economic Community of West African States (ECOWAS). GIABA's mandate includes adopting standards against money laundering and the financing of terrorism in accordance with acceptable international standards and practices and facilitating the adoption and implementation by member states of measures against money laundering and financing of terrorism, taking into account specific regional peculiarities and conditions (GIABA 2007). Other regional groups are the Middle East and North Africa Financial Action Task Force (MENAFAFT) and the Eastern and Southern Africa Anti-Money Laundering Group (ESAAMLG).

> *Several initiatives have been taken at the global and regional levels to combat money laundering, including in connection to financing for terrorism*

While GIABA and ESAAMLG have been granted observer status with the FATF, MENAFAFT is an associate member.[12]

All of these bodies aim to foster the adoption and implementation of standards, laws and policies to suppress money laundering and the financing of terrorism. Their actions have resulted in the creation of national follow-up committees in some countries, such as Côte d'Ivoire (Beket 2008).

Conclusion

Corruption remains a major challenge for many African countries. The general perception of the people is that many of the institutions of government are corrupt to varying degrees and the non-state institutions of civil society and the private sector are not insulated from the problem. Corruption remains the single most important challenge to the eradication of poverty, the creation of a predictable and favourable investment environment and general socioeconomic development. It continues to deepen poverty and impede reaching the Millennium Development Goals.

On a positive note there are remarkable efforts to address the problem. International and regional anti-corruption instruments and frameworks provide benchmarks and parameters by which African countries can tackle the problem. Many countries have passed anti-corruption laws, although those laws may not be up to the standards and requirements of the international and regional instruments.

Multiple anti-corruption institutions have been established in many countries—bodies charged with detecting money laundering, a dedicated anti-corruption body, a code of conduct bureau, an ombudsman and oversight agencies such as an auditor general. In addition, parliamentary committees and ad hoc investigative tribunals are regularly established to investigate specific cases of corruption or maladministration.

At the international level efforts to fight corruption include the Extractive Industries Transparency Initiative, the Publish What You Pay Campaign and the Kimberley Process. All three have improved the management and increased the transparency and accountability in the extractive sector. But corruption persists in the extractive industries, deepening the impact of poverty in many resource-rich countries.

The recovery and repatriation of stolen assets and resources to Africa from the West remains a dark spot in the global anti-corruption campaign. Western countries are not demonstrating a commitment to tackling the problem. The legal regime for asset repatriation is deliberately complicated and cumbersome in recipient countries, and the costs and time associated with the process make it an arduous, if not almost impossible, challenge for African countries to accomplish asset recovery. The provisions of the UN Convention Against Corruption on assets recovery must be duly enforced, while the United Nations Security Council must consider classifying the harbouring of stolen

> ‘ *Corruption remains a major challenge for many African countries. But there are remarkable efforts to address the problem*

assets from poor countries as a global security risk.

In the final analysis, the fight against corruption will involve considerable efforts by African countries in three areas:

- *Strong institutions.* Countries must build oversight institutions, namely the parliament, judiciary, office of the auditor general, the ombudsman, the public procurement system and the various anti-corruption bodies established for the purpose of tackling the multifaceted dimensions of corruption. Those bodies must have institutional autonomy, operational capacity, resources and a free and democratic environment in which to function. A freedom-of-information law is a major prerequisite for creating information flow and entrenching the culture of transparency and accountability in the conduct of public affairs.

- *A powerful anti-corruption constituency.* Civil society and the media, complemented by the key public institutions, can provide a powerful constituency in the fight against corruption in Africa. Regular exchange of ideas, information and collaboration should occur among all these actors and institutions involved in the national anti-corruption campaign.

- *Better remuneration for public servants.* Public-sector workers in Africa need to earn living wages in order to improve their morale and dedication to work and to prevent moonlighting and the temptation to subvert the public good through corrupt practices. In Uganda there is a popular sarcasm among civil servants, who say "my employer pretends that he is paying me, and I also pretend that I am working for him". The underlying factor is lack of commitment due to low wages. Both petty corruption and collaboration in grand corruption by civil servants are often bred by the need to augment poor salaries.

Notes

1. Thirty-three of the 53 African countries have ratified the United Nations Convention against Corruption: Algeria, Angola, Benin, Burkina Faso, Burundi, Cameroon, Central African Republic, Republic of the Congo, Djibouti, Egypt, Gabon, Ghana, Guinea Bissau, Kenya, Lesotho, Liberia, Libyan Arab Jamahiriya, Madagascar, Mauritania, Mauritius, Morocco, Namibia, Nigeria, Rwanda, São Tomé and Príncipe, Senegal, Seychelles, Sierra Leone, South Africa, Togo, Uganda, United Republic of Tanzania and Zimbabwe. The list of ratifying countries is compiled at the United Nations Treaty Collection, *Status of Multilateral Treaties Deposited with the Secretary-General.*

2. Twenty-seven states have ratified the African Union Convention on Preventing and Combating Corruption: Algeria, Benin, Burkina Faso, Burundi, Comoros, Republic of the Congo, Ethiopia, Ghana, Kenya, Libya, Lesotho,

Liberia, Madagascar, Mali, Malawi, Mozambique, Namibia, Nigeria, Niger, Rwanda, South Africa, Senegal, Seychelles, Tanzania, Uganda, Zambia and Zimbabwe. See African Union, *African Convention on Preventing and Combating Corruption: Status List.*

3. At the time of preparing this report, the two former presidents were still on trial in their countries for corruption charges.

4. In some cases, the appointment of a state official to the board of a private firm is postdated—held in trust until the public officer retires from the public service. This is common in the oil and gas sectors.

5. The Business Anti-Corruption Portal was developed by the Ministry of Foreign Affairs of Denmark, Deutsche Gesellschaft für Technische Zusammenarbeit and the Dutch Ministry of Foreign Affairs.

6. In the Nigerian case, the head of the anti-corruption agency—the Economic and Financial Crimes Commission—Mr. Nuhu Ribadu was recalled back to the police force (being a serving police officer). In the case of Kenya, John Githongo had to flee the country for fear of his personal safety.

7. See ECA country reports, 2007, for the countries cited and also USAID 2007.

8. See ECA Seychelles country report 2007.

9. These include the 2001 Nyanga Declaration and the 2006 Nairobi Declaration.

10. Although the Hague Convention recognizes the enforcement of foreign court orders, only three African countries are members of the Hague Convention on Private International Law. And generally for Western countries, the issue of assets reparation has been a serious political issue.

11. This prohibition is made explicit in article 6 of the African Union Convention on Preventing and Combating Corruption.

12. The list of FATF members and observers is available at www.fatf-gafi.org/document/52/0,3343,en_32250379_32237295_34027188_1_1_1_1,00.html.

References

Adejumobi, Said. 2007. "When Votes Do Not Count: The 2007 General Elections in Nigeria." *Nordic Africa Institute News*, No. 2 (May 2007).

AfDB (African Development Bank Group). 2003. "Proceeding of the Regional Learning Workshop on Combating Corruption in Africa." Paper presented at African Union Conference Center, Addis Ababa.

———. 2006. "Combating corruption in Africa: Issues and challenges." Concept paper for 2006 AfDB annual meeting. Ouagadougou: AfDB Operations Policy and Review Department.

African Union. *African Convention on Preventing and Combating Corruption: Status List.* www.africaunion.org/root/au/Documents/Treaties/List/African%20Convention%20on%20Combating%20Corruption.pdf.

Akomaye, Emmanuel. 2007. "Nigeria's Experience in Combating Corruption." Paper presented to the UNECA Ad Hoc Expert Group Meeting, "Deepening Judiciary Effectiveness in Combating Corruption." Addis Ababa: United Nations Economic Commission for Africa.

Amah, Madaki. 2005. "Curbing Corruption in Nigeria: Exploring

Alternative Strategies." Mimeo cited at www.nigeriannews. com/specialsmadakiOAmeh/ Madaki_O_Ameh_04_14_2005.

Annan, Kofi. 2003. "Message to the Third Global Forum on Fighting Corruption and Safeguarding Integrity." Speech delivered by Dileep Nair, Under-Secretary-General for Internal Oversight Services, 29 May 2003.

Ayamdoo, Charles. 2007. "Ghana's Experience in Fighting Corruption." Paper presented to the UNECA Ad Hoc Expert Group Meeting, "Deepening Judiciary Effectiveness in Combating Corruption." Addis Ababa: United Nations Economic Commission for Africa.

Beket, Patrice. 2008. "Lutte contre le blanchiment d'argent : un Comite de suivi intsalle." *Le Matin d'Abidjan,* 8 September 2008. www. lematindabidjan.com/visual_article. php?num_actualite=9519.

Bone, Andrew. n.d. "Conflict diamonds: The De Beers Group and the Kimberley Process." Press Release. London: De Beers Group Canada Inc. www.debeersgroup.com.

Botswana, Republic of. 2006. *Ombudsman Annual Report 2005/2006*.

Business Anti-Corruption Portal. www. business-anti-corruption.com.

CAFOD (Catholic Agency for Overseas Development). 1999. "The Rough Guide to Transparency and Natural Resource Revenues." Briefing paper. Berlin: CAFOD. www.cafod.org.uk.

———. 2006. "Unearth Justice: Counting the Coast of Gold." CAFOD report. Berlin: CAFOD. www.cafod. org.uk.

Coldham, Simon. 1995. "Legal Response to State Corruption in Commonwealth Africa." *Journal of African Law* 39(2):115–126.

Deinger, Klaus, and Paul Mpuga. 2004. "Does Greater Accountability Improve the Quality of Delivery of Public Services? Evidence from Uganda." World Bank Policy Research Working Paper. Washington D.C.: World Bank.

Doig, Watt, and Robert Williams. 2005. "Measuring 'Success' in Five African Anti-Corruption Commissions: The Case of Ghana, Malawi, Tanzania, Uganda and Zambia." Draft final report. Anti-Corruption Resource Center. www.U4 reports.

———. 2006. "Hands on or Hands Off? Anti-Corruption Agencies in Action, Donor Expectations, and a Good Enough Reality." *Public Administration and Development* 26:163–172. www.interscience.wiley.com.

———. 2007. "Why do Developing Country Anti-Corruption Commissions Fail to Deal with Corruption? Understanding the Three Dilemmas of Organizational Development, Performance Expectation and Donor and Government Cycle." *Public Administration and Development* 27:251–259.

ECA (United Nations Economic Commission for Africa). 2007a. "Deepening Judiciary's Effectiveness in Combating Corruption." Background Paper for UNECA Ad Hoc Expert Group Meeting, "Deepening Judiciary Effectiveness in Combating Corruption." Addis Ababa.

———. 2007b. Botswana country report. Addis Ababa.

———. 2007c. Djibouti country report. Addis Ababa.

———. 2007d. Malawi country report. Addis Ababa.

———. 2007e. Namibia country report. Addis Ababa.

———. 2007f. Senegal country report. Addis Ababa.

———. 2007g. Swaziland country report. Addis Ababa.

Extractive Industries Transparency Initiative. 2005. *Extractive Industries Transparency Initiative Source Book*. www.eitransparency.org.

———. 2008. Secretariat Work Plan. www.eitransparency.org.

Faull, Andrew. 2008. "Managing Corruption in the SAPS and Metro-Police Departments." *SA Crime Quarterly* No. 23.

Gbadamosi, Gbolahan. 2005. "Corruption Perception and Sustainable Development: Sharing Botswana's Anti-Graft Agency Experience." *South Africa Journal of Economics and Management Studies* 9(2): 262–276.

GIABA (Inter-Governmental Action Group against Money Laundering in West Africa). 2007. *Annual Report 2007*.

Githongo, John. 2007. "Kenya's Fight against Corruption: An Uneven Path to Political Accountability." Development Policy Briefing Paper No. 2, Center for Global Liberty & Prosperity.

Global Integrity. 2007. "Key finding: The wealthier G8 countries suffer from similar corruption charges as developing countries." *Global Integrity Report 2007*. http://report.globalintegrity.org/globalindex/findingd.cfm#g8.

Global Policy Forum. 2008. "Kimberley Process." Global Policy Forum Publications. www.globalpolicy.org.

Global Witness. 2005. "Make it Work: Why Kimberley Process Must Do More to Stop Conflict Diamonds." Available at www.globalwitness.org or www.globalpolicy.org

———. 2006. "The Kimberley Process at Risk." www.globalwitness.org.

Goldwyn, David, ed. 2008. "Drilling Down: The Civil Society Guide to Extractive Industry Revenues and the EITI." New York: Revenue Watch Institute. www.revenuewatch.org.

Guardian newspaper (Lagos).

Hansungule, Michelo. 2003. "*Anti-Corruption Initiatives in Africa: An Overview*." Good Governance Program, University of Pretoria, South Africa.

Heilbrunn, John. 2004. "Anti-Corruption Commissions: Panacea or Real Medicine to Fight Corruption." Washington D.C.: The World Bank.

Holman, Michael. 2006. "An Africa that takes care of itself." *Los Angeles Times*, May 23 2006, B13. http://articles.latimes.com/may/23/opinion/oe-holman23.

Hope, Kempe Ronald, and Bornwell C. Chikulo. 2000. *Corruption and Development in Africa*. New York: Macmillan Press Ltd.

Human Rights Watch. 2004. "Some Transparency, No Accountability: The Use of Oil Revenue in Angola and its Impact on Human Rights." www.hrw.org.

ISS (Institute for Security Studies). 1997. "Corruption: The Antithesis of Good Governance." In Lala Camerer, ed., *Costly Crimes: Commercial Crime and Corruption in Africa*. Monograph no. 15. www.iss.co.za/pubs/monographs/no15/section.html.

———. 2004. *Handbook. A comparative analysis: SADC Protocol against Corruption (2001), AU Convention on Preventing and Combating Corruption (2003), UN Convention against Corruption (2003)*. www.iss.co.za/dynamic/administration/file_manager/file_links/CORRUPT HANDBOOKNOV04.PDF.

Jain, Arvind, ed. 2001. *The Political Economy of Corruption*. London: Routledge.

Johnston, Michael. 1999. "A Brief History of Anti-Corruption Agencies."

In A. Schedler, L. Diamond, and M. Plattner, eds., *The self-restraining state: power and accountability in new democracies*. Boulder, CO: Lynne Rienner.

Kimberley Process, 2008. "Kimberley Process: From Conflict Diamonds to Prosperity Diamonds." Press release. Available at www.kimberleyprocess.com.

Klitgaard, Robert, 1988. *Controlling Corruption*. Berkeley: University of California Press.

Kofele-Kale, Ndiva. 2006. "Change or the Illusion of Change: The War Against Official Corruption in Africa." *The George Washington International Law Review* 38(4): 697–747.

Kyambalesa, Henery. 2006. "Corruption: Causes, Effects, and Deterrents." *African Insights* 36(2): 102–122.

Le, Tuan Minh. 2007. "Combating Corruption in Revenue Administration: An overview." In J. Edgardo Campos and Sanjay Pradhan, eds., *The Many Faces of Corruption*: *Tracking Vulnerabilities at the Sector level*. Washington D.C.: World Bank.

Levi, M., M. Dakolias, and T. Greenberg. 2007. "Money laundering and corruption." In J. Edgardo Campos and Sanjay Pradhan, eds., *The Many Faces of Corruption: Tracking Vulnerabilities at the Sectoral Level* . Washington, D.C.: World Bank.

Madise, Dingiswayo. 2007. "Challenges in the Fight against Corruption in Malawi: Some Thoughts." Paper Presented to the UNECA Ad Hoc Experts Group Meeting, "Deepening Judiciary's Effectiveness in Combating Corruption." Addis Ababa.

McPherson, Charles, and Stephen MacSearraigh. 2007. "Corruption in the Petroleum Sector." In J. Edgardo Campos and Sanjay Pradhan, eds., *The Many Faces of Corruption:*

Tracking Vulnerabilities at the Sector Level. Washington D.C: World Bank.

Michael, Bryane. 2004. "What Do African Donor-Sponsored Anti-Corruption Programs Teach Us about International development in Africa?" *Social Policy and Administration* 38(9): 320–345.

Moshi, H. 2007. *Fighting money laundering —the challenges in Africa.* Institute for Security Studies paper 152.

OECD (Organisation for Economic Cooperation and Development). 2008. *Corruption: A Glossary of International Standards in Criminal Law.* www.oecd.org/dataoecd/59/38/41194428.pdf.

Plummer, Janelle, and Piers Cross. 2007. "Tackling Corruption in the Water and Sanitation Sector in Africa: Starting the Dialogue." In J. Edgardo Campos and Sanjay Pradhan, eds., *The Many Faces of Corruption: Tracking Vulnerabilities at the Sector level.* Washington, D.C.: World Bank.

Publish What You Pay and Revenue Watch Institute. 2006. "Eye on EITI: Civil Society Perspectives and Recommendations on the Extractive Industries Transparency Initiative." New York: Revenue Watch Institute.

Publish What You Pay. Website. www.publishwhatyoupay.org/english.

RFI actualités. 2008. "Jacob Zuma parviendra-t-il à échapper à la justice ? " www.rfi.fr/actufr/articles/104/article_69347.asp.

Rogers, Elizabeth. 2006. "Conflict diamonds; Certification and corruption: a case study of Sierra Leone." *Journal of Financial Crime* 13(3).

Sardan, Oliver. 1999. "A moral economy of corruption in Africa." *Journal of Modern African Studies* 37(1).

Scher, D. 2005. "Asset recovery: Repatriating Africa's looted billions." *African Security Review* 14(4): 2005.

Shehu, Abdullahi. 2004. "Combating Corruption in Nigeria: Bliss or Bluster?" *Journal of Financial Crime* 12(1): 69–74.

Smillie, Ian. 2002. "Securing Sustainable Development: Trade, Aid and Security: Diamond Timber and West African Wars." Working paper, Ottawa: International Institute for Sustainable Development. www. iisd.org

———. 2005. "The Kimberley Process Certification Scheme for Rough Diamonds." In Verifor Case Studies. London: Overseas Development. www.verifor.org

Standing, Andre. 2007. "Corruption and the Extractive Industries in Africa: Can Combating Corruption Cure Resource Curse?" Institute for Security Studies Paper 153.

Stapenhurst, Rick, Nial Johnson, and Ricardo Pelizoo, eds. 2006. *Role of parliament in curbing corruption.* Washington, D.C.: World Bank.

Transparency International. 2006. "Report on the Transparency International Global Corruption Barometer." www.transparency.org.

———. 2007a. Corruption Perceptions Index. Regional Highlights: Africa. www.transparency.org/policy_research/surveys_indices/cpi/2007/regional_highlights_factsheets (accessed on 12 August 2008).

———. 2007b. "Mapping of Corruption and Governance Measurement Tools in Sub-Saharan Africa."

———. 2007c. Transparency International Global Perception Index.

———. 2008. "Promoting Revenue Transparency: Report on Revenue Transparency and Oil and Gas Companies." Transparency International in Focus. Berlin: Transparency International. www.transparency.org.

———. 2008. Kenyan Bribery Index 2008. www.tikenya.org/documents/KenyaBriberyIndex08.pdf.

U4 Help Desk. 2008. FAQs: Causes and Consequences of Corruption: What do we know about the causes and consequences of corruption?" www.u4.no/helpdesk.

United Nations. *Status of Multilateral Treaties Deposited with the Secretary-General.* http://untreaty.un.org/ENGLISH/bible/englishinternetbible/partI/chapterXVIII/treaty18.asp (accessed 12 August 2008).

USAID (United States Agency for International Development). 2007. "A Rapid Anti-Corruption Assessment Technique for USAID/Africa: Developing a Practical Checklist for USAID Missions in Africa." Washington D.C.: USAID.

Webb, Philippa. 2005. "The United Nations Convention Against Corruption: Global Achievement or Missed Opportunity?" *Journal of International Economic Law* 8(1).

Wright, Clive. 2004. "Tackling Conflict Diamonds: The Kimberley Process Certification Scheme." *International Peace Keeping* 11(4):697–708.

World Bank. 2008. "Implementing the Extractive Industries Transparency Initiative." Washington D.C.: World Bank.

In the early years of independence African countries made a deliberate effort to build human capacity. They established schools, health facilities, and universities dedicated to producing the human skills that the newly established states needed. Education was recognized as the bedrock of the future, producing the human capital to meet the needs of the continent.

The policy shift by international financial institutions in the 1980s de-emphasized the value of universities and pressured governments to invest less in higher education. As universities decayed, many trained professionals left for greener pastures. Between 1986 and 1996, of the 1,708 Africans awarded PhDs in U.S. and Canadian universities, only 687 returned to Africa (ECA n.d.-b). And the emergence of oppressive military and authoritarian regimes accelerated the brain drain, leaving many universities in dire need of human and financial resources to run even skeletal programs.

The structural adjustment programs of the World Bank and International Monetary Fund also had a devastating effect on the morale of civil servants. Governments were forced to reduce the public service, and many civil servants lost their means of livelihood. The freeze in recruitment that was subsequently instituted directly undermined capacity building for service delivery and severely undermined the caliber of the civil service.

The downsizing strategy promised a "lean and muscular civil service" with improved salaries for those who would remain in service. But Gelasi Mutahaba has observed:

> One singularly significant shortcoming was the conspicuous absence of effective pay and incentives reform, which remain critical to sustainable capacity building. Consequently, morale and discipline in the public service remained low, and unethical conduct in ways of bribery and corruption were on the rise. In the circumstances, service delivery continued to deteriorate in most countries throughout the 1990s (Mutahaba 2002, 12).

A need for new capacities was driven by the shift to market economies and to programs of economic growth led by the private sector, demands for transparency and accountability as part of good governance, the emerging global market and the advent of information technology. Despite many efforts, the capacity-building challenges for African countries continue to persist. The capacity deficit remains one of the major constraints to putting Africa on the path to accelerated growth and sustainable development. It is the critical missing link in Africa's development and democratization.

Human development entails enormous socioeconomic transformation, requiring the building of the appropriate capacities to ensure its achievement (Mohiddin 2007). African governments have recently launched capacity-building initiatives such as the New

Box 8.1 Definitions of capacity development

1. "Capacity building is the ability of individuals, groups, institutions and organisations to identify and solve development problems over time" (Peter Morgan 1996).

2. Capacity development is a concept which is broader than organisational development since it includes an emphasis on the overall system, environment or context within which individuals, organisations and societies operate and interact (and not simply a single organisation (UNDP 1998).

3. Capacity development is "any system, effort or process . . . which includes among its major objectives strengthening the capability of elected chief executive officers, department and agency heads and programme managers in general purpose government to plan, implement, manage or evaluate policies, strategies or programs designed to impact on social conditions in the community" (Cohen 1993).

4. "Capacity is the combination of people, institutions and practices that permits countries to reach their development goals. . . . Capacity building is . . . investment in human capital, institutions and practices" (World Bank 1998).

5. Capacity building is any support that strengthens an institution's ability to effectively and efficiently design, implement and evaluate development activities according to its mission (UNICEF-Namibia 1996).

6. "Capacity building is a process by which individuals, groups, institutions, organisations and societies enhance their abilities to identify and meet development challenges in a sustainable manner (CIDA 1996).

7. Capacity development: "The process by which individuals, groups, organisations, institutions and societies increase their abilities: to perform functions solve problems and achieve objectives; to understand and deal with their development need in a broader context and in a sustainable manner" (UNDP 1997).

8. Capacity strengthening is an ongoing process by which people band systems, operating within dynamic contexts, enhance their abilities to develop and implement strategies in pursuit of their objectives for increased performance in a sustainable way" (Lusthaus et al. 1995).

Source: From Lusthaus et al. 1999, 3.

African Partnership for Development (NEPAD) and the African Peer Review Mechanism (APRM). NEPAD promotes sustainable human development, eradication of poverty, continental and political integration and global competitiveness. APRM is a mechanism to promote the political, social and economic objectives of NEPAD and ensure that participating countries observe its principles and practices. To achieve NEPAD's objective of promoting sustainable human development, it is necessary to mobilize human and material resources and forge cooperation and partnership between government and civil society organisations (CSOs) at the national and international levels.

The African Governance Forum (AGF) that convened at Kigali, Rwanda, in May 2006 (AGF VI) recognized that capacity is key to ensuring good governance and the delivery of services. It dedicated its next forum, AGF VII, to issues of capacity building for development and the building of the capable state. From AGF VII, which convened at Ouagadougou, Burkina Faso, in October 2007, a consensus emerged that African governments must address capacity of the institutions of governance so that they can deliver services efficiently, effectively, equitably and predictably.

What is capacity building?

Capacity building—or "capacity development", the term widely used in the 1990s—has been defined in varying ways by different development agencies. Some use narrow definitions that focus on strengthening organisations and skills, while others use a broader definition that encompasses levels of capacity from the individual to the whole society. Box 8.1 is a sample of definitions from individuals and organisations.

Generally defined, capacity building is the ability of people, institutions and societies to perform functions, solve problems and set and achieve objectives. To be successful, capacity development needs to take place on the individual, institutional and societal levels (box 8.2). At the individual level capacity development relates to the knowledge, skills, values and ability of a person to perform set tasks in a conducive environment. At the organisational level it suggests the resources—human, material, physical and technological—available to perform organisational responsibilities effectively. At the societal level it involves the formal institutions, rules, procedures, processes and social and human infrastructures available for achieving collective goals defined by that society.

There are some core principles to guide effective capacity development at the organisational or societal level: ownership, sustainability, participation, mobilization of local resources and change processes. All capacity development efforts and training must be geared toward better performance of an institution or society in an inward looking, sustainable manner (see box. 8.3).

The capacity of an institution is essentially the product of the

Box 8.2 Key capacity notions and elements at three levels of capacity development

Level of capacity	Notion of capacity	Elements of capacity
Individual	The will and ability to set objectives and achieve them using ones own knowledge and skills.	Knowledge, skills, values, attitude, health, awareness.
Organisation	Anything that will positively influence organisational performance.	Human resources (capacities of individuals in organisations). Physical resources (facilities, equipment, material, etc.) and capital. Intellectual organisational resources (organisational strategy, strategic planning, business know-how, production technology, program management). Leadership of managers.
Environment	A conducive environment-political, legal, economic, social and cultural promotive of individual and organisational performance.	Formal institutions (laws, policies, ordinances). Informal institutions (customs, culture, norms). Social capital, social infrastructure.

Source: Adapted from UNESCO-IICBA 2006, 6.

dynamic interactions between the people managing the institution and the laws, rules, norms and traditions of the institution. The performance of the people will be determined by three factors: availability of supportive infrastructures, equipment and financial resources; their technical skills and professional competence and their commitment and integrity

Box 8.3 Principles of effective capacity development

Ownership. The people or organisation for which a capacity building project is meant must claim it, own it and drive it. Externally driven capacity development programmes are often fraught with tensions and contradictions and may not be durable.

Sustainability. In crafting capacity building programmes adequate attention and strategic planning should be focused on its sustainability.

Participation. Capacity development programmes must be participatory, especially for its recipients. Improving knowledge and skills, changing organisational culture and introducing modern techniques in institutions should be based on the active involvement of the major stakeholders of those projects.

Mobilization of local resources. Capacity development premised on external resources, whether human or material, is not sustainable. For capacity development to be indigenous, it must mobilize local resources in order to gain commitment.

Change process. Capacity development must be a change process. Ultimately, it should change the actions, processes and culture of an individual or organisation for better performance. This requires clear distillation of issues of capacity for whom, for what and in whose interests.

in observing the rules and regulations, norms and conventions of the institution (Mohiddin 2007).

In essence, capacity building is about people, who have to be trained, equipped, sufficiently remunerated and adequately motivated in the efficient uses and management of resources. It should also be recognized that capacity building is more than a technical exercise. It is rooted in the political economy as well as the legal and cultural traditions of the country, and any durable capacity building must take those factors into account. Equally important for capacity development is leadership that articulates strong national visions and values and creates an environment for human and institutional enhancement. Likewise, capacity-building efforts must necessarily be long-term and systemic. An evaluation of World Bank support for capacity building in Africa observed:

> The evaluation's findings underscore the importance of approaching capacity building in Africa as a core objective and ensuring that capacity building support is country-owned, results-oriented and evidence-based. The challenges to improving public-sector performance in Africa—posed by political and institutional characteristics, weak incentives, poor working conditions and emigration of highly skilled professionals—necessitate the priority of long-term efforts (World Bank 2005, xvii).

Capacity deficits in Africa

When they achieved independence, many African countries inherited weak and inefficient governance institutions, designed to serve colonial interests but of little value for post-independent states. From the beginning, the new African states needed to build capacity. But policies of the development donors did not have a positive impact on capacity building because they lacked internal ownership.

Authoritarian rule in many African countries in the early years of independence resulted in weak institutional capacity building and further undermined the already weak capacity bequeathed by colonial rulers. Military governments undermined institutions of good governance, namely, the constitution, political parties, the media and the judiciary. Finally, the structural adjustment programs of the Bretton Woods institutions in the 1980s undermined the capacity of public institutions in health and education, as well as the civil service and public enterprises (ECA 2005).

In the last few decades a great deal of resources has been committed to building capacity in Africa. The World Bank, the African Development Bank, the United Nations Development Programme, the Economic Commission for Africa, the Organisation for Economic Cooperation and Development and many governments under bilateral arrangements have been among the major players in advocating for, promoting or funding capacity building initiatives.

Almost a quarter of the US$55 billion of total annual overseas development assistance is directed to capacity building, mainly through technical assistance. The World Bank has also been a major provider of resources for capacity building by supporting a wide range of interventions through its country lending and non-lending programs and dedicated corporate and regional entities. "Between 1995 and 2004, the Bank provided some $9 billion in lending and close to $900 million in grants and administrative budget to support capacity building in Africa" (World Bank 2005, vii). The bulk

of this support has been directed toward the public sector.

How well has the World Bank's money been used? A Bank evaluation report noted: "[D]espite substantial progress in reforming the overall policy environment in the developing world and the steady improvement in the quality of project lending, development outcomes are still falling short of expectations, especially in Africa. Much of this shortfall is attributable to lagging capacity development" (World Bank n.d., 1). This suggests that capacity-development initiatives and strategy of the international development partners in Africa have been either inappropriate or ineffective in scaling up Africa's capacity to the required level for better economic management and performance. On the World Bank's role, the report further noted that "the Bank's support for capacity building in Africa remains less effective than it could be" (World Bank 2005, viii).

In many respects technical assistance measures and training have been found wanting. Technical assistance programs fill capacity gaps rather than build sustained country capacity. Thus they did not often lead to improved and sustained public-sector performance because they failed to apply the tools within a broad framework of human resource management and link them to organisational and institutional developments.

Seeing that the numerous training interventions and other capacity building initiatives over the years

> ' *Technical assistance programs fill capacity gaps rather than build sustained country capacity. Thus they did not often lead to improved and sustained public-sector performance*

have had little impact, some have started to question the value of continuing with such exercises. They doubt their effectiveness and whether new skills were acquired and translated into improved organisational performance. According to one report, "Training interventions have generally been funded without an organisational training needs assessment or a comprehensive trainings plan. Staff is being trained for specific tasks before they are in positions to use the training, or before measures have been taken to help retain them" (World Bank 2005, 32). The traditional approach, which focused on creating or reorganizing government units and building individual skills, could not by itself foster improved public-sector performance because it failed to address the institutional context in which organisations and individuals operated. The institutional context is critical to ensure that the necessary incentives and rewards are provided for improved public-sector performance. Training can be only part of the human capacity-building solution.

Capacity development has emerged in reaction to the poor results of initiatives based on technical cooperation. The new approach emphasizes that root causes of poverty, illiteracy and ill health are lack of capacity in government to design and implement proper development strategies and the inability of society to hold government accountable for its actions. It argues development achievements will be scalable and sustainable only if political and economic institutions function properly (World Bank 2005).

> *Capacity development has emerged in reaction to the poor results of initiatives based on technical cooperation*

Critical rethinking over the years has led to a growing global consensus that:

Capacity development is a long-term process, rarely amenable to seeking quick results through shortcuts. It is, above all, an endogenous course of action that builds on existing capacities and assets. As an endogenous voluntary process, capacity development can be supported or distorted by external interventions. Furthermore, to be successful, capacity development needs to take place at three cross-linked levels: the individual, institutional as well as societal levels.

A central element of this consensus is that capacity develops and takes root where incentives—monetary and non-monetary—are favorable, and dwindles where they are perverse. These incentives shape the demand for capacity, as when governance arrangements enable user, parliamentary, and citizen oversight to hold governments accountable for performance. Incentives also sustain the supply of national capacity as when pay polices reward highly-skilled professionals for remaining in the African public sector, and the enabling environment for private investment harnesses domestic entrepreneurial skills, rather than adding to "brain drain". As with the effectiveness of overall development assistance, ownership, local championship, commitment, and strong leadership are seen in the emerging consensus as prerequisites for sustainable capacity development. On the external side, the gap filling approach that tended to be donor driven needs to be replaced by a more "organic" approach that nurtures existing capacities (World Bank n.d., 2).

Capacity-building challenges

Africa's development in the 1980s was so disappointing that some characterized it as a lost decade for development. Several factors—ineffective policies, outright mismanagement (in some countries), a heavy external debt burden, poor governance and conflicts that precipitated the massive economic decline in the early 1980s—were responsible for the poor performance. But after some painful economic reforms as well as growing political liberalization and economic stability, some notable improvements have been registered in the last decade. But a lot more needs to be done to put Africa on the road to sustainable development.

The continent is still faced with the enormous challenges of poverty; the HIV/AIDS pandemic; promotion of democracy, rule of law, conflict prevention, management and post-conflict reconstruction; human capital flight; private-sector development; revitalization of universities and research institutions; regional cooperation and integration; trade; the burden of external debt; the

information revolution and technological progress (Sako and Ogiogio 2002). To deal with the challenges Africa needs capable states.[1] Yet the state in many African countries is weak, due to four related conditions described in a recent World Bank study:

First, the basic socioeconomic conditions in Africa, though improving in some ways, constitute a weak foundation for public sector capacities. The overall level of poverty both creates enormous need for effective public sector performance and limits the human and financial resources available to the public sector.

Second, specific political and institutional characteristics in African countries inhibit effective public sector performance. The state has yet to integrate formal rules with informal norms in ways that ensure good governance…

Third, . . . public sector in Africa exhibits low bureaucratic quality, weak mechanism of accountability, and high levels of corruption.

Last, globalization is widening gaps within Africa and between Africa and other regions. While globalization offers opportunities to help African countries to enhance their national capacities—through easier access to global knowledge—it also undermines their efforts by

> ' *Africa's development in the 1980s was disappointing, but after some painful economic reforms as well as growing political liberalization, some notable improvements have been registered in the last decade*

contributing to widening domestic income gaps, pulling highly trained talent out of Africa, and accentuating Africa's lack of competitiveness in international research and development and investment. About 70,000 highly qualified professionals and experts leave the continent annually. While migration brings in remittances, which help reduce poverty, it depresses public sector performance in such crucial areas as health, science and technology, and economic management (World Bank 2005, 2–3).

The challenges posed by the foregoing conditions require long-term, systemic approaches.

To promote development, many African countries have launched a Poverty Reduction Strategy Program (PRSP) and set their aims at the Millennium Development Goals (MDGs). The PRSPs require enhanced capacities to realize the economic and social foundations of poverty reduction. Because local governments are at the forefront of service delivery, particular attention needs to be given to building and enhancing their capacities. World Bank and IMF reviews of the PRSPs in 2002 underscored the poor capacity at the local government level and, more importantly, the inability to use existing capacity effectively, constraining preparation, implementation and monitoring and evaluation of PRSPs at the local level. MDGs, by setting specific development targets to be achieved by 2015, are contributing to

demands, not only for more effective capacity building, but also for these efforts to be more directly linked to results (World Bank n.d.).

Gaps in governance capacity in Africa

Good governance helps to create an environment of peace, stability and security in which people can be productive and creative, build wealth and employment and promote human development and alleviate poverty. For the institutions of governance to perform their functions effectively, they must be endowed with the appropriate capacities. Because sustainable development thrives in an environment of good governance, if African countries are to forge ahead with their development visions, they must build their governance capacities.

Some express doubt about the sincerity of African governments' alleged commitment to good governance. Political scientist Pierre Englebert asks, "[I]f we and African governments know that good governance promotes development and yet there have been no general improvements in governance, do African governments want development?" He adds, "[T]here is a potential contradiction here between the normative implications of the governance agenda and the self-interest maximization of all elites….We cannot take for granted the desire of governments to promote development" (Englebert 2005).

Improving the capacity of governance institutions poses a major challenge of development in Africa. To

> **If African countries are to forge ahead with their development visions, they must build their governance capacities**

strengthen governance, African governments have to commit themselves to meeting the capacity challenges. An ECA study argues "the major challenge . . . is to promote a culture of good governance necessary for sound economic management, efficient service delivery and social empowerment of the people. Governance capacity is needed to create a capable democratic state, a virile civil society and a thriving private sector with a good culture of corporate management" (ECA n.d.-b). This same position is echoed in an ACBF study that argues that capacity building will need to:

professionalize the voice of civil society and private sector representative institutions, empower women and civil society organisations, strengthen transparency and accountability, address political instability and provide skills for conflict resolution and management, enhance effectiveness and responsiveness of the public sector as well as the delivery of public services, reduce the burden of regulations, improve transparency, efficiency and effectiveness of the regulatory framework, encourage participation by all stakeholders in the development process, strengthen the rule of law, and effectively address the issue of corruption (Sako and Ogiogio 2002, 7).

One of the lessons learned from AGR I is that many of the governance institutions in Africa have a serious dearth of capacity. These include the legislature, executive, judiciary, civil service, political parties, civil society and the private sector. As such those governance institutions are weak, poorly accountable and prone to manipulations. While a major finding of AGR I is that governance has improved in Africa, its corollary is that there are several challenges for which capacity is the key. Sustaining and institutionalizing the modest gains in Africa will require substantial scaling up of capacity development efforts of those institutions (ECA n.d.-b).

Legislature

Entrusted with law making, allocation of resources and oversight functions, the legislature is the most important organ of governance. But the performance of many African legislatures is hardly satisfactory. Elected members often lack sufficient education, information and independence to perform their constitutionally mandated prerogatives. And parliaments lack adequate facilities, administrative and technical support and financial resources.

Weak caliber

Many legislators lack the education to understand their role and discharge their responsibilities. The Djibouti country study revealed that weak academic qualifications of elected officials resulted in their inability to initiate laws, analyze the budget and control the executive. Training programs that could upgrade their skills are often lacking or offered in an ad hoc manner with little durable impact. In Burkina Faso many elected officials are

'*The performance of many African legislatures is hardly satisfactory. Elected members often lack sufficient education and independence to perform their constitutionally mandated prerogatives*

The United States Agency for International Development (USAID) trained members of parliament and regional councils and parliamentary staff to strengthen their procedural, administrative, presentation and communication skills so they can make better use of committees, public hearings and fact-finding missions. It is hoped that the training will strengthen their ability to capture, analyze and incorporate input from civil society into the process of policy formulation, legislative decision making and regional and local planning. To ensure sustainability beyond its current support, USAID helped establish the Namibian Democracy Support Center, a cooperative partnership between selected government institutions and civil society organisations to further strengthen the interaction between the government and civil society in a coordinated and planned manner. The Center's objectives include outreach, planning, policy formulation and analysis. The program emphasizes the capacity of elected representatives to understand the implications and impact of HIV/AIDS on development and policymaking at national and regional levels and to analyze and provide interventions into legislative and policymaking process to reflect civic inputs.

Source: Namibia country report 2007.

reported to be illiterate, and their contribution is considered minimal. In Madagascar the legislators have minimum education and are unable to control the laws, finances and procedures proposed by the government. In Togo the management of the assembly's resources lack transparency, and the assembly lacks capacity to control the executive. The country report identified areas that need improvement—capacity to initiate laws, review policies and programs, communicate with the public and civil society, elaborate and control the budget and improve transparency and accountability in managing resources. The Seychelles report underscored the need to improve and enhance legislative capabilities on issues of national importance and recommended

training for members of both the government and opposition.

On the other hand, Namibia provides an encouraging example. Measures taken with the assistance of the United States Agency for International Development (USAID) are enhancing the competence of the parliament, which is regarded as one of the most professional in Africa. The USAID support enhances the skills of members of parliament and their staffs and deepens the parliament's democratic culture.

Weak technical and administrative support

The absence of administrative and advisory support for legislators undermines their ability to fulfil their responsibilities. In many African countries there is a short supply of professional staff capable of collecting, analyzing and converting data into meaningful information for legislators. Botswana lacks adequate technical and administrative support. A similar shortfall is reported in South Africa.

Poor facilities

Lack of facilities—buildings, offices, residential quarters and communication facilities— hampers the effectiveness of the legislature in many African countries. In Djibouti deputies do not have sufficient offices, residences, communication facilities such as telephone, fax, and Internet, a documentation center or interactive web site. Legislators in Madagascar lack an adequate library, computers, database, and access to the Internet. The national assembly in Nigeria lacks fully equipped office accommodations and a library. In Rwanda neither the Chamber nor the Senate have a resource center or research units staffed with professionals that can provide the necessary technical backup.

Facility constraint has been addressed in South Africa, where the national legislature has provided members with logistical support mechanisms including computers, communication facilities and travel services.

Inadequate financial resources

The inability to be acquainted with current developments in legislatures around the world and to have regular contact with constituencies through modern methods of communication significantly reduces the capacity and performance of legislators. In Burkina Faso legislators do not have the financial resources to attend international meetings that would expose them to best practices. As in Burkina, in Seychelles lack of foreign exchange has made it difficult for legislators to attend meetings and workshops abroad.

On the positive side, the National Assembly in South Africa, in accordance with section 57 of the constitution, grants financial assistance to each represented party in an amount relative to the party's strength, and senior party officers, such as the leader of the opposition, receive additional support. The money can be used for support and research staff, office administration and capital costs, enabling parties to establish and maintain a constituency outreach program. Because the support

was considered inadequate, assistance to parties has increased substantially from R71 million to R156 million in 2006/07 and will reach R278 million in 2009/10.

Lack of independence

Executive dominance significantly reduces the legislature's role in making laws and exercising oversight. In Togo the effectiveness of the parliament is hampered by the national assembly's lack of independence. In Zambia, where the capacity of parliament to operate independently is compromised by the ruling party's insatiable appetite for luring opposition members of parliament into its ranks, the legislature rarely initiates bills. Instead, it continues to be done by the executive.

Facing many constraints, parliaments are generally ineffective in Africa. Of the expert groups responding to the question on legislative effectiveness, it is not surprising that in only 8 of the 22 countries did more than 50% of the respondents regard it as effective. The overwhelming majority did not consider the legislature to be effective. (See chapter 4, "Institutional Checks and Balances".)

Executive

Because the executive is entrusted with initiating and implementing policy, any constraint of capacity of this branch could negatively impact development. But executives in Africa seem to be faced with many problems:

- Lack of sufficient capacity in policy analysis.

> ' *Facing many constraints, parliaments are generally ineffective in Africa. Executive dominance significantly reduces the legislature's role in making laws and exercising oversight*

- Lack of capacity to implement, manage and monitor and evaluate development programs.

- Personnel deficiency in managerial, financial and technical skills.

- Unmotivated and demoralized staff in the case of some countries.

- Inability to attract and retain capable staff.

- Weak statistical compilation and analysis capacity.

- Under-resourced and ineffective local governments.

- Lack of proper decentralization policy and strategy resulting in poor service delivery.

Many of these problems were flagged in AGR I but continue to constrain the executive.

Weak human resources and institutions

The Ghana country study revealed that politics plays a large part in the civil service and public officers were subjected to partisan pressure. Personnel often lack the requisite skills, training and resources to perform their duties competently. Performance is poor in several key areas and services are nonexistent in remote locations. In Botswana inability to attract capable staff and the low level of education, skills and experience of civil servants are major capacity constraints of the executive. In Zambia the performance

of the civil service was found to be below expectation and affected by a shortage of qualified personnel, politicization, demoralized workforce and poor working conditions. The public service delivery system is bloated, inefficient and ineffective in responding to the needs of the people.

In Djibouti weaknesses are found in human resources management, materials and logistics, internal controls, statistical capacity and budget preparation. In Nigeria the civil service is not results-oriented. There is a shortage of staff in economics, finance, policy analysis and general administration. The state lacks the capacity to provide security, protect individual rights and ensure adequate safeguard of property rights. And the police are inadequately trained and equipped.

In the Republic of Congo a lack of control in managing human resources contributes to corruption and fraud. In Madagascar there is a lack of competition in recruitment, unmotivated staff due to low pay, poor working conditions and lack of resources. The civil service does not have the procedures and strategy to attract competent personnel. The Namibian civil service remains perpetually short of competence in technical, managerial and leadership functions due to frequent turnover.

In Niger all levels of public administration suffer from shortage of human, material and financial resources. The number of civil servants fell by 10% from 2000 to 2004. Shortage of resources in local

> ' **Because the executive is entrusted with initiating and implementing policy, any constraint of capacity of this branch could negatively impact development**

governments has negatively impacted service delivery, and weak infrastructure renders law enforcement agencies ineffective. In Tanzania weak institutional and organisational frameworks, unclear roles between the central government and local government authorities and weak incentives for capacity development are constraints on the public service (ECA Tanzania country report).

Botswana lacks the capacity to generate evidence-based decision making and monitor and evaluate policy and program implementation. In Sierra Leone the government has a limited capacity to generate quality information for the analysis of development needs. There are few think tanks in the country—a result of the devastating war, which led to considerable brain drain. The universities have limited research activities into which policy analysis could feed. The capacity of the executive in Togo is weakened by poor rationalization of the state structure, weak decentralization, poor delegation of responsibility for economic management and poor human resources.

In Ghana the capacity to plan, initiate, implement and monitor local development remains weak. Local governments lack the authority to mobilize resources, and the central government's monitoring of local government and provision of technical assistance are weak. In the Republic of Congo local governments lack the capacity and independence to discharge their responsibilities. In Burkina Faso many local government entities exist only in name and do not have personnel

or facilities. The overwhelming majority of the experts from the surveyed countries did not consider local governments capable of delivering services.

Inadequate materials and infrastructure

It is reported in Nigeria that most departments of statistics lack vital data processing equipment like computers and other information technology facilities. The Republic of Congo lacks government buildings, office furniture and computers. In Cape Verde lack of resources (material and financial) to achieve the tasks assigned to the institutions is among the major constraints of the executive.

Efforts to cope with constraints

Some countries have tried to address their capacity constraints. For example, Namibia initiated measures aimed at achieving outcome-focused public service, inculcating professional and ethical behavior in civil servants and focusing on customer service. To achieve these reforms, a performance management framework is being piloted in two ministries.

In Cape Verde, within the context of the programme to modernize the state, several important measures were undertaken to improve its public administration system. These steps include the promulgation of a new law on the public administration system, a new plan for career development and salary increases for public servants, use of information technology in the public service and a new law on

> *Cape Verde has undertaken several important measures to improve its public administration system*

acquisitions and markets aimed at improving transparency in the procedure for acquiring property and services (ECA Cape Verde country report 2007).

To improve the quality of the public service and promote better service delivery in Kenya, a results-based management approach to public service reforms was introduced in 2004 under an initiative called the Results for Kenya Programme. The programme creates a citizen-focused, results-oriented public service to attain the country's Vision 2030 goals. Its components include promoting transformative leadership for better results and accountability, building institutional capacity in the public service, improving communication and education in the public service and structuring partnerships with public sector stakeholders (Nyamweya 2008). There have been some positive results in service delivery in Kenya.

Across project countries the poor quality of police equipment impedes the capacity to fight crime and protect lives and property. There is no country in which half (50%) the expert respondents felt that the police are well equipped. Even in the countries with the best scores, like Cape Verde, Botswana and Djibouti, only 40% to 45% of the experts considered the police to be well equipped.

Judiciary
Lack of independence, shortage of judges and magistrates, inadequate funding, poor remuneration and limited facilities continue

> *Lack of independence, shortage of judges and magistrates, inadequate funding, poor remuneration and limited facilities continue to constrain the effectiveness of the judiciary in Africa*

to constrain the effectiveness of the judiciary.

Lack of independence
An independent judiciary is a prerequisite for a functioning democracy and is central to good governance. Judicial independence is the foundation for the rule of law. It means that judges and magistrates are secure enough in their positions to dispense justice without political interference and cannot be dismissed or intimidated for taking a position that might have an adverse impact on the executive. Without independence, the judiciary is subject to the whims of political leaders.

Human resource constraints
In Sierra Leone magistrates, judges and other legal personnel are in short supply. In Namibia a shortage of magistrates, delays in appointing legal aid counsel due to lack of funds and extended investigation by the police constrain the effectiveness of the judiciary. And the drain of experienced prosecutors does not help the situation. Financial, human and material shortages are reported in Togo as a constraint on the judiciary. Although judges' competence and the independence of the judiciary are not in doubt in Cape Verde, it is nevertheless believed that judicial procedures are overly complex and excessively bureaucratic, resulting in delays in court decisions. Moreover, the court registry operates poorly because the number of officials is limited and they lack adequate qualifications, and disorganized files and limited use of information technology result in poor performance of the courts. In Botswana,

where magistrates, judges and other legal personnel are in short supply, the judiciary fails to retain qualified and experienced staff, leading to delays in the disposal of cases. In Madagascar lack of opportunities for career improvement, poor training, and poor working conditions, are among the serious constraints. In Seychelles a majority of the judges are foreigners with obvious implications for sustainable national capacity in the management of the judicial system. In South Africa the large backlog of cases across the country is attributed to inadequate funding, resources and capacity within the justice system. In Niger the ratio of judges to population is 1:70,000, well below the international standard of 1:7,000, and the number of judges has been increasing at the rate of only 25 per year.

Problems of infrastructure and facilities
Except in the capital city, court infrastructure, records management and the court system had collapsed in Sierra Leone as a result of the civil war. In Congo lack of transport, sufficient office furniture, typewriters and office facilities are reported to constrain the judiciary. In 2000 visits by the South African Human Rights Commission (SAHRC) to magistrate's courts in South Africa revealed poor security, lack of separate facilities for sensitive witnesses and children, nonfunctioning help desks and little essential equipment such as computers and recording machines.[2] In 2004 a parliamentary ad hoc committee on justice declared lack of resources to be the most important challenge faced by the courts. In

Nigeria the judiciary is incapacitated by lack of working facilities due to inadequate funding for modern amenities that could facilitate speedy delivery of justice. Almost all judges write notes in long hand except in Lagos State. Many lack access to computers and air-conditioned offices. Power outage is common, and writing materials are in short supply. Prisons are congested, largely by detainees awaiting trial.

Financial constraints
In Zambia poor funding has led to poor salaries and unattractive working conditions. Because the judiciary does not have financial autonomy, it has no leverage over its budget, let alone the rate and timing of disbursements. In Sierra Leone the judiciary also does not control its own budget. Consequently, there are long delays in adjudication and a large number of remand prisoners pervade the justice system.

In Ghana, however, some improvements in the judiciary are reported since AGR I, especially in building up infrastructure, establishing commercial courts, automating some of the high courts and improving management of the justice system. But executive dominance still blurs public confidence in some parts of the system. South Africa also has started to address the resource shortages that affect the performance of the judicial sector.

Non-state actors
Non-state actors can play an important role in consolidating and strengthening democracy. They play a vital role in mobilizing and

> *Non-state actors can play an important role in consolidating and strengthening democracy: mobilizing and articulating social demands, defending human rights and spearheading development*

articulating social demands, defending human rights, spearheading development activities and contributing to poverty alleviation. Although the hostile political environment they had to contend with for years has improved, many non-state actors in Africa lack skills, experience, organisational capabilities, financial resources and infrastructure. Many civil society organisations (CSOs) are weak, short of resources and dependent on foreign support.

Non-state actors require capacity to contribute to the formulation and implementation of development programs. In the 22 countries where expert opinion was solicited on how effectively CSOs contribute to promoting accountability and transparency, only in 6 countries—Mali (70%), Ghana (64%), Zambia (59%), Senegal (58%), Sierra Leone (52%) and Botswana (50%)—did a majority respond positively. In the 16 other countries the responses were below 50% and as low as 16.5% in Egypt.

Civil society organisations
Human resource and other organisational constraints. In Botswana lack of adequate skills, experience, creativity and funding are among the major constraints faced by CSOs. In Cape Verde civil society organisations suffer from poor management and lack of material resources. Improvement of management capacity requires permanent training schemes for CSO leaders. In Madagascar the CSOs suffer from insufficient organisational and leadership skills. In Sierra Leone civil society is weak in technical, strategic and advocacy skills. The majority

of CSOs lack a coherent mandate, functional boundaries, autonomy and managerial and programmatic procedures. In Namibia CSOs lack skills in organisational development, management, networking, lobbying, advocacy and research, monitoring and evaluation, and project identification and preparation. They are losing skilled managerial and professional staff to the public and private sectors due to low pay.

In Nigeria civil society is weak in organisation and highly susceptible to political manoeuvring, although it is active and engaged. There are about 175 prominent CSOs in the country, but few have solid organisational and managerial skills. CSOs play a limited role and make limited impact on policy formulation and implementation because few have a capacity for research or are computer literate. In Tanzania, despite the contribution of CSOs toward building a capable state, it is reported that even though many of the donor-supported projects for CSOs have built-in capacity development components, they reflect donor interest for short-term results rather than the development of sustainable organisations. Most small, indigenous CSOs do not have the capability to engage qualified administrative and financial managers to run their activities (ECA 2007b).

Financial and other constraints. Limited financial means and weak human resources are among the major constraints faced by CSOs in Burkina Faso, Cape Verde and Madagascar. In South Africa fragile funding has led to weakened CSOs,

> **Although the hostile political environment they had to contend with for years has improved, many non-state actors in Africa lack skills, experience and financial resources**

which have lost many of their competent staff to the government. In Tanzania CSOs are not financially self-sufficient and depend heavily on donors. The capacity of civil society in Kenya to engage the government has been undermined over the last four years by internal weakness, problems of ethnicity and capacity migration into government and formal politics and by resource shortages due to dependence on donors who prefer basket funding geared mostly toward supporting state institutions like the electoral commission during election periods rather than supporting CSOs.

Political parties

Political parties in Africa have little capability to articulate issues, engage in debate, promote their principles and vision of society or defend the interests and rights of their supporters. Most are not professionally organized and do not have functional democratic structures. Many lack competent and committed leadership. They suffer from severe funding problems and are exposed to harassment and intimidation by incumbent governments (ECA 2008).

Human resource and other institutional constraints. In Botswana political parties suffer from severe organisational problems. In Zambia weak internal leadership and management structures characterize most of the parties. In Djibouti political parties face problems of human resources. Likewise, in Madagascar, the political parties' internal capacity in organisational matters is weak and suffers from a shortage of trained staff. In Sierra Leone political

parties are deficient in institutional capacity. Many of them have existed merely for the purpose of contesting the 1996, 2003 and 2007 elections. Failing to win seats in parliament, they ceased to exist.

Financial and infrastructure constraints. Limited infrastructure and inadequate funding pose difficulties for the effectiveness of political parties. In Zambia they suffer from inadequate and uncertain funding, making it difficult to recruit full-time staff and purchase vehicles, office equipment, communication services and Internet connections. Similar shortages face parties in Botswana and Djibouti.

In South Africa funding for political parties is based on the size of a party. As a result, smaller and newer parties face capacity shortages, hampering their ability to compete. Madagascar also reported a lack of adequate finances and transparency of operation in parties. And in Senegal some parties do not even have decent headquarters; only the ruling party and a few opposition parties can afford accommodations. The system of financing political parties based on votes obtained has reduced chances that smaller parties can survive.

Although political parties are mushrooming in Africa, they mostly lack capacity and institutionalised procedures, processes and organisation. Without capable and efficient political parties that can promote informed debates, create alternative visions for society and rekindle hope in the democratic agenda, Africa's democratisation process will falter.

> *Political parties in Africa have little capability to articulate issues, engage in debate, promote their principles and vision of society or defend the interests and rights of their supporters*

Media

The media have grown in importance since the opening of political space and democratisation in the 1980s and 1990s, promoting accountability and transparency. (See chapters 1 and 4.) But constraints on the media continue. They suffer from deficiencies in skills, trained manpower in investigative journalism and quality reporting.

In Nigeria, though the quality of journalism is considered high, many media houses still lack equipment and facilities. The media are not adequately trained for handling sensitive and topical issues such as violent conflicts and gender issues, and professionals are poorly paid. Cape Verde reports the need to improve the training of journalists in order to enhance their independent performance.

In Kenya, however, there has been a substantial growth of the media with the licensing of private radio and television. The media have helped to promote transparency and accountability by exposing corruption and government scandals. They continue to indirectly influence policies and programs while highlighting conflict. Consequently, the ruling elites have attacked the media by using criminal elements and formal security structures to harass journalists, including attempts to gag them under the 2007 Media Bill.

Private sector

In the 1970s there was a strong belief that the public sector was the engine of growth, and the private sector did not have a significant role in the economies of many African countries. In some countries the ideological rationale was socialism. But after years of being marginalized the private sector is now acknowledged as the engine of economic growth. The past decade has witnessed a plethora of policies aimed at creating a more conducive environment for the private sector, and many countries have taken measures to enhance the sector's capacity to compete in global markets. Governments have also passed laws to attract investors and have improved the policy and regulatory environment.

Sustained economic growth and development in Africa requires an efficient and dynamic private sector. One report observed: "For the sector to play its role as an engine of growth, it needs to be encouraged by a conducive policy environment, the availability of functional and efficient infrastructure, effective public sector institutions, and security of investment. African countries need an enabling environment for both domestic and foreign private investment to flourish. The private sector needs improved management, better information on markets and investments, and a work force with the requisite skills and motivation. Supportive public policies and the efficient supply of infrastructure and services, as well as specific interventions to enhance private-sector institutions are direly needed" (Sako and Ogiogio 2002).

Despite today's relatively encouraging environment for the private sector, more needs to be done if the private sector is to play its expected role

> *After years of being marginalized the private sector is now acknowledged as the engine of economic growth*

as an engine of growth. The private sector in many of the countries is still fragile, lacking the capacity to compete in the global market. In Botswana undeveloped regulatory and institutional frameworks hamper growth and expansion of the private sector. In Seychelles the private sector needs better training in strategic fields. Capacity building in all sectors of the economy remains essential for long-term sustainable economic growth and social development. In Cape Verde administrative barriers, excessive bureaucracies, industrial legislation and high taxes constrain the private sector. In Sierra Leone the private sector operates in a difficult environment in two key respects: shortage of human resources and insufficient public utilities. For the majority of the citizens the informal sector is a means of their livelihood, but it has not been a beneficiary of reform initiatives by the government.

In South Africa, on the other hand, the informal sector, which constitutes an important part of South Africa's economy, benefits from programs and agencies to support people with money, business skills and technology to run their businesses. As the formal private sector expanded into the financial and service sectors, it experienced a shortage of skilled labor. As a result, the government launched the Joint Initiative for Priority Skills Acquisition to address the skills requirements of the country's expanding economy in several areas: planning and engineering of water, transport and other network areas; town and regional planning skills; training of engineers

and artisans; planning and management capacity in the health care and educational systems and education in mathematics and science.

Knowledge capacity for governance

In many African countries poor governance, a deteriorating economic situation—especially in the 1980s and 1990s—and poor social welfare have eroded the knowledge base and human capacity. First, research and educational institutions have witnessed a downturn in the quality of education and commitment to science. Budgets for education have dwindled, and funding for research has virtually dried up.

Second, emigration and brain drain have intensified, affecting governance capacity, especially in the delivery of social services. It is estimated that since 1990, 20,000 skilled professionals have left Africa each year. Yet Africa spends about US$4 billion per year (representing 35% of official development aid to Africa) to employ about 100,000 Western experts to perform functions generally referred to as technical assistance (ECA n.d.-a).

The costs and consequences of Africa's brain drain are enormous. For a continent with a dearth of financial resources, the huge costs of training skilled professionals are lost to the countries. In Kenya, for example, it costs about US$40,000 to train a doctor and US$10,000 to US$15,000 to educate a university student for four years, excluding tuition fees where such exists. The World Health Organization

' *In many African countries poor governance, a deteriorating economic situation and poor social welfare have eroded the knowledge base and human capacity*

estimates that delivery of basic health services requires 20 physicians per 100,000 people. While Western countries boast of about 222 physicians per 100,000 people, most African countries fall far short of the minimum standard (ECA n.d.-a). And the few physicians that Africa has are attracted to the West for better salaries, living conditions and professional fulfillment.

The knowledge shortfall on governance in Africa includes the skills to manage public institutions and businesses and to facilitate basic and applied research and innovative practices for better service delivery. A new incentive regime for better knowledge development in Africa must target the following:

- Better funding of research and educational institutions from the primary to tertiary levels.

- A merit system in education and research based on performance and output.

- Continuous training programmes for staff and officials in public institutions.

- Better remuneration for civil servants, public-sector workers and research and education staff in order to retain human capacity in Africa.

- A diaspora capacity programme that encourages donors and international development partners to engage and use the human capital of the African diaspora for technical assistance.

- Improvements in social welfare and governance, which will discourage human capital flight from the continent.

Given the diversity of African states and their differing levels of development and varying degrees of experiences in democratic governance, a "one size fits all" approach to capacity building is not appropriate. All countries share many capacity gaps, but the degree of complexity varies. The solutions will have to be appropriate to the historical, cultural and behavioural differences of each country.

Enhancing the capacity of parliament

The legislature, despite the constitutional prominence it enjoys, is still weak in initiating legislation and oversight. In many countries its effectiveness continues to be eroded by the dominance of the executive. If the legislature is to assume its constitutionally assigned role and become a vibrant institution, its capacity constraints have to be addressed as a matter of priority.

Strengthening skills of standing committee members

Given that most of the technical work of a parliament is handled at the committee level, targeting the committee members for more training makes sense. Training programmes should focus on issues such as:

- Reviewing legislation.

- Reviewing and approving the budget and expenditures of the government.

> **If the legislature is to assume its constitutionally assigned role and become a vibrant institution, its capacity constraints have to be addressed as a matter of priority**

- Scrutinizing the government's activities, policies and programs, and assessing whether they meet the intended objectives of legislation.

- Conducting investigations on special issues and reviewing appointments.

Strengthening technical and professional support

It is equally important to strengthen the technical support of the parliament. There should be a research wing to provide elected officials with the necessary briefs and elaboration of issues under consideration so they can make constructive inputs to legislation. The research wing should be endowed with good documentation resources, a well-stocked library and an Internet connection.

Strengthening relationships with constituencies

An important role for legislators is maintaining a close relationship with their constituencies and generating consideration at the parliamentary level of issues that specifically affect the people they represent. To maintain a close relationship with their constituency, the legislators need resources and logistics. Due to a lack of funding, in many countries this function is given only lip service.

Familiarizing newly elected members with the working of parliament

Parliaments are elected periodically. Turnover makes a training programme for new members quite a challenge. But regardless of cost it is important to organize training for new parliamentarians to familiarize them with the general principles of parliamentary operation.

Enhancing the capacity of the executive

Despite the key role it is expected to play in development, the executive seems to be dogged with many problems. Many of the issues flagged in AGR I continue. Although the constraints discussed earlier may be observed in many countries, their magnitude and intensity vary. Hence it is necessary to domesticate solutions to address the respective country problems. But there are some interventions that apply to all countries:

- Allocate sufficient resources to enhance skills in policy analysis, in formulating, managing and developing programs and in monitoring and evaluation.

- Strengthen the statistical office so it can generate reliable data for informed decision making.

- Develop think tanks to broaden the sources of vital and credible information for policy debates.

- Endow local governments with the resources to improve their service delivery to the public. Particularly, provide direct central government funding, then allow local governments the flexibility to use it to enhance their capacity for financial and fiscal planning and management, policy and program design, implementation, monitoring and evaluation and improved accountability.

Despite the key role it is expected to play in development, the executive seems to be dogged with many problems. Many of the issues flagged in AGR I continue

- Enhance the capacity of local governments to respond to the needs of the community, especially in developing a participatory planning and budgetary process that involves communities and other stakeholders in setting priorities and providing oversight.

- Improve the working conditions and remuneration of civil servants to boost morale and productivity.

- Harness information and communication technology to improve efficiency of service delivery.

- Build capacity in the executive to manage the changing role of the public sector in today's world of globalization, the market economy, multiparty democracy and information revolution.

Enhancing the capacity of the judiciary

Several measures are recommended to overcome constraints on the judiciary:

- Bolster the independence of the judiciary through legal and administrative reforms.

- Provide the resources to hire more judicial and support staff.

- Improve the remuneration system so qualified people can be attracted and retained.

- Implement a case management system and harness information technology to expedite case management and improve access to information.

- Provide continuous training at all levels to enhance the skills of the judicial staff.

- Provide convenient offices, court rooms, modern information-recording and retrieval systems and other facilities.

Enhancing the capacity of non-state actors

Several measures can be taken to boost the effectiveness of non-state actors:

- In consultation with civil society organisations, political parties, community-based organisations, the private sector and the media, devise policies and strategies to address their limitations in education, skills, experience, organisational ability and financing. Non-state actors need skills that will enable them to be effective in policy formulation and implementation, advocacy, negotiation and lobbying.

- Enhance CSOs' skills to participate in, and monitor, public service delivery.

- Consider funding political parties to ensure that small parties do not get discouraged due to financial shortage. For democracy to thrive, the existence of a vibrant multiparty system is necessary.

- Make Africa competitive. But today many African businesses are far from competitive. It is therefore important to enhance the capacity of the private sector to improve its efficiency and competitiveness.

- Attract foreign direct investment. Although there have been encouraging moves to improve the business environment, much more has to be done.

- Improve the private sector's competency for effective dialogue with other stakeholders in development, especially the public sector and civil society, in order to influence the policy agenda.

- Improve journalists' skills through support for appropriate training.

Conclusion

Africa entered the twenty-first century saddled with many challenges. To address these challenges, the continent must tackle its capacity deficits. Africa's brain drain was not solely triggered by poor economic conditions. It was also caused by political violence, repression of human rights and the lack of a productive professional and technological environment (Sako and Ogiogio 2002). One way to abate the brain drain is to address its root causes.

Despite a hostile environment, some skilled professionals opted to stick it out, but the lack of proper capacity often leads to frustration, forcing people to withdraw and remain inactive in spite of the critical skills they possess. It is thus important

that existing capacity is effectively utilized and that an environment that encourages capacity retention is put in place.

But capacity building by itself is not enough. Capacity has to be developed, effectively utilized and retained if it is to lead to appreciable changes in African countries. An ACBF study observed:

> The availability and effective utilization of the requisite capacity will determine Africa's ability to meet these challenges in the 21st century. What this implies, therefore, is that sustained structural transformation in Africa in the next two decades requires a significant leap in the quantum of support and commitment to capacity building as well as reforms for effective utilization of such capacity (Sako and Ogiogio 2002, 14).

The lessons identified in a study conducted in the early 1990s by ECA on capacity development can still serve as inspiration as Africa continues to tackle its capacity-building challenges:

- Capacity building requires a comprehensive approach that addresses needs in all critical sectors.

- Sound and stable economic policies are important for capacity building.

- National ownership of capacity building and responsibility

Africa entered the twenty-first century saddled with many challenges. To address these challenges, the continent must tackle its capacity deficits for its utilization is a necessary condition.

- While African governments should be in the driving seat of capacity-building efforts, the cost is so huge that they would not be able to achieve their objective without substantial external assistance. Mobilizing the resources from both domestic savings and external sources is needed to finance capacity building and utilization. But technical assistance for capacity building should complement—not compete with or substitute for—indigenous expertise. This concern was expressed in a recent ECA document which argues that "[w]hile foreign assistance is highly necessary and desirable, African states need to take the initiative, lead and mobilize strong internal efforts for capacity development. In other words, there are several capacity issues that can be addressed with good planning and strategy by African countries. Even where external support is required, such must be well-defined and focused in order to ensure the effectiveness of such intervention" (ECA n.d.-a, 6).

- An action plan for capacity building, with clear measures for monitoring and evaluating success, is needed.

- It is important to forge effective partnerships in capacity building involving the public and private sectors at the national level.

- National efforts in capacity building should be complemented by regional and sub-regional activities.

- Creating and maintaining a conducive economic and political environment is critical for capacity building.

- All actors involved in capacity building must agree on a mechanism for coordinating and harmonizing their initiatives in a manner that can effectively push forward the capacity-building agenda (ECA 2006).

There are great challenges confronting Africa and its international development partners in promoting capacity development on the continent. The first step in tackling those challenges has to come from Africa itself—harnessing its existing knowledge base, skills and diaspora human capital and improving the economic and social infrastructure necessary for institutional and societal capacity development. While Africa tackles the problem of brain drain, it should also take on the more serious challenge of brain retention, so people do not emigrate and there is a conducive environment for them to contribute to the development of their respective countries.

Notes

1. According to Mohiddin, the defining characteristics of a capable state are constitutionalism, democracy, intelligence, competence, legitimacy, flexibility and effectiveness. A capable state is well informed

> ' *There are great challenges confronting Africa. The first step in tackling those challenges has to come from Africa itself*

and knowledgeable, legitimate and firmly accommodated in society. It is capable of changing, adapting and adopting itself to emerging challenges. See Mohiddin 2007.

2. See ECA South African National Country Report, 2007, Chapter 9, p. 6).

References

ECA (Economic Commission for Africa). 2005. *African Governance Report 2005.* Addis Ababa.

———. 2006. "Capacity Building in Africa: Effective States and Engaged Societies." Report for joint workshop sponsored by African Development Bank, UNECA, and the World Bank, Addis Ababa, Ethiopia, February 24–25, 2006.

———. 2007a. Namibia country report. Addis Ababa.

———. 2007b. Tanzania country report. Addis Ababa.

———. 2007c. Togo country report. Addis Ababa.

———. 2008. Political Parties and Public Policies in Africa. ECA: Addis Ababa.

———. n.d.-a. "Brain Drain in Africa: Facts and Figures." Addis Ababa.

———. n.d.-b. "Capacity Development in Africa: Some Lessons from the African Governance Report." Unpublished paper. Addis Ababa.

Englebert, Pierre. 2005. "Notes on governance and capacity building." Paper for conference, "Aid, Governance and Development in Africa," Northwestern University, May 12–14, 2005.

Lusthaus, Charles, Marie-Helene Adrien and Mark Perstinger. 1999. "Capacity Development: Definitions, Issues and Implications for Planning, Monitoring and Evaluation." Universalia Occasional Paper No. 35.

Mohiddin, Ahmed. 2007. "Reinforcing capacity towards building the capable state in Africa." Concept paper for AGF VII.

Mutahaba, Gelasi. 2002. "International and African perspectives on public sector reform: Lessons for Rwanda." Paper presented in the Senior Policy Workshop for Secretary-Generals of the Government of Rwanda, Kigali, October 2002.

Nyamweya, Joyce. 2008. "Public Service Reforms in Kenya." Presentation at ECA, February 2008.

Sako, Soumana, and Genevesi Ogiogio. 2002. "Africa: Major Development Challenges & their Capacity Building Dimensions." ACBF Occasional paper No.1.

UNESCO (United Nations Educational, Scientific and Cultural Organization) and IICBA (International Institute for Capacity Building in Africa). 2006. "Capacity Building Framework." Addis Ababa: IICBA, 2006.

University of Namibia. 2007. Multidisciplinary Research Center, National Governance Report., 2007.

World Bank. 2005. *Capacity Building in Africa—An OED Evaluation of World Bank Support.* Washington, D.C.: World Bank Operations Evaluation Department.

———. n.d. "Towards a more strategic approach to capacity building in Africa." sitesources.worldbank.org/ INTCDRC/Resource/Africa.doc.

nex

A Project
Good
vernance:
oundwork,
ethodology
d Indices

The biennial *African Governance Report* (AGR) is a rigorous analytical study using a unique methodology to monitor and assess progress on governance in African countries. The AGR identifies capacity gaps in governance institutions, makes appropriate recommendations and seeks to enhance the capacity of governance institutions. The inaugural AGR I was published in 2005 and was widely acclaimed as a path-breaking and comprehensive work on governance in Africa.

Following AGR I, ECA held two technical workshops, "Lessons Learned and the Way Forward on Measuring and Monitoring Good Governance in Africa: The African Governance Report," in December 2004 and November 2006. The first workshop took an introspective view of the entire AGR process to better understand the weaknesses and limitations of the project and to identify the value-added of the project to ECA's member states. The second workshop reviewed and updated instruments and partnership modalities, bringing together a small group of partner institutions promoting good governance in Africa. The recommendations from both workshops fed into the review and implementation of the current report—AGR II.

The three research instruments—an opinion-based study using a national expert panel (C1), a national scientific sample household survey (C2) and desk-based research (C3)—were revised. C1 included new questions on public-private partnership, corporate governance, public financial management and accountability, integrity of monetary and financial systems and peace and conflict management. C2 added questions on HIV/AIDS. And C3 added questions on HIV/AIDS, corporate governance and economic and social rights.

Using the three research instruments, AGR II research was conducted in 35 countries, encompassing 9 new countries and an update from the 26 countries surveyed in AGR I.[1] In the new countries all three research instruments (C1, C2 and C3) were used to benchmark the baseline study. In the 26 AGR I countries the study was conducted using only C1 and C3.

Rationale and objectives of the project

The rationale for the AGR project is the emerging consensus that to meet the Millennium Development Goals by 2015, African states will have to create an enabling environment of good governance practices. In addition, the project provides a framework for implementing the various governance agendas that have been adopted by the Heads of State Implementation Committee of the New Partnership for Africa's Development (NEPAD). Since the AGR project represents the most thorough and empirically substantial attempt to measure governance in Africa to date, it is an invaluable tool for enriching policy content and dialogue across the continent.

Measuring and monitoring governance

The AGR project encompasses several objectives, and its scope includes all major stakeholders in the 35 AGR II countries.

Project objectives

- To promote a broad consensus on what constitutes good governance and the capable state.

- To provide a mechanism for monitoring efforts to create and sustain capable states and support broad-based growth, sustainable development and poverty reduction.

- To achieve a better understanding of governance processes, mechanisms and policies and promote an analytically based dialogue on governance.

- To maintain governance issues on the agenda of policymakers.

- To improve the capacity of African institutions to conduct analytical research and assessment on governance.

- To assist in assessing institutional capacity by identifying gaps and proposing policy interventions to address them.

Project scope

To ensure legitimacy for, and ownership of, the monitoring process within countries, a national research institution was selected to conduct the study in each country. The collaborating institutions were required to establish steering committees made up of major national stakeholders, including representatives of government, civil society, business and religious organisations. Those committees were established through the process of in-country workshops. Two workshops were convened: one on methodology, the other on validation. The former explained the methodology of the research for the national country study to stakeholders; the latter validated the findings of the study after the research has been completed and the report prepared.

AGR II project countries

- *New countries:* Cape Verde, Republic of Congo, Djibouti, Madagascar, Rwanda, Seychelles, Sierra Leone, Togo and Tunisia.

- *AGR I countries:* Benin, Botswana, Burkina Faso, Cameroon, Chad, Egypt, Ethiopia, Gabon, Gambia, Ghana, Kenya, Lesotho, Malawi, Mali, Mauritius, Morocco, Mozambique, Namibia, Niger, Nigeria, Senegal, South Africa, Swaziland, Tanzania, Uganda and Zambia.

Methodology

A research instrument with three components was designed to obtain information on the state of governance in Africa, as reflected by the political, economic and social affairs in each country. The three research components:

- *An opinion-based study* using a panel of 70–140 experts in each project country. Members of the expert panel were selected to ensure a cross-section in age, social status, education, political orientation, gender and ethnic, regional and religious background. The panel also represented both the private sector and civil society.

The research instrument was in "cafeteria" format (options for answering a question are already specified, and the respondent simply chooses one option). It was formulated and fine-tuned by groups of experts on Africa, then subjected to a pre-test in Benin and South Africa before being used in AGR I surveys. This instrument was then revised for AGR II. Once collected, the data from each expert panel study were subjected to further quality control to ensure that they were consistent and reliable.

- *A national sample survey* used a stratified, two-stage probability sample ranging from 1,300 to 3,000 households in each of the eight new project countries to represent a cross-section of the population (rural and urban, poor and middle class, educated and illiterate) to gauge perceptions of principal national problems and the accessibility, adequacy and efficiency of government services.

The questionnaire for the national household surveys was also in the closed cafeteria form. It was designed by experts at ECA and by external partners who have had experience in similar studies. But

implementation of the national household surveys was left to research collaborators in each project country, and ECA exercised close quality control to ensure that all household surveys had national coverage and were sound in scientific design and implementation.

The household sample survey in each project country was carried out either in close collaboration with the national statistical office, or with the principal sampling experts from it, to ensure that the survey utilised the official sampling frame, the official stratification and the overall survey infrastructure in order to enhance the credibility of the final outcome at all places and at all levels. Consistent with sound scientific survey practice, details on sampling methodology, copies of all research instruments and other relevant information are provided as an appendix in all country reports.

- *Desk-based research* of factual information and hard data supplemented and complemented the expert panel perceptions and national household surveys. The desk research is a critical review of existing literature and documented materials from both primary and secondary sources on the subject matter.

Calculating the indices

The indices are based only on the data from the expert panel study, which contains 85 indicators clustered by UNECA subject matter professionals.[2] Some sub-indices are not mutually exclusive.

The overall index is calculated using all 85 indicators for each project country. The index reflects only the perceptions of opinion leaders in each country. There is no input from other countries in the overall index of any country. Each governance index is constructed using average scores, which are put together and rescaled to bring each of them to a common range of 0–100 using the following approach:

Let

> T_i = sum of the mean scores of the indicators in cluster i, $i = 0$, 1, 2, . . . ,C, where C

is the total number of clusters in the study.

> K_i = the number of indicators in cluster i, $i = 1, 2, \ldots , C$

> Gi = Index of governance based on cluster i, $i = 0, 1, 2, \ldots , C$.

Then, G_i, $i = 0, 1, 2, \ldots , C$, the *index of governance* for the ith cluster, follows as:

$$G_i = \frac{T_i - K_i}{K_i(s-1)} * 100 = \frac{T_i - K_i}{4 * K_i} * 100, i = 0, 1, \ldots, C$$

where $K_0 = 85$, T_0 is the total of the average scores for all indicators in the study, and s, which is 5 in the Africa Governance Project, is the maximum possible score assignable for any of the 85 indicators, so that the corresponding overall index of governance will also be given by:

The weighted average formula is valid only if the C clusters are mutu-

$$G_0 = 100 * \frac{T_0 - 85}{340} = 100 * \sum_{i=1}^{C} w_i G_i , w_i = \frac{K_i}{\sum_{i=1}^{C} K_i}$$

ally exclusive and exhaustive. An index that is close to 100 is perceived to reflect good governance.

The data from the expert panel study are used to construct 23 sub-indices of governance for clusters of indicators. Each governance index is constructed using average scores, which are put together and rescaled to bring each of them to a common range of 0–100. An index that is close to 100 reflects good governance as perceived by the respective national opinion survey of the country concerned. Cross-country comparisons should be avoided since there are serious factors that negate the validity of such comparisons.

Clusters for index construction

Political representation

Political system. Democratic pluralism, mode of executive formation, parliamentary election mode, democratic framework acceptance, electoral system credibility.

Distribution of power. Parliamentary election mode, local assembly membership, status of constitutional checks and balances, legislative independence, legislative control, judicial independence.

Political party freedom and security. Parliamentary election mode, local assembly membership, acceptance of democratic framework, credibility of electoral system, electoral authority's legitimacy, election security, public media access, effectiveness of government programs against intrastate conflict.

Independence, credibility and transparency of electoral process. Electoral system credibility, electoral law credibility, electoral authority legitimacy, electoral authority's fairness, election security, public media access, election transparency, election control.

Institutional effectiveness and accountability

Legislative effectiveness. Status of constitutional checks and balances, legislative independence, legislative effectiveness, legislative control, strength of parliamentary opposition, legislative corruption, judicial independence, executive independence.

Judicial effectiveness. Legislative independence, judicial independence, mode of appointing judges, court access, justice access, judicial corruption, executive independence.

Executive effectiveness

Management of state structure. Legislative independence, judicial independence, executive independence, composition of senior appointees, executive corruption, government accountability, local government accountability, resource allocation, local government capacity, government responsiveness.

Civil service transparency, accountability and accessibility. Civil service management criteria, civil service

corruption, government accountability, government transparency.

Efficiency of government services. Access to services, relevance of services to poor and women, local government accountability, resource allocation, government responsiveness.

Decentralisation of structures. Local government accountability, resource allocation, local government capacity, community participation, government responsiveness.

Human rights and rule of law

Human rights. Democratic framework acceptance, court access, justice access, respect for human rights, effectiveness of human rights reporting, women's rights reporting, actions against human rights violations, actions against women's rights violations, effectiveness of watchdog organisations.

Respect for the rule of law. Status of constitutional checks and balances, leadership's respect for rule of law, police respect for human rights, citizens' confidence in law enforcement organs, civil society organisations' monitoring of violations by police and prisons, participation in conflict resolution, watchdog organisations' independence from executive, tax system equitability, tax system influence on local investment, tax system influence on foreign investment.

Law enforcement organs. Composition of police force, police equipment, corruption in law enforcement, watchdog organisations' independence from executive, effectiveness of watchdog organisations.

Civil society organisations and media independence

Civil society organisations' independence, role in conflict management, influence on policy and programs and promotion of accountability and transparency; mass media independence.

Economic management

Attractiveness of investment policies. Pursuit of sustainable development, government's drive for rural development, independence of management of public enterprises, corruption in public enterprises, private-sector participation in policymaking, confidence in management of public finances, transparency in government procurement, independence of central bank, soundness of central bank's fiscal policies, effectiveness of central bank, partnership of private and public sectors, competition in the economy, entrepreneurs' freedom of operation, restrictions to doing business, enforcement of contracts and property rights, transparency and accountability in corporate governance, protection of shareholders' rights, business access to land, credit and utilities.

Pro-investment tax policies. Pursuit of sustainable development, government's drive for rural development, tax system influence on local investment, tax system influence on foreign investment, tax system influence on business.

Tax system efficiency and corruption. Transparency in government procurement, tax system equity, tax collection efficiency, tax evasion.

Control of corruption

Legislative corruption, justice access, judicial corruption, executive corruption, civil service corruption, access to government services, corruption in law enforcement, independence of management of public enterprises, corruption in public enterprises, confidence in management of public finances, transparency in government procurement.

Project implementation

Preparation and updating of research instruments

Updating the research instruments for AGR II was completed by mid-2006. The updating was guided by the recommendations of experts, academics, partners and other stakeholders in the two workshops.

Selection of collaborating national research institutions

Because ECA had expended time and resources training in-country institutions for AGR I, it was agreed that engaging the same institutions for AGR II would reduce cost and ensure an excellent survey. In the nine new countries ECA, in line with its procurement rules and procedures, solicited institutions to submit a bid. Additionally, a capacity-assessment mission was undertaken to ensure that the institutions partaking in the highly competitive bidding would be able to undertake the AGR work if chosen. The selection of the collaborating research institutions was done in accordance with UN procurement rules and regulations.

Annex table: AGR II collaborating research institutions

Country	Research institution
Benin	Cellule d'Analyse de Politique Economique (CAPAN)
Botswana	Botswana Institute for Development Policy Analysis (BIDPA)
Burkina Faso	Centre pour la Gouvernance démocratique (CGD)
Cameroon	Centre d'Etudes et de Recherche en Economie Gestion (CEREG)
Chad	Recherche & Actions pour le Développement Société Anonyme (RAD– S.A)
Cape Verde	AFROSONDAGEM
Republic of Congo	Unité de Recherche en Analyse sociétale (URAS)
Djibouti	Université de Djibouti
Egypt	Faculty of Economics and Political Science, Cairo University
Ethiopia	Addis Ababa University (AAU)
Gabon	Institut Sous-Régional Multisectoriel de Technologie Appliquée de Planification et d'Evaluation de Projets (ISTA)
Gambia	University of the Gambia
Ghana	Ghana Center for Democratic Development (CDD-Ghana)
Kenya	African Center for Economic Growth (ACEG)
Lesotho	Institute of Southern African Studies (ISAS)
Madagascar	Cabinet d'Etudes de Conseils et d'Assistance à la Réalisation (ECR)
Mali	Koni Expertise
Malawi	Center for Social Research (CSR)
Mauritius	STRACONSULT
Morocco	Centre Africain de Formation et de Recherche Administratives pour le Développement (CAFRAD)
Mozambique	Centro de Estudos Estratégicos e Internacionais do Instituto superior de Realçoes Internacionais (CEEI-ISRI)
Namibia	Multidisciplinary Research and Consultancy Center (MRCC)*
Nigeria	Development Policy Center (DPC)
Niger	Cabinet d'Etudes, de Recherhes, Conseils, Analyse et Prospective (CERCAP)
Rwanda	Consortium formé de BEATER SARL et UNR Faculté des Sciences Economiques, Sociales et de gestion*
Senegal	Institut Africain pour la Démocratie (IAD)
Sierra Leone	Campaign for Good Governance (CGG)
Seychelles	STRACONSULT
South Africa	Institute of Democracy in South Africa (IDASA)
Swaziland	Uniswa Consultancy and Training Centre (CTC)
Tanzania	Department of Political Science and Public Administration, University of Dar-es-Salaam*
Tunisia	Center of Arab Women for Training and Research (CAWTAR)
Togo	Faculté des Sciences économiques et de Gestion (FASEG)
Uganda	Center for Basic Research (CBR)
Zambia	Center for Policy Research & Analysis (CePRA)

* Institutions not able to complete the survey in their respective countries.

Pre-launch workshops

Research institutions in the nine new countries were invited to a three-day training workshop to familiarize them with the methodology, objectives, descriptions, conditions and expectations of ECA. The training workshop was also meant to equip the participating institutions with the knowledge and information to execute a project of such magnitude while ensuring consistency and coherence as laid out in ECA's rules and regulations and the requirements contained in the request for proposal.

National launch workshops

The collaborating national research institution in each new country held an official launch workshop with representatives of government, civil society, the private sector, international partners and other relevant stakeholder groups to introduce the project, promote a suitable environment for implementation and encourage national ownership.

Steering committee

The collaborating institution in each of the new countries established a national steering committee composed of the various influential groups in the country to play an advisory role, facilitate popularization of the project and secure its support as the need may arise.

Preparation of country reports

The collaborating national research institutions collected the data, obtained ECA's quality-control clearance for them, analyzed them and produced a national country report in accordance with agreed-upon guidelines. ECA further provided technical oversight to ensure conformity with its detailed instructions, agreed-upon work plans and report formats, and reviewed the final results.

Preparation of country profiles

In the country reports the national research institutions also prepared draft country profiles, which are brief summaries of the governance situation in the countries, supported by data and concise information. These country profiles were reviewed by the ECA, with emphasis on quality control.

National stakeholder workshops

The collaborating national research institutions convened stakeholders' workshops to discuss the findings and draft report before the final report was submitted—an essential step in promoting national ownership and the report's credibility.

Collaborating research institutions

The institutional partners implemented the in-country governance surveys, prepared the country reports and profiles and facilitated the national stakeholders' consultations.

Notes

1. Surveys in Rwanda, Namibia and Tanzania were not completed, but the C3 research instrument was used.
2. Indices are calculated for only 26 countries, since data from some project countries were incomplete.